**NOT TO BE
TAKEN AWAY**

CONCISE
DICTIONARY
OF ART &
LITERATURE

Concise Dictionary of Art & Literature

of

Edwin Moore
Fiona Mackenzie Moore

TIGER BOOKS INTERNATIONAL
LONDON

© Geddes & Grosset Ltd 1993.

This edition published in 1993 by
Tiger Books International PLC, London.

ISBN 1-85501-325-8

Printed and bound in Slovenia.

A

Aalto, Alvar (1898–1976) Finnish architect who influenced 20th-century architecture away from the strong geometric shapes of CONSTRUCTIVISM towards softer curves and more irregular forms. He was also a designer of Artek furniture. In Finland he worked on postwar reconstruction in civic and industrial design. Major exhibitions were in Paris (1937) and New York (1938). He taught architecture at the Massachusetts Institute of Technology (1948–50). Important works include the War Memorial at Suomussalmi (1960) and the town hall at Saynatsalo (1950–2).

Abbey, Edwin Austen (1852–1911) American illustrator and painter of historical scenes. He worked both in the US and England and was the official painter at the coronation of Edward VII in 1902. He illustrated popular magazines, such as *Harper's,* and one of his best-known paintings is the portrait of *Richard, Duke of Gloucester*, and Lady Anne.

Abbey Theatre An Irish theatre founded in Dublin in 1904 by YEATS and Lady GREGORY. The Abbey quickly became the major venue for new Irish drama, staging plays by, notably, SYNGE, SHAW and O'CASEY as well as by Yeats and Lady Gregory.

Abelard, Peter (1079–1142) French theologian and philosopher. He began lecturing at Notre Dame in Paris in 1115 and soon gained a reputation as a formidable adversary in theological debate. He professed the new doctrine of nominalism, and was condemned for heresy twice, in 1121 and in the year he died. His love affair with his pupil Héloïse (1101–64), whose uncle had him castrated, with its combination of intellectual and physical passion described in their letters to each other, was to haunt the imagination of many poets, notably POPE in his *Epistle of Eloisa to Abelard*.

abstract art Art that intentionally avoids representation of the observed world. Abstraction has long been a feature of the decorative arts and to a large degree continues to dominate 20th-century art. There are two distinct trends: one towards an ordered, hard-edged CONSTRUCTIVISM, as in the works of MONDRIAN; the other leaning to a freer, more expressionistic reduction of forms, as e.g. in the CUBISM painting of CÉZANNE.

abstract expressionism Art that is based on freedom of expression, spontaneity and random composition and is characterized by loose, unrestrained brushwork and often indistinct forms, usually on large canvases. The works may or may not be figurative. The term mainly applies to an art movement of the 1940s in New York, although it was first used in 1919 with reference to the early abstract work of KANDINSKY. Inspired by SURREALISM, the movement represented a breakaway from the realism hitherto dominant in American art and went on to influence European art in the 1950s. Artists associated with the movement include DE KOONING, POLLOCK, KLINE and GORKY, as well as the COLOUR FIELD painters, ROTHKO and NEWMAN.

Absurd, Theatre of the A form of theatre, developed in the 1960s, that characterizes the human condition as one of helplessness in the face of an irrational, "absurd" universe. BECKETT, PINTER and IONESCO, whose characters communicate with one another in disjointed, inconsequential language, are among the best-known practitioners of the form, whose roots go back to Dadaism and the plays of JARRY. Absurdist drama reacts strongly against the conventions of NATURALISM. However, the only absurdist dramatist to become president of a country, Vaclav HAVEL, has argued that the form is in fact a very efficient vehicle for describing life realistically in a totalitarian society.

Académie française A literary academy founded by Cardinal Richelieu in 1635 to supervise and protect the purity of the French language. The Academy has 40 members ("the immortals") and is frequently quoted as an example of the rigidity or coherence of French culture, in contrast to the looser, less restricted cultures of other nations.

academy of art An institution of professional artists or scholars. The word derives from Greek and refers to a place of learning, but it was specifically the name of the grove where Plato taught his students. The first academy of art was the Accademia del Disegno, founded in Florence in 1563; MICHELANGELO was one of its first directors. Its purpose was to raise the artist's status from that of an artisan by teaching art theory as well as practical skills. Academies drew their authority and financial support from the church, royalty or rich families, like the MEDICI, and the proliferation of academies across Europe in the 18th century was largely under state control, the Royal Academy in the UK, founded in 1768, being an exception. The National Academy of Design was founded in the US in 1924 by a breakaway group of young members from the American Academy of Fine Arts, founded in 1802.

Achebe, Chinua (1930–) Nigerian novelist who became one of the most widely acclaimed African writers of the 20th century. Achebe's novels, e.g. *Things Fall Apart* (1958), have as their central theme the cultural clash between European colonialism and

African society. Achebe is a vivid and clever satirist, with a dark and often grim humour.

Acmeist group *see* **Akhmatova, Anna; Mandelstam, Osip**.

acrostic A type of poem, in which the initial letters of each line form a word reading downwards. The form was used by Roman poets, and the Elizabethan poet and statesman Sir John Davies (1569–1626) devised in *Hymns of Astraea* (1599) 26 verses, each spelling out the name of Elizabeth I ("Elisabetha Regina"). The form was also used by POE and LAMB.

acrylic paint A versatile synthetic paint that is quick-drying and can be used in thick, heavy layers or thin washes on almost any surface. A range of matt or gloss finishes can be achieved by the use of additives.

action painting A form of ABSTRACT EXPRESSIONISM in which the paint is applied to the canvas in the course of a series of actions or movements by the artist. This may involve dancing, cycling or rolling about on the canvas to spread and mix the wet paint. In a less random technique the artist might paint the silhouette of a model in various poses against the canvas. Jackson POLLOCK was a prominent exponent of action painting.

Acton, Sir Harold [Marino Mitchell] (1904–) English poet, historian and miscellaneous writer. The scion of an aristrocratic Anglo-Italian Roman Catholic family, Acton befriended John BETJEMAN and Evelyn WAUGH at Oxford University. Several characters in the latter's novels, notably Anthony Blanche in *Brideshead Revisited*, are partly based on Acton. Acton's reputation as a dandy and aesthete has tended to obscure the fact that he is both a gifted writer of lucid prose and a perceptive and knowledgeable critic of art and letters. His two volumes of memoirs, *Memoirs of an Aesthete* (1948) and *More Memoirs* (1970), are required reading for anyone interested in the so-called "Brideshead generation."

Adam, Robert (1728–92) Scottish architect famous for his individualistic interpretations of Palladian and RENAISSANCE styles in domestic architecture. He designed numerous town houses in London, e.g. 20 Portman Square (1777), formerly the Courtauld Institute of Art, and Chandos House (1771); and he transformed old houses, such as those at Syon (1726–9) and at Osterley (1761–80), both near London. He also worked on the layout of Charlotte Square (1791) and Register House (1774–92) in Edinburgh. His designs usually included interior decor and furnishings down to the smallest details, and his style has been widely imitated. His brother, **James Adam** (1730–94), worked with him as a draughtsman and also designed buildings of his own.

Adams, Ansel (1902–) American photographer. Born in San Francisco, he trained as a pianist before becoming a photographer in 1930. The clarity and detail of his landscapes, mainly of the southwest US of the 1930s, represented a move away from the painterly trends in mainstream art and photography. He helped to initiate the first photography departments in museums and colleges and wrote a number of technical handbooks on the subject.

Adams, Charles Samuel (1912–) American cartoonist. Born in New Jersey, he worked for *New Yorker* magazine from 1935 and became particularly well known for his humorously macabre style.

Adams, Henry Brooks (1838–1918) American historian, whose nine-volume *History of the United States During the Administration of Thomas Jefferson and James Madison* (1889–91) is a landmark in American historical writing. Adams' great-grandfather, John Adams, was the second US president, and his grandfather, John Quincy Adams, was the sixth. Adams' autobiography, *The Education of Henry Adams* (1907), is an enthralling account of the pitfalls of a progressive mid-19th century education.

Addison, Joseph (1672–1719) English essayist and poet. He achieved public recognition in 1704 with his poem on the battle of Blenheim, *The Campaign*, which earned him a minor government post (a not uncommon reward for politically useful poetry in those days). Addison swiftly demonstrated a fearsome proficiency in many literary fields; his neoclassical tragedy *Cato* (1713) was a huge critical and popular success. It was, however, as an essayist and moralist that Addison was to make his mark. He co-founded *The Spectator* with his old schoolfriend Richard STEELE in 1711, the tone of which is light and often very funny, as in the Sir Roger de Coverley papers, but is always concerned with proclaiming the virtues of reasonableness, common sense and benevolent moderation. Although Cyril Connolly described him (disparagingly) as the first Man of Letters (he made prose "artful and whimsical") in *Enemies of Promise*, Virginia WOOLF said of him in *The Common Reader*: "It is due to Addison that prose is now prosaic – the medium which makes it possible for people of ordinary intelligence to communicate their ideas to the world." His reputation as a moralist has proved less secure. He was unkind to his friend, the gentle Steele, and was foolishly unkind to the ungentle POPE, who hit back in the *Epistle to Dr Arbuthnot*: "Damn with faint praise, assent with civil leer, / And without sneering, teach the rest to sneer . . . Who must but laugh, if such a man there be? / Who would not weep, if Atticus were he?"

Aeken, Jerom van *see* **Bosch, Hieronymus**.

Aelfric (*c*.955–*c*.1020) English monk who wrote works in Old English on the lives of the saints, and trans-

lations from Latin homilies and the Bible. He also
wrote a Latin grammar which was still being used well
into the late Middle Ages. Aelfric has always been
highly regarded as a prose stylist.

Aeschylus (524–456BC) Greek dramatist, who is
regarded as the founder of Greek tragedy. Only seven
of his plays survive. These include *Seven Against
Thebes, Prometheus Bound* and the great *Oresteia* trilogy: *Agamemnon, Choephoroe (The Liberation Bearers)*
and the *Eumenides.* Aeschylus was regarded by the
Greeks as a less sophisticated playwright than the
other two great Greek tragedians, EURIPIDES and
SOPHOCLES, a judgment that largely prevailed until the
Renaissance. SHELLEY was heavily influenced by him,
and MARX regarded Aeschylus and SHAKESPEARE as
the two greatest dramatists of all time.

Aesop (*c.*620–564BC) Supposed Greek author of witty
fables in which human characteristics are satirized in
the form of dialogues between animals. Aesop's actual
existence is quite dubious; the fables themselves have
close parallels in many cultures.

Aestheticism The side of the debate that argues that
the value of a work of art is in its inherent beauty
and not in any moral, religious or political message it
might carry. Indeed, in the late 18th century, at the
height of the debate, it was suggested that any such
message actually detracted from the value of the work.
The famous court case between RUSKIN and WHISTLER
arose out of aesthetic controversy, although of a
slightly different nature. Since the beginning of the
20th century a more tolerant attitude has generally
prevailed.

Aesthetic movement A cultural movement which
developed in England in the late 19th century, characterized by a very affected and mannered approach to
life and the arts, a fondness for orientalism and deca-

dence, archaic language and pseudo-medievalism. The character Bunthorne in GILBERT and Sillivan's comic opera *Patience* (1881) is a conflation of all the features found ridiculous in the movement by contemporaries: "Though the Philistines may jostle, you will rank as an apostle in the high aesthetic band, / If you walk down Piccadilly with a poppy or a lily in your medieval hand." Oscar WILDE is the most prominent literary figure of merit associated with the movement.

aesthetics An area of philosophy concerning the ideals of taste and beauty and providing criteria for critical study of the arts. The term was coined in the mid-18th century by the German philosopher Alexander Baumgarten, and in the 20th century came to include a wider theory of natural beauty.

African art A term generally used to describe African tribal art in the countries south of the Sahara Desert. Much of this art is of a group nature, in that it has cultural and religious significance at its heart rather than individual ambition. Examples of typical art forms include richly carved wooden masks and figures. Body art is also important in tribal ritual and may involve scarring, tattooing or disfigurement of parts of the body, although it can also make use of paint, beads and feathers. Brightly coloured batiks and printed fabrics are a more recent feature of this rich heritage. African tribal art had a marked influence on 20th-century art styles, as in the works of PICASSO and CÉZANNE.

Aiken, Conrad Potter (1889–1973) American poet, novelist, short-story writer and critic. Collections of his poems include *Earth Triumphant* (1914) and *A Letter from Li Po* (1955). Novels include *Blue Voyage* (1927) and *A Heart for the Gods of Mexico* (1939). Aiken was a friend of T. S. ELIOT (his classmate at Harvard), and his work, often autobiographical in content, is regarded as representative of minor 20th-century modernist fiction and poetry.

air brush An atomizer, powered by compressed air, that is used to spray paint. It is shaped like a large fountain pen and produces a fine mist of colour, giving delicate tonal gradations and a smooth finish. Its principal use is in the fields of advertising and graphic design.

Akhmatova, Anna [pseud. of Anna Andreyevna Gorenko] (1889–1966) Russian poet who, with MANDELSTAM, was associated with the Acmeist group, a school of Russian poetry which first emerged as a coherent group with the formation of the Poets' Guild in Leningrad in 1911. In part a reaction to the more obscure aspects of SYMBOLISM, the group proclaimed the virtue of clarity of expression. Its founder, Akhmatova's ex-husband, Nikolai Gumilev, was executed by the Bolsheviks in 1921, and her son was arrested and imprisoned several times during Stalin's terror. Her great poem on the suffering of the Russian people under Stalin's rule, *Requiem*, was first published in Munich in 1963. She was denounced by Stalin's odious literary commissar, Zhdanov, as "a bourgeois relic" and "half-nun, half-whore." Akhmatova's poems are among the finest and most important of the 20th century, and she and Mandelstam are now recognized in the USSR as ranking among the greatest Russian poets.

alabaster A fine-grained type of gypsum that can be translucent, white or streaked with colour. It is soft and easy to carve and is therefore a popular medium for decorative artefacts and statues. It is not as strong or weather-resistant as marble, and is not often used for outdoor works.

Albee, Edward Franklin (1928–) American dramatist, whose early plays bore resemblances to the Theatre of the ABSURD. His best-known play, however, *Who's Afraid of Virginia Woolf* (1962, filmed 1966) is a semi-naturalistic study of marital breakdown against an academic background, which established him as a very individual voice in American drama.

Albers, Josef (1888–1976) German-born American painter and designer. He taught at the BAUHAUS until its closure in 1933, when he emigrated to the US, becoming an American citizen in 1939. His early work concentrated on stained glass, the design of utility objects and furniture. He took his Bauhaus ideas to the Black Mountain College in North Carolina and to Harvard University before moving to Yale University in 1950. He outlined his theories on colour relationships in *The Intersection of Color* (1963). His series of paintings entitled *Homage to the Square* explore these relationships through various compositions of flat squares set one inside the other.

Albert, Calvin (1918–) American sculptor in the school of ABSTRACT EXPRESSIONISM. Much of his work involved special metal welding techniques, and he undertook commissions for decorative sculptures in churches and synagogues. His one-man shows were in Chicago (1941) and New York (1944); a retrospective exhibition was shown at the Jewish Museum (1960) and he also participated in group exhibitions.

Alberti, Leon Battista (1404–72) Italian writer, architect, sculptor and painter. Born in Genoa, he worked mainly in Rome and Florence. His most famous written works are on art theory, including *On Painting* (*De Pictura*, 1435), *On Sculpture* (*De Statua*, c.1440) and his life's work, *On Architecture* (*De Re Aedificatoria*, 1485), the first treatise on architecture ever to be printed. His architectural designs include the facade of the Church of San Francesco in Rimini and that of Santa Maria Novella in Florence, but little of his painting or sculpture has survived. A prominent RENAISSANCE figure, his wide-ranging interests and talents, including music and athletics, are representative of the "universal man" ideal of his humanist views.

Alcott, Louisa M[ay] (1832–88) American novelist. She was an active social reformer and prolific author of novels, but is now remembered chiefly for her hugely successful children's novel, *Little Women* (1868–9), and its sequels, *Jo's Boys* (1886) and *Little Men* (1871).

Aldington, Richard (1892–1962) English poet and dramatist. His most highly regarded novel is *Death of a Hero* (1929), which is a thinly disguised semi-autobiographical account of the author's war experiences. His other works include a volume of IMAGIST poetry, *Images 1910–1915* (1915), and a bitter, debunking biography of T. E. Lawrence, *Lawrence of Arabia* (1955).

Aldrich, Thomas Bailey (1836–1907) American poet, novelist and editor of the *Atlantic Monthly* (1881–90). His most popular book was the semi-autobiographical novel, *The Story of a Bad Boy* (1870).

Alfieri, Count Vittorio (1749–1803) Italian poet and tragedian. His many works, including 21 tragedies, six comedies and an autobiography, display a strong enthusiam for Italian nationalism and reform.

Algardi, Alessandro (*c.*1595–1654) Italian BAROQUE sculptor. Born in Bologna, he worked in Rome from 1625 and was patronized by Pope Innocent X, mainly because his style of work was given less to contortion and violent action than his contemporary BERNINI. His major works include the tomb of Leo Xl (*c.*1645) in Rome and the sculptured group, *The Decapitation of Saint Paul*, in Bologna.

Alger, Horatio (1834–99) American author of boys' adventure stories, e.g. *Ragged Dick* (1867) and *From Canal Boy to President* (1881). As the title of the latter book indicates, Alger's works describe early poverty and adversity being overcome through manly (or boyish) fortitude.

Algren, Nelson [Nelson Algren Abraham] (1909–81) American novelist. He wrote four novels, two of which, *The Man with the Golden Arm* (1949) and *A Walk on the Wild Side* (1956), are classic portrayals of urban American underclass life. His first novel, *Somebody in Boots* (1935) is a tediously didactic work interlarded with chunks from the *Communist Manifesto*. His heroes and heroines are drifters, prostitutes and petty criminals. Algren was rated highly by his peers; Hemingway believed him to be one of America's best writers. His main flaw, which has led to his fall from subsequent critical esteem, is a rather over-sentimental view of his characters (he liked to describe himself as the "poor man's Dostoevsky" – *see also* Jim THOMPSON). He had a 17-year long love affair with Simone de BEAUVOIR.

alienation effect An effect which is supposed to occur upon an audience when the audience is reminded by action, dialogue or song that it is in fact an audience watching a play, and not, for example, waiting for a bus. The intention is to confront the audience with the artificiality of dramatic representation, through devices such as interrupting the action to address the audience, or by bursting into song, or by stylizing the stage set or action. The theory is especially associated with BRECHT, who claimed that his plays created an "alienating," distancing effect, enabling the audience to resist identifying emotionally with the characters on stage and therefore more capable of absorbing the message of plays, e.g. that traditional notions of morality simply represent "bourgeois" morality. "Alienation effects" of the kind described by Brecht have existed in drama since before ARISTOPHANES, and form an important element in the Theatre of the ABSURD. The value of

Brecht's formulation and use of the theory, however, is much debated. *See also* GRASS.

allegory A form of narrative in which the characters and events symbolize an underlying moral or spiritual quality, or represent a hidden meaning beneath the literal one expressed. BUNYAN's *Pilgrim's Progress* is the greatest English-language example of a sustained allegory.

Allen, Woody [pseud. of Allen Stewart Konigsberg] (1935–) American writer, actor and film director. His literary works, e.g. *Horse Feathers* (1976), display the obsessions with sex and psychiatry made familiar by his many films, but also show him to be a highly gifted parodist.

Allston, Washington (1779–1843) American landscape painter and leading figure in the beginnings of ROMANTICISM in the US. He worked mainly in Boston, apart from two lengthy periods in England, during the first of which (1801–8) he studied at the Royal Academy under Benjamin WEST. His work was large in scale and concentrated on the monumental, mysterious and dramatic elements of nature and religious subjects. Notable examples include *The Rising of a Thunderstorm at Sea* and *Dead Man Revived*. His later works were poetic and dreamlike in character, as in *Moonlit Landscape*. Samuel MORSE was his pupil. *See also* HUDSON RIVER SCHOOL.

Alma-Tadema, Sir Lawrence (1836–1912) Dutch-born painter who moved to England in 1870, where he enjoyed a highly successful career. He painted historical scenes, in particular of classical Greece and Rome, and designed stage sets for the Roman plays of Shakespeare. His paintings often included beautiful women, usually in a sentimental style but occasionally displaying eroticism, as in *In the Tepidarium* (1881). Most of his works contain an opus number in roman numerals.

Altamira The site in northern Spain of prehistoric rock paintings dating from about 13000BC, in 1879 the first ever to be discovered. Originally dismissed as forgeries, their age and authenticity were accepted as genuine only in the early 20th century. A variety of animals painted in a lively, naturalistic manner are depicted, including bison, aurochs and wild horses.

altarpiece A decorated wall, screen or sectional painting set behind the altar of a Christian church, a feature of church decor dating from the 11th century. There are two forms: a retable can be fairly large and complex, rising from floor level; a reredos is often smaller and may stand on the altar itself or on a pedestal behind it.

Altdorfer, Albrecht (1480–1538) German painter and printmaker. A major figure of the so-called Danube School of painters who developed the importance of landscape, his work is characterized by a fantastic inventiveness, distortion of figures and brilliant effects of colour and light. His themes were mainly religious, but his outstanding contribution to art is in the development of landscape painting as a genre in its own right. Notable among his paintings are *St George and the Dragon* (1510), *Susannah and the Elders* (1526) and *The Battle of Alexander and Darius on the Issus* (1529), which was a commission from Duke William IV of Bavaria.

Amis, Martin (1949–) English novelist, the son of Kingsley AMIS. His first novel, the gruesomely titled *Dead Babies* (1975), is a chilly little fable set in an imaginary England plagued by random killings. This and his later novels, e.g. *London Fields* (1989), are much admired by some critics; others regard them as essays in designer violence.

Amis, Sir Kingsley (1922–) English novelist and poet. His first novel, *Lucky Jim* (1953), a witty satire on academic life at an English university (see CAMPUS NOVEL), was a great success, its eponymous hero being seen as a type of ANGRY YOUNG MAN. Subsequent novels, e.g. *I like It Here* (1958) and his one novel with an American setting, *One Fat Englishman* (1963), are seen by some critics as displaying a progression from leftwing anti-establishment values towards a querulously reactionary position. His novels, however, are too complex and too good to be baldly categorized in this way. *The Anti-Death League* (1966) and *The Green Man* (1969), for example, are profound studies of the nature of death, love and God. (Amis is an avowed atheist, but few other modern novelists have written so passionately on the nature of God.) He is also a great comic writer, and is one of the best parodists in the English language. His *Collected Poems 1944–1979* were published in 1979. *See also* FLEMING.

Ammanati, Bartolomeo (1511–92) Italian sculptor and architect. He worked in Venice and Rome as well as in Florence, where he won a commission to create the famous fountain depicting a huge marble statue of *Neptune* with bronze nymphs. His architectural works include the Ponte Santa Trinité and the court of the Pitti Palace, both in Florence. In later life he destroyed many of his nude statues and recanted his secular works under the influence of counter-Reformation piety.

Anacreon (*fl.* 6th century BC) Greek lyric poet. His poems (mostly on love and wine, and many of doubtful attribution) were translated into French and English in the mid-16th century, and were much imitated, notably by poets of the METAPHYSICAL school.

Ancients, The A group of ROMANTIC artists working in England between 1824 and the early 1830s. PALMER was a leading member of the group, which also included RICHMOND and CALVERT. Their work was mainly pastoral in theme, much inspired by BLAKE's illustrations of Virgil.

Andersen, Hans Christian (1805–75) Danish writer. He wrote prolifically in many areas, but is now remembered solely for his fairy tales, such as "The Ugly Duckling" and "The Emperor's Clothes."

Anderson, Sherwood (1876–1941) American novelist and short-story writer. His greatest work is the novel *Winesburg, Ohio* (1919), which, like most of his fiction, focuses on the tragedies of small-town, mid-American life.

Andre, Carl (1935–) American sculptor whose Minimalist style emphasizes the real in art as opposed to the metaphoric. His systematic arrangements of single objects in horizontal pattern are intended to focus attention on the relationships between the objects and their surroundings. Famous among his works are his *144 Pieces of Lead* and *Equivalent VIII*, the "Tate bricks" that so outraged the British art public in 1976.

Andrea del Castagno (*c.*1421–57) Florentine artist. One of the leading painters of his generation, his potentially outstanding career was cut short by his death from plague. His earliest surviving works are the frescoes in San Terassio presso San Zaccaria in Venice, but his best-known works are in Florence, in particular the *Passion of Christ* (1445–50) in the convent of Santa Apollonia, which is now in the Castagno Museum. The monumental realism of his style is comparable with the work of DONATELLO, as in, for example, *The Vision of St Jerome* at SS Annunziata in Florence.

Andrea del Sarto (1486–1530) Florentine painter, a pupil of PIERO DI COSIMO and a contemporary of Fra BARTOLOMMEO who, along with RAPHAEL, influenced his elegant, classical style. His best-known works are his fresco cycles in the cloisters of the church of Santissima Annunziata and his Uffizi altarpiece, *The*

Madonna of the Harpies. A major figure of the high RENAISSANCE, his work was among the greatest examples of contemporary classical art.

Andrewes, Lancelot (1555–1626) English theologian and bishop. He was one of the most distinctive prose writers of his day (T. S. ELIOT quotes him in his poem "Journey of the Magi"), and was one of the translators of the AUTHORIZED VERSION of the Bible. His sermons combine a scholarly love of classical and scriptural reference with a gift for flowery, not always perfectly clear expression.

Angelico, Fra [Guido di Pietro] (*c.*1400–1455) Dominican monk and Florentine painter of the early RENAISSANCE. All his work is religious in character, one of the earliest and most famous being *The Annunciation* (1428). At the same time, his contribution to the understanding of perspective and the development of complex landscape settings is undeniably progressive and professional, as in *Descent from the Cross* (1440). His major work is the series of about 50 frescoes (most of them in the cells) in his monastery of San Marco, now a museum housing a large collection of his art.

Angelou, Maya [pseud. of Marguerite Johnson] (1928–) American dramatist, poet and short-story writer, whose works on her upbringing as a poor black female in St Louis, e.g. *I Know Why the Caged Bird Sings* (1970), have won her a large and appreciative audience.

Anglo-Saxon art A term for works of art produced in England between AD5 and 1066. The major source of surviving artefacts is the 7th-century excavation site at Sutton Hoo, and much of the Anglo-Saxon jewellery collection at the British Museum comes from there. The abstract plant and animal designs show the influences of Celtic art typical of Anglo-Saxon craft. The late 7th and early 8th centuries saw the production of

21

the Lindisfarne Gospels in the kingdom of Northumbria. These are famous for their delicate interwoven designs, reminiscent of Irish illuminations, as in the *Book of Kells*. The other centre for manuscript production was the Winchester school of the 10th century.

Angry Young Men A rather imprecise term used in mid-1950s Britain to denote a group of English writers who had little in common apart from vaguely leftish sympathies and a hatred of English provincialism and intellectual pretentiousness ("madrigalphobia"). Other characteristics of Angry Young Men included a liking for jazz, polo-neck sweaters, coffee bars, and compliant women – like their American counterparts, the BEAT GENERATION writers, Angry Young Men regarded women as appendages (although Doris LESSING and Iris MURDOCH were sometimes regarded as honorary AYM). Angus WILSON gives a meticulous dissection of the species in his short story "A Bit off the Map" (1957). Kingsley AMIS' *Lucky Jim* and OSBORNE's Jimmy Porter in *Look Back in Anger* were, like their creators, seen as Angry Young Men.

Anouilh, Jean (1910–87) French dramatist. His first play (in 1944) was an updating of SOPHOCLES's *Antigone*, in which the eponymous heroine becomes a thinly disguised representation of the spirit of France under German occupation. Anouilh's command of the technicalities of theatrical production has been much admired.

antinovel *see* **novel**.

Antique, The Remains of ancient art, in particular Greek and Roman statues, which were taken as a standard of classical order and beauty in the representation of the human form by RENAISSANCE and NEOCLASSICAL artists.

Antonello da Messina (*c.* 1430–79) Sicilian painter, whose work helped to popularize oil painting in Italy.

His work displays a strong Flemish influence in its light, atmosphere and attention to detail, as in some of his bust-length portraits. The composition and modelling of his figures, however, owe much to Italian sculpture. A good example of this combination is his *Crucifixion* in London's National Gallery.

Apelles Greek painter from the 4th century BC and court painter to Philip of Macedon and Alexander the Great. None of his work has survived and his fame is due to the enthusiasm of classical authors, whose detailed descriptions of his work later inspired RENAISSANCE artists such as BOTTICELLI and TITIAN.

Apollinaire, Guillaume (1880–1918) French art critic and writer of great influence among avant-garde artists and poets at the beginning of the 20th century. A friend of PICASSO and a champion of CUBISM, he published *The Cubist Painters* in 1913. He was also a supporter of ORPHISM and FUTURISM. He originated the term SURREALISM in 1917 in a preface to his play *The Breasts of Tiresias*. He was wounded in World War I and subsequently died of Spanish influenza.

Apollodorus Athenian painter from the 5th century BC called Sciagraphus because, according to Pliny, he was the first artist to depict light and shadow in the modelling of his figures, an important development in art history.

applied arts Art that serves a useful purpose or that ornaments functional objects; often a synonym for design. Subjects included under this term are architecture, interior design, ceramics, furniture, graphics, etc. These are usually contrasted with the **fine arts** of painting, drawing, sculpture printmaking, etc, and the division became more distinct at the time of the Industrial Revolution and the emergence of AESTHETICISM. This division is still a matter of important debate.

Apuleius (2nd century AD) North African Latin author

of a romance called *The Golden Ass* (or *Metamorphoses*), a satirical picaresque novel narrated by a man turned into an ass. The novel includes the story of Psyche's love and quest for Cupid, which has been adapted by many other authors, C. S. LEWIS's *Till We Have Faces* (1956) being a remarkable and haunting modern example.

aquarelle The French term for watercolour painting, where a water-based paint is applied to dampened paper in thin glazes that are gradually built up into areas of varying tone.

aquatint An etching technique where a resin-coated metal plate is placed in a bath of acid that bites into the resin, producing a pitted surface. The depth of tone intensifies the longer the plate remains in the acid, and areas required to be lighter in tone are "stopped out," using washes of varnish. The finished print resembles a watercolour wash, and the technique of overlaying separate plates of different colours can be used to build up a range of depth and colour. The process is often combined with linear etching.

Arabian Nights Entertainments *or* **The Thousand and One Nights** A compilation of stories, the earliest of which probably originated in Persia, that were translated into Arabic in the mid-9th century AD, and have become classics of Arab and world literature. The stories are told by Scheherazade to her husband, a king who has killed each previous bride following the consummation of the marriage. Scheherazade saves her life by keeping the king in suspense, postponing the conclusion of each story until the following night.

Aragon, Louis (1897–1982) French poet, novelist and essayist. Aragon was one of the founders of both Dadaism (*see* TZARA) and SURREALISM. He joined the Communist Party in 1927, after breaking with the Surealists in the early 1930s, and became a forceful exponent of socialist realism. His works include the novels *The Bells of Basel* (1934) and *Residential Quarter* (1936).

Arcadia A region of ancient Greece which became the archetypal setting for rural bliss and innocence in the arts. VIRGIL's *Eclogues* in the 1st century BC established the use of Arcadia as a literary device for this purpose, but the ironic undertone in Virgil's work (Arcadia is largely barren) is usually missing from later writers' use of the myth. Virgil's dark undertone returns to Western culture in the work of several 16th and 17th-century painters, e.g. Poussin, with reference to the phrase *Et in Arcadia Ego* ("And I [i.e. death] also in Arcadia").

Archipenko, Alexander (1887–1946) Ukrainian-born American sculptor who studied briefly at Kiev and exhibited in group shows in Moscow before moving to Paris. From 1910 he had links with CUBISM and was a member of the SECTION D'OR group. He opened his own school in 1912. The geometric style of his early work explored extreme simplifications of form and the importance of enclosed voids in sculpture. Experiments with a variety of media and with colour evolved into a polychrome relief style he called "sculpto-peinture." He became an American citizen in 1928 and taught in a number of establishments, including the New Bauhaus and his own schools in Chicago and New York. Later experiments in movement and light resulted in perspex sculptures lit from within. His influence on 20th-century European and American sculpture has been considerable.

Arden, John (1930–) English dramatist. His early plays, e.g. *Live Like Pigs* (1958) and *Serjeant Musgrave's Dance* (1959), were innovative assaults on the evils of social corruption and violence, and were widely praised for their very effective use of song, declamation and harshly poetic dialogue. His later plays are generally regarded as over-didactic, and are not so highly thought of.

Aretino, Pietro (1492–1556) Italian poet, whose name became a byword in Elizabethan times for witty licentiousness.

Ariosto, Ludovico (1474–1533) Italian poet. His *Orlando Furioso* (1532), an epic romance in verse set in Charlemagne's time, enjoyed European-wide popularity.

Aristophanes (*c*.448–380BC) Greek comic dramatist. Eleven of his great comedies survive. His work represents an early peak in comic satire that few subsequent dramatists have attained. The objects of his satire ranged from the "war party" (against the Spartans) in Athens to his fellow dramatists (EURIPIDES being a favourite target). The plays are also a valuable record of the intellectual debates of the day, e.g. the position of women in society and the nature of religious belief. The most popular of his plays in our own day has been *Lysistrata*, in which the women of Athens stage a "sex strike" against war. Aristophanes's powerful dramatic verse could also rise to great lyric heights, as in the chorus of *The Birds. See* COMEDY, GILBERT.

Aristotle (384–322BC) Greek philosopher. His writings, re-introduced to the Western world in the Middle Ages via Arabian scholarship, had great and occasionaly pernicious influence on almost every field of intellectual inquiry until the RENAISSANCE, when his authority ceased to be regarded as infallible. His *Poetics*, however, which resurfaced in fragmentary form during the Renaissance, was to become one of the cornerstones of literary NEOCLASSICISM, particulary in its strictures on the theatrical "unities." The plot of Umberto ECO's popular novel *The Name of the Rose* is based on the presence of a lost section of the *Poetics* in a medieval monastery.

Armory Show The international exhibition of modern art held at the 69th Regimental Armory in New York in 1913, one of the most influential exhibitions ever shown in the US. Organized by an association of painters and sculptors, including HENRI and DAVIES, it was effectively two exhibitions in one. It represented not only a fine cross-section of contemporary American art but also a massive selection of modern European art, a total of around 1,600 works. It toured the US, arousing great controversy and excitement among the 250,000 people who paid to see it, but it served the function of restoring the life and vitality of contemporary art and critical debate in the US.

Arnold, Matthew (1822–88) English poet and critic. He was the son of the educational reformer Thomas Arnold (1795–1842) and became one of the most important commentators on Victorian society. His literary and social criticism was influential on many 20th-century writers, notably T. S. ELIOT, but it is as a poet that he is chiefly remembered. His greatest poems, e.g. "Dover Beach," reflect the new uncertainties in religion and society created by the new industrial age.

Arnolfo di Cambio (1245–1302?) Italian sculptor and architect, who studied in Pisa under Nicola PISANO before moving to Rome in 1277, where he worked principally on Papal tombs. The best surviving example is that of Cardinal de Braye (d.1293) in San Dominico, which influenced the style of wall tombs for the next hundred years. He designed the altar canopies for San Paulo fuori le Mura (1285) and Santa Cecilia in Trastevere (1293), and was one of the architects of Florence Cathedral. The bronze statue of *St Peter* in Rome is also attributed to him, and he was one of the most important Italian architects in the Gothic style.

Arp, Jean *or* **Hans** (1887–1966) French abstract sculptor of great merit. He had early links with the BLAUE

REITER movement and later with CUBISM and SUR-
REALISM. Arp worked on the development of collage
together with the Swiss painter, **Sophie Taeuber**
(1889–1943), who later became his wife, and was a
founder of the Dada group. His later work involved
polychrome relief sculpture and a style he called
"creative abstraction," concerned with organic forms
while not actually representing plant or animal life.

Artaud, Antonin (1896–1948) French actor and theatre
director. His essays on the theatre, *The Theatre and Its
Double*, were published in New York in 1958 and have
had a lasting effect on Western drama. The essays lay
down guidelines for what he called a "Theatre of
Cruelty," i.e. a form of theatre which uses non-verbal
means of communication such as pantomine, light
effects and irrational language, to project the pain and
loss fostered by the modern world. His aim was to use
drama to subvert the idea of art as a set of concepts
separate from real life. An early SURREALIST, he later
rejected both that movement and the refuge of communist ideology into which so many of his fellow Surrealists fled. He suffered greatly from mental illness in
the last 15 years of his life.

Art Autre or **Art Informel** A name coined by art critic
Michel Tapie in *Un Art Autre* (1952); he used it to
describe nongeometric ABSTRACT EXPRESSIONISM.

Art Brut The work of anyone not linked to the art world
either as professional or amateur, for example psychiatric patients or prisoners, etc. The term can also
include graffiti and the work of young children. It
refers to any work uninfluenced by the art world and
its fashions. *See also* DUBUFFET.

Art Deco The decorative art of the 1920s and 1930s
in Europe and North America, originally called Jazz
Modern. It was classical in style, with slender, symmetrical, geometric or rectilinear forms. Major influ-

ences were ART NOUVEAU architecture and ideas from the ARTS AND CRAFTS MOVEMENT and the BAUHAUS. The simplicity of style was easily adaptable to modern industrial production methods and contemporary materials, especially plastics. This resulted in a proliferation of utility items, jewellery and furniture in an elegant streamlined form, as well as simplification and streamlining of interior decor and architecture.

Arthur (*fl.* 6th century AD) A possibly mythical Celtic warrior-king of post-Roman Britain, who may have organized resistance against the Saxon invaders. The Arthurian legend, with its tales of brave knights and holy quests, became enormously popular throughout Europe in the early Middle Ages, and its characters and legends have retained their significance in Western culture ever since. Notable users of the Arthurian myth since Sir Thomas MALORY include T. H. WHITE and TENNYSON.

Art Nouveau A style of decorative art influential and popular between 1890 and World War I in Europe and North America. Art Nouveau was primarily a design style with its main effects being seen in applied art, graphics, furniture and fabric design, and in architecture. In the fine arts it represented a move away from historical realism, but was not as vigorous or dominant as IMPRESSIONISM or CUBISM. Art Nouveau design is characterized by flowing organic forms and asymmetric linear structures, although architectural and calligraphic forms were more austere and reserved. Its principal exponents were the Scottish architect and designer **Charles Rennie Mackintosh** (1868–1928) and the American designer **Louis Comfort Tiffany** (1848–1933). Art Nouveau has enjoyed a revival of popularity in the 1970s and 1980s.

Arts and Crafts Movement An English movement in the decorative arts towards the end of the 19th century.

It was based on the ideas of the art critic John RUSKIN and the architect A.W. Pugin, with reference to the medieval guilds system, and took its name from the Arts and Crafts Exhibition Society formed in 1888. The motive was to re-establish the value of handcrafted objects at a time of increasing mass-production and industrialization. Designers in the movement, with a variety of styles, attempted to produce functional objects of an aesthetically pleasing nature. The most active and important leader of the movement was William MORRIS.

Arundel, Thomas Howard, 2nd Earl of (1586–1646) English patron of the arts, collector and antiquarian, and also a prominent figure at the court of Charles I. In 1613 he went to Italy to carry out archaeological work in Rome with the architect Inigo Jones. He was a patron of RUBENS and van DYCK, each of whom painted his portrait. His impressive art collection was broken up after his death, although the bulk of his classical sculpture is in the Ashmolean Museum in Oxford.

Ascham, Roger (c.1515–68) English educationalist and classics tutor to Elizabeth I. His book on education, *The Scholemaster* (1570), which criticizes corporal punishment, is a notable landmark in humanist educational theory.

Ashbery, John (1927–) American poet and critic. Volumes of his poetry include *Some Trees* (1956) and *The Double Dream of Spring* (1970). Ashbery's work is renowned for its vivid imagery.

Ashcan School A group of American painters of urban realism between 1908 and 1918. Its leading members were HENRI, LUKS, GLACKENS, and SHINN, although others were associated with them, including HOPPER, BELLOWS and MAURER. Their joint aim was to declare themselves primarily American painters, and they painted what they saw as American life, generally rejecting subject matter of academic approval. Among their influences were the works of DAUMIER and GOYA.

Asimov, Isaac (1920–92) Russian-born American science fiction author, whose many novels and short stories, e.g. *I Robot* (1950) have been very influential in the science fiction genre.

assemblage Any sculptural type of construction using found objects, from pieces of painted wood to old shoes. *See also* COLLAGE.

atelier The French term for an artist's studio. In 19th-century France, an *atelier libre* was a studio where artists could go to paint a model. No formal tuition was provided, and a small fee was charged. DELACROIX, COURBET and several of the Impressionists, e.g. PISSARRO and CÉZANNE, used the Atelier Julian, which was opened in 1860 and was later used by MATISSE, LÉGER and most of the NABIS.

attribution *or* **ascription** The assigning of an unsigned picture to a painter, using similarity of style or subject as the basis.

Atwood, Margaret Eleanor (1939–) Canadian poet and novelist, whose novel *Surfacing* (1972) established her as one of Canada's most important modern writers. Her works explore the common Canadian concern for cultural identity in relation to the US, and also the question of female identity in a male-dominated world.

Aubrey, John (1626–97) English antiquary and biographer. His *Lives of Eminent Men*, brief biographies of (mostly) his contemporaries, was first published in 1813, and is an invaluable and highly entertaining collection of biographical anecodotes, e.g. on SHAKESPEARE and JONSON.

Auden, W[ystan] H[ugh] (1907–73) English poet, who became an American citizen in 1946. His first verse collection, *Poems* (1928), was privately printed in a limited edition by his friend Stephen SPENDER, and is now one of the century's most sought-after first editions. Auden's reputation quickly grew, and by the early 1930s he was recognized as a highly original poet who was also the leading voice of a new generation of young poets, the "Auden generation" (or, derisively, the "Pylon School," so-called from their enthusiastic use of industrial imagery). Auden and his followers were concerned to develop a poetic aesthetic that would explain the world in leftiest terms. Apart from Auden, the most important figures were Spender, DAY-LEWIS and MACNEICE, followed by a host of lesser poets. (George ORWELL's essay *Inside the Whale* [1940] gives a caustic left-wing appraisal of Auden's politics – *see also* MACDIARMID.) In later years Auden became both a conservative and a Christian, and disowned many of his earlier left-wing poems (including "Spain," which Orwell had criticized for using the words "necessary murder").

Audubon, John James (1784–1851) American naturalist and artist. Born in the West Indies and brought up in France, he studied drawing with DAVID before moving to the US in 1803. He continued to draw and paint while working as a taxidermist, and his passion for ornithology resulted in the magnificent plates for his famous *Birds of America.* This was published by the London firm of Havell and Son between 1827 and 1838. A subsequent series, *The Viviparous Quadrupeds of North America*, was completed by his sons after his death. His drawings are lively and colourful and combine excellent draughtsmanship with scientific accuracy. *Birds of America* is among the most valuable and beautiful of illustrated books.

Auerbach, Frank (1931–) German-born British painter, he worked in England from 1939 and was influenced by BOMBERG, under whom he trained. Figures and portraits predominate in his work, executed either in chalk and charcoal or a heavy impasto of oil paint.

Austen, Jane (1775–1817) English novelist. Her six great novels were published in the following sequence: *Sense and Sensibility* (1811), *Pride and Prejudice* (1813), *Mansfield Park* (1814), *Emma* (1816), with *Northanger Abbey* and *Persuasion* being published posthumously in 1818. The novels are set firmly within the confines of the society in which Jane Austen lived, the well-bred middle class of Regency England, and usually feature the quest of young women for suitable husbands. Her reputation has increased sharply in the 20th century, and she is now seen as one of the greatest of all English novelists, with her masterly dialogue, finely tuned sense of satire and moral judgment. Even her juvenilia, e.g. the ferociously funny parody of the sentimental novel, *Love and Friendship* [sic], written when she was 14, displays a level of talent found in few other writers. Rudyard KIPLING's story "The Janeites" (1926) provides both the collective noun for her admirers and a perceptive analysis of her appeal. *See also* EPISTOLARY NOVEL.

Austin, Alfred (1835–1913) English poet, notorious for his inept, jingoistic verse. To the astonishment of the literary establishment, he was appointed POET LAUREATE in succession to TENNYSON in 1896. His verse was much parodied by his contemporaries.

Authorized Version *or* **King James Bible** A translation of the Bible published in 1611 in the reign of James I of England. The powerful and poetic language of the Authorized Version has made it perhaps the most influential book on writers in English from the early 17th century on. Although it is often said to be the greatest book ever written by a committee, the work is based for the most part on William Tyndale's (*c*.1495–1536) great translation of 1525.

autograph A term used to denote a painting by one artist only, and not assisted by pupils or assistants.

Automatistes *see* **Borduas, Paul Emile**.

Avery, Milton (1893–1965) American self-taught painter, whose early influences were MATISSE and the FAUVISTS. Although he later painted some landscapes in a more EXPRESSIONIST style, his work is mainly characterized by flat areas of thin paint in soft, rounded, flowing shapes, using closely keyed interacting colours. His best-known paintings include *Mother and Child* (1944) and *Swimmers and Sunbathers* (1945).

Ayckbourn, Alan (1939) English dramatist, noted for his often rather dark comedies of middle-class life in suburban England, e.g. *The Norman Conquests* (1974) trilogy, which depicts identical events through the eyes of different characters.

Ayres, Gillian (1930–) English painter much influenced in her early work by American ABSTRACT EXPRESSIONISM, particularly the work of Jackson POLLOCK. In the 1960s she moved towards tighter, organic forms, although her later work is again looser and more sensuous, concentrating on intensity of colours.

B

Babel, Isaac (1894–1941?) Russian writer, whose semi-autobiographical stories of his life as a Jewish intellectual with the Soviet Red Cavalry in the Russian Civil War, *Red Cavalry* (1923–5), have been highly praised for their portrayal of the harshness of war. Babel was imprisoned in 1939, and is assumed to have died in a Soviet labour camp.

Baburen, Dirck van *see* **Utrecht School**.

Bacon, Francis (1561–1626) English philosopher and statesman. He served both Elizabeth I and her successor James VI and I in various public offices until his conviction and disgrace for bribery in 1621, shortly after being created Viscount St Albans. Bacon's writings on philosophy and the need for rational scientific method, particularly in *The Advancement of Learning* (1605) and the *Novum Organum* (1620), are landmarks in the history of human thought, particularly in their insistence on argument based on fact and refusal to accept automatically any other authority. Bacon's prose is skilfully authoritative, with good rhetorical touches. This, and the fact that he was extraordinarily learned, gave rise to the theory in the late 19th century that he must have written SHAKESPEARE's plays, as only a genius could have written them. This theory, known as the **Baconian heresy**, is untenable, and is based purely on snobbery and a peculiar misapprehension of the nature of creative writing.

Bacon, Francis (1909–92) Irish-born British painter, who moved to London in 1925 where he set up as an interior decorator. His early work attracted little attention and he destroyed much of it. He later became famous almost overnight, in April 1945, when he exhibited *Figure in a Landscape* and the now well-known triptych, *Three Studies for Figures at the Base of the Crucifixion*. His works depict a horror-fantasy existence, concentrating on the repulsive aspects of human shape in weird landscapes or spaces, twisted and contorted in his handling of the paint, He also executed a series of paintings based on the portrait, by VELAZQUEZ, of Pope Innocent X. Bacon is an important but isolated figure in British art.

Bacon, Roger (*c*. 1214–92) English monk and philosopher, known as *Doctor Mirabilis* by his contemporaries for his wide learning and daring anti-scholastic speculation. Like his later namesake, Francis BACON (1561–1626), he advocated the supremacy of practical experience and experiment over the authority of ancient philosophers such as Aristotle. Bacon acquired the false reputation of being a magician, in which capacity he features in Robert GREENE's play *Friar Bacon and Friar Bungay* (1594).

Bagehot, Walter (1826–77) English social scientist and literary critic, whose works include *The English Constitution* (1867) and *Literary Studies* (1879–95). Bagehot is one of the finest Victorian essayists, and his analyses of such topics as the mystique of the monarchy and the appeal of nature poetry remain as lively and thought-provoking today as when they were first published.

Bainbridge, [Margaret] Beryl (1934–) English novelist. Her novels include *Another Part of the Wood* (1968), *The Dressmaker* (1973), *The Bottle Factory Outing* (1974) and *Young Adolf* (1978). Bainbridge's novels are grim little comedies of ordinary lives disrupted by macabre, and occasionally quite violent, incidents.

Bakst, Léon (1866–1924) Russian designer and painter. He trained at the Academy of Art in Moscow and, after a period in Paris, moved to St Petersburg in 1900. He established himself as a portraitist and illustrator, and designed spectacular ballet sets for the theatres, including the Russian Ballet. He also had his own school where Marc CHAGALL and the dancer Nijinsky were among his pupils. He was a close friend and associate of Diaghilev, and a member of the *Mir Iskusstra* group.

Baldung Grien, Hans (1484–1545) German engraver and painter thought to have worked in DÜRER's workshop and certainly influenced by him, as in *The Knight, Death and the Maiden* (1505). Later influences include GRÜNEWALD, and this can be seen in the use of colour and distortion in his major work, the altarpiece for the cathedral at Freiburg (1512–17). His teutonic taste for the gruesome and macabre is evident in the themes of his woodcuts, notably *The Bewitched Stable Boy* (1544).

Baldwin, James (1924–87) American novelist and essayist, whose works depict the problems of black and homosexual identity in the US. His novels include *Go Tell it on the Mountain* (1953) and *Another Country* (1962); his volumes of essays include *Notes of a Native Son* (1955) and *The Fire Next Time* (1963).

ballad A narrative poem or song in brief stanzas, often with a repeated refrain, and frequently featuring a dramatic incident. The songs sold by the vagabond Autolycus in Shakespeare's *As You Like It*, describing battles, public executions and the like, are typical examples of the sort of *broadside ballad* popular with the common people, up to (and a bit beyond) Victorian times. In 1765, the antiquary Thomas Percy (1729–1811) published his *Reliques of Ancient English*

Poetry (1765), a collection of ancient and not-so-ancient traditional English poems, songs and folk ballads that was to prove immensely influential. Its impact on English poets was deep and long-lasting. Examples of what has been termed the *literary ballad* soon began to appear. Notable examples include COLERIDGE's "Rime of the Ancient Mariner" and KEATS' "La Belle Dame sans Merci."

Among the greatest examples of the form are the *Border ballads*, which stem from the violent world of the English/Scottish borders from the late Middle Ages to the 17th century. Their merit had been recognized by the great Sir Philip SIDNEY in his *Defence of Poesie* (1595): "Certainly I must confess mine own barbarousness, I never heard the old song of Percy and Douglas, that I found not my heart moved more than with a trumpet." Sidney's opinion was to remain very much a minority one until the late 18th century, when the rediscovery of the great ballad heritage coincided with the birth pangs of the ROMANTIC movement, and with enthusiasm for the "noble" and "simple" truths of the world of traditional songs throughout Europe (*see also* MACPHERSON). Representative examples of the Border ballads are the laments "Sir Patrick Spens" and "The Bonny Earl of Murray," the haunting song of fairyland "Thomas the Rhymer," and the macabre "Twa Corbies."

The most important collection of the Border ballads is that issued (in three volumes) by Sir Walter SCOTT in 1802–3, *Minstrelsy of the Scottish Borders*. Many of the ballads here were written down at the dictation of the singers of the old songs themselves, one of whom, James HOGG's mother, complained that they would be spoiled for ever by being written down. As George MacDonald Fraser (*see* FLASHMAN) points out in his history of the Borders, *The Steel Bonnets* (1971), the characteristics of the ballads are those of an earthy, warlike folk: a restless turbulence and melancholy – "Now Liddesdale has ridden a raid / But I wat they had better hae stayed at hame, / For Michael of Winfield he is dead / And Jock o' the Side is prisoner ta'en."

Balzac, Honoré de (1799–1850) French novelist. His great collection of novels and short stories, written over a 20-year period, describes in masterly prose the lives of French men and women of every class. His collective name for the series, the *Human Comedy*, is meant to invite comparison with DANTE's *Divine Comedy*. The series comprises over 90 separate works, whose highlights include *Père Goriot* (1835) and *Cousin Bette* (1847). Balzac was a royalist, a Roman Catholic and a reactionary, and has been hailed by many critics (including MARX) as the greatest of all novelists.

Barbizon School A group of French landscape painters in the 1840s who based their art on direct study from nature. Their initial influences included CONSTABLE and BONINGTON as well as some of the Dutch landscape painters. Their advanced ideas represented a move away from academic conventions, and their interest in daylight effects and their bold use of colour helped prepare the way for IMPRESSIONISM. Leading members of the group included DAUBIGNY and Théodore ROUSSEAU.

Barker, George [Granville] (1913–) English poet, noted for his highly dramatic, often surreal verse. Volumes of his poetry include *Thirty Preliminary Poems* (1933), *Eros in Dogma* (1944) and *The True Confession of George Barker* (1950). The persona portrayed in his poems, that of an exuberantly devil-may-care Romantic poet, had a startling and long-lasting effect on Elizabeth SMART.

Barlach, Ernst (1870–1938) German EXPRESSIONIST

sculptor, who studied in Hamburg, Dresden and Paris and worked in Berlin until 1901. In 1906 he travelled in Russia and there was impressed by peasant building expressiveness. This led him to a simplified, block-like style of carving, intense in its emotional range and imbued with the atmosphere of the medieval gothic carvings that formed a vital part of his sculptural inspiration. Notable among his works is the war memorial at Gustrow Cathedral. His former studio at Gustrow and the Barlachhaus in Hamburg both contain collections of his work.

Barnard, George Grey (1863–1938) American sculptor. He studied in Chicago and Paris and was inspired by a line from Victor Hugo to produce his best-known work, *The Nature of Man,* which he exhibited in the Paris Salon in 1894. Other works in New York include *The God Pan,* in Central Park, and *Two Natures,* in the Metropolitan Museum.

Baroque A cultural movement in art, music and science in the 17th century. In terms of art history, the area of reference is slightly broader and takes in the late 16th and early 18th centuries. It specifically indicates the stage between the MANNERISM of the late High RENAISSANCE and ROCOCO, into which Baroque developed. As a style it is characterized by movement, rhetoric and emotion, stemming from the achievements of the High Renaissance, and it represented a reaction away from Mannerist attitudes and techniques. CARAVAGGIO was among its leading figures when it first began in Rome; BERNINI took prominence in High Baroque as the movement developed in the 1620s. RUBENS' series on the *Life of Maria de' Medici* marks a peak in Baroque painting, and REMBRANDT's work reflected Baroque trends for part of his career. Adjectivally, "baroque" can also be used to describe art from any age that displays the richness and dynamism associated with the movement.

Barrie, Sir J[ames] M[atthew] (1860–1937) Scottish playwright and novelist. His best-known play is the remarkable fantasy *Peter Pan* (1904), in which human children are taken to Never-Never Land by Peter Pan. Barrie's critical reputation shrank dramatically within his lifetime, principally in reaction to the sugary whimsy of much of his large output. The best of his work, however, e.g. *Peter Pan*, the strange little supernatural play *Mary Rose* (1920), the novel of class role-reversal *The Admirable Crichton* (1902), and the feminist play *What Every Woman Knows* (1908), are still popular.

Barry, James (1741–1806) Irish painter patronized and financed in his early career by the writer Edmund Burke. He was a history painter in the Grand Manner and professor of painting at the Royal Academy in London from 1782. His most famous and ambitious work is *The Progress of Human Culture* (1777–83), which he painted gratis for the Society of Arts. His uncompromising egotism caused his expulsion from the Academy in 1799.

Barthes, Roland *see* **Structuralism**.

Bartholdi, Frédéric Auguste (1834–1904) French sculptor, famous for his monumental sculptures, the most notable of which is *Liberty Enlightening the World*, the "Statue of Liberty" in New York Bay.

Bartolommeo, Fra [Baccio della Porta] (*c*.1472–1571) Florentine painter of the High RENAISSANCE and, from 1880, a monk in San Marco, the convent where Fra ANGELICO had worked. Bartolommeo was an excellent draughtsman, and his prolific, lively drawings communicate emotions more easily than his rather austere painting style with its solid, classical figures. He was a contemporary of RAPHAEL and had a notable influence on ANDREA DEL SARTO. Famous among his works are *The Vision of St Bernard, The Marriage of St Catherine* and the *Salvador Mundi.*

Basho [Matsuo] (1644–94) Japanese poet, master of the 17-syllable sequential verse form, whose component verses were to become known as *haiku.* A Basho haiku gave Ian FLEMING the title for one of his novels, *You Only Live Twice.*

Baskin, Leonard (1929–) American sculptor, graphic arts teacher and founder of the Gehenna press. A self-styled "moral realist," his work has affinities with EXPRESSIONISM and is concerned with the isolation and vulnerability of the human figure. A retrospective show of his work was held in 1962 at Bowdoin College Museum of Art.

Bassano, Jacopo da Ponte (*c.*1510–21) Italian painter, a prominent member of a family of painters from the town of Bassano. Jacopo trained with his father, **Francesco the elder** (*c.*1475–1539) and was briefly a pupil of VERONESE in Venice. Jacopo's early work is of Biblical scenes in a pastoral style, in which his vividly painted figures and animals are full of life. His style later became more refined during a vogue for prints after RAPHAEL and PARMIGIANINO, and he used chiaroscuro effects in his more mature compositions. His four sons were all artists, the most important being **Francesco** (1549–92), who continued the Biblical and pastoral themes of his father as well as being a painter of historical scenes, and **Leandro** (1557–1622), who also followed the rustic genre, but specialized in painting altarpieces. Both were important artists in the MANNERIST tradition.

Bauhaus German school of architecture and applied arts founded by the architect **Walter Gropius** (1883–1969) at Weimar in 1919. One of its aims, in common with the ARTS AND CRAFTS MOVEMENT in

England, was to narrow the gap between fine and applied arts; the other was to focus on architecture as the environment of art. Each student took a six-month foundation course in practical craft skills such as weaving, glass painting and metalwork. Among the first masters at Weimar were the EXPRESSIONIST painters KLEE and KANDINSKY. A more CONSTRUCTIVIST influence came with ALBERS and MOHOLY-NAGY, when the Bauhaus moved to Dessau in 1925. Later came a shift in emphasis from craftsmanship towards industrialized mass-production. Gropius resigned from the Bauhaus in 1928; it was moved to Berlin in 1932 and was closed by the Nazis in 1933. A number of Bauhaus masters emigrated to the US, where their ideas continued to be influential.

Bearden, Romare (1914–) American painter from Charlotte, North Carolina. His work is concerned with the life experience of black Americans. His COLLAGES and acrylic paintings are characterized by vibrant energy and expressiveness. One of his most successful works is *The Dove* (1946), and exhibitions include a retrospective in 1968 at the State University of New York and a one-man show in 1970 at the Museum of Modern Art, New York.

Beardsley, Aubrey Vincent (1872–98) English illustrator in the ART NOUVEAU style and a prominent figure of AESTHETICISM in the 1890s. Although he died at the early age of 25, he was a prolific artist. His distinctive use of black and white line and pattern, and his penchant for the morbid and grotesque made him one of the most controversial illustrators of his time. His first set of illustrations was for the *Mort d'Arthur* published by Dent, and he rose to fame with his work for Oscar Wilde's *Salomé* and the periodical *The Yellow Book*. Other notable works include drawings for *The*

Rape of The Lock, by Alexander Pope, and the magazine *Savoy*.

Beat Generation A term invented by Jack KEROUAC to describe a group of American writers, artists and musicians in the 1950s. Notable beat writers included Kerouac himself, whose novel *On the Road* (1952) became the "beat bible," the poets Allen Ginsberg (1926–) and Lawrence FERLINGHETTI, and the novelists Neal Cassady (1926–68) and William BURROUGHS. The beat writers were anti-Western in their values; they dabbled in communalism, loved modern jazz and took drugs (avidly). The term "beat" was said to denote (a) the weariness of struggling against materialist society, (b) jazz rhythm, which they tried to capture in their prose, (c) beautitude. The last quality is somewhat dubious, given the callous exploitation of women in which so many of the beats indulged. Ginsberg's poem "Howl" includes the surprising claim that American society destroyed the "beat minds" (i.e. the beats) of his generation, a judgment posterity has yet to confirm.

Beaumont, Sir Francis, *see* **Fletcher**.

Beauvoir, Simone de (1908–86) French novelist and essayist. Her novels and other writings explore the female predicament from the standpoint of existential feminism. Both her view of the female condition and her literary approach to it derive in large part from her longstanding relationship with SARTRE, which amounted to a lifetime's exercise in damage limitation in terms of ego and libido. Her essay *The Second Sex* (1949) is regarded as a cornerstone of the feminist movement. Her novel *The Mandarins* (1954) includes a thinly fictionalized depiction of her long affair with Nelson ALGREN.

Beckett, Samuel (1906–90) Irish dramatist and novelist. He moved to France in 1932, and subsequently wrote in French as well as English. Beckett described human suffering as the "main condition of the human experience"; this statement is the main signpost in the bleak territory of Beckett's works, where nothing much occurs except brilliant dialogues or monologues of despair. Beckett has been linked with both EXISTENTIALISM and the Theatre of the ABSURD, with his skill for combining highly sophisticated language with a starkly despairing message, with the occasional startling flash of Irish humour. His best-known play is *Waiting for Godot* (1952), in which two tramps await a third who never appears. Beckett was a friend of James JOYCE, and transcribed *Finnegan's Wake* from Joyce's dictation. He was awarded the NOBEL PRIZE for literature in 1969.

Beckmann, Max (1884–1950) German painter who studied at Weimar and also in Paris and Italy before moving to Berlin in 1904. Originally an IMPRESSIONIST and a member of the SEZESSION, his own experiences, and the misery and despair he witnessed during World War I led him to a more distorted, EXPRESSIONISTIC style reminiscent of German Gothic art, as in *The Night* (1919). His expressionism is not abstract but lies closer to social realism in its commitment to moral statements on human suffering and responsiveness. From 1932 he painted a series of nine triptychs outlining these themes, the best known being *Departure* (1932). He was one of the most important German expressionist painters.

Beerbolm, Sir Max (1872–1956) English critic, parodist and caricaturist. His parodies of contemporary writers such as Henry JAMES, KIPLING, H. G. WELLS and SHAW, in such collections as *A Christmas Garland* (1912), are regarded as amongst the finest examples of parody. Shaw, who was often his victim, called him the "Incomparable Max."

Behan, Brendan (1923–64) Irish dramatist, noted for

his plays based on his experiences as a youthful member of the Irish Republican Army, *The Hostage* (1958) and *The Quare Fellow* (1959), and for his auto-biographical account of life in borstal, *Borstal Boy* (1958).

Behn, Aphra (1640–89) English dramatist and novelist. Her most famous play, *Oronooka* (1688) attacks the horrors of slavery; other works, e.g. *The Forced Marriage* (1670), deal with the oppression of women in society. Her plays were very popular and are still highly regarded.

Bell, Vanessa (1879–1961) British painter and leading figure of the Bloomsbury group. Her early work is in a POSTIMPRESSIONIST style, but became more formal and design-orientated with her painting *Studland Beach* (1912). After a period of total abstraction, her later work returned to a more traditional form.

Bellamy, Edward (1850–98) American novelist. His best-known work, *Looking Backward, 2000–1887* (1888), describes a future America in which capitalism has disappeared and communal values have triumphed. The work was very influential on other "progressive" writers.

Bellany, John (1942–) Scottish painter who studied at Edinburgh College of Art and was a prominent figure in the renaissance movement in Scottish art in the 1960s. His work usually centres on the human figure, and human values are of prime importance. His early works, based on the working lives of fishermen, are full of dignity, portraying the heroic and the tragic in everyday human existence. His heritage is in the North European tradition and the influence of Max BECKMANN's "social realist" EXPRESSIONISM. This is apparent in the triptych *Allegory* and in Bellany's development of a symbolic "language" in his paintings.

Bellini, Giovanni (1430–1516) Venetian painter and

an important member of a family of artists. His early Gothic style derives from the teaching of his father **Jacopo** (c.1400–1470) but his later work involves a much more subtle use of tone and colour. He was influenced by his brother-in-law, MANTEGNA, and, in the use of oil paint, by ANTONELLO DA MESSINA, who visited Venice in 1475–76. His vision is of a classical, contemplative dignity, and an important feature of his work is the total integration of figures in a landscape that enhances the atmosphere. A common theme is the Madonna and Child, of which the *Barberini Madonna* is a notable example. GIORGIONE and TITIAN were among his pupils. His brother **Gentile** (c.1430–1507) was official painter to the Doge of Venice from 1474 and is known to have painted murals and portraits for Sultan Mehmet II while he was court envoy at Istanbul. Notable among his surviving works are *A Procession of Relics in the Piazza San Marco* (1496) and *The Miracle of Ponte da Lorenzo* (1500). Both artists were indebted to their father for the legacy of his two sketchbooks containing over 200 drawings that provided an invaluable source of inspiration for their compositions. The paintings by Mantegna and Giovanni of *The Agony in the Garden* are taken from Jacopo's drawings.

Belloc, Hilaire *see* **Chesterton, G. K**.

Bellow, Saul (1915–) Canadian-born American novelist. Bellow is recognized as a highly gifted writer, the dominant theme of his work being the gradual decay of the spiritual and physical fabric of 20th-century urban life. Representative novels are *The Adventures of Augie march* (1953), *Dr Sammler's Planet* (1969) and *Humboldt's Gift* (1975). He was awarded the NOBEL PRIZE for literature in 1976.

Bellows, George Wesley (1882–1925) American painter who was a pupil of HENRI and an important influence on the ASCHCAN SCHOOL. His painting is characterized by a bold, direct style, and the vigorous realism of his work is evident in *Stag at Sharkey's* (1909), one of a series of paintings of boxers. He was a progressive and outgoing artist and one of the organizers of the ARMORY SHOW.

Benét, Stephen Vincent (1898–1943) American poet, whose works include *John Brown's Body* (1928) and the short story *The Devil and Daniel Webster* (1937). His *Ballads and Poems* (1931) includes the poem "American Names," in which is his most famous line "Bury My Heart at Wounded Knee."

Bennett, Arnold (1867–1931) English novelist and dramatist. His most famous novels, e.g. *The Old Wives' Tale* (1908) and *Clayhanger* (1910), are naturalistic narratives of everyday people in the setting of the industrial society of mid-England; the setting being wholly suitable in the eyes of Virginia WOOLF, who dismissed Bennett's work as middle-class, middlebrow and of middling morality. His novels are in fact very readable, and display a remarkable gift for characterization and sharp observation of the dilemmas of human life.

Bentley, Edmund Clerihew (1875–1956) English civil servant, noted for his classic detective novel *Trent's Last Case* (1913) and for the invention of the verse form called the *clerihew*. Clerihews have two rhymed couplets of variable length and often encapsulate an unreliable biographical anecdote: "Mr Michael Foot/ Had lots of loot;/ He loved to gloat/ While petting his stoat."

Benton, Thomas Hart (1889–1975) American painter. He studied in Chicago and Paris and was for a time an abstract CONSTRUCTIVIST painter in the company of MACDONALD-WRIGHT. From the mid-1920s he became a champion of regionalist scene painting and developed his own dramatic style of social realism. Famous among his works are his mural commissions on *American Life* and a series of paintings, *Art of the West*. Jackson POLLOCK was his pupil.

Berger, Thomas (1924–) American novelist, best known for his novels contrasting the American dream with the actual American way of life, e.g. *Reinhart in Love* (1962), and for his remarkable novel of the American West, narrated by an ancient Indian fighter, *Little Big Man* (1963), the film of which is much sentimentalized.

Bernini, Giovanni Lorenzo (1598–1680) Italian BAROQUE sculptor, also painter, architect, designer and playwright. A precocious student, he trained with his father **Pietro** (1562–1629) and was patronized by Cardinal Scipione Borghese. His work demonstrates a tremendous insight, energy and virtuosity. Bernini's career and artistic dominance in Rome were established under Pope Urban VIII; he designed the *baldacchino*, or canopy, for St Peter's and built the huge *St Longinus* (1624–38). At this time he was effectively the leading sculptor in Rome. With the accession of Pope Innocent X, Bernini fell from favour to be replaced by ALGARDI. Subsequently his most successful commissions include *The Ecstacy of St Theresa* (1644–52) in the church of Santa Maria della Vittoria and the *Cathedra Petri* in the apse of St Peter's. He was an unrivalled portrait sculptor, whether depicting *Louis XIV of France* or his mistress, *Constanza Buonarelli* (c.1635), and his surviving paintings are also of outstanding quality.

Berryman, John (1914–72) American poet. His verse is intensely personal, self-critical and highly proficient. His work includes *The Dispossessed* (1948) and *Homage to Mistress Bradstreet* (1956).

Betjeman, Sir John (1906–84) English poet, whose nostalgia for pre-20th century England, coupled with a talent for sharp social satire, made him Britain's most popular poet. He became POET LAUREATE in 1972, by which time he had already achieved the status of a national institution in the UK, his work being very popular with the public yet receiving great acclaim from his peers and the critics. The titles of his collections, e.g. *Continual Dew* (1937), *A Few Late Chrysanthemums* (1954) and *A Nip in the Air* (1972), may give the impression of a slightly fey, eccentric and autumnal character (an impression he assiduously cultivated), but the poems within are often startlingly bleak and despairing. He also wrote widely and wisely on architectural conservation, and published a verse autobiography, *Summoned by Bells* (1960).

Beuys, Joseph (1921–86) German sculptor and important influence on 1970s avante-garde artists. He was a pioneer of "actions" or "happenings," with art as the catalyst that turned human consciousness on its head, as in *Coyote* (1974), in which he spent a week in New York having a conversation with a live coyote. Other performances included the deconstruction and reassemblage of his own works. A retrospective exhibition of his drawings toured Britain and Ireland in 1974. He was one of the leaders of the *Arte Povera* movement, and there is a collection of his assemblages at Darmstadt Museum.

Bewick, Thomas (1753–1828) English wood-engraver from Newcastle upon Tyne, who became famous for his illustrations of *A General History of Quadrupeds* (1790) and *A History of British Birds* I (1797–1804). He developed the art of wood-engraving into a viable process for clear printed illustrations, and his work is simple with bold tonal contrasts appropriate to the medium.

Bible, The *see* **Authorized Version**.

Biedermeier A style in art and architecture in Austria and Germany between 1815 and 1848. It took its name from a fictional character of the time, Gottlieb Biedermeier, who personified the philistine artistic taste of the middle classes. Architecture associated with the style is solid and utilitarian, paintings are meticulous and devoid of imagination.

Bierce, Ambrose (1842–1914?) American journalist and short-story writer. He was much influenced by POE, but the best of his stories, collected in *In the Midst of Life* (1898), have a macabre flavour all their own. The shocking twist at the end of his Civil War story, "An Occurrence at Owl Creek Bridge," has been widely praised and much imitated. His best-known work is *The Devil's Dictionary*, a collection of newspaper pieces first published in book form as *The Cynic's Word Book* (1906).

Bierstadt, Albert (1830–1902) German-born American landscape painter. From the US, he went to study in Düsseldorf and travelled in Europe, returning to the US in 1857. He was a member of the **Rocky Mountain School** of painters who painted landscapes of this formidable countryside, and is famous for his dramatic depiction of it, as in *Thunderstorm on the Rocky Mountains* (1859).

Bildungsroman (German for "education novel") A novel that describes the growth of a character (usually based on the author) from youthful naivety to a well-rounded (often rather smug) maturity. The term derives from GOETHE's *Wilhelm Meister's Apprenticeship*. Two notable examples in English are DICKENS' *David Copperfield* and JOYCE's *Portrait of the Artist as a Young Man*.

Bingham, George Caleb (1811–79) American painter from Missouri, he was a law and theology student and a cabinet-maker prior to entering the Academy of Fine

Arts in 1838. His early work is the most interesting. His precisely composed genre paintings of river life have a fresh and pleasing quality of zest and colour, as in *Fur Traders Descending the Missouri* (1845). His later compositions were influenced by German ROMAN-TICISM and lost something of their raw charm and individualism. He became professor of art at the University of Missouri in 1877.

Bishop, Isabel (1902–) American painter from Ohio, who studied in New York and taught at the Art Students' League in 1937. She was prominent during the 1930s as a painter of social realism, focusing on the transience of figures in the urban cityscape of Union Square, New York, as in *Waiting* (1938). A one-man exhibition of her work was shown in 1964 at the Brooklyn Museum.

Blackmore, R[ichard] D[oddridge] (1825–1900) English poet and novelist. The only one of his novels still read is the classic *Lorna Doone* (1869), a tale of love, outlawry and feuding set in 17th-century Exmoor.

Blair, Eric Arthur *see* **Orwell, George**.

Blake, Nicholas *see* **Day-Lewis, Cecil**.

Blake, William (1757–1827) English poet and artist in the tradition of ROMANTICISM. Blake trained as an engraver and scraped a precarious living as a book and magazine illustrator. His first book of poems, *Poetical Sketches* (1783), includes the remarkable lyric "How Sweet I Roamed," Blake's earliest poem on the themes that haunted his life: the crippling of innocence by cynical experience, and the imprisonment of visionary imagination by materialism. The requirements of his apprenticeship as an engraver led to an interest in church Gothic design and architecture, which inspired his love of precise line and pattern. From 1779 he studied at the Royal Academy, and in the 1780s began to publish his own poems with handwritten text and

drawings engraved on one plate in a new colour printing technique. His first engraved "illustrated poem"
was *Songs of Innocence* (1789), a slim, beautifully
hand-coloured volume, as were the books that followed,
such as *Songs of Experience* (1794), *The Marriage of
Heaven and Hell* (1791), and his longest mystical work,
Jerusalem (1804–20). These works had found a small
but highly appreciative band of admirers by the end
of his life, as did his no less innovative and lovely
watercolours.

Blake also painted in tempera, but never in oils. The
great feature of his work is the power of his visionary
imagination. He held that art, imagination and spiritual belief were interrelated, and this mysticism
characterizes all his work. He held a one-man exhibition in 1809 and published *A Descriptive Catalogue*,
in which he outlined his philosophy on art. In the last
decade of his life he was patronized by John Linnell,
and during this time he worked on engravings for the
Book of Job and his magnificent illustration of Dante's
Divine Comedy.

Blake is now recognized as one of the greatest of all
English poets. His influence on 20th-century poets has
been considerable, AUDEN and YEATS being notable
admirers of his work. In art, he was the source of inspiration for The ANCIENTS, a group of admirers that
included Samuel PALMER, and he has been considered
a forerunner of ART NOUVEAU.

Blakelock, Ralph Albert (1847–1919) American painter. He was self-taught, and his ROMANTIC landscapes
are dramatically lit and imbued with a sense of melancholy. His studies of Indians of the Far West were
unappreciated in his native New York, and by the time
his paintings had achieved recognition and popularity,
Blakelock had been committed to an asylum for the
insane. Representative works include *Indian Encamp-*

ment and Pipe Dance (1872) and *Moonlight Sonata* (1892).

blank verse A term sometimes used to denote any form of unrhymed verse, but normally applied to unrhymed verse in iambic pentameters, i.e. a line of verse with five short-long "feet," e.g. the actress Mrs Siddons's reputed remark: "You brought me water, boy; I asked for beer" (she was known to speak unconsciously in blank verse). The form was developed in English by the Earl of SURREY, and reached its highest peak in SHAKESPEARE's great plays. Other notable works written in blank verse include MILTON's *Paradise Lost* and WORDSWORTH's *The Prelude*.

Blaue Reiter, Der (German for "The Blue Rider") The name, taken from a painting by KANDINSKY, of a group of German EXPRESSIONISTS formed in Munich in 1911. Leading members of the group were Kandinsky, MARC, MACKE, KLEE and JAWLENSKY, who, although their working styles were diverse, were united by a philosophy of the creative spirit in European contemporary art. They organized two touring exhibitions in Germany in 1911 and 1912, and produced an *Almanac* (1912), which included major European avant-garde artists as well as tribal, folk and children's art. The idea of the *Almanac* was to unite music, art and literature in a single creative venture. It was intended to be the first in a series, but the group disbanded in 1914.

Blixen, Karen *see* **Dinesen, Isak**.

Bloomsbury Group *see* **Woolf, Virginia**.

Bluestocking An originally disparaging term denoting members of small, mostly female groups in English 18th-century social life, who held informal discussion groups on literary and scholarly matters. The term derives from the blue stockings worn by a male member of the groups, the botanist Benjamin Stillingfleet. Prominent female Bluestockings included Dr

JOHNSON's friends Hannah MORE, Elizabeth MONTAGU and Charlotte LENNOX.

Blume, Peter (1906–) Russian-born American painter, who studied at the Art Students League in New York. He used the imagery of Surrealism in a precise and meticulous style, and his work is concerned with the communication of ideas through storytelling. His most famous work is *The Eternal City* (1934–7), a satirical attack on the Fascist movement.

Blunt, Wilfrid Scawen (1840–1922) English poet and traveller, who became a staunch anti-imperialist and supporter of Indian and Irish independence movements. His verse collections, e.g. *Sonnets and Songs by Proteus* (1875) and *In Vinculus* (1889), reflect his two main interests, women and politics.

Boccaccio, [Giovanni] (1313–75) Italian poet and author, noted particularly for his collection of 100 short tales (*see* NOVELLA), the *Decameron* (1353), in which ten young Florentines, having fled Florence because of a plague, each tell a story to the others every day for ten days. The stories have flashes of occasionally gruesome and licentious wit, and have had considerable influence on English writers, notably CHAUCER.

Boccioni, Umberto (1882–1916) Italian FUTURIST painter and sculptor. He wrote *The Technical Manifesto of Futurist Painting* (1910) and *The Manifesto of Futurist Sculpture* (1912). One of his early and most important paintings is *The City Rises* (1910), but from 1912, under the influence of CUBISM, he developed a richer, semi-abstract style attempting to depict movement, as in *Dynamism of a Cyclist* (1913). A principal sculpture on the same theme is *Unique Forms of Continuity in Space* (1913). Boccioni died after a fall from a horse during World War I.

Böcklin, Arnold (1827–1901) Swiss painter. He studied in Düsseldorf and Geneva and established his reputation with the mural *Pan in the Reeds* (1875). His work is characterized by his use of mythological creatures to create a symbolic imagery relating to primeval human fears and emotions. Notable works include the five versions of *The Island of the Dead* (from 1880) and a staircase fresco (1868) in the Basel Kunstmuseum, which also houses a fine collection of his work. He had some influence on the Surrealist imagery of the 20th century.

body paint *see* **gouache**.

Böll, Heinrich (1917–85) German novelist, short-story writer and critic. His masterpiece is the novel *The Lost Honour of Katharina Blum* (1975), in which a young woman is hounded by the gutter press. The novel was Böll's response to the same gutter press's attempts to smear him as unpatriotic, his "crime" being a sharp analysis of postwar German society from a liberal standpoint. Other novels include *Billiards at half-past Nine* (1959) and *The Safety Net* (1979). He was awarded the NOBEL PRIZE for literature in 1972.

Bologna, Giovanni *or* **Giambologna** (1529–1608) Flemish-born Italian sculptor in the MANNERIST tradition. His earliest important piece of work is the bronze *Fountain of Neptune* in Bologna (1563–6), a commission by Pope Pius IV, but he is best known for his popular *Flying Mercury* and *The Rape of the Sabines* (1583), both in Florence.

Bolt, Robert [Oxton] (1924–) English dramatist. The best known of his plays is the historical drama *A Man for all Seasons* (1960), which deals with the conflict between Sir Thomas MORE's private conscience as a devout Roman Catholic and his public duty to Henry VIII as Lord Chancellor. In the play, as in life, More accepts martyrdom rather than give up his principles by accepting the monarch's divorce. Bolt's reputation went into partial eclipse during the 1970s, when his work became commonly labelled as "bourgouis," "humanist," "middlebrow" and so forth, despite an often grudging consensus that the plays were skilfully constructed. His central concern, however, the clash between individual morality and public tyranny, remains one of the important issues of the age, and the plays show every sign of outlasting their denigrators. Another important Bolt play is *State of Revolution* (1977), a study of the effect of power on the leaders of the Bolshevik Revolution.

Bomberg, David (1890–1957) English painter who studied at the Slade School of Art in London. His early work was highly abstract, as in *The Mud Bath* (1914). He had one-man shows in 1914 and 1919, and the lack of success of the latter forced him into a period of travel and work in isolation. He later abandoned abstraction for a more personal EXPRESSIONIST style. The value of this later work was not appreciated publicly until after his death, but he is now considered one of the pioneers of British expressionism and an influence on AUER-BACH.

Bond, [Thomas] Edward (1934–) English dramatist, notable for the extreme violence of his early work, e.g. in *Saved* (1965), in which a baby is stoned in a pram. The great public controversy over such plays as *Saved*, which was banned by the Lord Chamberlain from the stage, led in the end to the abolition of censorship of stage plays in Britain. Bond's other plays include *Bingo* (1974), in which Shakespeare condemns himself for not doing enough to reform society, and *The Fool* (1975), in which John CLARE, in his incarceration in an asylum, is portrayed as a victim of capitalist society. Bond's justification for the violence in his work – that it is needed to expose the rottenness of capitalism – has acquired an increasingly hollow tone over the years, while the plays themselves, like much of the work of his peers HARE and EDGAR, had by the end of the 1980s gathered an eerie aura of period atmosphere.

Bonington, Richard Parkes (1802–28) English painter. He lived in France from 1817 and was a pupil of GROS in Paris, where he became a close friend of DELACROIX. He was a first-class watercolourist, noted for the lightness and fluidity of his style. Along with CONSTABLE, whose work was shown in an exhibition alongside Bonington's at the "English" Salon in 1824, he became a strong influence on the BARBIZON SCHOOL as well as on Delacroix.

Bonnard, Pierre (1867–1947) French IMPRESSIONIST painter, a member of the NABIS group in Paris and a founder member of the Salon d'Automne. With the Nabis, he was influenced by GAUGUIN and Japanese art, and designed posters, stained glass and decorative panels. In stage decor he worked on *Ubu Roi* in 1896, and in the early 1900s he painted mainly landscapes. In 1915 a revision of his working style led him to reappraise his attitude to the study of form and composition, which he felt he had hitherto subordinated to a love of colour. He was elected a member of the London Royal Academy in 1940, and retrospective exhibitions of his work were held in 1947 in Paris and in 1966 at the Royal Academy.

Book of Common Prayer The once-official book of services for the Church of England, first published in 1549. The most loved version is that of 1662, the language of which, like that of the Authorized Version, has been very influential on English prose and poetry.

Border ballad *see* **Ballad**.

Bordone, Paris (1500–1571) Italian painter. He worked and studied in Venice from 1510 and was a pupil of TITIAN. In his day, his work was extremely popular and widely acclaimed for its use of chiaro-scuro and vibrant colour. Notable works are the *Presentation* *of the Ring of St Mark to the Doge* (1538) and *Portrait of a Young Lady* (c.1550).

Borduas, Paul Emile (1905–60) Canadian painter. He trained as a church decorator in Montreal and studied in Paris, his early work showing the influence of FAUVISM and SURREALISM. From 1933 he taught in Montreal until the publication of his *Refus Global* manifesto in 1948 aroused the wrath of the established Catholic Church and lost him his job. In the same year he formed the **Automatistes** with a group of young painters whose ideas were based on the spontaneity of creativity. During the 1950s he moved to New York and also held several one-man shows in different parts of the world. His later work was influenced by POLLOCK and RIOPELLE. Notable works include *Sous le Vent de l'Ile* (1947), *Floraison Massive* (1951), *Pulsation* (1955) and *The Seagull* (1957). A major exhibition, *Borduas et les Automatistes,* was held in Paris and Montreal during 1971.

Borges, Jorge Luis (1899–1986) Argentinian poet and short-story writer. Borges's (often very short) fiction is renowned for its use of fantastic themes (in a deadpan style), e.g. *Labyrinths* (1953), to make philosophical points – an approach that owes much to CHESTERTON. A favourite symbol is that of the labyrinth or maze, with a plot structure often based on the orthodox machinery of the detective story. Borges had an impish tendency to create imaginary authors, some of whom have found their way into scholarly works of reference.

Borglum, Gutzon (1867–1941) American sculptor famous for the portraits, at Mount Rushmore in South Dakota, of American Presidents Washington, Jefferson, Lincoln and Theodore Roosevelt. This massive feat of engineering began in 1930 and was not finished until after the artist's death. A monument to the Confederate Army was begun on Stone Mountain in Georgia but was never finished.

Borrow, George (1803–81) English novelist and travel writer. His best-known works are semi-autobiographical novels of gypsy life: *Lavengro* (1851) and *The Romany Rye* (1857), and his great travel book, *The Bible in Spain* (1843), which describes his experiences as a Bible distributor.

Bosch, Hieronymus [Jerome van Aeken] (*c.*1450–1516) Dutch painter, who took his name from the town of s'Hertogenbosch, where he lived and worked. Of his 40 surviving paintings, none is dated, which makes outlining his development difficult. More conventional paintings, such as the *Crucifixion* in the Musées Royaux in Brussels, may be early works or they may in some cases be commissions. His best-known and most intriguing works are bizarre and confusing, as in *The Garden of Earthly Delights*. His imagery is drawn from religious or moral allegories, folk tales and legends, but his imaginative use of the fantastic and grotesque is so strongly individualistic as to defy understanding. His work was collected by Philip II of Spain, and much of it is in the Prado Museum, Madrid. His influence reached from BRUEGEL in the mid-16th century to 20th-century SURREALISM.

Boswell, James (1740–95) Scottish lawyer and writer, whose fame largely rests on his *Life of Samuel Johnson* (1791), one of the greatest biographies ever written, Much of Boswell's private writings were suppressed by his descendants until the 20th century, due to their frankness about his sexual encounters. *See* JOHNSON.

Botticelli, Sandro (1445–1510) Florentine painter who studied under Filippo LIPPI and was influenced by VERROCCHIO. His earliest known commissioned work, in 1470, is a painted panel representing *Fortitude*, and his best-known example from this period is the *Ador-*

ation of The Magi. By 1480 he had his own studio with assistants, and during 1481–82 he worked on the *Moses* and *Christ* frescoes in the Sistine Chapel, Rome. *The Madonna of the Magnificat* (1480s), his best-known altarpiece, is one of several Virgin and Child paintings. He also did a series of mythological paintings for the Medici family, the most famous of which are *Primavera* and *The Birth of Venus* (1482–4). His early style is linear and graceful with elements of Gothic ornamentation, but in the 1490s his work became more dramatic and emotional, as in the intensity of *Pieté*, or the ecstasy of *Mystic Nativity* (1500). By the time of his death his popularity had declined, and his reputation was restored only in the late 19th century through the admiration of the PRE-RAPHAELITES and the esteem in which his work was held by RUSKIN.

Boucher, François (1703–70) French Rococo painter who trained as an engraver and was an associate of WATTEAU. In 1723 he took first prize at the Academy and became a member in 1734. From 1727 he was in Rome and was influenced by TIEPOLO. He became a leading interior designer and worked on the royal palace at Versailles as well as designing stage sets and costume details for the Paris Opera. From 1755 he was director of Gobelin's tapestry factory, and in 1765 he became court painter to Louis XV. Madame de Pompadour, of whom he painted several portraits, was one of his patrons. His work was elegant and frivolous, and he treated traditional mythological scenes with wit and humour. Accused by his critics of artificiality and a lack of originality, he responded that he never worked directly from nature because it was "too green, and badly lit." Notable among his works are *The Triumph of Venus* (1740), *The Reclining Girl* (1751) and *The Rising and the Setting of the Sun* (1753). FRAGONARD was his pupil.

Boudin, Eugene (1824–98) French painter from Le Havre, where he had a stationery and picture framing business. He always painted directly from nature, mainly beaches, skies and seascapes, and his light, spontaneous brushwork had a strong influence on the IMPRESSIONISTS; MONET and COROT were among his friends and customers who encouraged his painting. Some of his work was hung in the first Impressionist exhibition in 1874.

Bourdelle, Emile Antoine (1861–1929) French sculptor who studied at Toulouse and, after moving to Paris in 1884, exhibited at the Salon des Artistes Françaises. From 1896 he worked under RODIN, and his work up until about 1910 reflects Rodin's Romantic expressiveness. After this period, he developed a more classical style and worked relief sections of the Théâtre des Champs Elysées. Notable among his works are the several versions of *Beethoven, Tragic Mask* and the statue *Meracles Archer* (1910). A retrospective exhibition was held in 1928.

Bouts, Dieric (d.1475) Dutch painter from Haarlem, who lived and worked mainly in Louvain. His first major commission was an altarpiece for St Peter's Church there. Although influenced by van der WEYDEN and **Albert van Ouwater** (*fl.* 1450s–1470s), a Dutch landscape artist, his style is distinctive in its use of perspective, controlled composition, richness of colour and lyrical treatment of landscape. Notable works include *The Last Supper* from the Louvain altarpiece and *The Justice of Emperor Otto*. His treatment of themes such as *Mater Dolorosa* were popular and much copied.

Bowdler, Dr Thomas (1754–1825) Scottish physician and editor, who published *Family Shakespeare* in 1818. As the title might suggest, Bowdler's aim was to produce an edition of SHAKESPEARE suitable for family reading, i.e. with all indecency and blasphemy removed. The work was very successful, and the verb "to bowdlerize" became part of the English language. Bowdler's censorship was in fact decidedly erratic; many completely inocuous expressions are omitted, while he failed to recognize many of Shakespeare's grosser puns.

Bowen, Elizabeth (1899–1973) Anglo-Irish novelist and short-story writer. Her works, e.g. the novels *The Death of the Heart* (1938) and *The Heat of the Day* (1949), have been highly praised for their sharp, witty observation of upper-middle class life.

Bowles, Paul (1910–) American novelist, short-story writer and composer. His best-known work is the novel *The Sheltering Sky* (1949), a semi-autobiographical account of his marriage to the lesbian novelist Jane Auer Bowles (1917–73) and their life in Morocco. Bowles is commonly regarded as the spiritual father of the BEAT GENERATION, but is nonetheless an intriguing and highly skilful writer. His musical compositions include several very fine piano pieces, three operas (including two based on plays by Lorca), and "Blue Mountain Ballads" (lyrics by Tennessee WILLIAMS).

Boyd, William [Andrew Murray] (1953–) Ghanaian-born Scottish novelist. His highly regarded novels frequently feature expatriate Britons in exotic locations, and include *A Good Man in Africa* (1981), *Stars and Bars* (1984), *The New Confessions* (1987) and *Brazzaville Beach* (1990).

Bradbury, Malcolm [Stanley] (1932–) English novelist and critic. His best-known novels are satirical accounts of academic life, e.g. *Eating People is Wrong* (1959), *Stepping Westward* (1965) and *The History Man* (1975). His critical works include *Possibilities* (1973) and *The Novel Today* (1977).

Bradbury, Ray (1920–) American science-fiction

novelist and short-story writer. Long regarded as one of the finest writers in the science-fiction genre, his works include the novel *Fahrenheit 451* (1959), and a highly original collection of short stories describing the colonization of Mars, *The Martian Chronicles* (1950).

Bradford, Rev. E[dwin] E[mmanuel] (1860–1944) English poet and clergyman. Bradford's collections of verses, e.g. *In Quest of Love* (1914), extol the physical beauty of young boys in a very English manner. AUDEN and BETJEMAN were tongue-in-cheek admirers of his work; Hugh MACDIARMID, however, writing from a mysterious perspective all his own, was quite sincere in his description of Bradford's poems as "virile, useful work."

Brady, Nicholas *see* **Tate, Nahum**.

Bramante, Donate (1444–1514) Italian architect and painter, who was a leading and influential architect of the high RENAISSANCE, although the beginnings of his career were centred on painting. His *Men at Arms* frescoes (1480–5), now in the Brera in Milan, and the *Philosophers of the Palazzo del Podista* are examples of early works, and he is thought to have had an influence on Milanese painting. He designed the new St Peter's in Rome, although his plans were modified in the building. RAPHAEL was his pupil, and portrayed him as Euclid in *The School of Athens*.

Brancusi, Constantin (1876–1957) Romanian-born French sculptor, who trained at Crajaua and Bucharest before moving to Paris in 1904, where he met RODIN and worked briefly with MODIGLIANI. Influenced by the woodworking tradition of his native Romania and by the primitivist works of DERAIN and GAUGUIN, he abandoned modelling techniques in favour of direct carving, Working in marble, limestone and, later, in metals and wood, he allowed the materials to lead his craftsmanship and evolved a style of reduction of human and organic forms, as in *Sleeping Muse* (1910) and *The Seal* (1936). He made sculptures for the park at Tiju Jiu in Romania, including the huge *Endless Column* (1937). The essential simplicity of his style, his excellent craftsmanship and sensitivity to materials made him one of the most influential and well-respected sculptors of the 20th century.

Braque, Georges (1882–1963) French painter and, along with PICASSO, one of the founders of CUBISM. He was influenced by the FAUVES' use of colour in his early work, and in 1906 he saw and was impressed by the paintings of CÉZANNE. In 1907 he met Picasso and worked closely with him developing COLLAGE techniques in painting and introducing stencilled lettering, which emphasized the flatness of the picture plane. He was mobilized in 1914 in World War I and was severely wounded in 1917. His subsequent work concentrated on the classical traditions of still life, using his own unique structural methods. Later pieces show a broader handling of paint, elegance of pattern and restrained use of colour. Typical of his work are his series paintings of *Still Lifes* (1920s), *Atelier* (1948–50) and *Oiseaux* (1950–58).

Brecht, Bertolt (1898–1956) German dramatist and poet. His theory of "epic theatre" was developed in the 1920s, its basis being a loose structure of episodic scenes, connected by speeches or songs, which apply a commentary on the action, intended to demonstrate the falsity of any conclusion incompatible with supposedly Marxist dialectics. The purpose of Brecht's theatrical devices, borrowed from cabaret and popular theatre, is to "alienate" the audience into a state of objective receptivity to the playwright's message (*see* ALIENATION EFFECT). *The Threepenny Opera* (1928), for which Kurt Weill wrote the music, is an early example of the approach, which was further developed in plays such as *Galileo* (1938), and his best play, *Mother Courage* (1941). He settled in the U.S. during Nazi rule in Germany, returning to East Berlin in 1949, where he founded the Berliner Ensemble theatre. Brecht's main appeal has always been to Western leftwing or liberal audiences. Before the revolutions of 1989 in Eastern Europe, his plays were regarded as too gloomy by the governing commissars of socialist realism, and after, few find the plays to be of any relevance. *See also* GRASS.

Brenton, Howard (1942–) English dramatist. His plays, which are characteristic of 1970s left-wing "political" theatre, include *The Churchill Play* (1974). *The Romans in Britain* (1980) and (in collaboration with David HARE) a forceful condemnation of the right-wing press, *Pravda* (1985).

Breton, André *see* **Surrealism**.

Brideshead generation *see* **Acton, Sir Harold; Waugh, Evelyn**.

Bridges, Robert (1844–1930) English poet. Although very popular in his lifetime and appointed POET LAUREATE in 1913, Bridges's reputation has sunk to the point where he is largely remembered for having encouraged HOPKINS. His last long poem was *The Testament of Beauty* (1929), which he regarded as the summation of his work.

broadside ballad *see* **ballad**.

Brodsky, Joseph (1940–) Russian poet. Brodsky emerged as a major poet in the late 1950s, when many began to see him as following in the path of the great AKHMATOVA. He was arrested by the Soviet authorities in 1964 in the usual manner (for "parasitism"), was released after international pressure, and settled in the US, becoming an American citizen in 1977. Collections of his work include *Selected Poems* (with a fore-

word by AUDEN, 1973), and *A Part of Speech* (1980). He
was awarded the NOBEL PRIZE for literature in 1987.

Brontë, Anne (1820–49), **Charlotte** (1816–55) and
Emily (1818–48) English novelists and poets. With
their brother Branwell (1817–48), the sisters were
brought up by their father, an Irish curate, at Haworth
parsonage on the bleak Yorkshire moors, their mother
having died in 1821. Two elder sisters died in 1825,
and ill health dogged the surviving sisters and brother.
In 1846, the sisters published a volume of poetry
entitled *Poems by Curer, Acton and Ellis Bell*, the
pseudonyms repectively of Charlotte, Emily and Anne.
The volume attracted little attention, but in 1847
Charlotte's *Jane Eyre*, much of it based on her own
experiences at boarding school and as a governess, was
published to critical and popular acclaim. Emily's
Wuthering Heights and Anne's *Agnes Grey* were also
published in 1847, and in 1848, the year of Emily's
death from consumption, Anne published her second
novel, *The Tenant of Wildfell Hall*, in which she drew
on the character of Branwell. Charlotte survived her
sisters and brother and completed two more novels,
Shirley (1849) and *Villette* (1853). Of all the Brontës'
exceptionally fine novels, *Wuthering Heights* is the
greatest: a powerful romance with complex layers of
narration and meaning that is quite unlike any other
novel. Some of Emily's equally remarkable poems, e.g.
"Cold in the Earth," have the same strange emotional
intensity as her great novel.

bronze A metal alloy of bronze mixed with tin and
occasionally lead and zinc, which has been used as a
medium for sculpture since ancient times, when it was
cast solid using wooden models. Modern techniques use
hollow casting methods of sand casting or *cire perdue*
("lost wax").

Brooke, Rupert (1887–1915) English poet, whose

patriotic poems on the outbreak of World War I (*1914 and Other Poems*), published posthumously, 1915) were extremely popular during the war. He died of blood poisoning on his way to active service in the Dardenelles.

Brookner, Anita (1938–) English novelist and art historian. Her novels, e.g. *Hotel du Lac* (1984), *Friends from England* (1987) and *Latecomers* (1988), usually feature sensitive and refined heroines in love with men who become entangled with less sensitive and refined women. Her works on art include *Watteau* (1968) and *Jacques-Louis David* (1981).

Brooks, James (1906–) American painter who studied at Dallas and at the Art Students' League in New York. He worked as an artist-reporter during World War II, and his work in the 1930s with the Federal Arts Project was a colourful, monumental realism that developed into ABSTRACT EXPRESSIONISM during the 1940s. He turned to ACTION PAINTING in the 1950s and exhibited with others at the Peridot Gallery. A retrospective show of his work was in the Whitney Museum of American Art during 1963–4.

Brouwer, Adriaen (*c*.1605–38) Flemish painter who was a pupil of Frans HALS at Haarlem. His earliest work is richly coloured in the style of Flemish art. In 1631 he moved to Antwerp, and his palette took on the monochromatic tones associated with Dutch painting of the time. Brouwer provides an important link between the two traditions, and his humorous, low-life genre painting was much imitated, although his excellent characterization and brushwork were never matched. *The Smokers* (*c*.1637) and *The Five Senses* are representative of his work, which was collected by both RUBENS and REMBRANDT

Brown, Ford Madox (1821–93) English painter born in Calais. He studied at Antwerp, Paris and Rome before

settling in England in 1845. His early work is ROMAN-
TIC, as in *Execution of Mary, Queen of Scots* (1841), but
his links with the PRE-RAPHAELITES led to a develop-
ment of his painting in this style in his *Chaucer at the
Court of Edward III* (1851). His best-known picture is
The Last of England (1855), and his most detailed
piece, entitled *Work* (1863), took 11 years to complete.
He also designed glass and furniture for the William
MORRIS Company.

Browne, Sir Thomas (1605–82) English physician and
author. His two most famous works are *Religio Medici*
(1642), a meditation on Christian attitudes to life that
argues finely for religious toleration, and *Hydriotaphia
or Urn Burial* (1658), a quirky meditation inspired by
burial urns. Browne's ability to convey deep insights
in lightly flowing yet grandiloquent prose has been
much admired, and is almost impossible to imitate successfully (JOYCE comes close in a section of *Ulysses*).

Browning, Elizabeth Barrett (1806–81) English poet,
whose reputation grew rapidly in the early 1840s to
the point where she became regarded as a probable
successor to WORDSWORTH as poet laureate. She married Robert BROWNING in 1846, against the wishes of
her father. The marriage was an idyllic one; they spent
15 happy years together until her death in his arms.
Against all precedent, her creative life did not diminish
in her husband's shadow. Among the great works that
followed their marriage were *Sonnets from the Portu-
guese* (1850) and *Aurora Leigh* (1857). She also wrote
vigorously on social issues ("The Cry of the Children"
in her 1844 *Poems* was widely reprinted in campaigns
against child labour) and strongly supported Italian
independence.

Browning, Robert (1812–89) English poet, husband of
Elizabeth Barrett BROWNING. Browning's exuberant
and often bizarre poetic language, his gift for narra-

tive, strong sense of realism and innovative experiments in form, established him in his own lifetime as one of England's greatest poets. Many of his most anthologized poems, e.g. "Pippa Passes", are in his *Bells and Pomegranates* collection (1841–6), His masterpiece is *The Ring and the Book* (1869), a complex psychological study of a 17th-century murder in Italy. His *Men and Women* (1855) includes his great love poem "Love Among the Ruins," and the powerfully enigmatic "Childe Roland to the Dark Tower Came." His "child's story," *The Pied Piper of Hamelin* (1842), is perenially popular.

Brücke, Die (German for "The Bridge") An association of German artists founded in 1905 in Dresden by KIRCHNER and others. The name derives from Nietszche's idea that a man can be seen as a bridge towards a better future, and in this the artists saw themselves as a link with the art of the future, in a move away from realism and IMPRESSIONISM. They also wanted to integrate art and life and so lived together in community in the tradition of the medieval guilds system. Their influences included African tribal art and the works of van GOGH and FAUVISM. Their painting was mainly EXPRESSIONIST, although comprehending a variety of styles and techniques. They concentrated initially on figures in landscape and portrait, and made use of texture, clashing colour and aggressive distortion to powerful effect. With Emile NOLDE, they founded the Neue SEZESSION in 1910, a protest against the refusal of Nolde's *Pentecost* by the Berlin SEZESSION. Members of Die Brücke then split away from the Neue Sezession and exhibited as a group with Der BLAUE REITER. In 1913 the group disbanded because of conflicts over aims and policies in relation to the development of CUBISM.

Bruegel *or* **Brueghel, Pieter the Elder** (*c.*1525–69) Flemish painter and draughtsman and father of Pieter

BRUEGHEL [THE YOUNGER] and Jan BRUEGHEL. A
prominent figure in Flemish art in the mid-16th
century, he rated alongside van EYCK and RUBENS.
Bruegel studied under Pieter Coeck van Aelst and later
married his tutor's daughter. In 1551 he joined the
Antwerp Guild before travelling to France and Italy.
More influenced by landscape than southern art, his
drawings of the Alps demonstrate his sensitivity to
detail and his vision of space, which dominated his
subsequent landscape paintings. His print drawings
for James Cock in 1555 included such intriguing and
detailed drawings as *Big Fish eat Little Fish*, which
shows the influence of BOSCH. Paintings in this style
include *The Fall of the Rebel Angels* and *The Triumph
of Death*. He later moved to Brussels and was commissioned in 1565 by Nicholaes Jonghelsch for *The
Months*, a series of paintings that included the famous
Hunters in the Snow. This particular painting represents an important development in the form of landscape painting. His philanthropic and tolerant view of
humanity is ably depicted in his paintings of rustic
festivities and proverbial themes, such as *Peasant
Wedding Dance* (1566) and *The Misanthrope* (1568).
Only about 50 of his paintings survive, but he remains
one of the world's most admired and outstanding painters.

Brueghel, Jan (1568–1625) Flemish painter, also
called "Velvet" Brueghel, son of Pieter BRUEGEL THE
ELDER. He was trained by Mayeken Verhulst, his
grandmother, and patronized by Cardinal Borromeo in
his travels to Italy from 1594–96. He became Dean of
the Antwerp Guild in 1602. He painted mainly landscapes and still lifes, particularly flowers, which were
richly coloured and detailed. His landscape work was
often of wooded scenes peopled with mythological
characters or coaches and horses, usually on small can-

vases. He collaborated with other artists, including RUBENS, with whom he painted the *Garden of Eden.* David SEGHERS was among his pupils.

Brueghel, Pieter the Younger (1564–1638) Flemish painter, also called "Hell" Brueghel, son of Pieter BRUEGEL THE ELDER. He studied with Gillis van Coninxloo in the Antwerp Guild in 1585. Much of his work involved some copying of his father's works, which provided a source for his own compositions. He had a penchant for scenes of fire and brimstone, as in *The Burning of Troy,* and his work in general is of high quality.

Brunelleschi, Filippo (1377–1446) Italian sculptor and architect. He was a leading figure among the group of RENAISSANCE artists in Florence that included DONATELLO and ALBERTI. He trained initially as a goldsmith, and his earliest extant sculptures are of silver figures, dating from 1398–1400, in Pistoia Cathedral. In 1402 he was defeated by GHIBERTI in a competition to design new doors for the baptistry in Florence Cathedral; each of their entries is now in the Bargello, Florence. His subsequent achievements were mainly in the field of architecture. A major project was building the dome of Florence Cathedral. A later sculptural masterpiece is his painted wooden *Crucifix* (1412) in the church of Santa Maria Novella. He also made major contributions to the development of perspective.

brushwork The "handwriting" of a painter, i.e. the distinctive way in which he or she applies paint, either smoothly or roughly, thinly or thickly, in long strokes or short. Like handwriting, brushwork is individual to a painter.

Buchan, John, 1st Baron Tweedsmuir (1875–1940) Scottish novelist, statesman and Governor-General of Canada 1935–40. Buchan wrote voluminously on many subjects, but is now remembered chiefly for his adventure novels, such as *The Thirty-nine Steps* (1915), *Greenmantle* (1916) and *Sick Heart River* (1941). The novels often have a haunting, mystical element, particularly in landscape description, that is matched by few other writers.

Buck, Pearl S[ydenstricker] (1892–1973) American novelist. Her most famous work, based on her and her husband's experiences as missionaries in China, is *The Good Earth* (1938). She was a highly prolific author (over 80 books, very few of which are now read), and was awarded the NOBEL PRIZE for literature in 1938.

Buckingham, 2nd Duke of *see* **Villiers, George**.

Buffet, Bernard (1928–) French painter. He studied at the Ecole des Beaux-Arts in 1944, and in 1948 he shared the Prix de la Critique. He was a member of the Homme-Témoin group, and by the 1950s had held several successful exhibitions at the Drouant-David gallery. His distinctive linear style was popular and much admired by younger artists. The pessimistic atmosphere of his solitary, emaciated figures and distorted still lifes painted from a restrained and neutral palette seems to capture a sense of postwar futility that had great popular appeal. His later work has been criticized for its formularity and slickness.

Bulgakov, Mikhail (1891–1940) Russian novelist and dramatist. His novel *The White Guard* (1925) was staged in Moscow in 1926 (as *The Days of the Turbins*) and created a sensation through its sympathetic portrayal of the anti-Bolshevik forces in the Russian revolution. (With a tyrant's whimsy, Stalin protected the author against reprisal.) His masterpiece is the novel *The Master and Margarita* (published posthumously, 1966), a grimly comic fantasy in which the Devil creates havoc in modern Moscow, and befriends the lover of a sick author who is writing a novel about the

Crucifixion, scenes from which are interposed in the main plot.

Bunyan, John (1628–88) English author, whose *Pilgrim's Progress* (1678–84) is perhaps the greatest ALLEGORY in the English language. The book is a Puritan fable in which Christian, a pilgrim, abandons his wife and children to search for the Celestial City of salvation, meeting helpful and unhelpful characters along the way. Bunyan's language (influenced strongly by the AUTHORIZED VERSION) is simple and his vocabulary is restricted to common English words, yet his mastery of dialogue and chartacterization have made his book one of the greatest ever written.

Buonarotti, Michaelangelo *see* **Michaelangelo Buonarotti**.

Buonisegna, Duccio de *see* **Duccio di Buonisegna**.

Burchfield, Charles (1893–1967) American painter from Ohio, who studied at Cleveland Museum School of Art. During his early career he suffered from bouts of depression and obsessive fears that are reflected in work from this period, as in *Church Bells Ringing, Rainy Winter Night* (1917) and *Noontide in Late May* (1917). During the 1920s and 1930s his style became more documentary, although still retaining a sense of strangeness in perspective, as in *November Evening* (1934). His later work is more mystical and atmospheric, as in *Sun and Rocks* (1950).

Burgess [Wilson], [John] Anthony (1917–) English novelist, musician and critic. His output is huge and includes several important (usually satirical) novels, e.g. the nightmarish fantasy, *A Clockwork Orange* (1962) and *Earthly Powers* (1980).

Burke, Edmund (1729–97) Anglo-Irish statesman and philosopher. Burke entered Parliament for the Whig party in 1765 (via a rotten borough), and soon achieved high status within his party for his lively defence of constitutionalism and attacks on government abuses. His wise and prophetic attacks on government policy towards the American colonies established him as the dominant political thinker of the day. He was much admired even by his political enemies, and was a close friend of the strongly Tory Dr JOHNSON. His most important philosophical work is *A Philosophical Inquiry into the Origin of our Ideas of the Sublime and Beautiful* (1756), a work that was highly influential on many ROMANTIC writers and artists throughout Europe, e.g. on GOTHIC novelists such as Mrs RADCLIFFE, and on critics such as Gotthold LESSING. It identified physiological bases for the sublime and beautiful: terror is the source of the sublime, exciting "the strongest emotion which the mind is capable of feeling." The source of beauty is oddly defined: an object is beautiful if it has "the power of producing a peculiar relaxation of our nerves and fibres" (Burke's thinking is often obscure). His most significant political work is *Reflections on the Revolution in France* (1790), a treatise attacking the principles of the French Revolutionaries and their British followers and defending the slow, British approach to constitutional reform, which remains one of the most influential statements of conservative philosophy.

Burne-Jones, Sir Edward Coley (1833–98) English painter, designer and illustrator. He studied at Oxford University, where he met William MORRIS, who first interested him in art, and Dante Gabriel ROSSETTI, who remained a major influence on his style. He began to exhibit in 1877 and quickly became popular. From 1885–93 his work dwelt on escapist themes of myth and legend, imbued with a dreamlike, unreal quality of his own imagination. His later work was influenced by BOTTICELLO, especially in his portrayal of female beauty. He also designed tapestries and stained glass for William Morris's company.

Burney, Fanny [Frances, Madame D'Arbley] (1752–1840) English novelist. Her father, **Dr Charles Burney** (1726–1814), was a composer, author of *General History of Music* (1776–89), and a friend of many of the literary figures of the day, notably Dr JOHNSON, who also became a good friend of Fanny. Her first novel *Evelina* (1778), an epistolary novel on the usual themes of love and inheritance, was published anonymously and sold very well, as did her following novels, *Cecilia* (1782) and *Camilla* (1796). The novels were extravagantly praised by such figures as BURKE and Johnson, and Jane AUSTEN paid a fine tribute to her in *Northanger Abbey* (1803). She married General D'Arblay, a French refugee, in 1793. Her prose became increasingly tortuous over the years, and her last (five-volume) novel, *The Wanderer* (1814), has long been labelled unreadable. Her tragedy *Edwin and Elgitha* (1795) is an extremely odd work with three bishops among the dramatis personae and a death scene in which the heroine, played by the great actress Sarah Siddons, is brought from behind a hedge to die before the audience then carried back behind the hedge again. The first performance at Drury Lane ended in mass hysterics.

Burns, Robert (1759–96) Scottish poet. His father was a farmer in Ayrshire, where Burns was born. He worked as a farm labourer then an excise officer, and early on developed a reputation as a highly talented poet and convivial drinking companion. It was said of him that he "loved mankind in general, and women in particular." His fame rapidly spread after the publication of his first book of poems in 1786, *Poems, Chiefly in the Scottish Dialect*, and the former ploughman became the toast of Edinburgh society. The young

Walter Scott, who met him there, described him as having a "glowing eye," unlike any other he had ever seen. Burns wrote many of his best poems while still in his twenties, e.g. "The Cotter's Saturday Night," "The Twa Dogs," "The Jolly Beggars," and "To a Mouse." Apart from the first, these were written in Scots, which remained his best medium for poetry. Most of his poems in the standard vein of 18th-century poetic language (e.g. "Does Haughty Gaul Invasion Threat") are distinctly unmemorable. Critical opinion is divided as to his erotic collection of verse, *The Merry Muses of Caledonia*: some find them cheerfully bawdy, others wish he had never written them. This collection is still not included in most editions of Burns. His lyrical and satirical verse, however, is ranked with the world's finest poetry. *See also* CLARE.

Burroughs, William (1914–) American novelist, who became one of the leading figures of the BEAT GENERATION. His explicit and violent books, e.g. *The Naked Lunch* (1959), are based on his own experiences as a homosexual writer in the rough drug-culture underworld.

Butler, Gwendoline (1922–) English novelist, who has written around 30 crime novels, most notably the series of novels starring Inspector John Coffin, e.g. *Coffin's Dark Number* (1969), *Coffin on the Water* (1986) and *Coffin and the Paper Man* (1990). Butler's work is macabre, witty, and has weirdly offbeat touches: the action of *Coffin Underground* (1988), for example, revolves around a bizarre role-playing game.

Butler, Reg (1913–81) English sculptor, who originally trained in architecture, which he practised up until 1950. He began making sculptures, as an assistant to Henry MOORE, from 1947. A conscientious objector in World War II, he worked as a blacksmith and later made use of this experience in his welding techniques and metal sculptures, such as *The Birdcage* (1951). He rose to fame in 1953 after winning a competition for a monument to the *Unknown Political Prisoner*. His early style was fairly abstract, but later work is more figurative and sensuous.

Butler, Samuel (1613–80) English poet, author of a splendid satire on Puritan intolerance, *Hudibras* (1663), which achieved instant success in Restoration England. The poem, in three parts and based loosely on the narrative structure of *Don Quixote* (*see* CERVANTES), describes the adventures of a Presbyterian knight, Sir Hudibras and his "sectarian" squire Ralpho, with many digressions along the way on such topics as the Civil War, marriage and astrology. Butler's main target throughout, however, is what he sees as the religious intolerance and hypocrisy of the Puritans. *See also* VILLIERS.

Butler, Samuel (1835–1902) English novelist. Like many Victorians, Butler's religious faith was deeply troubled by Charles Darwin's theory of evolution. In later years, he attacked both Darwinian theory and established religion with equal vigour. His best novel is *Erewhon* (1872), a brilliant satire on Victorian hypocrisy in morals and religion, whose title is an anagram of "nowhere." His best-known book is *The Way of All Flesh* (published posthumously, 1903), an autobiographical family novel. *See also* HOMER.

Byatt, A[ntonia] S[usan] (1936–) English novelist and critic. Her novels include *The Game* (1967), a study of the relationship between two sisters, one an Oxford don and the other a successful novelist (Byatt's sister is Margaret DRABBLE) and *Possession* (1990).

Byron, Lord George Gordon (1788–1824) English poet. In his own words, "I awoke one morning and found myself famous," after the publication of his *Childe Harold's Pilgrimage* in 1812, a work that introduced the Byronic hero to the world: a lonely, handsome, melancholy, flawed man, fatally attractive to women, and remarkably similar to his creator. There followed a calamitous few years of great public scandal in which his half-sister Augusta had a child assumed to be his, he married and had a daughter, struggled with debt and public examination of his sanity, and finally left England (and his family) for good in 1816. He stayed with SHELLEY in Geneva for a while, before embarking on a life of romantic intrigue that scandalized Europe. He died of fever in Greece, while preparing to fight for Greek independence from Turkish rule. Byron's romantic verse epics are not now highly regarded, but his superb lyrics, e.g. "She Walks in Beauty Like the Night," and his great satirical poem *Don Juan* (1819–21) will always be loved. (*Don Juan* contains many biting comments on Byron's contemporaries, e.g. WORDSWORTH and COLERIDGE.)

C

Cabell, James Branch (1879–1958) American novelist, whose mock-courtly novels set in an imaginary medieval French kingdom had a huge following in the 1920s. The novels, e.g. *Jurgen* (1919), are complicated intellectual fantasies in which supernatural and mythological characters feature in bizarre plots of obscure import. Cabell's use of archaic language in the novels is in part a device to help him get away with some quite striking sexual imagery.

Cadell, Francis Campbell Boileau (1883–1937) Scottish painter. He was influenced by CÉZANNE and by POST-IMPRESSIONIST art, and from around 1910 he gradually developed his own colourist style. A friend and contemporary of PEPLOE, he went regularly to the island of Iona during the 1920s and 1930s, painting bold, clearly coloured landscapes in a geometrically simplified style. *Interior: The Orange Blind* (c.1928) is typical of his non-landscape works.

Calder, Alexander (1898–1976) American sculptor famous for his moving sculptures, or "mobiles"; non-moving ones he called"stabiles." Originally trained as an engineer, he began sculpting in welded metal in his mid-twenties. Early work consisted of portraits and animated toys in wood and metal, e.g. *The Brass Family* (1929). These were brightly coloured and organic, in a form suggestive of SURREALISM. His first exhibition was held in 1932 and thereafter he exhibited worldwide. Other notable works are *A Universe* (1934), *Mobile* (1958) and *The City* (1960).

Caldwell, Erskine (1903–87) American novelist, whose works, e.g. *Tobacco Road* (1932), are concerned with the lives of poor Whites in the southern US states.

Caliari, Paolo *see* **Veronese, Paolo**.

Calvino, Italo (1923–89) Cuban-born Italian novelist. The style of his work varies from a gruelling realism, e.g. his novel about a child caught up in the guerilla war against Fascism in Italy, *The Path of the Nest of Spiders* (1947), to later, highly complex explorations of fantasy and myth, e.g. *The Non-Existent Knight* (1959), and *Invisible Cities* (1972). *See also* Magic Realism.

Cambridge Platonists *see* **More, Henry**.

Campbell, Roy (1923–57) South African poet. He went to England in 1918 to study, but abandoned Oxford University to concentrate on his poetry. The virile, exuberant language of his first long poem, *The Flaming Terrapin* (1924), an allegory in which post-World War I civilization is seen as Noah's Ark, established his reputation within months of publication. The best of his succeeding verse is bitingly satirical (London literary figures being favourite targets), although he also wrote some fine lyric poetry. He went against the dominant literary current of the day by going to fight for the Fascists in the Spanish Civil War. His *Flaming Rifle* (1939), an unashamedly pro-fascist work, understandably received a chilly reception in the UK and the US. His poem "Zulu Girl," however, is a wonderfully moving (and prophetic) statement of the dignity and courage of black Africa.

Campin, Robert (*c.*1378–1444) Flemish painter, also known as the **Master of Flemalle**. Little is known of his real identity or the extent of his work. Two dated works are the wings of the *Welde* altarpiece (1438), now in the Prado, Madrid, and a painted stone *Annun-*

ciation (1428). Another probable piece is a triptych, *The Entombment* (*c*.1415–20). He may also have been a teacher of Rogier van der WEYDEN, and his development of perspective and chiaroscuro techniques had a considerable influence on the beginnings of the Netherlandish School.

campus novel A NOVEL with a university setting. Such novels are invariably satirical and are equally invariably written by former or practising academics. Early examples are Kingsley AMIS's *Lucky Jim* (1954) and Randall JARRELL's *Pictures from an Institution* (1954). Some novelists, such as David LODGE, whose *Small World* is perhaps the definitive example, have made a speciality of the genre. Another notable example is Malcolm BRADBURY's *The History Man* (1975). American examples tend towards anguish and "relationships"; the British are more concerned with casting a cold eye on the harsh world of academic politics.

Camus, Albert (1913–60) Algerian-born French novelist, dramatist and essayist. His work has strong links with the Theatre of the ABSURD in its portrayal of the helplessness of humanity in a world of random and brutal forces. The spirit of rebellion, however, is an equally strong element in Camus' work (*see* EXISTENTIALISM). His best-known works are the novels *The Stranger* (usually known in English as *The Outsider*) and *The Plague* (1948), and a very important essay on 20th-century totalitarianism, *The Rebel* (1951). He was awarded the NOBEL PRIZE for literature in 1957.

Canaletto, Giovanni Antonio Canal (1697–1768) Venetian painter who studied under Panini in Rome but worked in Venice, apart from a ten-year period in England. An unrivalled architectural painter with an excellent sense of composition, he was commercially successful due to the efforts of Joseph Smith, an English businesman who marketed his work for the tourist trade. Canaletto was a prolific and innovative artist, producing numerous drawings and etchings, not as preparatory sketches but as finished works in themselves. Smith also bought a large collection of his paintings, which he later sold to George III of England and much of this is still in the Royal Collection. Notable works include *The Stonemason's Yard* (*c.*1730) and *View of the Grand Canal*.

Canetti, Elias (1905–) Bulgarian-born German writer, a British citizen from 1952. Of Sephardic Jewish ancestry, Canetti escaped to Britain in 1939. His two best-known works are the novel *Auto da Fe* (1935), an allegory of the collapse of the civilized European mind in the face of the irrational dark forces of the 20th century, and the equally grim sociological study of mass behaviour, *Crowds and Power* (1960). He was awarded the NOBEL PRIZE for literature in 1981.

Canova, Antonio (1757–1822) Italian sculptor. His earliest work is naturalistic and emotional, as in *Daedalus and Icarus* (1779), but his first important commission, for the tomb of Pope Clement XIV (1783–7), shows the calm restraint and graceful contours that led to his becoming one of the major NEOCLASSICAL sculptors of the 18th century. Among his portrait sculptures are the *Emperor Napoleon I* and his sister, *Paulina Borghese*. Canova's considerable talent was out of fashion during the ROMANTIC period and has only subsequently achieved acclaim.

Capek, Karel (1890–1938) Czech novelist and dramatist. His best-known play is *R.U.R.* (1920), in which robots gain human emotions, rebel against servitude and destroy mankind. The play introduced the word "robot" into the English language (from the Czech *robota*, to work) and spawned a host of imitative science fiction works. With his brother **Josef Capek**

(1887–1945), he wrote *The Insect Play* (1921), a prophetic satire on totalitarianism.

Capote, Truman (1924–84) American novelist and socialite. His works include light romances such as *Breakfast at Tiffany's* (1958), and the bleak "faction" documentary novel *In Cold Blood* (1966), a chilling study of murder.

Caravaggio, Michaelangelo Amerighi da (1573–1610) Italian painter from Milan, who worked in Rome from 1592. His earliest paintings were small commissions, such as the *Music Party,* sharply focused but less dramatic than his mature work. The strong, bold, expressive use of light with which he made the technique of chiaroscuro his own is evident first in such works as *The Life of St Matthew* (1599–1602) and the *Crucifixion of St Peter* (1600–1608). After 1600 he painted only religious subjects, portraying ordinary people as Biblical characters, and working directly on to the canvas, to the horror of his religious patrons and his critics respectively. Initial versions of *St Matthew and the Angel*, the *Crucifixion of St Peter* and *The Conversion of St Paul*, all refused by the church authorities, were bought by Vincenzo Giustiniani. Caravaggio fled Rome in 1606 after killing a man in a fight, but his paintings from the last four years of his life include some remarkable works, notably the famous *Beheading of John the Baptist*. Caravaggio died of malaria, aged 37.

Carew, Thomas *see* **Cavalier Poets**.

caricature A drawing of a person in which his or her most prominent features are exaggerated or distorted in order to produce a recognizable but ridiculous portrait, possibly suggesting a likeness to another object. The technique was pioneered by Annibale CARRACCI in the late 16th century and flourished in the 18th and 19th centuries through the work of painters such as

HOGARTH and the caricaturists ROWLANDSON and DAUMIER.

Carlyle, Thomas (1795–1881) Scottish historian and essayist. Strongly influenced by German philosophy and literature, his early works include translations of GOETHE and *Sartor Resartus* (1833–4), a rather odd book which is mainly concerned with philosophical reflections on the appearance of things. This was followed by such works as *Heroes, Hero-Worship and the Heroic in History* (1841), *Chartism* (1839) and *Past and Present* (1843), and soon many began to hail him as the greatest social critic of the age. Carlyle hated the modern, materialistic age and condemned the exploitation of the poor in the Industrial Revolution. However, his adoration of "great men" and subsequent hatred of democracy have a sinister undertone for modern readers. His prose style is described by his admirers as exuberant, highly individualistic and dazzlingly eclectic; others subscribe to the critic Dwight Macdonald's view that his prose ("Carlylese") represents the death of the English language in the gutter.

Caro, Anthony (1924–) English sculptor. Originally trained as an engineer, he was an assistant to Henry MOORE from 1951–53. Influenced by DE KOONING and DUBUFFET, his early work is simplistic in form with an emphasis on surface texture. Later sculptures are prefabricated pieces of metal bolted or welded together and then painted, as in *Midday* (1960). His mature work shows a renewed interest in rusted and weathered materials. Caro has had a considerable influence on younger sculptors.

Carpaccio, Vittore (*c*.1450–1525) Venetian painter. His style shows the influence of Gentile BELLINI, in the series of paintings on *Scenes from the Life of St Ursula* (1490s). His sense of detail and command of perspective are evident in *St George Killing the Dragon,* as is his delicate and graceful use of light. He was a popular painter in his own day, and in the 19th century with the critic John RUSKIN. A notable favourite is *Two Courtesans*, a fragment of a larger painting, which was much copied.

Carpeaux, Jean-Baptiste (1827–75) French sculptor and painter. He won the Prix de Rome in 1854 and returned to Paris where he became a court favourite. He was commissioned for several portrait busts and also sculpted large groups, such as La *Danse* for the Opera and the relief *Flora* at the Tuileries. His work was expressive and emotional and represented a move away from neoclassical trends. He influenced RODIN. Notable works include *Neapolitan Fisherboy* (1858) and *Ugolino* (1860).

Carracci, Annibale (1560–1609) Bolognese painter, a brother of **Agostin** (1560–1608) and cousin of **Ludovico** (1555–1619), together with whom he founded a teaching academy in 1585. Their teaching concentrated on realistic representation of form drawn direct from nature, inspiring a new generation of Italian painters and forming the beginnings of the High RENAISSANCE in the 1600s. DOMENICO and RENI were among their pupils. Annibale, famous as the father of modern CARICATURE, rated alongside CARAVAGGIO in greatness and achievement. His early style of genre painting is direct and lively, as in *The Butcher's Shop* (c.1582). His work on the ceilings of the Farnese Palace in Rome (1597–1600), based on sources in antique sculpture, influenced early BAROQUE painting, and the treatment of landscape in his *Flight into Egypt* (c.1604) influenced the work of CLAUDE and POUSSIN. His brother Agostino was an engraver whose studies of the human body, published after his death, were used in teaching for the next two centuries. Like Annibale, he was a brilliant draughtsman and an important teacher at the Carracci Academy. Ludovico's style of work was much more painterly than that of his cousins, and he remained the driving force at the academy after the others had moved to Rome. His representations of light and texture influenced his pupil GUERCINO.

Carrè, Carlo (1881–1966) Italian painter. An advocate of FUTURISM (he wrote his own manifesto in 1913), he broke away from it in 1915 when he and de CHIRICO founded METAPHYSICAL PAINTING.

Carroll, Lewis [pseud. of Charles Lutwidge Dodgson] (1832–98) English author, clergyman and mathematician. His most famous works are the two remarkable "Alice" books, *Alice's Adventures in Wonderland* (1865) and *Through the Looking-Glass* (1872). The books describe the adventures of a young English girl in a bizarre dream world populated by characters such as Humpty Dumpty, the Red Queen and the Cheshire Cat. The works were written for children and have retained their status as classic children's books, but many modern critics see deeper, darker meanings in the text (*see The Annotated Alice*, 1960, by Martin Gardner).

Cartland, Dame Barbara (1901–) English romantic novelist. Over 500 million copies of her upwards of 500 published novels have been sold, making her one of the bestselling authors of all time. The novels have one basic theme: an innocent, virginal heroine in distress is rescued from her plight by a handsome stranger with a "past." She has explained her worldwide appeal as being due to the fact that "East of Suez everyone wants a virgin." From this perspective, critical disdain for her works may perhaps be seen as a form of cultural snobbery.

cartoon (1) A drawing, or series of drawings, intended to convey humour, satire or wit. Cartoons were commonly used from the 18th century onwards in newspapers and periodicals as a vehicle for social and political comment, and in comic magazines for children and adults in the 20th century. (2) A full-size preparatory drawing for a painting, mural or fresco. The drawing was fully worked out on paper and then mapped out on to the surface to be painted.

Carucci, Jacopo *see* **Pontormo**.

Carver, Raymond (1939–88) American poet and short-story writer. His collections of stories include *What We Talk About When We Talk about Love* (1981) and *Cathedral* (1983); volumes of poetry include *Where Water Comes Together With Other Water* (1985) and *In a Marine Light: Selected Poems* (1988). Carver's work is primarily concerned with the transient nature of American life, which is mirrored in the drifting, temporary relationships of his characters.

Cassady, Neal *see* **Beat Generation**.

Cassat, Mary (1845–1926) American painter, who lived and worked mainly in Paris, where she was associated with the IMPRESSIONISTS, particularly DEGAS, MONET and COUBET. Her draughtsmanship was excellent and her sense of design influenced by Japanese art. Notable works include *Lady at the Tea Table* (1885) and *Gathering Fruit* (1892). *Mère et Enfant* (1905) is representative of a favourite subject in her later career.

Castagno, Andrea del *see* **Andrea del Castagno**.

Cather, Willa Sibert (1876–1947) American novelist, whose novels of immigrant life on the American plains, e.g. *O Pioneers!* (1913) and *My Antonia* (1918), were based on her childhood experiences in Nebraska, and have been widely acclaimed for their realism.

Catlin, George (1796–1824) American painter, who was a lawyer before taking up painting in 1821. A self-taught artist, he painted portraits including over 500 of American Indians, among whom he lived from 1830–36. These were unappreciated in the US but their colourful directness was much praised when they were taken to France and England.

Cavalier Poets A loose grouping of lyric poets associated with the court or cause of Charles I during his clashes with the English Parliament and the ensuing Civil War. (Poets such as MARVELL and MILTON who supported the Parliament cause, however, are not known as Roundhead poets.) The most notable Cavalier poets are HERRICK, SUCKLING, **Thomas Carew** (c.1595–1640) and **Richard Lovelace** (1618–c.1658). The latter's witty and graceful "To Althea" is perhaps the most loved of the Cavalier poems.

Cave Paintings *see* **Altamira; Lascaux.**

Caxton, William (c.1422–91) English printer and translator. His *Recuyell of the Historyes of Troye* (printed at Bruges, 1475) is the first book to be printed in English. Soon afterwards, he began printing books at Westminster in London, with *Dictes or Sayengis of the Philosophres* (1477) being the first dated book to be printed in England.

Cellini, Benvenuto (1500–1571) Florentine MANNERIST sculptor and goldsmith. He made jewellery and medals to Papal commissions in his early career, but little of this has survived. In France in the 1540s he made a famous salt cellar with the gold and enamel figures of *Neptune and Ceres*, and he learned bronze-casting there, returning to Florence to create the great masterpiece of Mannerist sculpture, *Perseus* (1554), commissioned by Duke Cosimo Medici I. He also wrote a famous autobiography, which was found and published in 1728.

Cervantes [Saavedra], Miguel de (1547–1616) Spanish novelist, dramatist and poet. His satirical masterpiece, *Don Quixote de la Mancha* (first part 1605, second part 1615) describes the PICARESQUE adventures of the simple-minded gentleman Don Quixote, his more wordly squire Sancho Panza, and his horse Rosinante, in the course of which we are given the famous chivalric image of the elderly knight tilting at windmills, mistakenly believing them to be giants. Cervantes also wrote other very fine works, notably the short stories in *Exemplary Tales* (1613).

Cézanne, Paul (1839–1906) French painter. He studied in Paris, where he met PISSARRO, a lifelong friend, and the Impressionists MONET and RENOIR. Cézanne's early work, influenced by DELACROIX, was ROMANTIC in style, but from the late 1860s he introduced restraining discipline to his work and began painting directly from nature. He was more interested in form and structure than in the light effects that inspired IMPRESSIONISM. Notable works are views of *Mont Ste Victoire* and *L'Estaque*. He had a one-man show in 1875 and a retrospective was held in 1907. His work had a huge influence on CUBISM and 20th-century art generally.

Chadwick, Lynn (1914–) English sculptor, who experimented with "balancing sculptures" and mobiles in welded iron, inspired by animal and insect forms. He has had international acclaim and won the Sculpture Prize at the 28th Venice Bienniale. A retrospective exhibition was held in 1957.

Chagall, Marc (1887–1985) Russian-born French painter, who studied with BAKST in St Petersburg before moving to Paris in 1910, where he met MODIGLIANI, and DELAUNAY. His style suggests the influences of CUBISM and ORPHISM, but his unique, juxtaposed imagery is drawn from his own childhood memories. A notable early work is *Land the Village* (1911). He returned to Russia in 1914 and taught for a time, but found himself out of step with socialist-realist trends and from 1923 he moved between France and the US, teaching, illustrating books and designing stage sets and stained glass.

chalk A soft stone, similar to a very soft limestone, used for drawing. **Crayon** is powdered chalk mixed with oil or wax.

Champaigne, Philippe de (1602–74) Flemish-born French painter whose patrons included Queen Marie de Medici and Cardinal Richelieu. He was a successful portrait painter and also worked on frescoes at the Sorbonne and decoration for the Palais Royale in Paris. From 1643 to 1664, he produced some of his best work, its simplistic austerity influenced by Jansenist thought, e.g. *Ex Voto* (1662). This painting marks his daughter's miraculous cure from paralysis through the prayers of her fellow nuns at the convent of Port-Royale.

Chandler, Raymond Thornton (1888–1959) American novelist, educated in England, whose detective novels, e.g. *Farewell, My Lovely* (1940), have been widely praised for their sharp, wise-cracking dialogue. Most of his novels have been filmed, and his private detective hero, Philip Marlowe, the incorruptible loner, has become the most famous of the genre.

charcoal The carbon residue from wood that has been partially burned. Charcoal will make easily erasable black marks and is used mainly to make preliminary drawings, e.g. on walls. When used on paper it has to be coated with a fixative to make the drawing permanent.

Chardin, Jean-Baptiste Simeon (1699–1779) French painter, who became a member of the French Academy in 1728. Compared with the fashionable ROCOCO of contemporaries like BOUCHER, Chardin's small-scale genre paintings and still lifes were realistically direct and natural, as in *Rayfish, Cat and Kitchen Utensils* (1728). He later turned to pastel drawing because of failing eyesight and produced various portraits of himself and his wife. FRAGONARD was his pupil.

Chatterton, Thomas (1752–70) English poet, whose

pseudo-medieval poems (which he claimed were written by an imagined 15th-century poet, Thomas Rowley) were published poshumously in 1777. Chatterton's manner of death – he committed suicide while in distress – probably had more influence on Romantic literature (e.g. WORDSWORTH and BLAKE) than his poetry had, although it does show remarkable powers.

Chaucer, Geoffrey (c.1343–1400) English poet whose great narrative skill is displayed at its finest in *The Canterbury Tales* (c.1387). This masterpiece of wit and humour is set in a London inn, and consists of short stories, mostly in rhyming couplets, told to each other by various pilgrims from all social strata on their way to Canterbury. *See also* BOCCACCIO.

Chavannes, Puvis de *see* **Puvis de Chavannes**.

Cheever, John (1912–82) American short-story writer and novelist. Short-story collections include *The Enormous Radio and Other Stories* (1953), *The Brigadier and the Golf Widow* (1964) and *The World of Apples* (1973). His four novels are *The Wapshot Chronicle* (1957), *The Wapshot Scandal* (1964), *Bullet Park* (1969) and *Falconer* (1977). The main theme of Cheever's work, using his own comfortable background as a source, is the isolated discontent of life in affluent American suburbia, observed with a knowing, ironic and occasionally very funny eye.

The Stories of John Cheever (1978) won the Pulitzer Prize in 1979.

Chekhov, Anton Pavlovich (1860–1904) Russian dramatist and short-story writer. Chekhov's great plays deal with the lives and problems of the Russian middle classes. Summaries of their content, characterized by moods of indecision, helplessness and loss, can give only a faint impression of the universal appeal of their dramatic power, wit, and even occasional knockabout humour. Some famous examples are *Uncle*

Vanya (1900), *Three Sisters* (1901), and *The Cherry Orchard* (1904). Chekhov regarded his plays as comedies, but many critics see the tragic element as uppermost. As well as being one of the world's great dramatists, he was also one of its great short-story writers, his best being "My Life" (1896) and "The Lady with the Little Dog" (1899).

Chesterton, G[ilbert] K[eith] (1874–1936) English essayist, novelist, critic and poet. He was a highly prolific writer who acquired a remarkable facility for writing well in many modes during his early journalistic days. With his friend and collaborator **Hilaire Belloc** (1870–1953) – their partnership was called the "Chesterbelloc," "two buttocks of one bum" – he became known as a gifted disputant for what he saw as the glory of old, agricultural Roman Catholic England, as opposed to the new, industrial, cosmopolitan world, a position which unfortunately also led to his adoption of Belloc's unsavoury anti-Semitism. Chesterton's novels and detective stories, e.g. *The Innocence of Father Brown* (1911), and his weirdly anarchic *The Man Who was Thursday: a Nightmare* (1908), are highly entertaining in their paradoxical complications.

chiaroscuro An Italian word (literally "light-dark") used to describe the treatment of light and shade in a painting, drawing or engraving to convey depth and shape. It is particularly used of works by painters like CARAVAGGIO or REMBRANDT.

chinoiserie In the 16th and 17th centuries, trade with the Far East created a European market for Chinese art and influenced the development of a vogue for things Chinese. Pagodas and stylized scenes, plants and animals conceived to be in the Chinese style began to decorate pottery, furniture, fabrics and ornaments. These were finally mass-produced, both in Europe and the Far East, specifically for this market. A familiar product in this style is the famous Willow Pattern pottery range.

Chirico, Giorgio de (1888–1978) Greek-born Italian painter. He exhibited his series of "enigmatic" pictures in Paris in 1911. These are characterized by figures or statues in a townscape of strange perspectives and unnatural shadows. During World War I he was posted to Ferrara in Italy, where he met CARRÀ, with whom he founded METAPHYSICAL PAINTING. He later came to be seen as a forerunner of SURREALISM, but he himself abandoned modern art in the 1930s in favour of the tradition of the "Old Masters."

Christie, Dame Agatha [Clarissa Mary] (1890–1976) English detective-story writer, whose ingeniously plotted novels, e.g. *The Murder of Roger Ackroyd* (1926), established her as the finest writer in the field of the so-called "genteel" English murder mystery. Her two best-loved creations are the Belgian detective Hercule Poirot and the elderly amateur sleuth Miss Marple. Another recurring character worth noting is the crime novelist Ariadne Oliver, a figure clearly representing Christie herself (and with a good authorial joke: Oliver doesn't know why her detective is Finnish and a vegetarian, and wishes her readers wouldn't ask her why). Highlights of Christie's work include *Murder on the Orient Express* (1934) and *The ABC Murders* (both Poirot, as is *The Murder of Roger Ackroyd*), and *The Murder at the Vicarage* (1930) and *Murder is Easy* (1939) (both Miss Marple, and sharing a quite horrific atmosphere of outward respectability and actual corruption). The most famous of her works is probably the unfortunately named (and diabolically clever) *Ten Little Niggers* (1939). This latter work is the only one of the many Christie works renamed for the American market with a better title than the original: *And Then There Were None*. Critical opinion as to the merit of

Christie's novels varies widely: her popularity with the reading public, however, is unrivalled; her books have sold over a billion copies in English, and another billion in 44 other languages.

Christo Javacheff (1935–) Bulgarian-born American sculptor, who studied in Sofia and Vienna and was a member of the Nouveaux Realités group in Paris from 1958. He settled in Chicago in 1964 and continued his experiments with ASSEMBLAGE and "packaging." His initial "wrapped" objects were small in scale and intended to draw attention to the ambiguity of ordinary objects when parcelled up. He went on to wrap cars, trees, famous buildings, such as the Reichstag in Berlin, and areas of landscape, e.g. *Valley Curtain* in Colorado.

Church, Frederick Edwin (1826–1900) American painter, who studied under COLE, from whom he absorbed a sense of the grandeur of nature. He painted huge epic works based on sketches of South American scenery, e.g. *The Heart of the Andes* (1859). He also travelled Europe and Asia, and his most famous work, the *Falls of Niagara* (1857), was a huge success at the Paris Exhibition in 1867.

Churriguera, José Benito (1665–1725) Spanish sculptor and architect and prominent member of a family of artists famous for their ornate designs for church sculptures and altarpieces. He worked in Salamanca, where he built the high altar of the Church of San Estaban, and also in Madrid. The term *Churrigueresque* refers to any elaborate decoration of Spanish BAROQUE.

Cibber, Colley *see* **poet laureate**.

Cimabue [Cenni de Peppi] (*c.*1272–1302) Florentine painter. Possibly a teacher of GIOTTO, he is mentioned in Dante's *Divine Comedy* as being "eclipsed by Giotto's fame," but there is little documented evidence of his life and work. Part of a mosaic in Pisa Cathedral is known to be his work, and various others have been attributed to him, including the *Madonna of Santa Trinité* in the Uffizi in Florence.

cinquecento The Italian term for the 16th century.

Clare, John (1793–1864) English poet. While working as a labourer, he acquired a wide following in the 1820s and 1830s with such volumes as *The Shepherd's Calender* (1827). As with BURNS, Clare's popularity derived from his poems on rural life, and the fashionable appeal of the unlettered "ploughman poet" image (one much closer in reality to Clare's social status than Burns'). Clare spent most of his life in insane asylums from 1837 on, where he wrote many of the highly original and beautiful poems on which his reputation rests.

Classicism A style of art based on order, serenity and emotional control, with reference to the classical art of the ancient Greeks and Romans. It eschews the impulsive creativity and sponteneity of ROMANTICISM in favour of peace, harmony and strict ideals of beauty. Figures drawn in the classsical style were usually symmetrical and devoid of the normal irregularities of nature. *See also* NEOCLASSICISM.

Claude Gellée *called* **Claude Lorraine** (1600–1682) French painter who studied in France before settling in Rome in 1627. Early works were influenced by the MANNERISTS, e.g. ELSHEIMER, but, drawing from nature with great sensitivity to light, his style matured into a harmonious CLASSICISM. His pastoral landscapes were so popular that he produced a sketchbook of his paintings, *Liber Veritatis*, to guard against forgeries. He had a tremendous influence on 17th and 18th-century landscape painters. Notable works include *Landscape at Sunset* (1639) and *The Expulsion of Hagar* (1668).

Cleland, John (1709–89) English hack writer and

novelist, notable for his novel *Memoirs of a Woman of Pleasure* (1748–9), now known universally as *Fanny Hill*. This is a graphically detailed account of a prostitute's life in her supposed own words, which achieved huge underground sales in the 18th century and has appeared in countless (until our own times, illicit) editions since then. *Fanny Hill* is of interest for three reasons: (a) until modern times, it has been ignored by standard histories of English literature despite being one of the longest running bestsellers in the language; (b) its status as either erotica or pornography is relevant to the seemingly unresolvable modern debate over what, if anything, constitutes pornography; (c) it is, in parts, an enjoyable read, despite (or perhaps because of) Fanny's occasional indignant and entirely spurious moral observations (a technique perfected by Cleland that lives on in the world of tabloid journalism).

Clemens, Samuel Langhorne *see* **Twain, Mark**.

Clerihew *see* **Bentley, Edmund Clerihew**.

Close, Chuck (1940–) American painter and pioneer of "Superrealism" as a reaction against the strong emotions of ABSTRACT EXPRESSIONISM. His work involves projecting photographic images, usually portraits, on to a grid-patterned canvas that is then airbrushed in, a square at a time. These take months to complete and are representative of the Superrealist avoidance of painterly techniques.

Clouet, François (*c*.1510–72) French painter, son of Jean, or Janet, CLOUET. He was appointed court painter in 1541 and is thought to have painted the famous *King Francis I* (1542). His influences included the MANNERISTS, e.g. Pontormo. His excellence as a portraitist can be seen in his collection of drawings in the Musée Condé at Chantilly, and in his earliest signed portrait of *Pierre Quthe* (1562). Another notable work is *Lady in her Path* (c.1570).

Clouet, Jean *called* **Janet** (d.1540/1) French portrait painter and father of François CLOUET, who succeeded him as court painter to Francis I. None of his work is signed or documented, and they are attributed to him through a series of drawings thought to be his. These include *The Dauphin Francis* and *Man Holding Petrarch's Works*.

Clough, Arthur Hugh (1819–61) English poet. Like many Victorian poets (e.g. Matthew ARNOLD), Clough was much troubled by religious doubt and scepticism as to the worth of 19th-century civilization. His *Amours de Voyage* (1858) is a fascinating (and often very funny) exploration of the uneasy intellectual attitudes of the age, and his short poem "The Latest Decalogue" (published posthumously, 1862) remains the definitive assault on the citadel of Victorian hypocrisy. "Say not the struggle nought availeth" (also 1862) is his most famous title, if not poem.

Cobbett, William (1763–1835) English essayist and political reformer. His best-known work is *Rural Rides* (1830), a polemical collection of essays describing the poverty of the English countryside. Cobbett's prose has been much admired (even by his political enemies) for its lucidity and strength.

Cole, Thomas (1801–48) English-born American painter, founder of the HUDSON RIVER SCHOOL and pioneer of American landscape painting. He began his career with paintings from sketches of the Hudson River in 1825. Visits to Europe influenced his later depictions of religious and allegorical themes in dramatic settings as in the series paintings, *The Course of Empire* (1838) and *The Voyage of Life* (1840). CHURCH was his pupil.

Coleridge, Samuel Taylor (1772–1834) English poet. With his friend William WORDSWORTH he published

Lyrical Ballads in 1798, one of the most significant volumes in the history of English poetry. The authors rejected the notion of a special "poetic" language, and believed that poetry should be clear and accessible. Coleridge's main contribution to *Lyrical Ballads*, "The Rime of the Ancient Mariner," a highly dramatic and nightmarish account of a doomed sea voyage, is a typical product of ROMANTICISM and contrasts vividly with Wordsworth's poems of everyday life (a contrast the authors intended). From being an early sympathizer with revolutionary ideas, Coleridge became an active proponent of conservatism, and, with Wordsworth and SOUTHEY, was attacked for this by BYRON. His literary criticism was heavily influenced by German philosophy to the point of incomprehensibility but has flashes of brilliant insight into the creative process.

collage A piece of art created by adhering pieces of paper, fabric, wood, etc, on to a flat surface. The technique was popular with the Cubists, BRAQUE and PICASSO, and is a precursor of the more sculptural methods of ASSEMBLAGE.

Collins, [William] Wilkie (1824–89) English novelist, noted particularly for his remarkable and very influential detective novel *The Moonstone* (1868), one of the earliest and greatest examples of the genre, which introduced the first English fictional detective, Sergeant Cuff.

colour An effect induced in the eye by light of various wavelengths, the colour perceived depending on the specific wavelength of light reflected by an object. Most objects contain pigments that absorb certain light frequencies and reflect others, e.g. the plant pigment chlorophyll usually absorbs orange or red light and reflects green or blue, therefore the majority of plants appear to be green in colour. A white surface is one where all light frequencies are reflected and a black surface absorbs all frequencies. Artists' colours are made by combining pigments of vegetable or mineral extraction with an appropriate medium, e.g. linseed oil. The rarity of some mineral pigments has a direct effect on the prices of particular colours.

colour field painting a movement begun by ABSTRACT EXPRESSIONISTS including ROTHKO and NOLAN towards a more intellectual abstraction. Their paintings were large areas of pure, flat colour, the mood and atmosphere being created by the shape of the canvas and by sheer scale.

colourist A term in art criticism referring to an artist who places emphasis on colour over line or form. For example, TITIAN and GIORGIONE have been called the "Venetian Colourists." The term is, however, too vague to be applied consistently.

comedy A form of drama, usually of a light and humorous kind and frequently involving misunderstandings that are resolved in a happy ending. The first major examples known, those by ARISTOPHANES, are still among the greatest, and became known as **old comedy**. The roots of Aristophanes' work are ancient, based on fertility rituals, and often involve ferocious attacks on named individuals, e.g. EURIPEDES and SOCRATES. The outrage caused by Aristophanes' plays led to the Athenians banning the ridicule of named individuals on stage. The so-called **new comedy** that then developed in Greece, e.g. in MENANDER's plays, is known to us largely through adaptations of lost Greek originals by the Roman dramatists TERENCE and PLAUTUS. It is this new comedy, based upon ARISTOTLE's opinion that the business of Comedy is with people of no significance (who can be safely ridiculed), that was to prevail on the stage until the advent of CHEKHOV, IBSEN and STRINDBERG, with their downbeat comedies of middle-class life. These latter comedies may loosely be described as **tragicomedies**, although the term is normally reserved to denote those plays of the Jacobean period, such as Beaumont and FLETCHER's *Philaster* (1609) and *A King and no King* (1611), and SHAKESPEARE's "dark comedies," e.g. *Measure for Measure* (1604), in all of which the action seems to be leading inexorably towards a tragic ending, but resolves itself (more or less) happily at the end, after trials, tests and tribulations. Fletcher defined the form thus: "A tragicomedy is not so called in respect of mirth and killing, but in respect it wants deaths, which is enough to make it no tragedy, yet brings some near it, which is enough to make it no comedy, which must be a representation of familiar people, with such kind of trouble as no life be question'd; so that a god is as lawful in this as in tragedy, and mean [i.e. 'common'] people as in a comedy" (from the preface to *The Faithful Shepherdess*, 1610, which may be defined as a romantic pastoral with tragicomic elements).

Other notable forms of comedy include the comedy of HUMOURS, the COMEDY OF MANNERS, SENTIMENTAL COMEDY and COMMEDIA DELL'ARTE. *See also* MELODRAMA, MOLIERE; *compare* TRAGEDY.

comedy of humours *see* **humours, theory of**.

comedy of manners A form of COMEDY that features intrigues, invariably involving sex and/or money, among an upper region of society. The central characters are usually witty sophisticates, and there is often much mockery of characters from inferior stations who try to imitate the behaviour of their betters, e.g. a merchant trying to live the lifestyle of a gallant. The form is associated particularly with RESTORATION dramatists such as CONGREVE, ETHEREGE and WYCHERLEY. The finest of these *Restoration Comedies* is Congreve's *The Way of the World* (1700).

Commedia dell'arte A form of Italian COMEDY, popular

from the Renaissance until the 18th century, that used stock farcical characters (such as Harlequin and Columbine) and plots as a basis for improvization. Actors wore masks representing their particular characters, and were often skilled acrobats. The Commedia dell'arte form was given new life by GOLDONI. *See also* MEYERHOLD.

composition The arrangement of elements in a drawing, painting or sculpture in proper proportion and relation to each other and to the whole.

Compton-Burnett, Ivy (1884–1969) English novelist. Her 19 novels are composed almost entirely of dialogue and are mainly concerned with the traumas and dismal hypocrisies of upper-middle-class family life. Some critics regard her as a major novelist, others regard her works as oddities (a common complaint is that the dialogue is stylized to an exasperating degree). Her rather haughty criticisms of other novelists, e.g. of TOLSTOY, have not helped her reputation. The novels include *Brothers and Sisters* (1925), *Manservant and Maidservant* (1947) and *The Present and the Past* (1953).

concrete art A term used to describe severely geometrical ABSTRACT ART.

Congreve, William (1670–1729) English dramatist, whose comedies (*see* COMEDY OF MANNERS) are notable for their witty dialogue and sharp observation of social behaviour in Restoration England. His main theme was love (or its lack) and marriage. *The Way of the World* (1700), with its two evenly matched lovers, Mirabell and Millamant, is his best play.

Connolly, Cyril [Vernon] (1903–74) English critic, who edited the literary magazine *Horizon* (founded with SPENDER and another in 1939), one of the most discussed and influential magazines of the 1940s, in which several important works were first published, e.g. Evelyn WAUGH's *The Loved One*. Connolly's own works include a novel, *The Rock Pool* (1936), collections of essays such as *Enemies of Promise* (1938), and his best-known work, *The Unquiet Grave* (1944), a gloomy, faintly decadent "Word Cycle" of aphorisms and reflections on Western culture (the final issue of *Horizon* in 1950 includes the much quoted comment that "It is closing time in the gardens of the West and from now on an artist will be judged only by the resonance of his solitude or the quality of his despair"). Connolly features as "Everard Spruce" in Waugh's *Sword of Honour* trilogy. The portrayal of Connolly and his magazine (*Survival*, a "cultural beacon which blazed from Iceland to Adelaide") is a sardonic one, but also displays a wary respect for Connolly's sharp critical judgment.

Conquest, [George] Robert (1917–) English poet, historian and critic. His works include *Poems* (1955) and, with Kingsley AMIS, a highly entertaining comedy of sexual intrigue, the novel *The Egyptologists* (1965). He has also edited, with Amis, several important anthologies of science fiction stories. His most important work, however, is his study of Stalin's murderous policies in the Soviet Union in the 1930s, *The Great Terror* (1968, revised edition 1990).

Conrad, Joseph (1857–1924) Polish-born English novelist. English was Conrad's third language, after Polish and French. He qualified as a master mariner in the British marine service in 1894, and his first novels, *Almayer's Folly* (1895) and *The Outcast of the Islands* (1896), set the main pattern of his work: isolated (often outcast) characters tested to their limits in doom-laden exotic settings. His masterpiece is the great novella *Heart of Darkness* (1902), which describes the corrupting and destructive effects of European colonialism in Africa on both exploited and exploiter. (The story was used by Francis Ford Coppola as the basis for his Vietnam war film *Apocalypse Now*.)

Constable, John (1776–1837) English painter. He studied at the Royal Academy in London and while he admired GAINSBOROUGH and the Dutch landscapists, the main influence on his work was the English countryside. He was an ardent believer in studying nature directly, as demonstrated in *Cloud Studies* (1816–22) and full-size sketches for paintings like *View on the Stour* (1819) and *The Haywain* (1820). Initially less popular in England than in France, he influenced BONINGTON and DELACROIX and the BARBIZON SCHOOL, as well as providing a source of inspiration for the IMPRESSIONISTS. He became a member of the Royal Academy in 1829, and as a result of the death of his wife in the previous year, his mature work became more intense and dramatic, as in *Hadleigh Castle* (1829).

Constructivism A movement in ABSTRACT EXPRESSIONISM concerned with forms and movement in sculpture and the aesthetics of the industrial age. It began in post-World War I Russia with the sculptors PEVSNER, GABO and TATLIN. Their work, which made use of modern plastics, glass and wood, was intentionally nonrepresentational. Their ideas were published in Gabo's *Realistic Manifesto* (1920). Gabo and Pevsner left Russia in 1922 and 1923 respectively and went on to exert great influence on western art. Tatlin remained to pursue his own ideals of the social and aesthetic usefulness of his art, and in this he was later associated with RODCHENKO.

Constructivist theatre *see* **Meyerhold, Vsevolod**.

Cooper, James Fenimore (1789–1851) American novelist. Although most of Cooper's 33 novels are now almost completely unreadable, the series of five novels comprising the "Leatherstocking Tales" represents a major landmark in American fiction. The novels, e.g. *The Last of the Mohicans* (1826) and *The Deerslayer* (1841), describe the adventures of frontiersman Natty Bumpo (also known as Deerslayer, Leatherstocking, Hawkeye, Pathfinder). The dialogue within the books is strange to modern readers: the upper and middle classes speak in stilted, formal sentences, the lower classes in barbarous frontier jargon, while the Indians deliver sententious metaphor-laden speeches of solid teak. Once the language conventions are accepted, however, the novels can be read and enjoyed for what they are, the first lengthy fictional study of the frontier myth that continues to haunt the American mind.

Cooper, Samuel (1609–72) English painter of miniature portraits. He was an excellent draughtsman, and his distinctive style of BAROQUE composition made his work much sought after. The writer Samuel Pepys is thought to have paid £38 for a miniature of his wife. Cooper also painted slightly larger portraits of *Charles I* and the *First Earl of Shaftesbury*. His brother, **Alexander Cooper** (d.1660), although less well known was also a painter of miniatures.

Copley, John Singleton (1738–1815) American painter and one of the greatest portraitists of the 18th century. His reputation was established in Boston during the 1750s and 1760s with portraits of famous and professional people, such as Paul Revere and Samuel Adams. He settled in London in 1774 and entered the Royal Academy in 1779. His most popular English works were *Brook Watson and the Shark* (1788) and large dramatic scenes of contemporary events, e.g. *The Death of Chatham* (1780).

Corinth, Lovis (1858–1925) German painter who studied in Paris. His early work shows the influence of Frans HALS and RUBENS. He later developed a baroque style using IMPRESSIONIST techniques, as in *Salomé*

(1899). He was elected President of the Berlin SEZES-SION in 1911 and had a stroke later that year, which made painting more difficult for him. His subsequent work is more expressionist in style, as in *The Walchsee with a Yellow Field* (1921).

Corneille, Pierre (1606–84) French dramatist. The best known of Corneille's 33 plays are the tragedies *Le Cid* (1637), *Horace* (1640), *Cinna* (1641) and *Polyeucte* (1643). Corneille is regarded as the main founder of the form of French neoclassical tragedy (*see* NEOCLASSICISM), a form that reached its peak in the tragedies of RACINE. *Le Cid*, in particular, was enormously popular with the public, but the nefarious Cardinal Richelieu persuaded the ACADÉMIE FRANÇAISE to condemn the play for violating the Unities. Corneille's work was very influential on the course of English drama during the Restoration, particularly on DRYDEN's plays.

Cornelius, Peter von (1783–1867) German painter who studied at Düsseldorf and in Italy, and joined the NAZARENES in 1811. He was head of the Munich Academy from 1825 and later worked in Berlin. His early style was influenced by medieval art, but his later work owes more to RAPHAEL and MICHELANGELO. He revived German interest in monumental fresco painting, a notable example of which is the *Last Judgment* in the Ludwigskirche in Munich.

Cornell, Joseph (1903–73) American self-taught sculptor and pioneer of ASSEMBLAGE techniques. His best-known works are his shallow, upright boxes containing collaged pictures and small objects like pieces of Victorian antiques. A typical work is *Medici Slot Machine* (1942). His style is CONSTRUCTIVIST in approach with SURREALISM overtones.

Cornwell, David John *see* **Le Carré, John**.

Corot, Jean-Baptiste Camille (1796–1875) French painter. He was encouraged to draw from nature, and was influenced by classical landscape. As a result, some of his earliest work was already ahead of his time in originality, as in *The Farnese Gardens* (1826). He continued to produce highly popular landscapes, some more romantic in feeling than others, e.g. *Memory of Mortfontaine*, and was awarded the Légion d'Honneur in 1846. He greatly influenced landscape painting in the late 19th century.

Correggio, Antonio Allegri da (d.1534) Italian painter from Parma, a leading figure of the High RENAISSANCE. His early work suggests influences of MANTEGNA, LEONARDO and RAPHAEL, as in *The Madonna of St Francis* (1515), but it is his fresco work, along with commissions like *Jupiter and Io* (c.1530) and *The Rape of Ganymede*, which had the greatest influence on later BAROQUE and ROCOCO painters. In the cupolas of the church of San Giovanni Evangelista and the Cathedral at Parma he painted a central oculus, or illusory skylight, peopled with figures in flight, a technique copied from Mantegna but with the foreshortening and sense of illusion taken to new levels of ingenuity.

Cotman, John Sell (1782–1842) English painter and leader of the Norwich School of English landscape painters from 1806. He is best known for his sepia and watercolour landscapes, such as *Greta Bridge* (1805).

Cotton, Charles (1630–87) English poet, best known for his contribution (a dialogue) to the 5th edition of Walton's *The Compleat Angler* (1676), and for a translation of Montaigne's *Essays* (1685). Cotton was also a fine poet, whose charming landscape poems, e.g. *The Wonders of the Peak* (1681), were much admired by WORDSWORTH, COLERIDGE and LAMB.

Courbet, Gustave (1819–77) French painter. His early work was Romantic in style, but from the 1850s he became known for a brand of social realism that was as innovative as it was controversial. His large-scale genre paintings, such as The *Stonebreakers* (1850) and *Burial at Ornans* (1851), were criticized as focusing too much on the ugly and distasteful, but these works were important in their deliberate move away from CLASSICAL and ROMANTIC themes, and they influenced the representation of everyday subjects in art. Another notable and controversial piece was *The Artist's Studio* (1855). His later work was less intense and includes more landscape and seascape paintings. A retrospective of Courbet's work was held in 1880.

Coward, Sir Noel [Pierce] (1899–1973) English dramatist, actor and songwriter, best known for his witty "sophisticated" comedies of life on the fringes of English upper-middle-class society, e.g. *Private Lives* (1930) and *Blithe Spirit* (1941), and musicals such as *Bitter Sweet* (1929). Coward's dry, cynical wit has only slightly dated, but his "patriotic," uplifting works, e.g. the play *Cavalcade* (1931) and the film *In Which We Serve* (1942), are now only of note as period pieces. His languid skill as an actor is seen at its best in the film version (1959) of Graham GREENE's novel *Our Man in Havana*.

Cowley, Abraham (1618–67) English poet. His most important works are *The Mistress* (1647), a collection of DONNE-inspired METAPHYSICAL love poems, "Davideis," a Scriptural epic in rhymed couplets on the story of David, and several PINDARic odes, e.g. *Ode, upon the Blessed Restoration* (1660), which were very influential on later 17th-century poets, notably DRYDEN.

Cowper, William (1731–1800) English poet. Cowper was best known in his own day as an engaging satirist and nature poet, but his darker religious poems, mostly written during periods of mental instability, e.g. "The Castaway" (1799, published posthumously, 1803), are now seen as of more lasting importance. Cowper is also now regarded as an important transitional figure between the 18th century and the romantic era.

Crabbe, George (1754–1832) English poet. His poem *The Village* (1783) presents a bitter and true picture of rural poverty in England. The work is a scathing riposte to the more idyllic portrayal of village life given by writers such as GOLDSMITH, and was published with the help of Dr JOHNSON and Edmund BURKE. The "Peter Grimes" section of his poem *The Borough* (1810) inspired Benjamin Britten's great opera (1945) of the same name. Although he wrote mainly in standard 18th-century rhymed couplets, Crabbe's social indignation and subject matter place him, like COWPER, as a bridge between the 18th century and the romantic era.

Cranach, Lucas (1472–1553) German painter, whose early works were dramatic compositions, such as *Crucifixion* (1503) and *Rest on the Flight* (1504), inspired by the wooded landscape of the Danube around Vienna. He became court painter to the Elector of Saxony and painted portraits of classical subjects like *Apollo and Diana* (1530). He also designed woodcut prints for the Protestant cause, as well as painting a number of portraits of Martin Luther.

Crane, [Harold] Hart (1899–1932) American poet. He published only two volumes of verse, *White Buildings* (1926), a series of poems on life in New York City, and *The Bridge* (1926), a WHITMAN-inspired epic series of poems on the "Myth of America," exemplified in such figures as Pocahontas and Rip Van Winkle, with Brooklyn Bridge as the unifying symbol.

Crane, Stephen [Townley] (1871–1900) American journalist, poet and novelist. Crane's greatest work is *The Red Badge of Courage* (1895), a study of the shattering impact of the Civil War upon a young soldier. His volume of poems, *The Black Riders and Other*

Lines (1895), draws on Emily D<small>ICKENSON</small>'s verse in American poetry.

Crashaw, Richard (1613–49) English poet. He converted to Roman Catholicism around 1645, and his often highly florid and elaborate "baroque" imagery was inspired by his reading of Spanish mystical writers. His main work is *Steps to the Temple* (1646), which includes the much derided description of Mary Magdalene's eyes (in "The Weeper") as "two portable fountains."

Crawford, Thomas (1814–57) American sculptor in the N<small>EOCLASSICAL</small> tradition. He lived and worked mainly in Rome, where he designed the famous bronze Ar*med Liberty* (1863) for the dome of the Capitol in Washington.

crayon *see* **chalk.**

Crivelli, Carlo (d. *c*.1500) Venetian painter, who exiled himself following imprisonment for adultery in 1457. He was probably trained in Venice and possibly in Padua too, and in his exile worked in Dalmatia, in Croatia, before moving back to Italy, to the Marches region, his first documented work there being a polyptych for a church in Massa Fermana (1469), which is still in situ. His works, all religious, are stylized and rich in iconography, and many feature metal or plaster details. His most important work is *The Annunciation with St Emidius* (1486), now in the National Gallery, London, with its tightly controlled composition and deep perspective holding together harmoniously various religious and political elements.

Cronaca, Il *see* **Pollaiuolo, Antonio del.**

Cruelty, Theatre of *see* **Artaud, Antonin.**

Cubism An art movement started by P<small>ICASSO</small> and B<small>RAQUE</small>, and influenced by African tribal masks and carvings, and by the work of C<small>ÉZANNE</small>. They moved away from R<small>EALIST</small> and I<small>MPRESSIONIST</small> trends towards a more intellectual representation of objects. Hitherto, painters had observed subjects from a fixed viewpoint, but the Cubists also wanted to represent a more cerebral understanding of their subject. The result was an explosion of multi-viewpoint images, often broken up into geometric shapes and realigned to suggest faces full on and in profile together, to explain the three-dimensional variety of an object or to imply movement, as in DUCHAMP's series, *Nude Descending a Staircase*. Such fragmented images could be highly complicated. Cubism had an enormous and continuing influence on 20th-century art, and other notable exponents of the movement were GRIS, Leger, and DELAUNAY.

Cudworth, Ralph *see* **More, Henry**.

cummings, e[dward] e[stlin] (1894–1962) American poet, novelist and artist. His autobiographical novel *The Enormous Room* (1922), which describes his wrongful three-month imprisonment for treason in France, won him international recognition, and his subsequent experimental free verse and distinctive use of typography was to prove of great influence. His name is given above in the lowercase form he preferred.

Cunninghame Graham, Robert Bontine (1852–1936) Scottish travel and short-story writer, essayist and politician. The son of a Scottish laird and a half-Spanish mother, he ranched in Argentina and married a Chilean poet in 1879. Graham's remarkable political career included service as a Liberal MP, imprisonment after a demonstration against unemployment (Bloody Sunday, 1887), and the first presidency of the Scottish Labour Party. His travel books include *Mogreb-el-Acksa* (1898), a description of exploration in Morocco that inspired George Bernard SHAW to write *Captain Brassbound's Conversion*. His many other books include *Thirteen Stories* (1900), *Scottish Stories* (1914) and *The Horses of the Conquest* (1930). His friend

Joseph CONRAD used him as the model for Charles Gould in *Nostromo*.

Curry, John Steuart (1897–1946) American painter, who trained as an illustrator before starting to paint scenes of American life in the midwest. He worked on the Federal Arts Project in the 1930s, painting murals that established his reputation as a regionalist painter. His works, influenced by RUBENS, are occasionally over-dramatic. Typical of his work is *Baptism in Kansas* (1928).

Cuyp, Aelbert (1620–91) Dutch landscape painter, the outstanding member of a family of artists from Dordrecht. His work was inspired by the river landscapes of northern Europe, of the Maas and the Rhine, his favourite subjects being fields of cows. He had a strong sense of composition and light, creating warm, still scenes of great dignity and grandeur, e.g. *The Maas at Dordrecht*. His father, **Jacob Gerritz Cuyp** (1594–1651) was principally a painter of portraits, such as *Boy with a Hawk* (1643), while his uncle, **Benjamin Gerritz Cuyp** (1612–52), was a genre painter of Biblical scenes, like *Adoration of the Shepherds*.

Cyrano de Bergerac, Savinien (1619–55) French soldier, poet and dramatist. His works include two fantasies, *Comical History of the States and Empires of the Moon* (1656) and *Comical History of the States and Empires* (1661), satires on contemporary social customs which were influential on both SWIFT and VOLTAIRE. He is most famous for having an enormous nose, and for reputedly fighting around a thousand duels. *See also* ROSTAND.

D

Dada An art movement that began in Zurich in 1915, its name randomly chosen from a lexicon. Dada represented a reaction to postwar disillusion with established art. Leading figures included Jean ARP and the poet TRISTAN TZARA, and, when the movement spread to New York, PICABIA and DUCHAMP. Its aim was to reject accepted aesthetic and cultural values and to promote an irrational form of non-art, or anti-art. The random juxtapositions of COLLAGE and the use of ready-made objects suited their purpose best. A notable example is Duchamp's *Fountain* (1917), which was an unadorned urinal. Dada gave way to NEUE SACHLICH-KEIT around 1924 as the artists associated with the movement diversified. It led, however, to the beginnings of SURREALISM and is the source of other movements in ABSTRACT ART, such as "happenings" (*see* BEUYS, KAPROW) and ACTION PAINTING.

Daddi, Bernardo (*fl.*1290–1349) Florentine painter, whose earliest documented work is *The Madonna Enthroned* (1328), which shows the influence of his older contemporary GIOTTO. A larger *Madonna* is in the Or San Michele. Daddi's other small panels are happier and more lyrical than the work of Giotto, and his popularity and influence continued into the late 14th century.

Dahl, Roald (1916–90) English author (of Norwegian

parentage), who is known primarily for his entertaining and unpatronizing children's stories, such as *Charlie and the Chocolate Factory* (1964), *Danny, Champion of the World* and several brutally funny collections of poems for children (often illustrated by Quentin Blake). His collections of short stories (definitely not for children), e.g. *Over to You* (1946), *Kiss, Kiss* (1960) and *Switch Bitch* (1974) include several suberbly macabre tales, and a few haunting air war stories (Dahl served as an RAF fighter pilot during World War II).

Dali, Salvador (1904–89) Spanish painter, whose early influences included CUBISM and metaphysical painting before he joined the SURREALISTS in 1928. His work is precise and academic in execution, giving weight and emphasis to the hallucinatory neuroses of his subject matter. Notable works include *Limp Watches* (1931), *The Last Supper* (1955), and the famous *Christ of St John of the Cross* (1951). Although he was expelled from the Surrealists in 1938, he is popularly thought of as *the* representative Surrealist painter.

Dante [Alighieri] (1265–1321) Italian poet, whose earliest work, *Vita Nuova* (1290–94), tells of his love for "Beatrice," probably Bice Portinari, a girl whom he hardly knew but who became for him a symbol of beauty and purity. Expelled from his native Florence for political reasons, Dante wrote his masterpiece, the *Divine Comedy*, during 20 years of wandering exile. It is an allegorical description in three parts of the poet's journey through Hell, Purgatory and Paradise. He is guided by VIRGIL through Hell to the summit of Purgatory from where his idealized earthly love Beatrice, a representative of the divine, conducts him to the presence of God. One of the world's great poets, his influence was enormous, and he was responsible for making Tuscan the language of literary Italy.

Danube School *see* **Altdorfer, Albrecht**.

D'Arblay, Madame *see* **Burney, Fanny**.

Daubigny, Charles Franéois (1817–79) French painter, member of the BARBIZON SCHOOL and a pioneer
of *plein air* landscape painting. His early work was
influenced by CLAUDE among others, but later paintings have an open and light atmosphere more associated with Dutch landscape, and these became a source
of inspiration to the IMPRESSIONISTS. He had a studio-
boat from which he painted his favourite river and
canal scenes, such as *View from the Seine* (1852).

Daumier, Honoré (1808–97) French cartoonist, painter
and sculptor. He worked for the Republican magazine
Caricature in which his cartoons depicting King Louis
Philippe as *Gargantua* caused him six months imprisonment. After the suppression of *Caricature* he made
bourgeois society his target in *Le Charivari*. He was
proficient and prolific in the newly developed medium
of lithography, producing over 4,000 lithographs in the
course of his career. He was also an original and innovative painter and sculptor. *Washerwoman* is typical of
his sympathetic but unsentimental treatment of the
pathos of day to day life for the poor. Daumier influenced the works of MILLET and COROT, and he spent his
last years, blind and impoverished, in a cottage given
to him by the latter.

Davenant *or* **D'Avenant, Sir William** (1606–68) English dramatist. None of his plays, with the possible
exception of the comedy *The Wits* (1633) is of much
interest. Davenant is worthy of note, however, for (a)
evading the Puritan ban on plays with an early English opera (*see* HEROIC TRAGEDY), *the Siege of Rhodes*
(1656); (b) introducing women actors on to the public
stage (and more elaborate, movable scenery); (c) the
possibility that Shakespeare may have been his real
father, a rumour current amongst his contemporaries

that Davenant himself encouraged. He succeeded to JONSON's unofficial position of POET LAUREATE, and to his pension, in 1638.

David, Jacques Louis (1784–1825) French NEOCLASSICAL painter. He won the Prix de Rome in 1775. His earliest work was in the ROCOCO tradition, but a more realistic approach and appreciation of the ANTIQUE are evident in some of his best-known works, e.g. the *Oath of the Horatii* (1784) and *Death of Socrates* (1787). He was the leading artist of the French Revolution and was imprisoned after the death of Robespierre; *View of the Luxembourg Gardens* (1794) was painted at this time. He survived to become painter to Napoleon Bonaparte and painted *The Coronation of Napoleon* (1805–7), but after the Battle of Waterloo he fled to Brussels, where he died in exile. GROS and INGRES were his pupils.

Davie, Alan (1920–) Scottish painter. He studied at Edinburgh School of Art, and early influences include POLLOCK and DE KOONING. His own style of mystical EXPRESSIONISM is vigorous and dynamic. He has held many one-man shows in Europe and the US, and has won many awards, including Best Foreign Painter at the San Paulo Bienniale in 1963.

Davies, Arthur Bowen (1862–1928) American artist, whose early influences include WHISTLER, BOTTICELLI and PUVIS DE CHAVANNES, as in *Unicorns* (1906), although his later work was more affected by CUBISM. He was a member of The EIGHT and also helped organize the ARMORY SHOW. He later worked on the establishment of the Museum of Modern Art in New York.

Davies, Sir John *see* **acrostic**.

Davis, Stuart (1894–1964) American painter, whose early work was influenced by the ARMORY SHOW and the work of LÉGER, as in *Lucky Strike* (1921). He later developed a more precise, hard-edged style, but his mature work is brighter and more decorative, as in *Oah! In Sao Pao* (1951).

Day-Lewis, Cecil (1904–72) Irish-born English poet. In the 1930s he belonged to the "AUDEN generation" of leftwing poets, and proclaimed the glories of revolutionary socialism in such volumes as *The Magnetic Mountain* (1933), with a rather bloodthirsty enthusiasm. As with most of his peers, his socialist ideas gradually eroded over the years; he became POET LAUREATE in 1968. He also wrote highly regarded detective novels under the pseudonym "Nicholas Blake," e.g. *A Question of Proof* (1935).

Deconstruction *see* **Structuralism**.

Defoe, Daniel (1660–1731) English novelist and pamphleteer. Embroiled in many controversies, Defoe was a skilled and prolific propagandist for whichever political faction was paying his wages at the time. His tract *The Shortest Way with the Dissenters* (1702), which argues with deadly irony for the ruthless extirpation of all religious dissenters (he was one himself), was taken at face value by the authorities and he was pilloried and imprisoned. His two greatest novels are marvellously detailed first-person narratives: *Robinson Crusoe* (1719), which has been described as the first real novel (also the first survivalist manual), and *Moll Flanders* (1722), in which an ex-prostitute describes her misadventures in English low life and her eventual happy settlement in Virginia.

Degas, Edgar (1834–1917) French painter and sculptor. He studied at the Ecole des Beaux-Arts in Paris, and the Old Masters and Renaissance painters formed his early influences. During the 1860s he met MONET and began exhibiting with the IMPRESSIONISTS, although he was less interested in *plein air* effects of light than in capturing movement or gesture. He is famous for his many paintings and pastel drawings of racehorses and ballet dancers, e.g. *Ballet Rehearsal* (1874). In later life he turned to sculpture because of failing eyesight, although ballet remained a favourite theme, e.g. *The Little Fourteen-year-old Ballet Dancer* (1881). Degas' merits were recognized early, and his achievement has endured. A retrospective exhibition of his work was held in Paris in 1937.

Dekker, Thomas (*c*.1570–*c*.1632) English dramatist and pamphleteer. His best-known play, *The Shoemaker's Holiday* (1600), in which a shoemaker becomes Lord Mayor of London, is typical of his work in its sympathetic and uncondescending treatment of the lives of ordinary people. His great tragedy, *The Honest Whore* (1604–5), was written in collaboration with MIDDLETON.

De Kooning, Willem (1904–) Dutch-born American painter, a member of the New York School and a major exponent of ABSTRACT EXPRESSIONISM. He came to prominence in the 1940s with his strong, enigmatic paintings of female figures. These subjects and landscapes have dominated most of his work, as in his *Woman* series of the 1950s. He has had widespread influence on the work of other abstract artists.

Delacroix, Eugène (1798–1863) French painter whose early influences included GÉRICAULT and RUBENS. His early work, while ROMANTIC in subject matter, owes much to CLASSICAL composition, as in *The Barque of Dante* (1822). He was a friend of BONINGTON, and with him studied the work of CONSTABLE in England. He also visited North Africa, which inspired works such as *Women of Algiers* (1834). He undertook commissions for murals and portraits, notably of *Paganini* (1832) and *Chopin and George Sand* (1838). He also kept a journal of his work and influenced other artists, particularly those of the BARBIZON SCHOOL.

De la Mare, Walter (1873–1956) English poet and

novelist. The best of his work, e.g. *The Listeners* (1910), *The Return* (1910) and *Memoirs of a Midget* (1921), has a delicately eerie quality that is quite unlike any other writer's work. Much of his work was written for children, e.g. the poetry collection *Peacock Pie* (1913), and the loss of childhood innocence and happiness is the dominant theme in his fiction and poems.

Delaunay, Robert (1883–1935) French painter and originator of ORPHISM, along with his wife, **Sonia Delaunay-Terk** (1885–1979). His early experiments with CUBISM, NEOIMPRESSIONISM and FAUVISM combined to influence the development of his style, as in his series paintings of the *Eiffel Tower* (1910) and *Windows. Circular Forms* (1912) was a more abstract development. His work inspired many of the German Expressionists, including MACKE and KLEE.

Demuth, Charles (1883–1935) American painter and leading precisionist artist. His work embraced a variety of styles, and his influences include CÉZANNE and DUCHAMP in paintings such as *Acrobats* (1919) and *Box of Tricks* (1920). He was also a proficient illustrator and his best-known work, based on a poem by William Carlos Williams, is *I Saw the Figure Five in Gold* (1928). Demuth lived and worked mainly in Paris.

Denis, Maurice (1870–1943) French painter and founder member of the NABIS group. He studied at the Atelier Julien, where he met BONNARD and SERUSIER. One of his best-known works, *Hommage à Cézanne* (1900), portrays members of the Nabis. He also founded the *Ateliers d'Art Sacré* and painted frescoes in the Church of St Paul in Geneva, and *Catholic Mystery* (1890). His works in general display a sense of priority of line and colour over realistic representation of form.

De Quincey, Thomas (1785–1859) English essayist and critic. His best-known work is his *Confessions of an English Opium Eater* (1822), which describes his opium addiction and poverty in the London slums. His essays are among the most entertaining in the English language, and include such gems as "On Murder Considered as One of the Fine Arts" and "On the Knocking on the Gate in 'Macbeth'."

Derain, André (1880–1945) French painter, who studied at the Académie Carriére and, along with MATISSE, founded FAUVISM. VAN GOGH was an influence in his early work, as in *Mountains at Colliours* (1905), and he was one of the first to be influenced by African tribal art, creating granite masks and block-like figure sculptures. His mature works owe more to CÉZANNE and to RENAISSANCE art, becoming more CLASSICAL in style.

Derrida, Jacques *see* **Structuralism**.

De, Stijl *see* **Stijl, De**.

deus ex machina A Latin term meaning "god from the machine," i.e. a god introduced into the action of a play to resolve some intractable situation in the plot. The device was used commonly in both Greek and Roman drama. In Greek drama, the intervention took the form of the god being lowered onto the stage via some kind of stage machinery. EURIPIDES seems to have been particularly fond of the device, but it was rarely used by AESCHYLUS and SOPHOCLES. The term has come to denote any twist in a plot which resolves or develops the action in an unexpected way. The device became an extremely common feature of Victorian literature and drama, in the form of legacies from long-lost relatives enabling otherwise impossible marriages to take place and foiling innumerable wicked schemes. The device has been rarely used in modern serious literature, except for ironic effect, as at the end of David LODGE's novel *Nice Work*.

Dickens, Charles (1812–70) English novelist. He achieved immediate popularity with *The Posthumous Papers of the Pickwick Club* (1836–7), the first of his 14

great novels, most of which were published in instal-
ments in periodicals. His popularity with the reading
public in both Britain and America was quite remarkable, with, for example, crowds of New Yorkers waiting
at the docks for the latest instalment of *The Old Curi-
osity Shop* (1840–1); the news of Little Nell's death
sent a tidal wave of grief across the country. Dickens'
critical reputation has grown steadily since the 1930s.
His faults were always apparent: an often ludicrous
adulation of women ("the angel in the house") and
occasional gross wallows in sentiment; however, his
narrative skill, characterization, dialogue and social
analysis place him firmly in the first rank of all novelists. The novels include *Oliver Twist* (1837), *Martin
Chuzzlewit* (1843–4, which includes a section set in
America with some caustic comments on American culture and society), the semi-autobiographical *David
Copperfield* (1849–50), *Bleak House* (1852–3, a stunning panorama of English life), *Great Expectations*
(1860–1) and *Our Mutual Friend* (1864–5).

Dickinson, Emily (1830–86) American poet. A virtual
recluse from her late twenties onward, only seven of
her *c*.2,000 poems were printed in her lifetime.
Editions of her poetry began to appear in the 1890s, an
the startling originality and worth of her work gradually became recognized. Her strange aphoristic lyrics
with their individualistic punctuation – with dashes
– and a highly personal imagery derived from inner,
obliquely described torment – are among the greatest
produced in the US.

Diderot, Denis (1713–84) French philosopher. With
others, he edited the great *Encyclopédie*, 17 volumes
of which appeared under Diderot's overall direction
between 1751 and 1772, despite attempts on the part
of reactionary elements, including the Church, to sup-
press its publication. Diderot's other works include

several rather dull "bourgeois" plays, e.g. *The Father of the Family* (1758), which show the influence of LILLO, several novels and *Rameau's Nephew* (1761), an intriguing philosophical tract in the form of a dialogue between Diderot and the composer Rameau's nephew, in which the moralistic ideas of the former are opposed to the latter's sensuality, with each party gradually becoming aware of the validity of the other's argument and/or of the dualism of man's nature (the work is also a wide-ranging satire on contemporary intellectuals).

Dinesen, Isak [pseud. of Baroness Karen Blixen] (1885–1962) Danish short-story writer. Her elaborate fantasy stories, e.g. *Seven Gothic Tales* (1934) and *Winter's Tales* (1942), with their tone of aristocratic amusement and vaguely decadent air, have an occasionally almost 1890s atmosphere about them. Her autobiographical account of life on a Kenyan coffee farm, *Out of Africa* (1937), was made into a very successful film in 1985.

diptych A pair of paintings or carvings on two panels hinged together so that they can be opened or closed.

Disraeli, Benjamin [1st Earl of Beaconsfield] (1804–81) British statesman and novelist. His father, **Isaac Disraeli** (1766–1848) wrote several notable works, including *Curiosities of Literature* (1813). Benjamin was baptized a Christian at 13, but remained proud of his Jewish ancestry and heritage throughout his life. His political novels, e.g. *Coningsby* (1844) and *Sybyl* (1845), were written as manifestos for "Young England" Toryism, and show a strong sympathy for the plight of the poor in the "two-nation" society created by the Industrial Revolution. He became prime minister of the United Kingdom in 1868 and 1874–80.

distemper An impermanent paint made by mixing colours with eggs or glue instead of oil.

Divisionism *see* **Postimpressionism**.

Dix, Otto (1891–1969) German painter in the social-realist tradition of the NEUE SACHLICHKEIT. His work is meticulously detailed and realistic, his criticism of society undiluted, as in *The City* triptych (1927–8). His expressive use of distortion heightened the ugliness of themes such as *The War* (1923–4). He brought the same direct forcefulness to his portraits, e.g. *Sylvia von Herden* (1926). His work was denounced as degenerate by the Nazis, but he returned to his career after 1945.

Dodgson, Charles Lutwidge *see* **Carroll, Lewis**.

Doesburg, Theo van (1883–1931) Dutch painter, founder member of the De STIJL group and editor of its magazine. His early work was influenced by FAUVISM and POSTIMPRESSIONISM, but his style became increasingly abstract under the influence of MONDRIAN, whom he met in 1915. He wrote about, and lectured on, De Stijl, and influenced ideas from the BAUHAUS to modern ABSTRACT ART. Examples of his work include *The Cow* (1916–17) and *Counter-composition in Dissonances no. XVI* (1925).

Domenichino [Domenico Zampiere] (1581–1641) Italian painter and pupil of Annibale CARRACCI, at whose academy in Rome he studied. From 1610 he was the city's leading painter. He painted The *Life of St Cecilia* fresco (1611–14) in the Church of San Luigi dei Francesca, which is CLASSICAL in style, and the BAROQUE *Four Evangelists* (1624–8) in the Church of San Andrea della Valle. His popularity declined after the 1620s, but was revived for a time in the 18th century. Other notable works include *Landscape with Tobias and the Angel* (c.1615) and *Last Communion of St Jerome* (1614).

Domenico Veneziano (c.1400–1461) Italian painter and contemporary of CASTAGNO, he was influenced by DONATELLO. His best-known surviving work is the *St Lucy* altarpiece (c.1445), with its strong perspectives and fully rounded figures. His use of soft pastel colours contributes to the light atmosphere of the work. PIERO DELLA FRANCESCA was his assistant.

domestic tragedy A form of TRAGEDY that appeared in the Elizabethan period, which focuses on the crises of middle-class domestic life in an unpatronizing and sympathetic manner. Early examples include the anonymous *Arden of Faversham* (1592) and HEYWOOD's *A Woman Killed with Kindness* (1607). LILLO's *The London Merchant* (1731), which was much admired and very influential throughout Europe (*see* Gotthold LESSING), established the genre as a highly popular (and profitable) one. The form is closely related to SENTIMENTAL COMEDY, and was also influential on the development of MELODRAMA.

Donatello [Donato di Niccolò] (1386–1466) Florentine sculptor, who trained with GHIBERTI and became the leading figure of the early RENAISSANCE. An early commission for a series of statues for Florence Cathedral (1408–15) and the Or San Michele (1411–13) includes the *St Mark*, the seated *St John the Evangelist* and the famous *St George*, which surmounts a relief demonstrating the technique of *stiacciato*, a method of low-relief drawing in marble, which Donatello brought to prominence. His most classical work is the bronze *David* (1430s), but his reaction against classical principles is evident in later works, e.g. *St John the Baptist* (1457), *Judith and Holofernes* (1456–60) and *St Mary Magdalen* (1465), which are powerful in their emotional intensity.

Dongen, Kees van [Cornelius Theodorus Marie] (1877–1968) Dutch painter. He settled in Paris in 1897 and his early infuences include MONET and IMPRESSIONIST art. His landscapes of the early 1900s are Impressionist in approach, but towards the end of the decade he had introduced a bolder technique in the bright impasto of the FAUVIST style. From 1910 he painted mainly nudes and society portraits, e.g. *Women on the Balcony* (1910).

Donleavy, J[ames] P[atrick] (1926–) American-born Irish novelist. His works include *The Ginger Man* (1955), a comedy of undergraduate life in Dublin, and *The Beastly Beatitudes of Balthazar B* (1968).

Donne, John (1572–1631) English poet and divine. Brought up a Roman Catholic, he converted to Anglicanism in the mid-1590s. The pattern of most of his life, as with most ambitious men of his age, is an unsettled one, punctuated by occasional hazardous adventures such as accompanying Sir Francis Drake on his raid on Cadiz (1596). He became dean of St Paul's in 1621 and was one of the most popular preachers of his time. His poetry is regarded as amongst the finest METAPHYSICAL verse, and displays a love of paradox and self-questioning doubt with regard to spiritual and philosophical beliefs. Few other poets have his ability to take a metaphorical description to its limits, e.g. his comparison of his mistress's body with a landscape in "Going to Bed," without being ridiculous.

Doré, Gustave (1832–83) French sculptor, painter and illustrator. He worked originally as a caricaturist for *Le Journal Pour Rire* and became well known for his illustrations of such works as Dante's *Inferno* (1861) and Cervantes' *Don Quixote* (1862). His realistic drawings of London's slums (1872) were used in a government report. His most notable sculpture is the memorial to Alexandre Dumas (1883). Doré's work was admired by van GOGH and the SURREALISTS.

Dos Passos, John (1896–1970) American novelist. His masterpiece is his great trilogy of American life, *U.S.A.*, comprising *The 42nd Parallel* (1930), *1919* (1932) and *The Big Money* (1936).

Dostoevsky, Fyodor (1821–81) Russian novelist. Like many Russian intellectuals, he was a revolutionary in his youth but converted to a mystical faith in Russian Orthodoxy and the "slav soul" while exiled for his beliefs in Siberia. His exile was preceded by a macabre mock-execution by firing squad, an encounter with death that affected him deeply. His novels are profound explorations of sin and redemption through suffering. They include *Crime and Punishment* (1866), *The Idiot* (1868), *The Possessed* (1872) and *The Brothers Karamazov* (1880).

Dou, Gerrit (1613–75) Dutch painter who studied with REMBRANDT, on some of whose works he may have collaborated, e.g. *The Blind Tobit and his Wife Anne* (c.1630). Dou's later works are on a small scale, smoothly and precisely painted: he sometimes used a magnifying glass for the fine detail of his carefully composed interiors.

Douglas, Lord Alfred *see* **Wilde, Oscar**.

Dove, Arthur Garfield (1880–1946) American painter who studied in Paris, returing to the US in 1910. There he made his living with commercial illustration work while developing his own ABSTRACT painting style based on organic forms, e.g. *Nature Symbolized No. 2* (1914). The development of his style is comparable with the abstract art of his contemporary KANDINSKY. His later work concentrates less on abstract forms and more on the interrelation of areas of colour, as in *High Noon* (1944).

Doyle, Arthur Conan (1859–1930) Scottish physician, novelist and short-story writer. His most famous creation is the amateur detective Sherlock Holmes, who solves mysteries by a mixture of deduction and intuitive perception. The stories have been translated into practically every major language, and were collected in various volumes, e.g. *The Adventures of Sher-*

lock Holmes (1892) and *The Hound of the Baskervilles* (1902).

Drabble, Margaret (1939–) English novelist. Her novels, which frequently feature the dilemmas and life crises of intelligent, married career women, are often snootily dismissed as "old-fashioned," "middlebrow" or "traditional," but have many admirers. The novels include *The Millstone* (1965), *The Ice Age* (1977) and *The Middle Ground* (1980). She also edited the long-awaited fifth edition of *The Oxford Companion to English Literature* (1980), which is now established as the essential reference guide to the subject. *See also* BYATT.

Drayton, Michael (1563–1631) English dramatist and poet. Little of his huge and wide-ranging output is now read, except for a few fine short poems, notably the sonnet beginning "Since there's no hope, come let us kiss and part," and "Agincourt," whose first line is "Faire stood the wind for France." His plays were often written in collaboration with other dramatists, e.g. MIDDLETON.

Dreiser, Theodore (1871–1945) American novelist. Dreiser was a naturalistic novelist with an ultra-mechanistic view of human nature as defined and governed by the natural laws of biology and social conditioning, a view expressed with stolid conviction in such novels as *Sister Carrie* (1904). His later novels, and non-fiction documentary works such as *America is Worth Saving* (1941), are more optimistic, reflecting his transition from nihilism to socialism. His masterpiece is *An American Tragedy* (1925), a doom-laden narrative in which a factory worker is inexorably led by fate to drown his girlfriend.

Dryden, John (1631–1700) English poet, dramatist and critic. Dryden was the most important literary figure of late-17th century England, as well as a highly significant contributor to the political and religious controversies of the day. His verse satires, e.g. *Absalom and Achitophel* (1681), the social comedies, e.g. *Marriage à-la-Mode* (1672), and the verse tragedies, e.g. *All for Love* (1678), are among the finest of their respective genres. He was also the first great English critic, and a poet of great stature. He became POET LAUREATE in 1668 but lost the post in 1688 in the political upheaval surrounding the replacement of King James II by William and Mary.

Dubuffet, Jean (1901–85) French painter who studied in Paris in 1918 but began painting seriously only in 1942. His work represents a deliberate rejection of established values in art in favour of a naive style using mixed media. His collection of ART BRUT reflected his interest in the works of primitives, psychotics and children, and his ideas about pure, untrained art influenced trends in modern ABSTRACT and SURREALIST art.

Duccio di Buonisegna (*fl.*1278–1318) Italian painter, little of whose work is clearly documented apart from his masterpiece, the *Maesté* (1311) for the Siena Cathedral altarpiece. Other works have been attributed to him by comparison with the *Maesté*, including the *Rucellai Madonna* (1285) in the Uffizzi in Florence and the small *Madonna of the Franciscans* (1290). The liveliness and movement in Duccio's work represents a move away from Byzantine traditions towards Gothic expressiveness and can be compared with the direction of the work of GIOTTO in Florence.

Duchamp, Marcel (1887–1968) French-American artist, founder of the SECTION D'OR group and a prominent figure in American DADA. His early work was influenced by CUBISM, and his *Nude Descending a Staircase No.2* (1912) represents a move away from this towards an interest in movement that prefigures FUTURIST trends. He achieved notoriety in the US with "ready-mades," such as *Bicycle Wheel* (1913) and with the submission, which was rejected, to the Society of Independent Artists Exhibition of a urinal under the title *Fountain* (1917). *Large Glass: The Bride Stripped Bare by her Bachelors, Even* (1915–23), although uncompleted, is considered to be his masterpiece.

Duchamp-Villon, Raymond (1876–1918) French sculptor. The brother of Marcel DUCHAMP and Jacques VILLON, and an important member of the SECTION D'OR group. His earliest work is expressively naturalistic, but from 1910 he became a prominent CUBIST sculptor. His sculptures, based on the human figure, concentrated on masses rather than details. His most famous masterpiece is *The Horse* (1912–14). His promising career was cut short by his death from typhoid at the end of World War I.

Dufy, Raoul (1877–1953) French painter and designer. His early work followed the trends of IMPRESSIONISM, FAUVISM and CUBISM before he developed his own witty, idiosyncratic style during the 1920s. His preferred subjects were racing and boating scenes and the life and high society of the Riviera, painted in bright lively colours and dextrous lines. Notable works include *Riders in the Wood* (1931) and *L'Histoire de l'Electricité* (1938).

Dumas, Alexandre [Dumas père] (1802–70) French novelist and dramatist, whose entertaining romantic novels, e.g. *The Three Musketeers* (1844) and *The Count of Monte Cristo* (1845) achieved instant and lasting popularity. His illegitimate son, also called **Alexandre Dumas** [Dumas fils] (1824–95), also wrote novels and plays, his masterpiece being the play *Camille*, an adaptation of his own novel (1848), which caused a sensation when it was staged in 1852, and was the basis for Verdi's opera *La Traviata* (1853).

Du Maurier, Dame Daphne (1907–89) English novelist and short-story writer. Several of her very popular stories and novels have been filmed, e.g. *Jamaica Inn* (1939), *Rebecca* (1940) and "Don't Look Now" (1973). Once dismissed as a writer of superficial interest, the critical reputation of her work is steadily growing. Her gift for creating an atmosphere of supernatural menace (as in "Don't Look Now") is especially good.

Dunbar, William (*c*.1465–*c*.1530) Scottish poet and divine, noted mainly for his very fine poem "Lament for the Makaris" (*c*.1507), an elegy primarily for his fellow dead poets (*makar* is the Scots word for "poet").

Dunsany, Edward, 18th Baron (1878–1957) Anglo-Irish novelist, dramatist and short-story writer. He was acquainted with YEATS, who encouraged him to write for the ABBEY THEATRE. The best of his work, e.g. the fantasy stories in *The Book of Wonder* (1912), is rated above the ruck of the "Celtic Twilight" fantasy of some of his Irish contemporaries. His readership and critical reputation increased sharply with the growth of the fantasy market in the 1960s.

Duoduo [pseud. of Li Shizheng] (1951–) Chinese poet. Duoduo (the name is that of his dead daughter) is regarded as a unique figure in modern Chinese poetry, in that he is a strong admirer of Western poets such as Dylan THOMAS and Sylvia PLATH and has assimilated their influence in his work, yet is still very much a traditional Chinese poet, albeit one working in the modernist vein. His poems, e.g. those in *Looking Out From Death* (1989), are characterized by a restrained yet impassioned intensity. He has lived in exile since the Tiananmen Square Massacre of 1989.

Durand, Asher Brown (1796–1886) American painter. He trained first as an engraver, and his early portrait and landscape prints established his reputation in this field. From the 1830s he painted detailed landscapes after the tradition of the HUDSON RIVER SCHOOL. He was a founder, and later a president, of the National Academy of Design. Notable works include *Kindred Spirits* (1849).

Dürer, Albrecht (1471–1528) German engraver and painter. A leading figure of the Northern RENAISSANCE, his work is outstanding in its attention to detail and its emotional content, heightened by his masterly development of a wide range of tonal gradations and textures, e.g. *Melancholia I* (1514). In painting, his influences included the Italian masters, such as Giovanni BELLINI, as in *The Festival of the Rose Gardens* (1506). Later paintings illustrate his sympathies with the Lutheran Reformation, e.g. *Four Apostles* (1526). The scope and variety of his work, both theoretical and practical, was unrivalled in Northern Europe, and his albums of engravings exerted a tremendous influence on North European art.

Durrell, Lawrence (1912–90) English poet, novelist and travel writer. His most famous work is the series of novels comprising the *Alexandria Quartet*, i.e. *Justine* (1957), *Balthazar* and *Mount Olive* (both 1958), and *Clea* (1960). The quartet is typical of Durrell's work in its use of lush, baroque language and complex sexual intrigue. Durrell was an admirer of Henry MILLER, with whom he exchanged letters of extravagant mutual admiration.

Dyck, Sir Anthony van (1599–1641) Flemish painter. His early painting was partly influenced by Rubens, in whose studio he worked, but following a period spent in Genoa from 1621 to 1628 he developed his own unique and influential style of portraiture, investing his sitters with extraordinary character and refinement of detail. After 1632, he was court painter to Charles I of England, and his portraits of the nobility influenced court painting and portraiture for the next two hundred years. Most of his English works remain in the Royal Collection, including two portraits of Charles (c.1638). Another notable work is *Iconography*, an album of etchings of famous contemporaries, which was completed after his death with reference to his oil sketches and drawings.

E

Eakins, Thomas (1844–1916) American painter. He studied in Paris and was greatly influenced by the works of VELAZQUEZ and RIBERA, which he saw in Madrid. His own work is strongly realistic, as in *The Gross Clinic* (1875), although his portraits show a more dramatic interest in the use of tonal contrasts, reminiscent of REMBRANDT's work, e.g. *Max Schmitt in a Single Scull* (1871). He was a revolutionary and influential teacher at the Pennsylvania Royal Academy from 1876–86. Other notable works include *The Writing Master* (1881), a portrait of his father, and *The Biglen Brothers Racing* (1873).

Eardley, Joan (1921–63) English-born Scottish painter. She studied at Glasgow School of Art before moving to Catterline on the northeast coast of Scotland, where she spent the rest of her life. Her best-known works are landscapes and seascapes around this area, freely and boldly executed, and conveying the power of the sea and the elements. Her sketches and portraits of the Samson children of Glasgow are sensitive, touching and often amusing.

Earl, Ralph (1751–1801) American painter, who studied in London with Benjamin WEST, but was largely uninfluenced in his own strictly realist style. The bulk of his works are portraits of members of wealthy Connecticut families, e.g. *Oliver Ellsworth and his Wife* (1782).

Eco, Umberto (1932–) Italian critic and novelist. Eco first made his mark as a writer on semiotics, in such works as *A Theory of Semiotics* (1972). His best-known work of fiction is *The Name of the Rose* (1981, filmed 1987), a best-selling medieval detective story overladen with theological and language puzzles, in which an English monk, appropriately named William of Baskerville, solves a series of murders in a monastery. *See also* ARISTOTLE.

Edgar, David (1948–) English dramatist. His two most important works are *Destiny* (1976), a long, absorbing and cold-eyed study of fascism and British society that remains one of the few worthwhile plays on the subject, and his adaptation of DICKENS' *The Life and Adventures of Nicholas Nickleby* (1980), which achieved huge critical and popular success, and is remembered with great affection by many people. Edgar's work differs from that of fellow left-wing dramatists of his time, such as BOND and HARE, in that he has a much superior gift for characterization, and, perhaps more notably, has a sense of the ridiculous, e.g. in his short sketch *Ball Boys* (1975).

Edgeworth, Maria (1768–1849) Irish novelist. Her many works include a treatise on education, children's stories and romantic novels, but her greatest and most influential works were her historical novels of Irish life, notably *Castle Rackrent* (1800), which with its exuberant, realistic dialogue and concern for social harmony and justice, set a pattern that was to be followed by other historical novelists, such as SCOTT. Her books were much admired by her contemporaries, and are highly readable.

Edwards, Jonathan (1703–58) American divine, whose rigidly predestinarian writings, e.g. *The Freedom of the Will* (1754), had a strong and somewhat depressing influence on many 18th and 19th-century writers, e.g. HAWTHORNE.

Ehrenburg, Ilya (1891–1969) Russian war correspondent and novelist. His greatest novel is *The Thaw* (1954), which is the first major work published in the USSR to address the horrors of the Stalin era.

Eight, The A group of American painters comprising GLACKENS, HENRI, LUKS, SLOAN, DAVIES, and others. For the most part they were realist painters and campaigned vigorously on the development of progressive art away from the strictures of academic tradition. Only one exhibition of their work was held, at the Macbeth Galleries in New York in 1908. *See also* ASHCAN SCHOOL.

Eilshemius, Louis Michel (1864–1941) American painter. His earliest works were IMPRESSIONIST-style landscapes, but he later developed a more primitivist approach, e.g. *New York at Night* (1917). He had a one-man show at the Société Anonyme in 1920, but his work subsequently went out of fashion and was restored to popularity only in the 1930s.

El Greco [Domenikos Theotocopoulos] (1541–1614) Cretan-born Spanish painter, sculptor and architect. He studied in Italy, where he was possibly a pupil of TITIAN, although TINTORETTO and MICHELANGELO undoubtedly influenced his work. From 1577 he lived and worked in Toledo. In the main he painted religious subjects, including many portrayals of St Francis. His style was emotional and spiritually evocative, and his palette idiosyncratic in its predominating cold blues and greys at a time when the vogue was for warmer colours. Notable works include *The Burial of Count Orgaz* (1586) and *The Assumption* (1613).

Eliot, George [pseud. of Marry Ann Evans] (1819–80) English novelist. Eliot's novels deal with the problems of ethical choice in the rapidly changing rural environment of 19th-century England, and are regarded as amongst the finest in the language. Her novels include *Adam Bede* (1869), *The Mill on the Floss* (1860), and her masterly study of 1830s English life *Middlemarch* (1871–2), which was described by Virginia WOOLF as "one of the few English novels written for grown-up people." *See also* REALISM.

Eliot, T[homas] S[tearns] (1888–1965) American-born British poet and critic, whose early work was heavily influenced and shaped by his friend Ezra POUND. His early volumes of poetry, notably *Prufrock and Other Observations* (1917) and *The Waste Land* (1922), are concerned with what Eliot saw as the breakdown of civilization and its values in the cultural "Jazz Age" disarray of the post-World War I era. The poems struck an immediate and responsive chord throughout Europe and America, and by the time he became a British subject in 1927, he was established as the most influential poet of the age. He also attempted to revive the art of verse drama, in such works as *Murder in the Cathedral* (1935) and *The Family Reunion* (1939). Eliot's work has been attacked as being over-replete with often highly recondite allusions and a fashionably slick despair, but he remains one of the most important poets in the language. His critical works, e.g. *The Sacred Wood: Essays on Poetry and Criticism* (1920), are equally important landmarks in the field of criticism. He converted to High Anglicanism in the late 1920s, and was regarded as a pillar of the British establishment for the rest of his life. He was awarded the Nobel Prize for literature in 1948.

Ellis, Alice Thomas [pseud. of Anna Haycraft] (1932–) Anglo-Welsh novelist, regarded by many critics as one of the wittiest modern British writers. Her novels include *The Sin Eater* (1977), *the Birds of the Air* (1980) and *Unexplained Laughter* (1985). Ellis's work is fey, witty and often hauntingly sad, with occasional super-natural elements. Her collection of articles from *The Spectator* magazine, *Home Life* (issued in four volumes 1986–90), is virtually unique among such compilations in not being depressingly twee.

Ellison, Ralph (1914–) American writer, whose KAFKAesque and partly autobiographical novel *Invisible Man* (1952) describes the alienated life of a young black man in New York.

Elsheimer, Adam (1578–1610) German painter and etcher. His early work is in the Flemish Realist tradition, but Italian art influenced the lyricism of his later landscapes and genre paintings. He often combined engraving and painting on copper, working on a small scale, and his attitude is simple and direct, in contrast with the MANNERIST fashion of the time. Notable works include *Rest on the Flight into Egypt* (1609), and he had an important influence on other artists, including RUBENS and REMBRANDT.

Emerson, Ralph Waldo (1803–82) American philosopher, essayist and poet. He was an exponent of Transcendentalism, a characteristically American philosophy compounded of cloudy, generalized mysticism (showing the influence of CARLYLE) and optimism. He was much revered by contemporaries such as THOREAU, who saw him as one of the greatest 19th-century thinkers. His ideas are contained in his early work *Nature* (1836) and *Essays, First and Second Series* (1841, 1844).

Empson, Sir William (1906–84) English poet and critic. His *Seven Types of Ambiguity* (1930, written while he was studying mathematics at Cambridge) is a modern classic of literary criticism that has been much enjoyed for its witty insights into the language used by writers such as DONNE and SHAKESPEARE.

Engels, Friedrich *see* **Marx, Karl**.

engraving A technique of cutting an image into a metal
or wood plate using special tools. When ink is applied
to the plate, the raised parts will print black and the
engraved parts white. The term is also used for a print
produced in this way.

Ensor, James (1860–1949) Belgian painter from
Ostend. His early work was Impressionistic in the
Belgian style, but he gradually lightened his palette
and began using a bizarre and fantastic symbolism.
His work was exhibited through his membership of Les
VINGT, but the strongly expressionistic *Tribulation of
St Anthony* (1877) and *Entry of Christ into Brussels*
(1888) caused his work to be rejected even by them,
and he subsequently gave up painting. The importance
of his work was later recognized, and he is considered
as a forerunner of EXPRESSIONISM and SURREALISM.

epic theatre *see* **Brecht, Bertolt**.

epistolary novel A novel in the form of a series of
letters written to and from the main characters, sometimes presented by the author in the anonymous role
of "editor." The form flourished in the 18th century,
examples including RICHARDSON's *Pamela* (1741) and
BURNEY's *Evelina* (1778). The best parody is Jane AUS-
TEN's *Love and Friendship* (written when she was 14),
closely followed by FIELDING's (much larger) *Shamela
Andrews* (1741). Jane Austen toyed for a while with
the form: *Lady Susan* (written 1793–4), a minor work
by her own high standards, ends with a lovely send-up
of the form's conventions in the "Conclusion," and the
first draft of *Sense and Sensibility* (1797–8), entitled
Elinor and Marianne, was originally in epistolary
form, but the form was too weak for what she planned
to write.

Epstein, Sir Jacob (1880–1959) American-born British
sculptor in the Romantic tradition. A great part of his
work aroused controversy in public opinion because of

its alleged indecency, e.g. *The Monument to Oscar Wilde* (1912) in Paris. His portrait busts, conversely, were much admired. Important influences on his style include Wyndham LEWIS and some of the Cubist artists. Notable works include *Christ* (1919), *Genesis* (1931), and *Adam* (1939).

Ernst, Max (1891–1976) German painter and sculptor. He was self-taught and, with Jean ARP, founded DADA in 1914; CHIRICO was among his early influences. He produced bizarre and surreal images in lithograph and photomontage, e.g. *The Elephant Celebes* (1921). He was a founder member of SURREALISM with BRETON in 1922 and moved to the US in 1941. Later works, such as *The Temptation of St Anthony* (1945), reveal the development of a grotesque, twisted imagery.

Escher, Mauritz Corneille (1898–1970) Dutch graphic artist famous for his popular optical-illusion drawings, such as *Endless Staircase*, which persuade the viewer to see and accept a totally illogical image, or to see one image "hidden" in another.

Estes, Richard (1936–) American painter. His work depicts American streets in a "superrealist" style, revealing an interest in juxtaposed photographic images and the interrelation of objects seen behind glass or reflected in it, e.g. *Foodshop* (1967).

etching A technique of making an ENGRAVING in a metal plate, using acid to bite out the image rather than tools. Tones of black or grey can be produced, depending on the extent the acid is allowed to bite. The term is also used for a print produced in this way.

Etherege *or* **Etheredge, Sir George** (*c*.1634–91) English dramatist, whose play *The Comical Revenge* (1664) established the main pattern of RESTORATION comedy, i.e. witty, cynical characters in the amoral world of fashionable society. His best play in this vein is *The Man of Mode* (1676).

Etty, William (1787–1849) American-born English painter, notable mainly for his nude female paintings, which, despite having attracted criticism for weakness in draughtsmanship, display a fine sense of sensual form, texture and colour. He also produced large, complex compositions, such as *The Combat* (1825). Other important works include *Ulysses and the Sirens* (1873) and the *Joan of Arc* triptych (1847).

Euripides (480–406BC) Greek dramatist, the youngest of the three great Greek tragedians, the others being AESCHYLUS and SOPHOCLES. His popularity lasted until well into the Byzantine era, and 19 of his (perhaps 92) plays are extant, the most notable being *Alcestis, Medea, Orestes* and *The Trojan Women*, the last of which describes the fate of the captive Trojan women after the Greek victory over Troy. It has had several major productions since the end of World War II, resonant as it is with the aftermath of holocaust. Euripides adopted a more rationalist, questioning approach to the gods and their divine affairs than his great predecessors, and was clearly more concerned with the business of everyday human beings, for which he was mercilessly satirized by ARISTOPHANES.

Eusden, Laurence *see* **poet laureate**.

Evans, Mary Ann *see* **Eliot, George**.

Eyelyn, John (1620–76) English author an diarist. His diary was first published in 1818, and first published in full in 1955. Like the diary of his friend PEPYS, it is full of valuable details of domestic and social life in 17th-century England.

Evergood, Philip (1901–75) American painter. His early works are of Biblical or genre scenes, but from the 1930s he developed a unique linear style with vibrant colour, consisting of awkwardly drawn figures in a shallow perspective. His preferred subject matter was social-realist issues, e.g. *Lily and the Sparrows*.

Existentialism A philosophical position based on a perception of life in which man is an actor forced to make choices in an essentially meaningless universe that functions as a colossal and cruel Theatre of the ABSURD. The main writers associated with Existentialism are French, notably SARTRE and CAMUS, and the bilingual BECKETT. The roots of Existentialism are complex; one important source is NIHILISM, the influence of which is apparent in Camus' great novel *The Outsider* (1942), described by its author as "the study of an absurd man in an absurd world." Another important source is the Danish theologian Søren Kierkegaard (1813–55), who observed that life must be lived forwards, but can only be understood backwards. Life is therefore a continual act of faith in which choices are made for a series of actions, the consequences of which must remain unclear.

Camus' quest for meaning in life and art led him to an accommodation with Christianity, detailed in his great anti-totalitarian essay *The Rebel* (1951), whereas Sartre came to an uneasy alliance with Marxism; Beckett, however, kept on ploughing his unique and lonely furrow, free of political or religious comfort, until his death.

Discussion about Existentialism in the Arts tends to degenerate into bad-tempered squabbles about the motivation, meaning and effect of the particular piece under examination, a process complicated by the often pervasive role of violence in works labelled "Existentialist." Thus, the film director Sam Peckinpah was probably sincere in describing his films as Existentialist dramas in the quasi-Marxist mode of Sartre; for most viewers, however, they are simply glorifications of violence.

Expressionism A term, derived from the character of some 20th-century Northern European art, which was coined in a description of an exhibition of Fauvist and Cubist paintings at the Berlin SEZESSION in 1911, but quickly came to be applied to the works of Die BRÜCKE and Der BLAUE REITER. Expressionist works represented a move away from the observational detachment of realism and, to an extent, Impressionist trends, and were concerned with conveying the artist's feelings and emotions as aroused by his subject. Any painting technique that helped to express these feelings was considered a valid medium and included bold, free brushwork, distorted or stylized forms, and vibrant, often violently clashing, colours. The term *expressionist* also refers to an expressive quality of distortion or heightened colour in art from any period or place. *See also* ABSTRACT EXPRESSIONISM.

Eyck, Jan van (d.1441) Dutch painter. Little is known of his early career, but he was court painter to Philip, Duke of Burgundy, from 1425 to about 1430, and all his dated works are from the 1430s, when he lived in Bruges. He was a master in the medium of oil painting, and his representation of light and detail remains unsurpassed. His paintings, while strongly realistic, are imbued with a serene, spiritual atmosphere, as in the famous *Arnolfini Marriage* (1434). Other notable works include the Ghent altarpiece (completed 1432) and *The Man in the Red Turban* (1433).

F

Fabriano, Gentile da *see* **Gentile da Fabriano**.

Fabritius, Carel (1622–54) Dutch painter who studied in REMBRANDT's studio. His earliest work shows the influence of his master, although he later developed his own style based on a cooler palette. His subject matter included portrait, genre and still lifes as well as animal paintings, of which *Goldfinch* (1654) is a notable example. He was killed in the explosion of the Delft ammunition factory.

Faes, Pieter van der *see* **Lely, Sir Peter**.

Fantin-Latour, Henri (1836–1904) French painter and lithographer. He is best known for his paintings of flowers and his group portraits, such as *Homage to Delacroix* (1864). He also did imaginative lithographic illustrations inspired by the works of Romantic composers like Wagner.

Farquhar, George (1678–1707) Irish dramatist. His plays are the best of the late Restoration comedies. They are also the most good-natured, without lacking anything satirical bite, and there have been many successful modern productions of them. His best plays are *The Recruiting Officer* (1706) and *The Beaux' Stratagem* (1707), both of which are important transitional works between the witty bawdiness of Restoration comedy and the more decorous, moralistic plays of the 18th century.

Farrell, J[ames] T[homas] (1904–79) American novelist. Most of his work is set in the Irish slums of Chicago, where Farrell was brought up. His best-known work is the "Studs Lonigan" trilogy, a grim saga (in the naturalistic mode) of the life of a small-time hoodlum in Chicago: the three novels are *Young Lonigan* (1932), *The Young Manhood of Studs Lonigan* (1934) and *Judgment Day* (1935).

Faulkner, William (1897–1962) American novelist. His first novel, *Soldier's Pay* (1926), was written with Sherwood ANDERSON's encouragement. His next two novels, *Sartoris* and *The Sound and the Fury* (both 1929), began the famous series of works dealing with the history of a fictional Mississippi county, Yoknapatawpha, which ended with *The Reivers* (1962). The series deals with the political, social, racial and sexual tensions created in the South in the aftermath of the Civil War. The critical reputation of Faulkner's work has grown considerably since the 1940s, and is now seen as a significant examination of the crisis of the fragmentation of American society. He was awarded the Nobel prize for literature in 1949.

Fauvists a group of French painters including MATISSE, DERAIN, VLAMINCK and others, who painted in a particularly vivid and colourful style. The term *fauve* ("wild animal") was coined as a form of derogatory criticism of an exhibition held at the Salon d'Automne of 1905. Their use of strong, bright colours to express their response to the fierce light of the Mediterranean coast owes something to the influence of GAUGUIN and van GOGH, but they were less interested in representing what they saw and more concerned to express their own feelings in the boldness and freedom of their compositions. Other artists whose work included a Fauvist period were van DONGEN and DUFY. Although Matisse continued to explore Fauvist techniques, the other artists soon diverged, and the movement as such was fairly short-lived. It was, however, influential in CUBIST and EXPRESSIONIST art.

Federal Arts Project A series of American government aid schemes to assist artists during the years of the Depression, 1933–43. Initially they sponsored civic work on public buildings, but were augmented in 1935 to include a wide range of talents and projects. Most of the US's contemporary major artists of the time were involved in the schemes.

Feige, Albert Otto Max *see* **Traven, B**.

Feininger, Lyonel (1871–1956) American painter. He was in Europe from 1887 until 1937, and worked as a cartoonist before taking up serious painting in 1911. He was involved with Der BLAUE REITER. From 1919 to 33 he taught at the BAUHAUS. His work incorporates CUBIST and FUTURIST features, e.g. *Raddampfer II* (1913), although later pieces, such as *Deep, Sonnenuntergang* (1930), are cooler and more CONSTRUCTIVIST in approach. He often achieved a delightful sense of EXPRESSIONIST fantasy reminiscent of his early satirical drawings.

Fergusson, John Duncan (1874–1961) Scottish painter, one of the Scottish COLOURISTS. His earliest works show the influences of WHISTLER and the GLASGOW SCHOOL. Later work, dating from a period spent in Paris (1907–14), is more FAUVIST, as in the bold use of colour and free brushwork of *Rogan Harbour, Evening*, or the dynamics of his group paintings, e.g. *Rhythm* (1911). An important collection of his work was gifted to Stirling University.

Ferlinghetti, Lawrence (1919–) American poet and publisher, whose City Lights Bookshop in San Francisco was a breeding ground for BEAT GENERATION writers, of whom he is a typical example, in the 1950s. His own works also include the more lyrical *A Coney Island of the Mind* (1958).

Feuchtwanger, Lion (1884–1958) German novelist. His best-known work is the historical novel *Jew Suss* (1925), which describes the rise and fall of a Jewish politician in 18th-century Germany. Being Jewish, a pacifist and a socialist, Feuchtwanger fled Nazi Germany to Vichy France, from where he escaped to the US. He was a friend of Bertolt BRECHT, with whom he collaborated on several plays.

Fielding, Henry (1707–54) English novelist and dramatist. His satirical plays, e.g. *Pasquin* (1736) and *The Historical Register for 1736* (1737), both of which were cruelly funny attacks on the Walpole administration, provoked the British Government into passing the strict Licensing Act of 1737 to censor stage plays. Fielding then continued his attack on corruption and hypocrisy by turning to novel-writing. His first novel, *Joseph Andrews* (1742) was a very successful send-up of Samuel RICHARDSON's *Pamela* in which the conventions of male and female virtue are reversed; the second, *Jonathan Wild* (1743), re-assails the British Government by presenting the career of a criminal as an allegory of political vice; and his greatest work, *Tom Jones* (1749), surveys the whole of English society with masterly insight, humour and compassion. He is one of the great innovators of the novel, and his works remain hugely entertaining. In his last novel, *Amelia* (1751), the most sombre and realistic of his books, Fielding once again stood convention on its head by having the eponymous heroine disfigured – he was concerned to show that outer and inner reality did not always match up. He also wrote many important tracts on social problems, and worked tirelessly as a magistrate to improve judicial standards.

figurative art *or* **representational art** Art that recognizably represents figures, objects or animals from real life, as opposed to ABSTRACT ART.

Filipepi, Alessandro di Mariano *see* **Botticelli, Sandro**.

fine arts *see* **applied arts**.

Firbank [Arthur Annesley] Ronald (1886–1926) English novelist. His weirdly exotic works bear the stamp of the AESTHETIC MOVEMENT, but are unlike any others in the language in their oblique, flickering dialogue and fantastic characters. Typical examples are *Valmouth* (1919) and *Concerning the Eccentricities of Cardinal Pirelli* (1926). He influenced, among others, WAUGH and HUXLEY.

Fitzgerald, Edward (1809–83) English poet. His best-known work is his very free translation of *The Rubaiyat of Omar Khayyam* (1859). This enormously successful work is one of the most quoted poems in the language, although Fitzgerald's version is more resonant of Victorian doubts and fears than of the bright scepticism of the 12th-century Persian Omar.

Fitzgerald, F[rancis] Scott [Key] (1896–1940) American novelist and short-story writer. His works are moralistic fables of extravagance and glamour set against the background of Fitzgerald's own world of 1920s "Jazz Age" High Society. *The Great Gatsby* (1925), the story of a mysterious financier, and *Tender is the Night* (1934), a fictional reworking of Fitzgerald's own problems (his wife Zelda became mentally ill), are his best-known works.

Fitzgerald, Penelope (1916–) English novelist. Her novels include *The Bookshop* (1978), *Human Voices* (1980) and *The Gate of Angels* (1990). *Human Voices*, a very funny yet moving account of life at the BBC during the Blitz, is perhaps her most representative novel.

Flashman, Sir Harry Paget (1822–1914) English soldier and travel writer. Flashman only produced three books in his lifetime, the best-known of which is *Dawns* *and Departures of a Soldier's Life* (1880). A huge manuscript containing his memoirs was discovered in 1965, from which several volumes, edited by the Scottish historian **George MacDonald Fraser** (1925–), have been presented to the public, e.g. *Flashman* (1969) and *Flashman at the Charge* (1973). The memoirs contain many fascinating anecdotes about prominent 19th-century figures, e.g. Lincoln, Bismarck and DISRAELI, and have been described as "deplorably readable." The famous soldier reveals himself to be an incorrigible coward and sexual adventurer, but he is also a remarkably fine writer. His description in *Flashman and the Redskins* (1982) of the "forty-niners" in Kansas is comparable to DICKENS at his best.

Flaubert, Gustave (1821–80) French novelist. His masterpiece is his first published novel, *Madame Bovary* (1857), one of the greatest of all 19th-century novels, a story of romantic self-deception, adultery and suicide in rural France. Flaubert's meticulous concern for finding exactly the right word, and for objective, impersonal narrative, a fluid style and artistic integrity, have earned him a niche all of his own in world literature.

Flaxman, John (1755–1826) English sculptor and designer. He studied at the Royal Academy in London and worked for Josiah Wedgwood, where his low-relief design and portraits developed his strong sense of line and detail. He was also a proficient illustrator, and his work on the *Iliad* and the *Odyssey* (1793) influenced continental artists, such as INGRES. From 1810 he occupied the newly created chair of sculpture at the Royal Academy. Important monuments include those of the Earl of Mansfield (1801) at Westminster Cathedral, Nelson (1810) at St Paul's, and the delicate relief of Agnes Cromwell (1800) at Chichester.

Flecker, James Elroy (1884–1915) English poet and

dramatist. The title poem in his collection *The Golden Journey to Samarkand* (1913) is his best-known work, although his verse play *Hassan* (1922) was staged in 1923, with music by Delius.

Flemalle, Master of *see* **Campin, Robert**.

Fleming, Ian [Lancaster] (1908–64) English journalist and novelist. His series of novels featuring the secret agent James Bond, e.g. *Live and Let Die* (1954) and *Goldfinger* (1964), were enormous popular successes and have all been filmed. The novels have been attacked for their slick treatment of sex and violence; Kingsley AMIS gives a spirited defence of them in his *The James Bond Dossier* (1965), but, characteristically, manages to point out all of Fleming's lapses in taste along the way.

Fletcher, John (1579–1625) English dramatist. Fletcher was one of the most popular dramatists of his day, and frequently collaborated with other dramatists, most notably Sir Francis Beaumont (1584–1616), from 1606 to 1613. Their best-known works are the tragicomedies (a genre they had a significant influence on) *The Maid's Tragedy* (1610–11) and *A King and No King* (1611) (*see* COMEDY). Fletcher also collaborated with SHAKESPEARE on *The Two Noble Kinsmen* (first published 1634) and Henry VIII (1613), the firing of a cannon during the production of the latter causing the burning down of the Globe Theatre.

Flirts and Straights A distinction between authors who specialize in showing off to their readers (**flirts**) and those whose main concern is getting on with telling the story (**straights**). A flirt will play with conventions and expectations, and disrupt the narrative with disquistions on the meaning of life or on what the author had for breakfast. A straight will, for the most part, maintain the agreed conventions between author and reader. A writer of detective stories, in which genre the conventions are fairly rigorous, is almost always a straight, though inferior crime writers will make their heroes secret readers of PROUST or NIETZSCHE. Many writers combine both elements: George ELIOT is a straight in character development, but a flirt in digression.

Florio, John (*c.*1553–1625) English author. His father was an Italian Protestant refugee who settled in London. He compiled an Italian–English dictionary, *A World of Words* (1598). His translation of MONTAIGNE's *Essays* (1603) was of great influence (Shakespeare quotes from them in *The Tempest*).

Fo, Dario (1926–) Italian dramatist and director. Fo's satirical farces, e.g. *Accidental Death of an Anarchist*, (1970) have as their target such social issues as police corruption and the oppression of women. Influences on Fo include BRECHT, COMMEDIA DELL'ARTE and Mayakovsky.

Foote, Samuel (1720–77) English actor and dramatist, whose plays and performances frequently satirized his contemporaries. A representative work is *The Minor* (1760), an anti-Methodist satire.

Forain, Jean Louis (1852–1931) French painter and caricaturist. He made his living with the Paris journals, *Le Scapin* and *La Vie Parisienne*, and was influenced in his early paintings by REMBRANDT and GOYA. His work reveals the cartoonist's economical sense of line and gesture. He exhibited with the Impressionists, although he used a less colourful palette, and his main influences were MANET and DEGAS. Notable works include *The Tribunal* (1884), and *Counsel and Accused* (1908).

Ford, Ford Madox (1873–1939) English novelist, editor and critic. His most important works are the novels *The Good Soldier* (1915) and the tetralogy *Parade's End* (published in one volume 1950). Ford had great influence on his contemporaries in his role of editor and critic (he founded the *Transatlantic Review* in 1924 and was a generous source of encouragement to many writers), and the reputation of his own writings (greatly revered by Graham GREENE) is steadily growing.

Ford, John (1585–*c.* 1639) English dramatist, notable for such REVENGE TRAGEDIES as *'Tis Pity She's a Whore* and *The Broken Heart* (both 1633). Ford's bleak, objective vision of human suffering and his command of blank verse were highly praised by T. S. ELIOT.

Forster, E[dward] M[ontagu] (1879–1970). English novelist and critic. His novels, e.g. *The Longest Journey* (1907) and *Howards End* (1910), are mainly concerned with moral and ethical choices and personal relationships within groups of educated, middle-class people. His best-known work is *A Passage to India* (1924), which describes the clashes and prejudices between the British and Indians under the British Raj.

found object *or* **objet trouvé** A form of art that began with DADA and continued with SURREALISM, where an object, either natural or manufactured, is displayed as a piece of art in its own right.

Fouquet, Jean (*c.*1420–81) French painter. Little of his work is documented, and while he is known to have travelled in Italy and to have painted a portrait, since lost, of Pope Eugenius IV, his style was largely uninfluenced by Italian art. His early patrons include Etienne Chevalier, who commissioned his *Book of Hours* (1460) and the Melun diptych, *Madonna and Child* (*c.*1450). He was also court painter to Louis XI from 1475. His work is dominated by his excellent draughtsmanship, bringing a grace and purity to miniatures and larger works alike, as in Josephus' *Jewish Antiquities* (1470–76).

Fowles, John [Robert] (1926–) English novelist. The

film rights to his first book *The Collector* (1963), a creepy psychological study of a butterfly collector turned kidnapper, were sold while the book was still in proof stage. His next novel, *The Magus* (1966), in which an English schoolteacher on a Greek island is subjected to a series of sinister "happenings" by a god-like millionaire, and his third, *The French Lieutenant's Woman* (1969), a quasi-historical narrative written for the most part in pastiche Victorian prose, and with two separate endings, have established him as one of the major novelists of our time.

Fragonard, Jean-Honoré (1732–1806) French painter. One of the greatest exponents of ROCOCO, he studied with CHARDIN and BOUCHER. His early works were historical scenes on a grand scale, e.g. *Coreseus Sacrificing himself to Save Callierhoe* (1765), but he is best known for his smaller, picturesquely pretty canvases, such as *The Swing* (1766). His patrons included Madame de Pompadour and Madame du Barry, for whom he painted the four *Progress of Love* paintings (1771–3). His frivolous style went out of vogue during the French Revolution, and he died in poverty.

Frame, Janet [Paterson] (1924–) New Zealand novelist and short-story writer. Frame spent eight years in a psychiatric institution after being labelled as schizophrenic, and only narrowly escaped being leucotimized thanks to the publication of her collection of short stories, *The Lagoon: Stories* in 1952. Her work includes ten highly regarded novels, e.g. *Owls Do Cry* (1957) and *Intensive Care* (1970). Her autobiographical volumes, *To the Island* (1982), *An Angel at my Table* (1984) and *The Envoy from Mirror City* (1984), are, like her novels, moving explorations of the anarchic borderlands between sanity and mental breakdown.

France, Anatole [pseud. of Jacques Anatole Thibault] (1844–1924) French novelist, who specialized in social and political satire. His best-known work is *Penguin Island* (1908), an allegory of the evolution of society. He was awarded the Nobel prize for literature in 1921.

Francesca, Piero della *see* **Piero della Francesca**.

Francis, Sam (1923–) American painter. After service in World War II and a period in hospital, he studied in California and Paris, where he met RIOPELLE. Other influences included Japanese art and American abstract expressionists, such as Jackson POLLOCK, e.g. *Big Red* (1953). His first one-man show was in 1952 in Paris, and he had several retrospective exhibitions during the 1960s.

Frankenthaler, Helen (1928–) American painter. Her early influences included GORKY and POLLOCK, and her work forms a significant link between ABSTRACT EXPRESSIONISM and COLOUR FIELD PAINTING. From Pollock she learned a canvas-staining technique, which she developed with the use of strong acrylic colours to create a complete synthesis of colour and surface. Notable works include *Mountains and Sea* (1952).

Franklin, Benjamin (1706–90) American author, scientist and statesman. He helped draft the Declaration of Independence, and played an active role in American political life for most of his long life. His best-known works are *Poor Richard's Almanack* (1733–58), a witty blend of commonsense philosophy and satire, and his masterpiece, the highly entertaining *Autobiography* (first published in England in 1793, and in America in 1818).

Fraser, George Macdonald *see* **Flashman**.

Frayn, Michael (1933–) English dramatist and novelist, noted for his dry, sardonic humour. Representative novels include *The Tin Men* (1965), a satire on robotics and computers, and *A Very Private Life* (1968), a futuristic, anti-Utopian fantasy. His plays include *Noises*

Off (1982), which uses the conventions of farce to send up theatrical life.

Frazer, Sir James George (1854–1941) Scottish scholar and anthropologist. His study of religious customs and myth, *The Golden Bough* (1890–1915), was a major influence on many 20th-century writers, notably T. S. ELIOT and JOYCE, and his belief that faith and ritual must be set in the context of religions influenced FREUD's theories.

free verse *or* **vers libre** Any form of verse without traditional metrical or stanzaic form. Free verse is usually characterized by the use of rhythmic "natural speech" cadences, is dependent on alliteration and the subtle placing of syllabic stresses, and can be rhymed or unrhymed. T. S. ELIOT described free verse as not a liberation from form, but a "revolt against dead form." The SYMBOLIST MOVEMENT placed great emphasis on free verse, which has a very long ancestry. The "Song of Songs" in the Authorized Version is in free verse, as is Milton's *Samson Agonistes*. Whitman's huge epic poem *Song of Myself* (1855) is another notable example.

French, Daniel Chester (1850–1931) American sculptor, best known for his civic commissions. These include *The Minute Man* (1875) in Concord, Massachusetts, and the seated figure of *Abraham Lincoln* (1922) in Washington DC.

fresco A painting directly painted on to a wall that has previously been covered with a damp freshly laid layer of lime plaster, the paint and plaster reacting chemically to become stable and permanent. Fresco painting worked particularly well in the warm, dry climate of Italy, where it reached its peak in the 16th century.

Freud, Lucien (1922–) German-born British artist, who settled in England in 1931. His expressive linear style is evident in *Girl with Roses* (1947–8) and has been described as "hyper-realist." Later works display a more painterly style and freer brushwork, without, however, losing their hypnotic intensity, e.g. *Francis Bacon* (1952).

Freud, Sigmund (1856–1939) Austrian psychiatrist, who founded psychoanalysis. His works, which include *The Interpretation of Dreams* (1900) and *The Ego and the Id* (1923), have been of enormous influence in the 20th century. *Freudian literary criticism* is the study of literature according to the precepts and insights of Freud's theories on the hidden imperatives of the unconscious (Freud's own writings on literature, e.g. on Hamlet and Oedipus in *The Interpretation of Dreams*, are of great value). *See also* FRAZER, JUNG.

Friedrich, Caspar David (1774–1840) German Romantic painter, who studied at Copenhagen and settled in Dresden in 1798. He was largely uninfluenced by other artists or trends, and his work was highly controversial due to his treatment of landscape, e.g. *The Cross on the Mountain* (1808). His works have a melancholy atmosphere peculiar to the Northern European temperament: land, sea and sky are fused in strange crepuscular light or hazy mist, out of which emerge trees and ruins. The strong sense of emotion and spiritual feeling in his work was an important development in landscape painting, although Friedrich himself died in poverty and his significance was recognized only towards the end of the 19th century.

Frost, Robert Lee (1874–1963) American poet. Frost's work is concerned mainly with the people and landscape of New England; his best poems, e.g. "The Death of the Hired Man" and "Stopping By Woods on a Snowy Evening" have a quiet, lyrical quality that won him many admirers. Later critics, such as Lionel TRILLING, have pointed out the dark, enigmatic nature of much of his symbolism. Representative volumes include *A Boy's Will* (1913), *North of Boston* (1914), both these volumes being first published in the UK, where Frost lived 1912–15, *A Witness Tree* (1942) and *In the Clearing* (1962).

Fry, Christopher [Harris] (1907–) English dramatist, whose verse dramas such as *A Phoenix too Frequent* (1946) and *The Lady's Not for Burning* (1949) were popular with both critics and the public, and are frequently revived.

Fry, Roger *see* **Postimpressionism.**

Fugard, Athol (1932–) South African dramatist, whose plays explore the tragedy of racial tension caused by apartheid in South Africa. His works include *The Blood Knot* (1961), *Boesman and Lena* (1968), *Sizwe Bansi is Dead* (1972) and *Master Harold . . . and the Boys* (1982). He has also written film scripts and a novel, *Tsotsi* (1980), the latter being a study of a young black criminal's growing social and moral awareness.

Fuseli, Henry (1741–1825) Swiss painter. He originally trained for the priesthood but took up painting and settled in England in 1765. He was much influenced by the great painters of the Italian RENAISSANCE, particularly MICHELANGELO, and his paintings are mannered and romantic with a strange sense of the grotesque and macabre, which was later to appeal to SURREALIST artists. He was professor of painting at the Royal Academy in London, where ETTY, LANDSEER and CONSTABLE were among his pupils. Notable works include *The Nightmare* (1872) and *The Witches in Macbeth*.

Futurism A movement of writers and artists, originating in early 20th-century Italy, that extolled the virtues of the new, dynamic machine age, which was reckoned to have rendered the aesthetic standards of the past redundant. The founding document of the movement is the poet Filipo Marinetti's (1876–1944) *Futurist Manifesto* of 1909, which, in literature, called for the destruction of traditional sentence construction and the establishment of a "free verse in free words" (*parole in libertà*) owing nothing to the literary standards of the past (*see* TZARA); the new relationship between words was to be in terms of analogy alone. The English variant of Futurism is *Vorticism*, which included writers such as Wyndham LEWIS and Ezra POUND. The Russian variant, *Russian Futurism*, was led by the poet Vladimir Mayakovsky (1893–1930), whose curious love affair with the Soviet dictatorship ended with his suicide (Lenin described him as "incomprehensible"; once he was safely dead, Stalin lauded him as a great Bolshevik poet).

Futurism became a spent force by the 1930s, largely because of its close association with Fascism and the establishment of the Futurist hero Mussolini's dictatorship in Italy (Marinetti's vision of war as "the hygiene of the world" is also Mussolini's). The relationship between Italian Fascism, Soviet Communism, and Futurism, it should be noted, was actually a very close one. The Italian critic (and founder of the Italian Communist Party) Antonio Gramsci (1891–1937), praised Marinetti and his cronies for their destructive onslaught on traditional culture ("clearly revolutionary . . . absolutely Marxist"), as did the Soviet cultural commissar Anatoly Lunacharsky, who described Marinetti as "the one intellectual revolutionary in Italy," while the Soviet avant-garde journal *Lef* asserted that "In Italy Mayakovsky would have been Marinetti, and in Russia Marinetti would have been Mayakovsky" (*see* Igor Golomstock's *Totalitarian Art*, 1990, for an extended analysis of the unsavoury relationship between such banalities and 20th-century totalitarianism). *See also* REALISM.

In art, BOCCIONI and CARRÉ were among the painters in the group, whose aim was to convey a sense of movement and dynamism, as in Boccioni's *The City Rises*

Futurism

(1910). As a group, the Futurists published manifestos on various aspects of the arts, and exhibitions toured Europe during 1911–12. The original group of painters had broken up by the end of World War I, but their work and ideas had a resounding influence on subsequent art movements.

G

Gabo Naum [Naum Neemia Pevsner] (1890–1979) Russian-born sculptor. He initially studied medicine and engineering but took up sculpture in 1916. His early works were based on a kind of geometric CUBISM which came to be seen as the origins of CONSTRUCTIVISM. He was one of the first to experiment with KINETIC ART and to make use of lightweight and transparent modern materials to enhance the delicate balance and sense of weightlessness of his work. In Russia, together with his brother Antoine PEVSNER, he published their *Realistic Manifesto* (1920), which set out the principles of Constructivism. It represents a turning away from the style of TATLIN and MALEVICH, whose work they found too utilitarian in approach. In 1922 Gabo moved to Berlin and exhibited there, in Paris (1924) and in the US (1926) with van DOESBURG and Pevsner. He had a one-man show in 1938 at the London Gallery before settling in the US, where he taught at Harvard and was elected to the Institute of American Academy of Arts and Letters. Important commissions include sculptures for the Baltimore Museum of Art (1951) and a relief for the United States Rubber Company in the Rockefeller Center, New York (1956).

Gainsborough, Thomas (1727–88) English painter. His earliest influences were WATTEAU and the ROCOCO painters. Mature works such as *The Blue Boy* (1770) show some influence of RUBENS and van DYCK, but essentially Gainsborough's own individual style is predominant. He worked as a portrait painter, first in his native Suffolk and later in Bath, before moving to London in 1774 where he was a founder member of the Royal Academy. His keen interest in landscape painting pervades most of his work, his sitters often being portrayed in an outdoor setting, e.g *Mr and Mrs Andrews* (1748). He developed a light, rapid painting style based on a delicate palette and at all times demonstrating his own delight in painting. Later works include his "fancy" paintings or imaginary landscapes and portraits, e.g. *Peasant Girl Gathering Sticks* (1782). Other major masterpieces include *Mary, Countess Howe* (1774), *The Cottage Door* (1780) and *The Watering Place* (1777).

Galsworthy, John (1867–1933) English novelist and dramatist. His plays, e.g. *Strife* (1909) and *Justice* (1910), are realistic, hard-hitting campaigning works designed to expose social injustice (the furure over *Justice* resulted in UK prison reform). His plays are excellently constructed, recognize the complexity of human motivation, and there have been several successful revivals. His most lasting achievement, however, is his *Forsyte Saga* trilogy, *The Man of Property* (1906), *In Chancery* (1920) and *Awakening* (1920). The trilogy is centred on the life of Soames Forsyte, a suburban London solicitor, and examines the brutality beneath the veneer of seemingly civilized middle-class life. An adaptation of the *Forsyte Saga* by the BBC in 1967 achieved remarkably high viewing figures throughout the world. He was awarded the NOBEL PRIZE for literature in 1932.

Galt, John (1789–1839) Scottish novelist. He described his novels as "theoretical histories" of the changing social patterns of Scottish country life. His best novel is *Annals of the Parish* (1821), in which a clergyman, with much unconsciously funny deadpan detail, describes incidents in the humble lives of his parishioners (the philosopher J. S. Mill took the term "utilitarian" from this book).

Garrick, David (1717–79) English actor and dramatist. He was a pupil of Dr JOHNSON at Lichfield, and accompanied him to London in 1737. He made his mark as an actor within a few years, his performance as Richard III in 1741 making particular impact. He dominated the English theatre for the rest of his life, and was actor-manager of Drury Lane Theatre from 1747 to 76. The farces he wrote are now of little interest, but his letters (published 1831–2) provide fascinating portraits of his contemporaries, who were in no doubt as to his acting genius: the actress Kitty Clive said of him, "Damn him, he could act a gridiron!"

Gaskell, Mrs Elizabeth (1810–65) English novelist. Her novels about English country life, e.g. *Mary Barton* (1848) and *North and South* (1855), are often concerned with the injustices of the "two-nation" society (*see* DISRAELI) of 19th-century England. Her most popular novel, however, was (and is) *Cranford* (1851–3), a gentle and entertaining study of life in a small village. She became a friend of Charlotte BRONTË, whose biography she wrote (1857).

Gauguin, Paul (1848–1903) French painter, printmaker and sculptor, one of the greatest exponents of POSTIMPRESSIONISM. He was brought up in Peru and worked as a stockbroker before taking up painting in 1873. He exhibited in three IMPRESSIONIST exhibitions before he began to develop his own simplistic, richly coloured style. *The Vision after the Sermon*, or *Jacob wrestling with the Angel* (1888), inspired by the lifestyle of Breton peasants at Pont-Aven, marks the beginning of this development. During his Breton period he exerted a powerful influence on other artists, in particular the NABIS and the SYMBOLISTS, and this influence has also extended into 20th-century EXPRESSIONIST painting. Gauguin's interest in primitive and simplistic art led him to make his home in the South Pacific Islands where, despite illness and poverty, he painted some of his most important masterpieces, including *Where do we come from? What are we? Where are we going?* (1897).

Gay, John (1685–1732) English dramatist and poet. His masterpiece is *The Beggar's Opera* (1728), a ballad opera based upon an observation by his friend SWIFT that a "Newgate pastoral" might make an "odd pretty sort of thing." The work was a huge success, its popularity due in part to the fact that characters and incidents in the play are drawn from real life – notably, from the life of the prime minister, Walpole, who gritted his teeth on this occasion but banned the play's sequel, *Polly* (1729). The play was said to have made Gay rich, and the producer John Rich gay. BRECHT's *Threepenny Opera* is based on Gay's play.

Genet, Jean (1910–86) French dramatist and novelist. His best-known novel, *Our Lady of the Flowers* (1943), describes homosexual life in prison in loving detail, and, like all of his novels, was banned in the US until the 1960s. His plays, e.g. *The Maids* (1947) and *The Balcony* (1957) are remarkable examples of the Theatre of the ABSURD, and suffered much from censorship.

genre painting A painting that has as its subject a scene from everyday life, as opposed to a historical event, mythological scene, etc. Genre paintings appear in the backgrounds of Medieval paintings, but it was the Dutch painters, e.g. BRUEGEL, BOSCH and VERMEER, who were the first to specialize in them and to continue the tradition. In France, CHARDIN used genre scenes to great effect, but they did not become really popular with painters until the Realists, e.g. COURBET and MILLET. British painters, e.g. HOGARTH, GAINSBOROUGH and WILKIE, painted genre scenes, but gradually the distinction between such scenes and other genres of painting has blurred.

Gentile da Fabriano (*c*.1370–1427) Italian painter in the INTERNATIONAL GOTHIC tradition. Little of his work has survived, but he is thought to have established his reputation with frescoes, since lost, for the Doge's Palace in Venice. He was held in high regard in Siena, Florence and Rome. His best-known surviving masterpiece is the *Adoration of the Magi* (1423), now in the Ufizzi in Florence. He was a contemporary of GHIBERTI and exerted a great influence on younger artists: PISANELLO, BELLINI and Fra ANGELICO were among his pupils and followers.

Gentileschi, Orazio (1563–1639) Italian painter, his earliest work was MANNERIST in style but the major influence on his art was his friend and older contemporary CARAVAGGIO. His paintings were poetic and clearly drawn, as in the graceful *Annunciation* (*c*.1623). He moved to England in 1626, where he was commissioned by Charles I to paint the ceilings of the Queen's house. His work at this time was less Caravaggesque in style and lighter in colour and mood. His daughter **Artemisia Gentileschi** (1593–*c*.1652), however, was a powerful exponent of the Caravaggesque style and was responsible for its predominance in Naples, where she settled in 1630. Her earliest known masterpiece is *Susannah and the Elders* (1610) and a favourite theme was *Judith and Holofernes*, which she represented in several paintings.

Gerhardie, William (1895–1977) English novelist. Gerhardie was highly thought of by his contemporaries, notably WAUGH. The novels, especially *The Polyglots* (1925), are full of strange characters and events which are often straight renderings of incidents in Gerhardie's own rather bizarre life.

Géricault, Théodore (1791–1824) French painter. He studied in the classical tradition and his early work was influenced by RUBENS, but his mature style took its direction from his admiration of the works of MICHELANGELO. The realism and baroque dynamism of *The Raft of the Medusa* (1819) caused nearly as much outrage as its political overtones, and his powerful, direct oil sketches, such as *The Derby at Epsom* (1820), exerted a huge influence on younger painters. Géricault is seen as the originator of ROMANTICISM in painting.

Ghiberti, Lorenzo (1378–1455) Florentine sculptor. The span of his work covers the late Gothic and early Renaissance periods, of which times he was an outstanding and highly talented figure. His masterpieces are the two sets of gilded bronze doors for the Baptistry in Florence. He worked on these from 1401 to 1452, giving training and employment to most of the major contemporary artists in his workshops. The difference of approach between the two pairs of doors aptly illustrates Ghiberti's early Gothic style and the later predominance of Renaissance principles. Other important works include life-size bronzes of *St John the Baptist* (1412–16); *St Matthew* (1419) and *St Stephen* (1425–29). He also wrote two *Commentaries*, one a history of Italian art and the other an autobiography. DONATELLO, UCCELLO and MASOLINO were among his pupils.

Ghirlandaio, Domenico (1449–94) Florentine painter, who ran a workshop, together with his brothers **Benedetto** (1458–97) and **Davide** (1452–1525), where he produced frescoes and altarpieces for a number of churches in Florence, e.g. *The Life of St John the Baptist* (1845–90) in the Church of Santa Maria Novella, as well as in San Gimigniano and in the Sistine Chapel in Rome: *The Calling of the Apostles* (1481–2). He was also a portraitist of some stature and his tempera studies are detailed and compassionate, as in *The Old Man and his Grandson*. An interesting feature of his major works is his use of contemporary portraits in his frescos. His son **Ridolfo** (1483–1561) was also a portrait painter, and MICHELANGELO was his pupil.

Giacometti, Alberto (1901–66) Swiss painter and sculptor. He studied in Paris, experimenting in CUBISM and CONSTRUCTIVISM, and was a member of the SURREALISTS from 1930 to 1935. From this period his highly individual style developed and was finally widely recognized after a major exhibition in New York in 1948. Representative works include *Four Women on a Base* (1950), *Café* (1931) and *The Cage (Woman and Head)* (1950). Throughout his career he struggled with the problems of representing more than the the visual reality of his subject, particularly in portraiture. In sculpture he was also concerned with space and perspective in relation to the scale of his figure groups. While Giacometti's work is thoroughly unique and individual, he is perhaps best described as an existentialist artist.

Giambologna *see* **Bologna, Giovanni**.

Gibbon, Edward (1737–94) English historian. His masterpiece is his *History of the Decline and Fall of the Roman Empire* (1776–88), a work which, in breadth of narrative and erudite analysis, remains one of the greatest of all historical studies. Gibbon's sceptical and ironical tone while describing the rise and establishment of Christianity gave much offence to many of his contemporaries.

Gibbon, Lewis Grassic [pseud. of James Leslie Mitchell] (1901–35) Scottish novelist. His masterpiece is his trilogy *A Scots Quair*, i.e. *Sunset Song* (1932), *Cloud Howe* (1933) and *Grey Granite* (1934), which charts the progress of Chris Guthrie, a Scottish farm girl, through broken marriages and parenthood to life in the city. The underlying philosophy of the trilogy is a bizarre blend of Scottish nationalism, Marxism (the structure is based on MARX's "progressive" theory of history, and Chris's son joins the Communist Party) and an elemental mysticism that faintly echoes Emily BRONTË's *Wuthering Heights* (the work ends with Chris apparently becoming one with the land). Gibbon was much influenced by MACDIARMID.

Gide, André (1860–1951) French novelist. Brought up under a strict Protestant family regime, Gide early on developed a strong but confused moral sense, and decided he was a homosexual after reading Oscar WILDE. His novels, e.g. *Fruits of the Earth* (1897) and *Strait is the Gate* (1909), are usually short and are fascinating studies of sexual and social self-deception. He flirted with communism for a while, but condemned the horrors of the Soviet system in his *Return from the U.S.S.R.* (1936), a work which, in its integrity and lack of bigotry, is one of the key political books of the 1930s. He was awarded The NOBEL PRIZE for literature in 1947.

Gilbert, Sir W[illiam] S[chwenck] (1836–1911) English dramatist and librettist. His collaboration with the composer Sir Arthur Sullivan (1842–1900) resulted in the "Savoy operas," e.g. *Trial by Jury* (1875) and *The Gondoliers* (1889), of which there are 13 in all. The operas are such fun, and the tunes so good, that the extreme sharpness of social comment and essential impropriety of much of the dialogue, tends to be missed. Gilbert is probably the only dramatist to have operated at the same level of satire as ARISTOPHANES, and the enormous popularity of the operas with the Victorian middle classes remains something of an enigma. Gilbert was also one of the finest English parodists, and wrote much excellent light verse. *See also* AESTHETIC MOVEMENT.

Ginsberg, Allen *see* **Beat Generation**.

Giorgione del Castelfranco (1475–1510) Venetian painter. Virtually none of his work is accurately documented and little has survived, but he is accepted as having been one of the most influential painters of his time. He is thought to have studied with BELLINI, and was a contemporary of TITIAN. He painted the *Castelfranco Altarpiece* in his native town, and other works, authenticated by surviving fragments or engravings or by the writings of Marcantonio Michiel and VASARI, include paintings for the Doge's Palace (1507–9) and frescos for the Fondaco dei Tedeschi in Venice (1508). The bulk of Giorgione's work was in small private commissions, typical of which are *The Tempest* and *The Three Philosophers*. *The Concert Chapitre* may have been painted by Giorgione or Titian. The critical importance of Giorgione's work is in his treatment of landscape; he was one of the first to imbue landscape painting with strong atmospheres and moods to which the detail is subordinated, and in this he was much admired and imitated by younger and succeeding generations of Venetian painters.

Giotto di Bondone (1267–1337) Florentine painter and architect. Little of his work is documented, but his known and accredited works show a development of spatial perspective and fully rounded figures that represent a departure from the flat, decorative imagery of the Byzantine era. The most important works accepted as his are the frescos of *The Life of the Virgin, St Anne and St Joachim* and *The Life and Passion of Christ* (1313) in the Arena Chapel in Padua, but great controversy surrounds the attribution of *The Life of St Francis* frescos in the Church of San Francesco at Assisi (*c*.1290s). Among the many panel paintings thought to be by Giotto is the *Ognissanti Madonna* (*c*.1308) in the Uffizi, Florence. Giotto exerted an enormous influence over the next generation of Florentine painters, and his work is now taken to represent the starting point of modern western art.

Giovanni Bologna *see* **Bologna, Giovanni.**

Gissing, George (1857–1903) English novelist. His novels are unrelentingly grim works designed to expose the horrors of social injustice and often have as their central character an artist or hack writer (like Gissing himself) struggling to survive in a sea of indifference and poverty. His two best-known novels are *New Grub Street* (1891), a bitter portrayal of the literary world's underclass, and *The Private Papers of Henry Ryecroft* (1903).

Giulio Romano *see* **Raphael.**

Glackens, William James (1870–1938) American painter. He studied at the Pennsylvania Academy of the Fine Arts and was influenced and encouraged as a serious artist by his friend Robert HENRI, whom he met in 1891, although he continued to earn his living by art journalism and illustration. He was a member of the New York Realists and The EIGHT, and a leading figure of the ASHCAN SCHOOL, although his work has a strong Impressionist style, as in *Chez Mouqin* (1905). He was involved in organizing the ARMORY SHOW, in which he exhibited, and a memorial exhibition of his own work was held at the Whitney Museum of American Art in 1938.

Glasgow, Ellen (1873–1945) American novelist. Her novels are usually set in her native Virginia and are closely observed dramas of social and political tension. Representative examples include *Virginia* (1913) and *Barren Ground* (1925).

Glasgow Boys *or* **Glasgow School** A group of painters centred in Glasgow in the 1880s and 90s. They represented a move away from academic strictures and were inspired by the *plein air* BARBIZON SCHOOL. They established an outpost of the European vogue for naturalism and romantic lyricism in landscape painting, and their influence extends into the 20th century, particularly in Scottish landscape painting. Members of the group included LAVERY, HENRY, HORNEL and GUTHRIE.

Goes, Hugo van der (d.1482) Flemish painter from Ghent, where he joined the painters' guild in 1467 and became dean in 1475 before entering a Brussels monastery. His major work, on which attribution of others is based, is the Medici commission for the *Portinari Altarpiece* (1746), now in the Uffizi in Florence, which shows a rich sense of decorative surface texture combined with outstanding perception of space and depth of composition. The subject is the *Adoration of the Child*, and the landscape of the centre panel extends to the wings, where the saints and the patron's family are depicted. Other important works include *The Adoration of the Magi* (1470) and *The Death of the Virgin* (1480).

Goethe, Johann Wolfgang von (1749–1832) German poet, dramatist, novelist, philospher, scientist and statesman. He was one of the most learned and influential figures of his time. His novel *The Sorrows of Young Werther* (1774) is a morbid tale of unrequited love that supposedly inspired a wave of suicides of oversensitive young men throughout Europe (*see also* MACPHERSON). Other great works include the novel *Elective Affinities* (1809), the verse drama *Egmont* (1788) and much great poetry. His masterpiece, the verse drama *Faust*, was published in two parts in 1808 and 1832.

Gogarty, Oliver St John (1878–1957) Irish poet and novelist, remembered principally for being the model for the rumbustious Buck Mulligan in James JOYCE's *Ulysses*, and for *As I was Going Down Sackville Street* (1937), a valuable memoir of Dublin's literary world.

Gogh, Vincent van (1853–90) Dutch painter. He originally studied theology and was a lay preacher before taking up painting in 1880. He studied at the Antwerp Academy, but his work remained thoroughly unacademic in its realist subject matter and bold, expressionistic style, e.g. *The Potato Eaters* (1885). He moved to Paris in 1886 where his work was variously influenced by DEGAS, GAUGUIN and SEURAT, although without compromising his enigmatic use of colour and powerful impasto brushwork. He spent the last two years of his life in the south of France, partly in an asylum at St Rémy; it was a time of intense creativity arising out of personal anguish, e.g. *The Cornfield* (1889). His importance in the establishment of a new direction to EXPRESSIONIST and ABSTRACT ART is enormous, and his work had a resonant and continuing influence on 20th-century art worldwide.

Gogol, Nikolai (1809–52) Russian short-story writer, dramatist and novelist. His two great works are the play *The Government Inspector* (1836), a scathing satire on Russian bureaucracy and obsequience, and *Dead Souls* (1842), a novel in which the names of dead peasants are bought by a young man scheming for an inheritance. He also wrote some exceptionally fine stories, e.g. "The Nose" and "The Overcoat," in which his favourite theme of confusion between appearance and reality is used to wildly comic effect.

Golding, Sir William (1911–) English novelist. His first novel, *Lord of the Flies* (1954), describes the reduction to primal brutality of a party of British schoolboys stranded on a desert island; his second, *The Inheritors* (1955), a savage fable of man's origins, established him as a master of dark allegories concerning man's propensity for evil. He was awarded the NOBEL PRIZE for literature in 1983.

Goldoni, Carlo (1707–93) Italian dramatist. He wrote

over 250 plays (in French as well as Italian), and some operas. Around 150 of his plays are comedies, invariably set in his native Venice and frequently featuring satirical attacks on the aristocracy. Goldoni's comedies are generally seen as adapting the form of COMMEDIA DELL'ARTE to a more realistic approach with greater appeal to the tastes of the middle-class audiences of the mid to late 18th century.

Goldsmith, Oliver (1730–74) Irish poet, essayist and novelist. He settled in London in 1756, where he became a hack reviewer and writer for periodicals. His two greatest works are the novel *The Vicar of Wakefield* (1764), a cunningly structured blend of virtue and humour that became one of the most popular of all 18th-century novels, and his hugely successful play *She Stoops to Conquer* (1773), which is one of the most popular of all English comedies.

Gopaleen, Myles na *see* **O'Brien, Flann**.

Gorenko, Anna Andreyevna *see* **Akhmatova, Anna**.

Gorky, Arshile [Vosdanig Manoog Adoian] (1905–48) Armenian-born American painter who studied and taught at the Grand Central School of Art in New York. His early work shows the influence of his friend DE KOONING and of CUBIST art, as in *The Artist and his Mother* (1926–9). He worked on the FEDERAL ARTS PROJECT in the 1930s, painting an abstract mural, now destroyed, for Newark Airport. In the 1940s he began to establish his own bright, free-flowing style from the assimilation of Cubist and more organic abstract forms, typified by a series of paintings of *Garden in Sochi* (1941) and *The Liver is the Cock's Comb* (1944). Gorky's later works are more subdued in colour range following a series of personal crises and disasters. He committed suicide.

Gorky, Maxim (1868–1936) Russian novelist, dramatist and short-story writer. He was born into poverty, self-educated, and his works deal with the plight of the poor and society's outcasts in Czarist Russia. His best-known works are *The Mother* (1906–7), a story of awakening political consciousness, the autobiographical trilogy *Childhood* (1913), *Among People* (1915) and *My Universities* (1923), and his great play *The Lower Depths* (1902). His works were later used as templates by many practitioners of socialist realism, a doctrine he helped formulate in the 1930s (*see* MARX). The best of his former colleagues were killed by the Soviet regime in the 1930s.

Gossaert, Jan *called* **[Jean de] Mabuse** (*c.*1478–1533) Flemish painter from Mabeuge. He was a master of the Antwerp Guild and Philip of Burgundy was his patron. His early work shows the influence of van EYCK and van der GOES, but he later included elements of Italian art, and his work is a curious yet dignified admixture of Flemish portraits and figures in classical poses, as in *St Luke* (1515) and *Danaë* (1527). He undertook several royal commissions, for which he travelled widely, and he had a notable influence on European art. Major works include *Adoration of the Magi* (1507–8).

Gothic A style of architecture that lasted from the 12th to the 16th centuries in Northern Europe and Spain. Its effect on art was to produce the INTERNATIONAL GOTHIC style.

Gothic novel A type of NOVEL that was enormously popular in the late 18th century, combining elements of the supernatural, macabre or fantastic, often in wildly ROMANTIC settings, e.g. ruined abbeys or ancient castles. The heroes and/or heroines, whether medieval or modern, for the most part speak in a formal, stilted language curiously at odds (for the modern reader) with the appalling situations they find themselves in. Horace WALPOLE's *The Castle of Otranto*

(1764) and Ann RADCLIFFE's *The Mysteries of Udolpho* (1794) are among the best-known examples of the genre. Jane AUSTEN's *Northanger Abbey* (1818) remains the definitive parody.

gouache *also called* **poster paint** *or* **body paint** An opaque mixture of watercolour paint and white pigment.

Goujon, Jean (*c.*1510–68) French sculptor, who was responsible for developing a sculptural parallel to the MANNERIST traditions then in vogue in writing and painting. Nothing is known of his early life and works, although it seems likely that he travelled in Italy and had a knowledge of Italian architecture and sculpture. He was also looked on as an authority on the ANTIQUE. Notable works include the pillars in the Church of St Maclou near Rouen, and the caryatids at the Louvre in Paris. Goujon fled France as a Protestant exile after 1562, and is thought to have died in Bologna.

Goya y Lucientes, Francisco de (1746–1828) Spanish painter and printmaker, who studied in Madrid, where he finally settled in 1775. Early works contain elements of NEOCLASSICAL and ROCOCO styles, but the major influences on his art were TIEPOLO and VELAZQUEZ, who inspired his strong, free-flowing technique and powerful pictorial style. Early pieces include frescos for the Church of San Antonio da Florida and portraits of the royal family, to whom he was court painter from 1786. Important later works include the etchings *Los Caprichos* (1799) and *Disasters of War* (1810–20), and reveal his dislike of the established church and state, as well as his later outrage at the behaviour of an invading French army. The famous paintings of *May 2nd 1808* and *May 3rd 1808* also form a dramatic and moving record of wartime atrocities. His works of later years, known as his "Black Paintings," also demonstrate an abhorrence of human cruelty. Goya spent his last years in exile in France.

Grahame, Kenneth (1859–1932) Scottish author of the classic children's stories *The Golden Age* (1895), *Dream Days* (1898), and (his masterpiece) *The Wind in the Willows* (1908). Grahame became Secretary of the Bank of England, writing his stories in his spare time to entertain his only son.

Gramsci, Antonio *see* **Futurism**.

Granville-Barker, Harley (1877–1946) English dramatist, producer, critic and actor. The best of his plays are the naturalistic dramas *The Voysey Inheritance* (1905) and *Waste* (1907). His productions, especially those of SHAKESPEARE, broke new ground in their concern for textual authenticity and disdain for over-elaborate sets. His *Prefaces* to Shakespeare's plays were published in four volumes, 1927–45, and are the first major study of Shakespeare from the viewpoint of a drama producer.

Grass, Gunter [Wilhelm] (1927–) German novelist, dramatist and poet. His best-known novel is *The Tin Drum* (1959), a grimly comic satire on the collapse of Hitler's Third Reich, as seen through the eyes of a dumb boy. His plays include *The Plebians Rehearse the Uprising* (1966), a satire on BRECHT's dramatic and political theories, set during the Berlin workers' rebellion against the East German dictatorship. Grass's own political views are staunchly socialist but democratic, with a consistent and wholly admirable opposition to totalitarianism of all varieties.

Graves, Richard (1715–1804) English clergyman and author of *The Spiritual Quixote* (1773), an entertaining PICARESQUE NOVEL that describes the experiences of a dissenter travelling through England. The work satirizes the "enthusiastic" preaching and conduct of the more extreme Methodists, particularly George Whitefield, who is disowned in the book by John Wesley himself.

Graves, Robert [von Ranke] (1889–1985) English poet, novelist and critic. His great autobiography *Goodbye to all That* (1929) was one of the first accounts of World War I soldiering to make a major impact from an antiwar standpoint. In his poetry, Graves developed a highly idiosyncratic voice based on his belief in a primal matriarchal principle that had been suppressed by rational, superficial, patriarchal values, a view in which he was influenced by the American poet **Laura Jackson Riding** (1901–), with whom he lived from 1927 to 1939. He describes his beliefs in *The White Goddess* (1948). His poems were extensively revised by him throughout his life (five collected editions between 1938–75). His two great historical novels, *I, Claudius* and *Claudius the God* (both 1934) are very highly regarded.

Gray, Thomas (1716–71) English poet. His best-known poem is "Elegy Written in a Country Churchyard" (1751), a meditation on the graveyard at Stoke Poges, which is one of the most quoted from poems in the language.

Green, Henry [pseud. of Henry Vincent Yorke] (1905–73) English novelist. His strange, highly original novels have been much praised by his peers, notably UPDIKE and WAUGH. His most remarkable quality is his fluid and confident use of the rhythms and expressions of ordinary speech. The novels include *Living* (1929), *Loving* (1945) and *Back* (1946).

Greene, Graham (1904–91) English novelist, who is regarded as one of the greatest modern novelists. He converted to Roman Catholicism in 1926, and his religious beliefs (or disbeliefs: his "faith" is indistinguishable from atheism for many) play an important part in his fictional world, the so-called "Graham

Greeneland," a seedy, often exotic world of spiritually tainted not-quite-heroes. His wartime experiences as a British Intelligence Agent in Africa during World War II, a role ideally suited to Greene, also shaped his fiction. Greene's division of his novels into "entertainments," e.g. *Brighton Rock* (1938), and works to be classed as more serious, e.g. *The Heart of the Matter* (1948), is generally disregarded by both readers and critics.

Greene, Robert (*c*. 1558–92) English poet, dramatist and pamphleteer. Greene's tracts on the Elizabethen underworld are valuable for their descriptions of criminal life and language. He is also noted for his attack on SHAKESPEARE in his "Groat's Worth of Wit" (1592), in which he warns his fellow university-educated dramatists against the "upstart Crow" Shakespeare. The publisher of the tract apologized publicly for the remark.

Gregory, Lady Augusta (1852–1932) Anglo-Irish dramatist. She was a founder and director of the ABBEY THEATRE and a close friend of, and collaborator with, YEATS. Her plays, many of which are based on Irish legends, include *The Kiltartan Molière* (1910) and *Irish Folk History Plays* (1912). Her memoir *Our Irish Theatre* (1913) is a vivid and very entertaining account of the spectacular ego clashes of Anglo-Irish literary life.

Grieve, Christopher Murray *see* **MacDiarmid, Hugh**.

Gris, Juan [José Gonzalez] (1887–1927) Spanish painter who studied in Madrid before moving to Paris in 1906. ART NOUVEAU was an early influence on his work prior to meeting PICASSO in 1910. His work in the CUBIST style developed into the more abstract form of Synthetic Cubism, and he was an early experimenter in COLLAGE. Most of his paintings have a constructivist approach, as in *Homage to Picasso* (1912), but later works, such as *Violin and Fruit Dish* (1924), are more freely painted. Gris also designed stage sets and costumes for Diaghilev's Ballet Russe.

grisaille A monochrome painting made using only shades of grey, often used as a sketch for oil paintings.

Gropius, Walter *see* **Bauhaus**.

Gros, Antoine Jean (1771–1835) French painter who studied under DAVID and was influenced by RUBENS and the Venetian painters. In 1793 he met Napoleon and became his official war painter, travelling with the armies and recording battle campaigns in a bold and vivid manner that won him great acclaim. He is seen as a forerunner of the ROMANTIC movement in France, although he later tried to revert to his early classical training, the lack of success of which lead to his suicide in 1835. Notable works include *The Plague at Jaffa* (1804) and *The Battle of Aboukir* (1806). He also decorated the cupola of the Pantheon in Paris. BONINGTON, DELACROIX and GÉRICAULT were all pupils of Gros.

Grossmith, George (1847–1912) *and* **Weedon** (1852–1919) English theatricals and authors of *A Diary of a Nobody* (text by both, illustrations by Weedon), which first appeared (to immediate acclaim) in *Punch* magazine in 1892. The diary solemnly recounts the humdrum experiences, and small triumphs and disasters, of Charles Pooter, a lower-middle-class clerk, in suburban London. The work is generally regarded as a classic of English humour.

Grosz, George (1893–1959) German painter, cartoonist and illustrator. He was a prominent member of DADA and established his early reputation with caricatures for the satirical press. Important collections of his work, such as *The Face of the Ruling Class* (1821) and *Ecce Homo* (1927), represent his fiercely anti-fascist and anticapitalist views. He settled in the US in the 1930s and taught at the Art Students' League, New York. Later paintings are more mellow and less political in approach, as in a number of café and street scenes, e.g. *New York Harbour* (1936), although some works are still surreal and terrifying, e.g. *The Pit* (1946). Grosz has been hailed by critics as a satirist ranking alongside DAUMIER, GOYA and HOGARTH.

grotesque A term for a style of ornamentation that began in Roman times and reached its height with ROCOCO. It consisted of a series of figurative or floral ornaments in decorative frames that are linked by festoons.

Grünewald, Matthias [Mathis Godhardt-Niethardt] (*c.*1460–1528) German painter, whose few surviving works include religious paintings and altarpieces, most important of which is the altarpiece commissioned for the monastery at Isenheim (1515), now in the Musée d'Unterlinden, Colmar. His competent use of perspective, gothic imagery, strong colour and an expressionistic style of distortion all combine to produce a powerful and intensely emotional vision of Christ's suffering. He is also known to have produced a number of smaller paintings, although unlike many North European artists of the time, he did little in the way of engraving. He was an influential painter among younger contemporaries such as BALDUNG GRIEN, DÜRER and Hans HOLBEIN the Younger.

Guardi, Francesco (1712–93) Venetian painter. He is known mainly for his views of Venice, painted in a free, expressive style in contrast to the detailed compositions of his older contemporary CANALETTO. Guardi was a prolific artist, painting historical and religious subjects, still lifes and imaginary views, but his patrons and agents were not significant enough to raise him out of the obscurity and poverty in which he eventually died. His brother **Giovanni Antonio** (1699–1760) ran the family studio, and it is uncertain which of the brothers painted the outstanding *Story of Tobit* (*c*.1755) in the Church of San Raffaele.

Guercino, Il [Giovanni Francesco Barbieri] (1591–1666) Italian BAROQUE painter from Centro. His early influences include the Venetian painters and Ludovico CARRACCI, and his works are distinguished by their dramatic sense of light and colour, soft, well-rounded forms and excellent draughtsmanship. His best-known work is the *Aurora* ceiling fresco (1621–3) in the Villa Ludovisi in Rome, where he lived at that time. He later settled in Bologna, where his mature work took on a more classical aspect although remaining painterly in style, and his career was long and successful.

Guston, Philip (1913–80) American painter. His early figurative works are concerned with social issues, and he worked on murals for the WPA (the Works Progress Administration), set up under the FEDERAL ARTS PROJECT. Later works are more abstract and lyrical, concerned with the interaction of colours, and his mature work includes pieces of a more sinister atmosphere, notably his series on the Klu Klux Klan.

Guthrie, Sir James (1859–1930) Scottish painter and member of the GLASGOW SCHOOL. He spent much of his time in the village of Cockburnspath, inspired by the *plein air* painting of the BARBIZON SCHOOL. He later moved to Glasgow, where he enjoyed a successful career in portrait painting. His works are subtle in tone and full of realism without sacrificing a good sense of decorative line and colour. Along with the other Glasgow Boys, he has had an influence on younger generations of Scottish painters.

Gwathmey, Robert (1903–) American painter whose work is linear and colourful in a stylistically simplified style. A common theme is the life of southern black workers, as in *Workers on the Land* (1947).

H

Haggard, Sir H[enry] Rider (1856–1925) English novelist. He wrote 34 adventure novels, of which *King Solomon's Mines* (1886) and *She* (1887) are the best known. The novels are exciting, well-constructed narratives, and occasionally display a strong empathy with African culture.

Hague School *see* **Mauve, Anton**.

Haiku *see* **Basho**.

Hall, [Marguerite] Radclyffe (1883–1943) English novelist. Her novel *The Well of Loneliness* (1928) was one of the first significant works of fiction to describe lesbianism openly and sympathetically; it was banned in the UK until 1949, but not in the US. She also published four volumes of poems and seven other novels, notably *Adam's Bread* (1926).

Hals, Frans (*c*.1581–1666) Dutch painter. His early life and works are not well documented, but he is thought to have studied in Haarlem. His first major work is *The Banquet of the St George Civic Guard* (1616), a lively and innovative group portrait and a move away from formal trends in group portraiture. His fresh, natural spontaneity and a sound understanding of the works of CARAVAGGIO combine in the famous *Laughing Cavalier* (1624). His mature works, while still freshly and sensitively composed, are more sombre in colour and mood, e.g. *The Regents* and *The Regentesses of the Almshouse* (both *c*.1664). Hals had a large family and all his numerous commissions could not keep him out of the poverty in which he eventually died. Several of his sons became painters.

Hamilton, Gavin (1723–98) Scottish painter. He trained in Scotland before settling permanently in Rome from 1775, where he was involved in the NEO-CLASSICAL circle of MENGS. His influences included the ANTIQUE and the works of POUSSIN, and his history paintings were copied in engravings and were influential among succeeding generations of Neoclassical painters, including DAVID.

Hammett, [Samuel] Dashiell (1894–1961) American novelist. Like Raymond CHANDLER (whom he influenced), Hammett wrote tough "hard-boiled" realistic crime novels, that are based on his own experiences as a Pinkerton detective and that won a wide following. Examples include *The Maltese Falcon* (1930) which featured the laconic private eye Sam Spade, and *The Thin Man* (1932), whose hero was the contrastingly urbane Nick Charles.

Hamsun, Knut (1859–1952) Norwegian novelist, poet and dramatist. His best-known novel is *Hunger* (1890), a vivid, almost surreal autobiographical work narrated by a starved clerk, which includes scenes set in the US, where Hamsun had worked as a tram conductor in Chicago. Other works, e.g. *Pan* (1894) and *Growth of the Soil* (1917), display a mystical absorption in nature that darkened in later years to support for the irrational, occult aspects of Nazism. He was awarded the NOBEL PRIZE for literature in 1920.

Hanson, Duane (1925–) American sculptor famous for his realistically detailed figures modelled out of fibre-glass resin, and using real garments and objects as props. The themes of most of these works tend to be American stereotypes of one kind or another, e.g. *Tour-*

ists (1970) represents middle-class lack of taste or self-awareness.

Hardy, Thomas (1840–1928) English novelist, short-story writer and poet. His novels are set for the most part in his native Dorset (the "Wessex" of the novels). The greatest of the novels are *Far from the Madding Crowd* (1874), *The Return of the Native* (1878), *The Mayor of Casterbridge* (1886), *Tess of the D'Urbervilles* (1891) and *Jude the Obscure* (1896). Hardy was the first major English novelist to suffer from censorship; editors of the magazines in which many of the novels were originally published (in parts) often demanded cuts on the ground of propriety, which Hardy would later restore in volume form. Hardy's novels are generally characterized as gloomy studies of doomstruck characters struggling in vain against a hostile fate in an uncaring environment, and they usually end in death ("the President of the Immortals . . . had ended his sport with Tess"). The merits of the novels have been constantly debated since they were published; Henry JAMES, for example, described *Tess* as full of "faults and falsity." Few other novelists, however, have written prose which displays a more deeply moving empathy with all living creatures, an empathy which produced in his later years some of the greatest English poetry, e.g. *Wessex Poems* (1898), *Time's Laughing-stocks* (1909), *Satires of Circumstances* (1914) and *Winter Words* (1928). The *Collected Poems* (1930) contains more than 900 poems produced over a period of 60 years, poems of a quite remarkable variety of form, but all alike in their strange, dignified and lyrical descriptions of humankind and our tortured relationship with other forms of life and the environment. He is now ranked as one of the three great poets in English of the 20th century, the others being YEATS and ELIOT.

Hare, David (1917–) American sculptor. He originally

trained as a photographer and was involved with the SURREALIST MOVEMENT in the 1940s. His best-known pieces are metalwork sculptures, such as *Juggler* (1950), which show his concern with linear and spatial forms.

Hare, David (1947–) English dramatist. His plays include *Slag* (1970), *Knuckle* (1974), *Teeth 'n' Smiles* (1975), *Plenty* (1978), and "films for television," *Licking Hitler* (1978) and *Dreams of Leaving* (1980). A recurring theme in Hare's work is the proposition that Britain lost a unique opportunity at the end of World War II for creating a genuinely egalitarian society. *See also* BOND, BRENTON.

Harris, Frank (1856–1913) Irish born Anglo-American writer and editor, whose best-known work is his autobiography *My Life and Loves* (1922–7), an entertaining, sexually explicit and thoroughly unreliable auto biography describing Harris's life as, among other things, a cowboy in the West and a literary editor in London. He edited the *Saturday Review* from 1894–8, and his friends (who usually became ex-friends) included WILDE, SHAW and WELLS.

Harris, Joel Chandler (1848–1908) American writer, whose Aesop-like "Uncle Remus" stories, e.g. *Uncle Remus and Br'er Rabbit* (1906), are based upon a deep and sympathetic knowledge of the folklore of Southern Blacks.

Harris, Thomas (c.1940–) American novelist. His gripping thrillers, *Red Dragon* (1983) and *The Silence of the Lambs* (1988), are superbly plotted psychological studies of serial killers and their FBI hunters. *The Silence of the Lambs* was described by Roald DAHL as the "best novel for years," and by another reviewer as a "literary nasty." The central character of these haunting studies of "children of a nightmare" is the psychotic psychiatrist Dr Hannibal Lecter, a monstrous comic/macabre creation who has been described as a cross between Dracula and Sherlock Holmes.

Harte, [Francis] Bret[t] (1836–1902) American poet and short-story writer, noted especially for his shrewdly observed stories of Californian gold miners in *The Luck of Roaring Camp and Other stories* (1870). The best of his humorous verse, e.g. "Plain Language from Truthful James" (1870) is still highly regarded.

Hartley, L[eslie] P[oles] (1895–1972) English novelist. His novels include the "Eustace and Hilda" trilogy, i.e. *The Shrimp and the Anemone* (1944), *The Sixth Heaven* (1946), and *Eustace and Hilda* (1947). His best-known work is *The Go-Between* (1953), a subtle portrayal of social and sexual intrigue in Edwardian England.

Hartley, Marsden (1877–1943) American abstract painter. He travelled to Paris and Berlin from 1912 to 1915, and was associated with KANDINSKY. His earlier works are bright and decorative, as in *A German Officer* (1914), but mature pieces include more atmospheric, troubled landscapes dependent on mass and line, e.g. *Lobster Fishermen* (1940–41).

Hasek, Jaroslav (1883–1923) Czech novelist and short-story writer. His masterpiece is *The Good Soldier Svejk* (1925), a brilliantly mordant PICARESQUE novel based on Hasek's own experiences as a soldier in the Austro-Hungarian army. Svejk's cunning talent for extracting himself from difficult situations resulted in him becoming an unofficial national symbol in 20th-century Czechoslovakia. Hasek's own improbable career included service in the Bolshevik Red Army as a political commissar.

Havel, Vaclav (1936–) Czech dramatist and statesman. Havel's plays of the 1960s and 1970s, e.g. *The Garden Party* (1963), used the techniques of the Theatre of the ABSURD to satirize the brutality and corruption of Czech communism, with an ORWELLian-like emphasis on the corruption of language under totalitarianism. Like KUNDERA and other Czech writers, he enjoyed a brief spell of artistic expression during the "Prague Spring," but was imprisoned for several years after the Soviet invasion of 1968. In one of the most astonishing turnarounds in literary, political, or any careers, Havel was elected President of Czechoslovakia in 1990. *See also* IONESCO.

Hawthorne, Nathanael (1804–64) American novelist and short-story writer. He was born in Salem, Massachusetts, where his ancestors had helped persecute the so-called "Salem witches," and his consciousness of the dark side of New England Puritanism (*see also* EDWARDS) profoundly shaped his life and work. His masterpiece is *The Scarlet Letter* (1850), a psychological novel on the guilt-ridden consequences of adultery in 17th-century New England. Other notable novels include *The House of the Seven Gables* (1851), which also explores the dark recesses of his sense of ancestral guilt, *The Blithesdale Romance* (1852), a sardonic reworking of his experiences at the Brook Farm Transcendentalist colony, and *The Marble Faun* (1860), a historical novel set in Renaissance Italy. His short-story collections include *Twice-Told Tales* (1837) and *Mosses from an Old Manse* (1846). He also wrote comparatively light-hearted stories for children, e.g. *Tanglewood Tales* (1853).

Haydon, Benjamin Robert (1786–1846) English painter, whose talents did not quite match his aspirations to raise the timbre of British history painting to the Grand Manner. He was a ROMANTIC and a friend of the poets Keats and Wordsworth, whose portraits he painted. He is known to have been an eloquent lecturer and writer, passionate in his defence of the arts. His own paintings, however, tended to be awkward and melodramatic. A typical work is *The Maid of Sara-*

gossa. He was thwarted in his ambition to decorate the Houses of Parliament with frescoes. He finally developed a paranoia that led to suicide.

Hazlitt, William (1778–1830) English essayist and critic. Highly influential in his own day, Hazlitt remains one of the most important literary critics, especially valued for his essays on his contemporaries and on SHAKESPEARE. His works include *Characters of Shakespeare's Plays* (1817), *Lectures on the English Comic Writers* and *Political Essays* (both 1818) and *The Spirit of the Age* (1825). His personal relations with his great contemporaries, e.g. WORDSWORTH, were often strained, due to his impulsive nature and high opinion of the critic's worth.

Heaney, Seamus [Justin] (1939–) Irish poet and critic, regarded by many critics as the finest Irish poet since YEATS. Heaney's collections include *Eleven Poems* (1965), *Death of a Naturalist* (1966), *Wintering Out* (1972) and *Station Island* (1984). Brought up a Roman Catholic in Northern Ireland, Heaney now lives and works in the Republic of Ireland. The two dominant themes of his poetry are the recurring patterns of "tribal revenge" rooted in Irish culture and the decay of traditional Irish country life.

Heine, Heinrich (1797–1856) German poet and critic. His masterpiece is his *Book of Songs* (1827), which includes some of the greatest lyric poems ever written, many of which have been set to music, notably by Schubert. One of his great achievements as a poet was to combine high lyricism with a dry sense of irony, as in "The Lorelei." He had a cautious friendship with MARX, who observed of Heine that poets were a breed apart. Although strongly radical in his politics, Heine had an equally strong (and prophetic) distrust of the intolerance and anti-Semitism of German radicalism.

Heller, Joseph (1923–) American novelist. His experiences as a USAF bombardier during World War II formed the factual basis for his first remarkable novel, *Catch-22* (1961), a grim, surrealist satire on military life and logic. His other novels include *Something Happened* (1974) and *Good as Gold* (1979).

Héloïse *see* **Abélard, Peter**.

Hemingway, Ernest (1899–1961) American novelist and short-story writer. His first important work was *The Sun also Rises* (1926), a novel set among what his friend Gertrude STEIN called the "lost generation" of expatriate American writers and artists in 1920s Paris. Hemingway's laconic narrative style, with its "tough guy" dialogue and macho values, made a big impression on his contemporaries, an impression consolidated by his next novel, *A Farewell to Arms* (1929), a tragic love story set on the Italian Front during World War I (in which Hemingway served as an ambulance driver). His subsequent collections of short stories, *Men Without Women* (1927) and *Winner Take Nothing* (1933), were also highly acclaimed. He supported the Republican government during the Spanish Civil War, his reporting experiences there forming the basis for his great novel *For Whom the Bell Tolls* (1940). He settled in Cuba in 1945, and was sympathetic to Castro's revolution of 1959 (Castro won first prize in a 1960 fishing competition; Hemingway presented him with it). He committed suicide in the US in 1961. His influence on other American writers, both in prose and lifestyle, has been immense, but often pernicious. He was awarded the NOBEL PRIZE for literature in 1954.

Henley, W[illiam] E[rnest] (1849–1903) English poet, critic and editor. Henley was an interesting minor poet with a talent for unusual rhymes. Some of his poems, e.g. "Invictus," will always retain their popularity, but his role as a mentor to younger writers is more significant. Both KIPLING and STEVENSON (the latter based Long John Silver in *Treasure Island* on Henley) spoke feelingly of Henley's support and encouragement.

Henri, Robert [Robert Henry Cozad] (1865–1929) American painter who studied at the Pennsylvania Academy of Art and at the Ecole des Beaux-Arts in Paris. Early influences included Thomas EAKINS and Frans HALS. He also admired the works of MANET and pioneered the movement to bring art out of the academies to the people in America. He was a leader of The EIGHT and a founder member of the ASHCAN SCHOOL. The major import of his work is the social realism of his subject matter, based on a deeply held belief that artists should paint life around them as they saw it. Typical of his work is *West 57th St., New York* (1902). Some of his best works are portraits, such as *Laughing Child* and *The Masquerade Dress: A Portrait of Mrs Robert Henri* (1911).

Henry, George (1858–1943) Scottish painter and member of the GLASGOW SCHOOL. One of his best-known paintings is *Galloway Landscape* (1889), illustrating a favourite theme of cattle in landscape. His approach is simplistic in style, highlighting a strongly decorative sense of line and colour. He collaborated on two paintings with his friend HORNEL: *The Druids* (1889) and *The Star in the East* (1890). He later settled in London, where he founded the Chelsea Art Club.

Henry, O *see* **O Henry**.

Hepworth, Dame Barbara (1903–75) English sculptor. She trained at the Royal College of Art in London, where she was a contemporary of Henry MOORE and of Ben NICHOLSON, to whom she was married (1932–51). Her preference was for direct carving rather than the hitherto favoured techniques of modelling and casting sculptural pieces. An early work, *Figure in Sycamore* (1931), demonstrates her acute sensitivity to the natural appropriateness of the material to the subject in her work. Pierced holes and scooped-out hollows in wood and stone carvings were experiments in depth and perspective that she later developed by painting parts of the hollows and stretching strings over the openings, as in *Pelagos* (1946). Along with Moore, she was one of the most innovative and celebrated British sculptors of the 20th century. After her death in a fire, her studio and garden at St Ives were established as a museum of her work.

Herbert, George (1593–1633) English Anglican priest and poet. Herbert's poems were published posthumously as *The Temple: Sacred Poems and Private Ejaculations* (1633) and are among the greatest devotional poems in the language. He described his poems as "a picture of the many spiritual conflicts that have passed betwixt God and my soul." The poems display the characteristics of METAPHYSICAL POETRY in their subtle, paradoxical exploration of spiritual themes. The simple piety of Herbert's life and the intellectual power of his poetry makes him one of the most appealing of all English poets. The popularity of his work with both Puritans and High Anglicans in late 17th-century England was quite unusual.

heroic tragedy A form of TRAGEDY that became very popular during the RESTORATION. Such tragedies were usually written in bombastic rhymed couplets, and featured the adventures in love and war of improbably noble characters in exotic locations, past and present. The characteristic conflict at the heart of such plays was the clash between the equally imperious commands of love and duty. The first appearance of the form was DAVENANT's "opera in the manner of the ancients," *The Siege of Rhodes*, in 1656. The form was used by dramatists of the stature of DRYDEN and

OTWAY, but eventually collapsed under the satirical onslaught of VILLIERS' *The Rehearsal* in 1671.

Herrick, Robert (1591–1674) English Anglican priest and poet. His sacred and secular poems were collected in a joint volume published during the Commonwealth period, *Hesperides* and *Noble Numbers* (both 1648). Many of the poems are surprisingly direct in their sympathy for the traditional (virtually pagan) customs of English country life. The delicate sensuality of his poems places him high among the English lyric poets. *See also* JONSON.

Hesse, Hermann (1877–1962) German-born Swiss novelist, short-story writer and poet. Hesse's fiction reflects his fascination with oriental mysticism, spiritual alienation and worldly detachment. In the 1960s, he was seen as a major prophet of "alternative" culture values. His novels include *Steppenwolf* (1927), *Narziss and Goldmund* (1930) and *The Glass Bead Game* (1943). He was awarded the NOBEL PRIZE for literature in 1946. His works were blacklisted by the Nazis in 1943, but (as with JUNG, who influenced him) controversy remains active over his relationship with Nazism.

Heywood, Thomas (*c.*1574–1641) English dramatist. His two best-known plays are the DOMESTIC TRAGEDY *A Woman Killed with Kindness* (1603), once described as the first "bourgeois tragedy," and an uproarious adventure comedy, *The Fair Maid of the West* (1600–1603). Charles LAMB described him as "a sort of *prose* Shakespeare."

Higgins, George V[incent] (1939–) American novelist and short-story writer. His experiences as a reporter and assistant district attorney in Boston form the background to Higgins's highly acclaimed crime fiction. Notable works include the novels *The Friends of Eddie Coyle* (1972) and *Impostors* (1986). Higgins's masterly low-life dialogue has no equal; his sense of irony and fate has been compared to that of the great Greek tragedians.

Highsmith, Patricia (1921–) American novelist. Her most famous creation is the charming villain Tom Ripley (virtually a psychopath), who features in such novels as *The Talented Mr Ripley* (1956) and *Ripley's Game* (1974).

Hill, Reginald (1936–) English novelist. His series of detective novels featuring the Yorkshire policemen Dalziel and Pascoe, e.g. *A Clubbable Woman* (1970) and *Bones and Silence* (1990), have been much admired for their skilful plotting, characterization, and sharp social comment on modern Britain.

Hilton, Walter *see* **Julian of Norwich, Dame**.

history painting A GENRE of painting that takes as its subject a scene from history (particularly ancient history), religious or mythological legend, or from great works of literature, e.g. by Dante or Shakespeare.

Hobbes, Thomas (1588–1679) English philosopher, whose materialist views were strongly influential on his contemporaries. He was born in the year of the Armada, and once noted that he and "fear came into the world at the same time." Hobbes' most notable work is *Leviathan* (1651), a study of society, observing that the life of man outside the constraints of civilized society is "poor, nasty, brutish and short," and concluding that men live best under strong leadership (Cromwell became Lord Protector in 1653). A great deal of subsequent political theory, continuing into our own time, consists of attempts to either refute or accommodate Hobbes' bleak conclusions on human nature. Hobbes' prose is very fine, with a sure feel for the telling image: "The Papacy is not other than the Ghost of the deceased Roman Empire, sitting crowned upon the grave thereof." He wrote his autobiography in Latin verse when he was 85. *See also* Henry MORE.

Hochhuth, Rolf (1931–) German dramatist. The best known of his plays are *The Deputy* (1963), an attack on Pope Pius XII for his supposed unwillingness to condemn the Nazis' mass murder of the Jews during World War II, and *Soldiers* (1967), which, with no basis, implied that Winston Churchill was involved in assassinating the Free Policy leader, General Sikorsky, in 1943. The plays have little merit but are of interest as examples of the "drama documentary" of the 1960s and 1970s.

Hockney, David (1937–) English artist, whose versatility in the fields of painting, printmaking, photography and design makes it hard to confine him to any one category. His unorthodox artistic development and infinite variety of sources are all underpinned by his outstanding draughtsmanship. Hockney achieved distinction while still a student at the Royal College of Art in London, winning a number of prestigious awards. Public acclaim came with the exhibition in 1963 of a set of 16 etchings entitled *Rake's Progress*. He designed sets and costumes for Jarry's *Ubu Roi* in 1966. His early works are stylistically naive, and here he acknowledges a debt to DUBUFFET, but to classify Hockney as a Pop artist is to miss the point of his depth and diversity. Paintings such as *We Two Boys Forever Clinging* (1961) and *Peter getting out of Nick's Pool* (1966) illustrate the recurring themes in his work of homosexuality and a fascination with the reflective surface of water. Hockney has held teaching posts at the universities of Iowa, Colorado and California, where he lives.

Hoffmanstahl, Hugo von (1874–1929) Austrian poet, dramatist, and librettist for six of Richard Strauss's operas, e.g. *Elektra* (1909) and *Rosenkavalier* (1911).

His works were rooted in a deep Roman Catholic faith
and display a concern for artistic integrity and a growing concern for social issues. His plays, e.g. *The Tower*
(1925), were highly praised by T. S. ELIOT.

Hogarth, William (1697–1764) English artist. He
trained first as an engraver in the ROCOCO tradition,
and by 1720 had established his own illustration business. He then began his series of paintings known as
"conversation pieces," e.g. *A Scene from The Beggar's
Opera* (late 1720s) of which there is a version in the
Tate Gallery, London. By the 1730s he was also painting some fine portrait commissions in a lively and
direct manner, e.g. *Captain Coram* (1740). The reason
he did not achieve the status of a successful portraitist
is that he was not inclined to flatter his sitters. Also
about this time he began to produce his series paintings comprising six to eight pictures that followed a
sequential narrative in the manner of tableaux in a
stage play. They tended to illustrate vice and punishment and to satirize moral values. The best known of
these is *Marriage à la Mode* (1742–4). He also wrote a
treatise on aesthetic principles entitled *The Analysis
of Beauty* (1753). Hogarth was an influential figure in
painting, and his contribution to the development of
satiric art is immeasurable.

Hogg, James (1770–1835) Scottish novelist and poet.
Hogg was a self-educated shepherd (nicknamed the
"Ettrick Shepherd" by his contemporaries), who
rapidly became a leading light of Edinburgh's literary
world from 1810. Sir Walter SCOTT (who gave him early
encouragement), and WORDSWORTH were among his
friends. Hogg produced some quite remarkable works,
including (his masterpiece) the novel *The Private
Memoirs and Confessions of a Justified Sinner* (1824),
a macabre study of religious mania and murder that
has gained sharply in reputation this century, and *The*

Three Perils of Man (1822), a bizarre and highly entertaining precursor of the "sword and sorcery" genre. He also wrote some marvellous parodies of his fellow poets.

Holbein, Hans [the Younger] (*c.*1479–1543) German painter. He began his career in Basel, where Erasmus was one of his major patrons. He painted mainly portraits and religious paintings, the most important of which is *The Death of Christ* (1521), memorable and moving in its realism. His portraits were minutely detailed and exactly drawn, as in the painting of *Thomas More as Lord Chancellor* (1527), which he painted on a visit to England. He also painted *Sir Thomas More and his Family* (1527), which is thought to be the first ever domestic group portrait. In Basel he had produced a set of 51 woodcuts entitled *The Dance of Death*, the egalitarian message of which gained popularity with the spread of the Reformed Church. At the same time church patronage declined, and Holbein moved to England where he became court painter to Henry VIII, and painted the full-length portrait that has come to be the representative image of that monarch. He painted numerous royal portraits, but unfortunately many of his original works have been lost or destroyed and are now only represented by original sketches or copies. Holbein was also a great miniaturist and designer, and an outstanding influence on succeeding generations of painters.

Holmes, Oliver Wendell (1809–94) American essayist, noted especially for the light, humorous discourses of *The Autocrat of the Breakfast Table* (1858) and its sequels, e.g. *The Professor of the Breakfast Table* (1860).

Holub, Miroslav (1923–) Czech poet, critic and scientist. Widely regarded as one of Europe's greatest living poets, Holub's work combines a scientifically rigorous approach to observation with a vivid poetic imagination. Like all important East European poets, much of his work had to be published abroad until the 1989 Revolution. He has published many volumes of verse and several important collections of essays, e.g. *The Dimension of the Present Moment and other Essays* (1990). His scientific works include *The Immunology of Nude Mice* (1989).

Homer (*c*.800BC) Greek poet, author of the two great epic poems *The Iliad*, the story of the Greek war against Troy, and *The Odyssey*, which describes the adventures of the Greek hero Odysseus (known to the Romans as Ulysses) on his voyage home from the war. The characters and events of the poems have had a profound influence on Western literature. Homer was reputedly blind, and born on the island of Chios, but nothing about him is known for certain, not even his existence – or sex; Samuel BUTLER (1835–1902) believed Homer was a woman .

Homer, Winslow (1836–1910) American painter. He trained first in lithography and worked as a war illustrator for *Harper's Weekly* during the Civil War. His first paintings owe something to the directness and detachment of early photography, but he was subsequently influenced by the works of MANET. Clear, bright paintings like *Breezing Up* (1876) are typical of his style and show the sea as a favourite theme. He spent 1881–2 in the northeast of England before settling on the coast of Maine in the US, painting powerful oils and watercolours of dramatically stormy seas, e.g. *Northeaster* (1895).

Honthorst, Gerrit van (1590–1656) Dutch painter from Utrecht. He spent the years 1610–20 in Italy and was deeply influenced by the work of CARAVAGGIO, evidenced in the paintings *Christ before the High Priest* (1617) and *Samson and Delilah* (1620). Thereafter he returned to Holland, where he was a prominent figure in the UTRECHT SCHOOL, and over the next decade his tonal range became lighter and less dramatic. From the 1630s he was court painter at The Hague and painted a number of royal portraits there and abroad, including Charles I of England and members of the Danish royal family. While his later career was internationally successful, his early Caravaggesque period was to have more lasting influence on future artists.

Hooch or **Hoogh, Pieter de** (c.1629–c.1684) Dutch painter from Rotterdam, who is thought to have trained in Haarlem. His still, peaceful interior and garden-figure compositions are absolutely typical of Dutch painting of the time, e.g. *The Courtyard of a House in Delft* (1658). He was an older contemporary of VERMEER but was probably influenced by the younger artist. His later works are more ambitious but lack the quality of his early pieces, e.g. *A Musical Party* (1675–7).

Hood, Thomas (1799–1845) English poet. His humorous verses, e.g. *Odes and Addresses to Great People* (1825), were very popular in their day, and Hood is still recognized as a master of light, satirical, skilfully punning verse, as in "Faithless Sally Brown." Some of his serious poems, e.g. "The Song of the Shirt," which exposed the appalling working conditions of seamstresses, and "The Dream of Eugene Aram," a nightmarish study of a murderer, also achieved great popularity.

Hooker, Richard (c.1554–1600) English divine. His *Laws of Ecclesiastical Polity* (1593–7), written in response to Puritan attacks on Anglican moderation, remains the most readable theological work of its size in English, thanks to Hooker's beautifully constructed prose and humane tolerance.

Hopkins, Gerard Manley (1844–89) English Jesuit priest and poet. Hopkins converted to Roman Catholicism in 1866. His poems frequently express the keen conflict he felt between his desire to serve God as both priest and poet, and his deeply felt inadequacies, particularly in the "Dark Sonnets" of the mid-1880s, e.g. "No worst, there is none." Other well-known poems are "The Wreck of the Deutschland," inspired by the death of nuns in a shipwreck, and "The Windhover," a spiritually charged celebration of a falcon hovering.

Hopper, Edward (1882–1976) American painter. He studied at the Chase School of Art with Robert HENRI and was a member of the ASHCAN SCHOOL. His initial influences include MANET and DEGAS. Early etchings and watercolours are concerned with the urban realism that was to dominate his later work. His major paintings have a quiet presence intensified by the use of strong morning and evening light. The heavy stillness of deserted streets and the passive isolation of his figures, as in *Early Sunday Morning* (1930), give rise to feelings of intense sadness.

Horace [Quintus Horatius Flaccus] (65–8BC) Roman poet and satirist. Like his friend VIRGIL, he looked to the literature of Greece for inspiration, but the sardonic, realistic and tightly controlled language of his poems' language is wholly Roman. His *Odes, Satires* and *Epistles* have been much imitated by poets of all ages, e.g. POPE.

Hornel, Edward Arthur (1864–1933) Scottish painter and member of the GLASGOW SCHOOL. He collaborated with his friend George HENRY on *The Druids* (1889) and *The Star in the East* (1890) as well as travelling with Henry to Japan. Japanese art further influenced the development of the colourful and linear quality of his work. A favourite theme was children playing in fields of flowers or by streams, usually painted in a rich colourful decorative impasto.

Houdon, Jean-Antoine (1741–1828) French sculptor

who studied with PIGALLE and won the Prix de Rome in 1761. In Rome from 1764 to 1768 he achieved initial fame with the figures *L'Ecorche* (1764) and *St Bruno* (1767). He then went on to establish his reputation in portrait busts, examples of which are *Gluck* (1775), *Voltaire* and *Benjamin Franklin* (1778). He was commissioned for a marble statue of *George Washington* (1791) for the Virginia State Capitol in Richmond. Houdon survived the French Revolution but achieved little of note afterwards.

Household, Geoffrey (1900–1988) English novelist and short-story writer. The typical Household narrative is an adventure story, frequently involving a lengthy pursuit or duel, written in the first person, and with revenge as the most common motivation. His masterpiece is *Rogue Male* (1939), in which the narrator sets out to assassinate Hitler; the sequel, *Rogue Justice*, following 42 years later. One of Household's most unusual gifts is his ability to create an atmosphere of conflict that borders chillingly on the supernatural, as in *The Dance of the Dwarfs* (1968). Also of note is his superb collection of short stories, *The Europe That Was* (1979), a masterly evocation of vanishing (or vanished) patterns of European life.

Housman, A[lfred] E[dward] (1859–1936) English poet and neoclassical scholar. Housman's poetic output was small: *A Shropshire Lad* (1896), *Last Poems* (1922), and *More Poems* (1936) are all slim volumes containing short, elegiac lyrics expressing a pessimistic outlook on life. The poems often describe young labourers or soldiers meeting an untimely end. He also spent 27 years of his life (1903–30) preparing an authorized five-volume edition of a very minor Roman poet, Manilius, a project that baffled his colleagues. His criticism of his fellow scholars' work could be extremely cutting, and is often very funny.

Howard, Henry, Earl of Surrey *see* **Surrey, Earl of**.

Howells, William Dean (1837–1920) American novelist, critic and editor. He wrote 35 novels of which the best known are *A Modern Instance* (1882), *The Rise of Silas Lapham* (1885) and *A Hazard of New Fortunes* (1890). The novels show a general progression towards a kind of TOLSTOYAN socialist idealism. He was very influential in his role as associate editor of *Harper's Magazine* (1886–91), and encouraged, among others, Mark TWAIN and Henry JAMES.

Hudson, W[illiam] H[enry] (1841–1922) Argentinian-born British novelist and naturalist. His nonfiction works include *The Naturalist in La Plata* (1892), *Idle Days in Patagonia* (1893), and his fascinating account of his childhood, *Far Away and Long Ago* (1918). His masterpiece is the novel *Green Mansions* (1904), a strange tale of love and death set in the Venezuelan jungle.

Hudson River School A group of American landscape painters active in the mid-19th century. Leading figures were COLE and DURAND, and their work was concerned with the beauty and mysticism of nature, expressed in romantic terms on a grand and noble scale. They were influenced by the writers Fenimore Cooper and Washington Irving as well as by TURNER.

Hughes, James Langston (1902–67) American poet. He is best known as a chronicler of the sufferings of poor urban Blacks. His works include *The Weary Blues* (1926) and *One-Way Ticket* (1949).

Hughes, Ted [Edward James Hughes] (1930–) English poet, noted for his violent poetic imagery drawn from the natural world in such collections as *The Hawk in the Rain* (1957) and *Crow* (1970). Most of his poems about animals have bloody conclusions, which led one critic to conjecture that he would eventually run out of animal subjects. His appointment as POET LAUREATE in

1984 following the death of BETJEMAN was greeted with some surprise (his work, however, is no more death-haunted than Betjeman's). He married Sylvia PLATH in 1956, whose suicide in 1963 led to Hughes becoming the target of a peculiarly nasty campaign of vilification by self-appointed guardians of Plath's memory.

Hugo, Victor (1802–85) French novelist, dramatist and poet. The production of his play *Hernani* (1830), a highly romantic and unconventional poetic drama, was marked by inflamed squabbles between supporters and opponents of the new formally looser and more socially challenging drama. The ensuing controversy established Hugo as the leader of French literary romanticism. His best-known novels are *The Hunchback of Notre Dame* (1831) and *Les Misérables* (1862).

humours, theory of (in medieval medical theory) Any of the four body fluids: blood, phlegm, yellow (choleric) bile, and black (melancholic) bile. This theory is the basis for the *Comedy of Humours*, notably Ben Jonson's *Every Man in his Humour* (1598), in which the characters have names and behaviour appropriate to their eccentrically dominant "humour" or personality trait. For humour in the modern sense, *see* **wit**.

Hunt, [James Henry] Leigh (1784–1859) English poet and essayist. With his brother **John Hunt** (1775–1848), he founded in 1808 a very successful weekly paper called *The Examiner*, which promoted reformist politics. Hunt also produced some charming light verse, e.g. "Jenny Kissed Me," and the two ingenious sonnets "To a Fish" and "A Fish Replies." He published BYRON and SHELLEY when other editors regarded them as beyond the pale, and was very encouraging to KEATS. DICKENS used his less attractive characteristics as the basis for the character Harold Skimpole in *Bleak House*.

Hunt, William Holman (1827–1910) English painter
and a founder of the PRE-RAPHAELITE movement.
Along with his friend MILLAIS, he was opposed to the
frivolity of established trends in contemporary art and
sought to express the Pre-Raphaelite aims of direct
study from nature and natural composition. He is
known to have made several journeys to the Middle
East to paint accurate detail for his Biblical scenes. He
was deeply religious, and his paintings have a strong
moralistic message and symbolic attention to detail, as
in *The Light of the World* or *The Awakening Conscience*
(1854). His work generally lacks grace and sensitivity
in its colour and composition, and apart from its
strength of conviction, is not now held in particularly
high regard.

Hunt, William Morris (1824–79) American painter
who studied in Paris and was associated with the BAR-
BIZON SCHOOL. He returned to the US where he promoted the Barbizon artists and exerted considerable
influence on his American contemporaries through his
own landscape and figure paintings. Much of his work
was lost in a fire in 1872, and his only extant works of
any note are his murals in the New York State Capitol,
Albany. The writer Henry James was his pupil.

Hunter, George Leslie (1877–1931) Scottish painter
and member of the group referred to as the Scottish
COLOURISTS. He was influenced by FAUVIST painting,
and his delight in the richnesses and relationships of
colour is evident in most of his work. A typical example
is *Reflections, Balloch.* Landscapes and still lifes with
fruit or flowers were common themes.

Huxley, Aldous [Leonard] (1894–1963) English novelist, short-story writer and essayist. His early novels
and stories, e.g. *Crome Yellow* (1921) and *Mortal Coils*
(1922), are sardonic, waspish satires on the brittle post-
World War I world of English intellectual life. These

and succeeding works, e.g. *Antic hay* (1923) and *Point Counter Point* (1928), often feature thinly disguised portraits of Huxley's friends and associates, e.g. D. H. LAWRENCE and the critic **John Middleton Murry** (1889–1957), the latter seriously contemplating challenging Huxley to a duel over his portrayal as "Burlap" in *Point Counter Point*. Huxley's masterpiece is *Brave New World* (1932), a chilling fable of a future totalitarian state based on a scientifically contrived caste system. Huxley's later works, e.g. the Utopian novel *Island* (1962), are rather more optimistic in tone. His nonfiction works include *The Doors of Perception* (1954) and *Heaven and Hell* (1956), in which he records the spiritual insights he claims to have received as a result of taking hallucinogenic drugs. *See also* Sir Thomas MORE.

I

Ibbetson, Julius Caesar (1759–1817) English painter
who established himself in London copying other
works for dealers and imitating the Dutch landscape
painters and GAINSBOROUGH. From 1800 he settled in
his native Yorkshire, where he painted landscapes and
coastal scenes with figures. His work is essentially
English and picturesque in style. He also painted some
portraits, typical of which is one of the poet Robert
Burns in a Scottish landscape setting.

Ibsen, Henrik (1828–1906) Norwegian dramatist.
Ibsen's great plays fall into three groups: the early
verse dramas, which culminated in *Brand* (1866) and
Peer Gynt (1866); the plays of social realism dealing
with such issues as venereal disease, municipal corruption and female emancipation, e.g. *A Doll's House*
(1879), *Ghosts* (1881), and *An Enemy of the People*
(1882); the late symbolic plays, e.g. *The Wild Duck*
(1884), *The Master Builder* (1892), and *John Gabriel
Borkman* (1896), in which the realism of the middle
period is mixed with an introspective, disturbing symbolism which draws upon folk traditions. *Hedda Gabler*
(1890) marked a powerful return to realism in its depiction of the menace of intellectual arrogance. Ibsen's
plays have been heavily influential upon 20th-century
drama. He particularly influenced SHAW, whose *Quintessence of Ibsenism* (1891) is a lively summation of
Ibsen's achievement.

icon *or* **ikon** A religious image, usually painted on a wooden panel, regarded as sacred in the Byzantine Church and subsequently by the Orthodox Churches of Russia and Greece, where they survive. The word comes from the Greek *eikon*, meaning "likeness," and strict rules were devised as to the subject, generally a saint, and to the form of the painting and its use, so although icon painting flourished in the 6th century it is extremely difficult to date icons painted then or later. A reaction to what was considered idolatry took place in the 8th century, resulting in **iconoclasm**, the destruction of such images.

iconography (1) The study and interpretation of representations in figurative art and their symbolic meanings (also called **iconology**). It is particularly important in the understanding of Christian art, especially of the medieval and Renaissance periods, e.g. the dove signifying the Holy Spirit, or the fish symbolizing Christ. (2) The album of etchings of his contemporaries by van DYCK.

Imagism A poetry movement of the early 20th century which advocated using everyday language and precise representation of the image of the subject discussed. Imagist poems were short and to the point, anti-ROMANTIC and anti-Victorian in tone, and could be on any subject under the sun (as in William Carlos WILLIAM's "The Red Wheelbarrow"). Prominent Imagists included Williams, Ezra POUND and Amy LOWELL, whose *Tendencies in Modern American Poetry* (1917) has the best introduction to the movement. Ford Madox FORD, who is sometimes described as an Imagist, had a row with Amy Lowell at a fund-raising *Imagiste* dinner, after which he claimed that no one really knew what an Imagist was.

impasto An Italian word used to describe the thickness

and textures that can be achieved with ACRYLIC or OIL PAINT.

Impressionism An art movement originating in France in the 1860s, centred on a fairly diverse group of artists who held eight exhibitions together between 1874 and 1886. The main artists were CÉZANNE, DEGAS, MANET, MONET, MORISOT, Camille PISSARRO, RENOIR and SISLEY, although they did not all show paintings at all eight exhibitions. The name of the movement was coined by critics from a painting by Monet in the 1874 exhibition entitled *Impression: Soleil Levant*. Members of the group were variously influenced by the BARBIZON SCHOOL, the works of TURNER and CONSTABLE, and the realism of COURBET. The advent of photography and scientific theories about colour also had their impact on the painters' approach to their work. The Impressionists were concerned with representing day-to-day existence in an objective and realistic manner, and they rejected the Romantic idea that a painting should convey strong emotions. They wanted to record the fleeting effects of light and movement, and so their usual subjects were landscapes or social scenes like streets and cafés. They chose unusual viewpoints and painted "close-ups," probably influenced by photography. They were on the whole much freer in their use of unusual colours and a lighter palette; their subject matter was also less weighty, and they came in for some criticism over the lack of intellectual content of their painting. Impressionism has had an enormous influence on almost every subsequent major art movement: on CUBISM via Cézanne; on the synthetic art of GAUGUIN through SEURAT and the NEOIMPRESSIONISTS, and on EXPRESSIONISM through the works of van GOGH. This influence has continued in a large proportion of 20th-century art.

Ingres, Jean-Auguste-Dominique (1780–1867) French

painter, one of the greatest exponents of NEOCLASSICAL art. He studied at the Académie Royale in Toulouse and worked in DAVID's studio before winning the Prix de Rome in 1801 with *The Ambassadors of Agamemnon*. He was in Rome from 1806 to 1824 and was greatly influenced by the works of RAPHAEL. His paintings during this period had variable receptions, and he earned his living with pencil portraits of French and English tourists. He returned to Paris in 1824, where he established his reputation with *The Vow of King Louis VIII*. From 1834 to 1841 he was director of the French Academy in Rome and he later became a professor at the Ecole des Beaux-Arts in Paris. He presented a powerful opposition to the ROMANTICISM of DELACROIX and his circle, although some of his later portraits, e.g. *Mme Moitessier* (1851, 1856), and nudes, e.g. *The Turkish Bath* (1859–62), have an anatomical distortion and sensuousness of line that is not austerely classical. He strongly influenced DEGAS, PICASSO and MATISSE through his excellent draughtsmanship.

Inness, George (1825–94) American painter whose early landscapes were influenced by the HUDSON RIVER SCHOOL, as in *The Delaware Valley* (1865). He later adopted a freer, less detailed approach following a visit to Italy and to the BARBIZON SCHOOL in France. *The Monk* (1873) is impressionistic in its loosely painted dark masses and soft lights, while still retaining something of the mysticism of the Hudson River tradition. His work was widely admired in the US.

Innes, Michael *see* **Stewart, J. I. M**.

intaglio The cutting into a stone or other material or the etching or engraving on a metal plate of an image; the opposite of RELIEF. Intaglio printing techniques include ENGRAVING and ETCHING.

interior monologue *see* **Richardson, Dorothy**.

International Gothic A predominant style in European art covering the period between the end of the Byzantine era and the beginning of the RENAISSANCE, i.e. *c*.1375–*c*.1425. Some variations in styles occurred regionally, but the most influential centres were Italy, France and the Netherlands. Ideas spread widely due to an increase in the art trade, to travelling artists, and to a certain amount of rivalry over royal commissions. The Dukes of Berry and Burgundy were among the major patrons of the time. International Gothic style was characterized by decorative detail and refined, flowing lines; figures were often elongated or distorted to increase an appearance of elegant charm and the use of gilts and rich colours figured strongly. Scale and perspective were more symbolic than naturalistic, although naturalism began to take hold in the later works of the period, as in GENTILE DA FABRIANO's *Adoration of the Magi* (1423).

Ionesco, Eugène (1912–) Romanian-born French dramatist of the ABSURD. His plays include *The Old Soprano* (1950), *The Lesson* (1951) and *Rhinoceros* (1959), all of which have become firm favourites in the theatrical repertoire. Ionesco's passionate hatred of both left and right totalitarianism and his distrust of political didacticism have made him a rather isolated figure in French intellectual circles. When President HAVEL visited Paris in 1990, Ionesco pointed out (with great relish) that Havel was now being feted by the very intellectuals who had denounced his plays as giving ammunition to the right; a true absurdist situation.

Iron, Ralph *see* **Schreiner, Olive**.

Irving, Washington (1783–1859) American essayist and short-story writer. His best-known stories are "Rip Van Winkle" and "The Legend of Sleepy Hollow," both of which are included in *The Sketch-Book of Geoffrey*

Crayon (1820). He also wrote a five-volume biography of George Washington (1855–9).

Isherwood, Christopher (1904–86) English-born American novelist and dramatist. His best-known works are the novels *Mr Norris Changes Trains* (1932) and *Goodbye to Berlin* (1939), the latter forming the basis for the film *Cabaret* (1972). He also wrote works in collaboration with his friend AUDEN, e.g. the verse drama *The Ascent of F6* (1936).

J

Jacobean tragedy A development of REVENGE TRAGEDY in the Jacobean period. The distinction between "Jacobean" and "revenge" tragedy is a disputed one, hinging on the supposed wave of cynicism and pessimism that is alleged by some historians to have accompanied the accession of James VI of Scotland to the English throne, and the end of the Elizabethan era. The debate is a complex one, but it is undoubtedly the case that tragedies such as SHAKESPEARE's *Hamlet*, TOURNEUR's *The Revenger's Tragedy*, MIDDLETON's *The Changeling*, and WEBSTER's *The White Devil* and *The Duchess of Malfi*, are obsessed with political and sexual corruption to a virtually pathic degree. The language of these plays is highly sophisticated, ironic, and coldly brilliant.

Jacobs, W[illiam] W[ymark] (1863–1943) English novelist and short-story writer. Many of his stories are humorous, but he is particularly noted for the macabre little story "The Monkey's Paw," in *The Lady of the Barge* (1902).

James, Henry (1843–1916) American-born British novelist, short-story writer and critic. James settled in England in 1869 and became a British citizen in 1914, after the outbreak of World War I. His works fall into three main groups: the first deals with the contrast between American innocence and brashness, and the older, more cynical European culture, e.g. *Daisy Miller*

(1879) and *Washington Square* (1880); the second group examines, with often obsessive detail, the minutiae of English upper-class social life and character, e.g. *The Spoils of Poynton* (1897) and *The Awkward Age* (1899); the third group, e.g. *The Ambassadors* (1905) and *The Golden Bowl* (1904), returns to the American/European contrasts of the first period. (An alternative grouping of the works was said to be James the First, James the Second, and the Old Pretender.) James also wrote over 100 short stories, including the classic ghost story, *The Turn of the Screw* (1898). James' meticulous concern for finding exactly the right word to convey his precise meaning has often been ridiculed, but his concern for personal integrity and for making the right choice between right and wrong actions, and his profound understanding of the moronic nature of evil, e.g. in *What Maisie Knew* (1897), make him one of our greatest writers.

James, M[ontague] R[hodes] (1862–1936) English scholar and ghost-story writer. His stories, e.g. *Ghost Stories of an Antiquary* (1904) and *More Ghost Stories of an Antiquary* (1911), have a unique atmosphere: a mix of dry, scholarly wit (his protagonists are invariably old-fashioned, donnish gentlemen) with a horrifically reticent undertone of supernatural terror. His story "Casting the Runes" was memorably filmed by Jacques Tourneur in 1957 as *The Night of the Demon*.

James, P. D. [pseud. of Phyllis Dorothy James White] (1920–) English novelist. Her crime novels, particularly those starring her poet/policeman Inspector Adam Dalgleish, have acquired a wide and appreciative following. The novels include *A Mind to Murder* (1963), *The Black Tower* (1975), *Death of an Expert Witness* (1977) and *A Taste for Death* (1986). The last, a sombre piece which is as much about religious faith as traditional detection, has been hailed as her master-piece.

James, William (1842–1910) American philosopher, brother of Henry JAMES. His *The Varieties of Religious Experience* (1902) includes the phrase "stream of consciousness," which has been adapted by literary critics to denote a fluxive method of narration in which characters voice their feelings with no "obtrusive" authorial comment and with no orthodox dialogue or decription. The term has particular reference to the work of JOYCE and WOOLF.

Janssens, Abraham (1575–1632) Flemish painter. A contemporary of RUBENS, he lived and worked mainly in Antwerp, apart from one or two brief visits to Italy. His early works were MANNERIST in style, as in *Diana and Callisto* (1601), but later pieces are more classical in their clear modelling of figures and powerful lighting: *Scaldis and Antwerpia* (1609). His most memorable work is *Calvary* (*c.*1620). SEGHERS was his pupil.

Jarrell, Randall (1914–65) American poet, critic and author of a satirical novel on the piranha bowl of academic life, *Pictures from an Institution* (1954), which, like Kingsley AMIS's *Lucky Jim*, is an early example of the so-called CAMPUS NOVEL. His volumes of poetry include *Losses* (1948) and *The Woman at the Washington Zoo* (1960).

Jarry, Alfred (1873–1907) French dramatist of the ABSURD. The first performance of his anarchic farce *Ubu Roi* (1896), a savage and surreal version of *Macbeth*, is memorably described by YEATS in *The Trembling of the Veil* (1926). Supporters and opponents of Jarry's work came to blows as an actor impersonated an opening door. Jarry's subversive, extravagant and often brutal work has had much influence on modern drama.

Jawlensky, Alexei von (1864–1941) Russian painter.

He lived in Munich from 1896 and was associated with KANDINSKY and Der BLAUE REITER group, although his own style was more simply abstract with linear design and flat areas of strong colour e.g. *Girl with Peonies* (1909). From 1929 his works became more mystical, as in the series *Night* (1933). His work was always of an independent nature, slightly removed from the trends of the time.

Jazz Modern *see* **Art Deco**.

Jeffers, [John] Robinson (1887–1962) American poet. The dominant theme in his poetry is his doctrine of "Inhumanism," in which mankind is portrayed as being of little significance in the great wheel of uncaring natural forces. His works include *Roan Stallion* (1925) and several influential adaptations of Greek tragedies, e.g. *Medea* (1947).

Jerome, Jerome K[lapka] (1859–1927) English dramatist, essayist and novelist. His most enduring work is *Three Men in a Boat* (1889), a light-hearted tale of three men and a dog on a rowing holiday, which is regarded as a classic of humorous writing.

John, Augustus (1878–1961) English painter and younger brother of Gwen JOHN. He studied at the Slade School of Art, where he was an outstanding draughtsman and became a champion of radical and revolutionary art. He taught at the School of Art at University College, Liverpool, for a time, but much of his life was spent in nomadic journeyings in various parts of England, Ireland and Wales. A typical work of this period is *The Way down to the Sea* (1909–11). He later visted Provence in the South of France, producing a large number of oil sketches: *Provencal Studies*. While the quality of his work, especially his drawings, received intermittent praise in the UK, he had 38 paintings exhibited in the ARMORY SHOW of 1913, an indication of his stature abroad. His innovations in painting were often misunderstood and maligned. *The Smiling Woman* (1908) and *Marchesa Casati* (1919) are notable examples of his best portraits.

John, Gwen (1876–1939) English painter and elder sister of Augustus JOHN. She studied at the Slade School of Art and at WHISTLER's studio in Paris. She was a close friend of the sculptor, RODIN. A quiet and unassuming person, her paintings reflect her personality, sensitively painted in muted tones reminiscent of Whistler's palette. Her preferred subjects were young women in interior settings, and she creates a persuasive atmosphere of peace, stillness and quiet dignity, as in *A Lady Reading* (1907–8). In 1913 she converted to Roman Catholicism and lived in increasing seclusion at Meudon in France. She exhibited three paintings in the ARMORY SHOW of 1913, and her only one-man show was in London in 1926, but memorial and retrospective exhibitions held in 1946, 1952, 1968 and 1976 have done much to redress the balance of acclaim and appreciation she deserves.

Johns, Jasper (1930–) American painter, sculptor and printmaker. His early works are ABSTRACT EXPRESSIONIST pieces, but his style took on a new direction under the influences of RAUSCHENBERG and the composer John Cage. Famous among his avant-garde works are his *Target* and *Flag* paintings (1954–5), including *Target with Four Faces* (1955). His works, especially in sculpture, anticipate pop and conceptual art in its use of real objects. Some of his paintings incorporate objects like beer cans applied directly to the canvas. His mature works are more subtle in approach.

Johnson, Marguerite *see* **Angelou, Maya**.

Johnson, Dr Samuel (1709–84) English critic, lexicographer and poet. One of the greatest literary figures of the 18th century, his works include the *Dictionary of the English Language* (1755), a highly important edition of *Shakespeare* (1765), *Lives of the Most Eminent Poets* (1779–81), several wonderful essays, e.g. in *The Rambler* (1750–2), and the great verse satires *London* (1738) and *The Vanity of Human Wishes* (1749). In 1763 he met James BOSWELL. Johnson was the great moralist of the age, a devout Christian tormented by self-doubt, an English Tory with Jacobite sympathies, who once drank a toast to the "next slave rebellion in the West Indies"; Boswell was dissolute, a rapacious sexual predator, associated with radicals, and was a Whiggish Scot who saw slavery as a necessary part of life. An unlikely friendship was formed, and Boswell began recording Johnson's conversations. After Johnson's death, Boswell published the greatest biography in the English language, his *Life of Samuel Johnson, L.L.D.* (1785). In 1773, Johnson and Boswell travelled to the Scottish Hebrides, the tour resulting in two books, Boswell's *Journal of the Tour of the Hebrides* (1785), and Johnson's *Journey to the Western Isles* (1775). Johnson's only novel, *Rasselas* (1759), is a melancholic little fable which sums up its author's philosophy thus: "Human life is everywhere a state in which much is to be endured, and little to be enjoyed." *See also* GARRICK, VOLTAIRE.

Johnston, Jennifer (1930–) Irish novelist. Her first (and best) novel, *The Captains and the Kings* (1972), a remarkable study of the doomed relationship between an old, haunted Anglo-Irishman and a young boy, has been very highly praised for its skilfully crafted blend of pathos and humour. Johnston's other novels include *The Gates* (1973), *Shadows on our Skin* (1977) and *The Invisible Worm* (1991).

Jonson, Ben[jamin] (*c.*1572–1637) English dramatist and poet. After a turbulent early life, in which he "trailed a pike" in the Flanders campaign, and killed a fellow actor in a duel, Jonson settled down to writing the "comedies of HUMOURS" (i.e. plays featuring characters who personify a particular quality or vice) that established him as one of the great dramatists. The plays are especially noted for their satirical dialogue. The most frequently staged examples are *Volpone* (1616), *The Alchemist* (1616) and *Bartholomew Fair* (1614). He was appointed the first POET LAUREATE in 1616, in which year he published a folio edition of his poetic and dramatic works, setting a highly important precedent: his friend SHAKESPEARE's first folio followed in 1623. Jonson was much admired by the younger generation of poets, such as HERRICK, who called themselves the "Sons of Ben."

Jordaens, Jacob (1593–1678) Flemish painter, engraver and designer whose style was greatly influenced by his older contemporary RUBENS. He established a workshop in Antwerp in the 1620s, but he also assisted Rubens on major projects. Jordaens' own works include genre paintings, portraits and altarpieces, and he undertook large numbers of commissions including *The Triumph of Frederick Hendrick* (1652) for the Huis ten Bosch Villa at The Hague.

Jorn, Asger (1914–73) Danish painter and engraver. He studied in Paris and was involved with the Paris International Exhibition of 1937. Early influences include KLEE, ENSOR and AFRICAN tribal art. His works became more expressive in style during the 1940s. From 1955 he lived mainly in Paris. His paintings from the 1950s and 1960s are vibrant and explosive in their powerful brushwork and colour, as in *Green Bullet* (1960).

Joyce, James [Augustine Aloysius] (1882–1941) Irish novelist and short-story writer. Educated in Jesuit schools and at Dublin University, he left Ireland in 1902, returning briefly twice, once for his mother's death and burial, and once to oversee the publication of his short stories. Their publication was suppressed from (justified) fear of libel, the collection finally appearing as *Dubliners* (1914) in London. (His first published work had been a collection of slight but charming lyrics, *Chamber Music*, in 1907). His first great novel, *Portrait of the Artist as a Young Man*, in which the hero, Stephen Dedalus, is based on Joyce himself, appeared in 1914–15. By the time his masterpiece, *Ulysses* (1922), was published in Paris, he was widely seen as a world-class writer. *Ulysses* was banned in the US until 1933, and in the UK until 1936. The novel describes the experiences of two men in Dublin during one day, 16 June 1904: Leopold Bloom, a Jewish advertisement salesmen, who represents the common man, and Stephen Dedalus, who reappears to represent the artist. The supposed "difficulty" of the book has been much exaggerated. The structure is based on HOMER's *Odyssey*, and the text is saturated with literary references from Joyce's wide reading, but the book can be read and enjoyed with no recourse to scholarly explanation. The same cannot really be said of *Finnegans Wake* (1939), which uses a vast repertoire of difficult, punning and alliterative language to create an effect of all actual and possible human experience. The best way into it is to listen to Joyce's own recording of the "Anna Livia Plurabelle" section of the wake. *See also* BECKETT, Dorothy RICHARDSON.

Judd, Donald (1928–) American conceptual artist who studied at Columbia University and at the Art Students' League, New York. His geometric sculptures consist of painted cubes or other solid forms arranged in sequence on floors or low down on walls. His contention was that the shape, colour, volume or surface of an object were viable in themselves as works of art. He had his first one-man show at the Green Gallery in

New York in 1964, and a retrospective at the Whitney Museum, New York, in 1968.

Jugendstil The German form of ART NOUVEAU. *See also* KIRCHNER; KLINGER.

Julian of Norwich, Dame (*c.*1342–*c.*1413) English anchorite. Her *Sixteen Revelations of Divine Love* (1393) examines the contradiction between her mystical revelations of the proximity of Christ to her, and the chasm between Christ and man caused by the sins of humanity. T. S. ELIOT quoted her thoughts on the mystery of sin and redemption in his *Four Quartets* ("Little Gidding"): "Sin is behovely [i.e. necessary], but all shall be well and all shall be well and all manner of things shall be well." Julian was one of a number of 14th-century English mystical writers, notably the Augustinian Walter Hilton (d.1396), the hermit Richard Rolle (*c.*1300–1349), Margery Kempe (*c.*1373–*c.*1439), and the anonymous author of the much admired *Cloud of Unknowing*.

Jung, Carl Gustav (1875–1961) Swiss psychiatrist, who began his career as a follower of FREUD, but split with him after challenging Freud's concentration on the sex impulse. His theory of the "collective unconscious," a sort of reservoir in the unconscious mind filled with memories and instincts common to all humans, and his use of the term "archetype" to denote an image or symbol drawn from this store, have had a great influence on many writers, e.g. HESSE and PRIESTLEY. Jung also wrote some very interesting literary criticism, notably on SHAKESPEARE and JOYCE. Jung's relationship with the Nazi regime in Germany during the 1930s is still a matter of intense debate.

Juni, Juan de (*c.*1510–77) Spanish sculptor who trained in Italy and Burgundy and settled at Valladolid in 1540. He was one of Spain's most important sculptors of the time. His style is expressive and graceful, and he executed a large number of sculptures on religious themes. Notable works include two representations of *The Entombment*, one at Valladolid, 1539–44, and one at Segovia Cathedral, 1571.

Justus of Ghent [Joos van Wassenhove] (*fl.*1460–80) Flemish artist. He was a member of the guilds of Antwerp and Ghent and a friend and contemporary of Hugo van der GOES. Notable among his early works are *The Crucifixion* and *The Adoration of the Magi*. He was in Italy from 1473 to 1475, working for the Duke of Urbino, when he painted *The Communion of the Apostles* (1473–4); this work was to form an important link between the painting of Italy and The Netherlands.

K

Kafka, Franz (1883–1924) Prague-born German novelist and short-story writer. His novels *The Trial* (1925) and *The Castle* (1926), and several of his short stories, notably "Metamorphosis," are established classics of 20th-century literature. The atmosphere of his fiction, in which characters are often trapped in bureaucratic totalitarianism, is oddly prophetic of the era of the dictators; many of his family were to die in Hitler's camps. His unfinished novel *Amerika* (1927) is a surprisingly light-hearted Chaplinesque affair set in the US (which he never visited).

Kandinsky, Wassily (1866–1944) Russian-born painter and art theorist who originally graduated in law from Moscow University before going to study painting in Munich in 1896. Typical of his early work is *Blue Mountain No. 84* (1908). He joined the Berlin SEZESSION in 1902, and returned to Berlin after a time travelling in Europe and Africa. By 1910 he was creating the beginnings of ABSTRACT EXPRESSIONISM, with nonfigurative paintings whose significance depended on the interrelation of colours and forms. He formed Der BLAUE REITER with Franz MARC before returning to Russia in 1918 to teach and to set up the Russian Academy of Artistic Sciences. With the imposition of social realism in Russia, Kandinsky returned to Germany in 1922, where he taught at the BAUHAUS until its closure in 1933. He then settled in France. Kandinsky's writings have been as influential as his paintings on 20th-century art, in particular *Reminiscences* (1913) and *Concerning the Spiritual in Art,* written in 1910, but not published until 1947. His ideas also spread to Europe and the US via a number of his exiled Bauhaus students.

Kane, Paul (1810–71) Irish-born Canadian painter. He travelled in Canada for the Hudson Bay Company in the late 1840s and returned with an astonishing collection of sketches, which he used as a source for his bizarre paintings. He borrowed imaginatively from well-known European artists, as in *Blackfoot Chiefs*, where the composition is reminiscent of the works of RAPHAEL. Indian portraits painted by Kane bear an uncanny resemblance to the European aristocrats painted by REYNOLDS and RAEBURN. He published an account of his travels entitled *The Wanderings of an Artist* (1859), and by the time of his death had become something of a legend.

Kaprow, Allen (1927–) American artist, famous as the inventor of "happenings" (*see* ACTION PAINTING). His earliest influences include ABSTRACT EXPRESSIONISM and the theories of chance and randomness expounded by the composer John Cage. In the late 1950s he began creating complicated assemblages and environmental pieces. The first happening took place in New York in 1959 and involved acted-out fantasies and responses by various "performers"; it was called *Eighteen happenings in six parts*. Kaprow has had an acknowledged influence on 20th-century art since the 1960s.

Kaufmann, Angelica (1741–1807) Swiss painter. Her early travels in Switzerland and Italy with her father engendered an appreciation of NEOCLASSICAL art, which she later applied to her work. She was in London from 1776 where she was a popular artist, doing portraits and scenes from Shakespeare and Homer as well as history paintings. She was a friend of REYNOLDS and a founder of the Royal Academy. She also decorated house interiors for architects like Robert ADAM. After her marriage in 1781 to the Italian landscape painter **Antonio Zucchi** (1726–95), she settled in Rome. Notable among her best portraits are those of the German writer Goethe and REYNOLDS.

Keats, John (1795–1821) English poet. He abandoned his apprenticeship as an apothecary to concentrate on poetry in 1816, the year he met Leigh HUNT, who published the young poet's work in *The Examiner*. He also became friendly with many of Hunt's friends, notably SHELLEY. His poems were savagely attacked by *The Examiner's* literary and political rivals; Keats seems to have been deeply affected by the criticism, which was based purely on class spite and cultural snobbery (the "Cockney School" of poetry was one sneering description). Keats, who was never in good health, died of tuberculosis in Rome, where he is buried. Most of his great poems, e.g. "The Eve of St Agnes" and "To a Nightingale," are included in *Lamia and Other Poems* (1820).

Keinholz, Edward (1927–) American sculptor. He studied in Washington and then went to Los Angeles where he opened the Now Gallery and the Ferus Gallery. He was initially a painter but moved on to three-dimensional constructions in the 1960s. His works are mainly tableaux built up with real objects and figures in plaster or other media. They are realist in approach, featuring some sordid aspects of society and illustrating his dislike of the superficial, materialistic side of American life. Notable works are *The State Hospital* (1966) and *Portable War Memorial* (1968).

Kelly, Ellsworth (1923–) American painter who studied in Boston and at the Académie des Beaux-Arts, Paris. He returned to the US in 1954, where he became a leading figure among the "hard-edge" group of ABSTRACT painters. His work consists of flat, bright areas of colour bounded by sharp edges, black and white geometric compositions, and panels of colour placed adjacently, e.g. *Blue, Green, Yellow, Orange, Red* (1966). He also did some sculptures and low-relief works along similar lines.

Kemal, Yashar (1923–) Turkish (Kurdish) novelist and short-story writer, whose exhilarating tales of blood feuds, banditry and social change in rural Turkey have been labelled, with some justice, as Tolstoyan in characterization and landscape description (Kemal's paternal forebears were feudal lords, his mother's were brigands; at the age of five, he saw his father murdered). The novels include *Memed, my Hawk* (1955), *The Lords of Akchasaz* (1974) and *The Saga of a Seagull* (1976).

Kempe, Margery *see* **Julian of Norwich, Dame**.

Keneally, Thomas (1935–) Australian novelist. His novels include *The Chant of Jimmie Blacksmith* (1972), a grim, bloody tale of a young aborigine's violent response to the shabby ambiguities of his role in white society; *Confederates* (1979), an American Civil War saga; and *Schindler's Ark* (1982), his remarkable non-fictional study of the unlikeliest Scarlet Pimpernel in history, Oskar Schindler, a German businessman whose Cracow factory became a place of refuge for imprisoned Jews.

Kennerly Jr, Thomas *see* **Wolfe, Tom**.

Kent, Rockwell (1882–1971) American painter and draughtsman. He trained in architecture at Columbia University, where he was a student of Robert HENRI and helped with the first Independents Show in 1910. His early landscapes owe something to the works of Winslow HOMER, although with more solidity of form and contrasting tones. The works of the EIGHT and the

ASHCAN SCHOOL also had their influence, as in *The Road Roller* (1909). His black and white book illustrations are also well known and admired.

Kerouac, Jack (1922–69) American novelist. One of the best known of the BEAT GENERATION, his most popular work is the semi-autobiographical novel *On the Road* (1957), a typically meandering, episodic account of the ramblings across America of a young writer and his friend. His other works include *The Dharma Bums* (1958) and volumes of poetry.

Kierkegaard, Søren *see* **Existentialism**.

kinetic art An art form in which light or balance are used to create a work that moves or appears to move. Kinetic artists include GABO, CALDER and CHADWICK. More complicated kinetic art objects are made to move by electric motors.

King James Bible *see* **Authorized Version**.

Kingsley, Charles (1819–75) English clergyman and novelist. His works include historical novels such as *Westward Ho!* (1855) and *Hereward the Wake* (1866), and reformist-orientated novels of industrial society such as *Alton Locke* (1850). His masterpiece, however, is his children's story *The Water Babies* (1863), a bizarre fantasy about a young chimney sweep's adventures in an underwater world (apparently after drowning). The work is popular with both children and FREUDIANS.

Kinsella, Thomas (1928–) Irish poet. His collections include *Another September* (1958), *Downstream* (1962) and *Peppercanister Poems: 1972–1978* (1979).

Kipling, Rudyard (1865–1936) Indian-born English short-story writer, poet and novelist. Born in Bombay, he was sent home to be educated, then returned to India where he rapidly made a name for himself as a superb journalist and caustic observer of Anglo-Indian society. He returned to England in 1889, where he achieved celebrity status with his poems of army life, *Barrack-Room Ballads* (1892), which established him as an unofficial spokesman for the (then much despised) British soldier and for the British Empire. From this period until his death, Kipling's reputation was to vary according to the political climate. In the 1940s, however, both T. S. ELIOT and George ORWELL, who differed widely in their politics, wrote essays giving high praise to his work, and subsequent critics have tended to agree with their opinions of his worth. The poems and short stories are particularly good, the best of which, e.g. the poems "Gethsemane" and "The Buddha at Kamakura," and the stories "The Wish House" and "They" have a strange, occasionally quite eerie beauty all their own. His most enduringly popular works are his children's books, e.g. *The Jungle Book* (1894) and *Just So Stories* (1902). He was awarded the Nobel Prize for literature in 1907.

Kirchner, Ernst Ludwig (1880–1938) German painter and engraver. He studied at Dresden and Munich and was a founder of Die BRÜCKE. His initial works are in the *Jugendstil*, or German ART NOUVEAU manner, but he was also influenced by late Gothic German woodcuts, and this pervaded the works of Die Brücke. Other influences on Kirchner's early individual style were primitive art and the works of GAUGUIN and van GOGH, but his stylized drawing technique and strong juxtapositions of colours owe a great deal to the works of MUNCH and to MATISSE and the FAUVISTS. Kirchner's approach was impetuous and direct, concerned with expression of emotion, for which he developed personally symbolic images or "hieroglyphs" as a kind of pictorial language to describe emotions. Fears and anguish feature strongly in the years prior to World War I, and his woodcuts became more harsh and distorted. He suffered a nervous breakdown in 1914 and spent the rest of his life at a sanatorium. In the 1920s he painted more tranquil landscapes, but the last decade of his life saw a return to the abstract. Nazi condemnation of his work as "degenerate" sparked a return of mental illness, which led to his suicide.

Kirkup, James (1923–) English poet and travel writer. The publication in 1977 of his poem "The love that dares to speak its name" (describing the physical love of a centurion for Christ) in the British homosexual periodical *Gay News*, resulted in the first prosecution for blasphemous libel for half a century (*Gay News* was fined and its editor given a suspended prison sentence). His most highly regarded work is the title poem of *A Correct Compassion* (1952), a wonderful celebration of a masterly surgeon working "with proper grace/Informing a correct compassion." His autobiographical novel, *The Only Child* (1957), based on his working-class childhood, is a rarity among such works in being a largely happy one. He has also written widely on Japan, where he has taught for many years.

Klee, Paul (1879–1940) Swiss painter. He studied in Munich and travelled in Italy before returning to his native Berne. By 1906 he was back in Munich, and in 1911 became involved with Der BLAUE REITER, showing works in their second exhibition in 1912. Early works were influenced by CUBISM, ORPHISM and SYMBOLISM and were largely monochromatic, but the event that affected the character of much of his work was a trip to Tunisia with MACKE in 1914, which inspired a new approach to colour abstraction. He taught at the BAUHAUS and at the Düsseldorf Academy but was dismissed by the Nazis and returned to Berne in 1933. His work was included in the exhibition of allegedly "degenerate" art in 1937, and he suffered a severe depression thereafter. His later works are larger and darker and lack the joyful sparkle of earlier pieces, although his imaginative style and technical genius were undiminished. Through the outstanding quality of his own work and through his teaching, Klee has exerted an enormous influence on modern art, making him one of the most innovative and important artists of the 20th century.

Klimt, Gustav (1862–1918) Austrian painter who studied at the Vienna school of Arts and Crafts and was one of the founders of the Vienna SEZESSION. His early works were variously influenced by IMPRESSIONISM, SYMBOLISM and ART NOUVEAU, but were often misunderstood, and occasionally rejected by the commissioners, as happened with his murals for Vienna University (1900–1903). He also exhibited at the Sezessions of 1903 and 1904 despite increasing controversy and isolation. One notable commission still in place is the mosaic mural for the Palais Stoclet in Brussels (1911). Klimt was an excellent draughtsman and had a great influence on younger artists such as KOKOSHKA and SCHIELE.

Kline, Franz (1910–62) American painter who studied in Boston and trained as a painter at the Heatherly School of Art in London. His earliest works were mainly city views and landscapes painted in heavy impasto, but from the 1950s he developed a style not unlike an enlarged and modified form of Chinese calligraphy. Working mainly in black and white, although he did experiment with colours, his paintings have an expressive fluidity of brushwork and boldly structured composition, as in *Chief* (1950) and *Ninth Street* (1951).

Klinger, Max (1857–1920) German painter, sculptor and illustrator. He studied at Karlsruhe and Berlin, travelling to Paris (1883–6) and Rome (1888–93) before settling in Leipzig. His early training was in the classical tradition, which he adapted to his own development of ART NOUVEAU, and he is now thought of primarily as a *Jugendstil* or German ART NOUVEAU artist. His etchings contain elements of fantasy reminiscent of BÖCKLIN, which anticipate surrealist imagery, as in *Adventures of a Glove* (1881) and his illustrations to Brahms' *Fantasias*. His most famous sculpture is the Beethoven monument (1899–1902), and a noteworthy painting is *The Judgement of Paris* (1885–7).

Koestler, Arthur (1905–83) Hungarian-born British author and journalist. A former Communist, he wrote widely on a range of interests, but his masterpiece, and one of the greatest of all political novels, is *Darkness at Noon* (1940), which describes the trial and execution (under Stalin's regime) or an old Bolshevik called Rubashov, who is a fictional composite of several real victims of Stalin, notably Nikolai Buhkarin, former head of the Communist International. A believer in the right to euthanasia, Koestler and his wife died in a suicide pact.

Kokoshka, Oskar (1886–1980) Austrian painter who studied in Vienna where he met KLIMT and other SEZESSION artists and was influenced by ART NOUVEAU. A typical early work is the lithograph *The Dreaming Boys* (1908). He painted still lifes and a series of portraits renowned for a depth of insight into the personality of the sitter, whether innate or projected by the artist being a matter of debate; a typical example is *The Marquis of Montesquieu* (1909–10). He also did a number of graphic illustrations for *Die Sturm* magazine. He taught at the Dresden Academy until 1924 and then travelled around Europe and North Africa, painting landscapes in an expressionist style and doing "portraits" of cities and towns from unusual viewpoints e.g. *Jerusalem* (1929–30). He moved to England in 1938 after the condemnation of his work by the Nazis; his painting *Self Portrait of a Degenerate Artist* (1937) is typical of the defiant eccentricity that characterizes much of his work.

Kollwitz, Käthe Schmidt (1867–1945) German engraver and sculptor. Her strong social convictions and compassion for the poor and oppressed in society are central to the import of her art (she was married to a doctor). Notable early works include *Weavers' Revolt* (1897–8) and *Peasants' War* (1902–8), two series of etchings that aroused considerable political controversy. *Mother and Child* was a common theme handled with sensitivity and gentleness in drawings and sculptures, e.g. *Pietà* (1903). Her pacifist views are evident in the lithograph cycles *The War* (1923) and *Death* (1934–5), which were in part the cause of her expulsion from the Prussian Academy of Berlin in 1933.

Kuhn, Walt (1877–1949) American painter who studied in Paris and Munich and taught at the New York School of Art. He was associated with Robert HENRI and helped to organize the ARMORY SHOW of 1913. His earlier works are realist in approach, but in the 1920s and 1930s the influences of PICASSO, DERAIN and MATISSE became more apparent. Favourite themes include circuses and clowns in bright colours, as well as landscapes and still lifes; a typical work is *Clown with Black Wig* (1930).

Kundera, Milan (1929–) Czech novelist. His novels include *The Unbearable Lightness of Being* (1985), which is set against the background of repression that followed the Soviet invasion of Czechoslovakia in 1968, and *Immortality* (1991).

Kuniyoshi, Yasuo (1893–1953) Japanese-born American painter who studied art in Los Angeles and New York. He also earned a living as a photographer until his works achieved wider recognition in the 1930s after the Modern American Artists Exhibition of 1929. His works are decorative, full of symbolic imagery and reminiscent of naive art in depth and perspective. A typical work is *I'm Tired* (1938). His works became extremely popular in Japan during the 1960s.

Kupka, Frank (1871–1957) Czech painter. He studied in Prague and Vienna, and worked as an illustrator in Paris, where he lived from 1895. He was associated with Marcel DUCHAMP and became interested in the problems of depicting movement, which he explored in the series *Girl with a Ball* (1908). He continued the same theme in *Amorpha, Fugue in Two Colours* (1912), which was an innovation in the development of ABSTRACT painting. ORPHISM also influenced his work in terms of its mysticism. A notable piece in his mature style is *Working Steel* (1921–9), conveying a sense of the power and movement of the machine age.

Kyd, Thomas (1558–94) English dramatist. His most important work is his REVENGE TRAGEDY *The Spanish Tragedy* (1588–9), which was very popular on the early 17th-century stage and very influential on the work of many dramatists, most notably on SHAKESPEARE, whose *Titus Andronicus* (1592–3) is modelled on the Kyd play. (Kyd may also have written a lost *Hamlet*, on which it is suggested Shakespeare's play was based.)

Kyd's history is a curious one. With Shakespeare, he was attacked by Robert GREENE in *Greene's Groatsworth of Wit* (1592) as one of a new breed of non-university educated dramatists who were subverting the livelihood of their betters. He became closely associated with Christopher MARLOWE, with whom he lodged for a while, and was arrested and tortured in 1593 following the discovery of some papers, attributed to Marlowe by Kyd, denying the divinity of Christ. Kyd was released a month after Marlowe's murder in the same year, and died in poverty the following year; his parents refused to administer his estate.

L

Lacan, Jacques *see* **Structuralism**.

Lachaise, Gaston (1882–1935) French sculptor who studied in Paris and settled in the US in 1906. He had his first one-man show at the Bourgeois Gallery, New York, in 1918. He was responsible for renewing enthusiasm for direct carving methods in American sculpture, and his work represents a move away from academic forms and strictures. He was known for his perceptive portrait busts and for his female figure studies. These were large and smoothly articulated with a voluptuous femininity reminiscent of the paintings of Renoir, e.g. *Standing Woman* (1912–27).

Lafarge, John (1835–1910) American painter. He studied in Paris and derived his influences from a variety of sources, including oriental art. His first major commission was to decorate Trinity Church, Boston, where he devised murals and stained glass windows. He was associated with William MORRIS and the PRE-RAPHAEL-ITE movement in his approach to art. Notable works include *Maua—our Boatman* (1891).

Lamb, Charles (1775–1834) English essayist and critic. Lamb was a much loved friend of HAZLITT, Leigh HUNT, WORDSWORTH and COLERIDGE, and many of his writings display the great charm his friends describe. With his sister **Mary Anne Lamb** (1764–1847), he wrote a prose version for children of Shakespeare's plays, *Tales from Shakespeare* (1807), which has retained its popularity. In 1796, in a fit of insanity, Mary killed their mother, and Charles looked after her until her death. His *Specimens of English Dramatic Poets* (1808), was an important contribution to the reasessment of Shakespeare's contemporary dramatists.

Lampedusa, Giuseppe di (1896–1957) Italian novelist. His most famous work is *The Leopard* (1958), which describes the decline of aristocratic society in Sicily following the island's annexation by Garibaldi in 1860 during his unification of Italy.

Lancaster, Sir Osbert (1908–86) English cartoonist and author of several satirical studies of British architectural history, e.g. *Progress at Pelvis Bay* (1936) and *Draynfleete Revealed* (1949). Lancaster's reputation as one of the deadliest and wittiest critics ever of architectural folly is secure. His two autobiographies, *All Done from Memory* (1953) and *With an Eye to the Future* (1967), are minor classics of the genre. His aesthetic tastes largely matched those of his friends BETJEMAN and WAUGH.

Landor, Walter Savage (1775–1864) English poet and essayist, noted for his classically inspired lyrics and epigrams, and for his *Imaginary Conversations* (1824–9), a collection of around 150 imagined dialogues between such people as Francis BACON and Richard HOOKER, and DANTE and Beatrice. DICKENS used him as the model for the bad-tempered yet lovable eccentric Boythorne in *Bleak House. See also* SPENSER.

Landseer, Sir Edwin (1802–73) English painter of precocious talent who was a student of HAYDON and won acclaim while still a child for his animal drawings, including the Society of Art silver palette at age 11. His etchings and paintings were technically very well observed and draughted, but tended towards a gross sentimentality in humanizing animals, particularly dogs, e.g *The Old Shepherd's Chief Mourner* (1937), a quality that was the source of his widespread popularity throughout his career. He was Queen Victoria's favourite painter, and his works were well known through engraved copies. Other notable works include *The Monarch of the Glen* (1850), and the the lions modelled for Trafalgar Square in 1867.

Lang, Andrew (1844–1912) Scottish scholar, essayist and poet, remembered chiefly for his anthropological works, e.g. *Myth, Ritual and Religion* (1887), which FREUD drew from, and his fairy stories for children, e.g. *The Blue Fairy Book* (1889).

Langland, William (*c*.1332–*c*.1400) English poet, reputed author of the allegorical religious poem *Piers Plowman*. Virtually nothing is known of Langland for certain. The poem, written in alliterative verse, is one of the greatest works in medieval literature and contains passages of great beauty.

Lanier, Sidney (1842–81) American poet, noted for his study of the connection between music and poetry, *The Science of English Verse* (1880), and for his verse collection, *Poems* (1877), which experiments with metrical forms that resemble musical forms.

Lardner, Ring (1885–1933) American journalist and short-story writer, whose stories of American low life, e.g. *What of It?* (1925), are noted for their cynical wit.

Larkin, Philip [Arthur] (1922–85) English poet. His early verse e.g. *The North Ship* (1945), shows the influence of YEATS. His later, far greater poems, owe more to the influence of HARDY, but Larkin's later voice, as became apparent in *The Less Deceived* (1955), is all his own: a dark, sardonic lyricism combined with disconcertingly colloquial turns of phrase. Two further important volumes followed: *The Whitsun Weddings* (1964) and *High Windows* (1972), establishing him as the greatest of all postwar English poets. Larkin's poetry is wryly observant of social change, e.g. "Sexual intercourse began in 1963 / Somewhere between the end of the Lady Chatterly ban, / And the Beatles' first LP" (from "Annus Mirabilis"), and is often very bleak. Larkin also wrote two novels, *Jill* (1946) and *A Girl in Winter* (1947); a collection of essays on jazz, *All What Jazz?* (1970); and edited *The Oxford Book of Twentieth Century Verse* (1971), an exhilaratingly off-beat anthology.

Lascaux The site, in Dordogne, France, of some outstanding paleolithic cave paintings and rock engravings. Dating from *c*.15000BC, they have survived in remarkably good condition and depict local fauna, etc, on a large scale and in a bold, direct style.

La Tour, Georges (1593–1652) French painter who worked in Luneville under the patronage of the Duke of Lorraine. Around 40 of his works have survived, but only two are dated, which complicates any assessment of his artistic development. He was strongly influenced by CARAVAGGIO, and probable early works include *Peasant* and *Peasant's Wife* (*c*.1620). These feature strong, dramatic lighting, whereas those thought to be later paintings have a monumental air of stillness with figures lit by a single candle, e.g. *St Sebastian tended by the Holy Women* (*c*.1650). La Tour's works are possessed of a more classical serenity than the late MANNERIST paintings of his contemporaries.

Lavery, Sir John (1856–1941) Irish-born Scottish painter and member of the GLASGOW SCHOOL. He studied in Paris and *plein-air* painting had a strong influence on his work. WHISTLER was another major influence, as is evident in Lavery's commissions celebrating the visit of Queen Victoriato the Glasgow International Exhibition of 1888. His well-draughted compositions are light and relaxed in atmosphere, e.g. *The Tennis Party* (1885). The main output of his later career was in portraiture.

Law, William (1686–1761) English divine. His masterpiece is *A Serious Call to a Holy and Devout Life* (1728),
which uses sharply drawn portraits ("characters") to
illustrate how the Christian life should be lived (and
how it should not). Law's beautifully simple prose, and
gentle, undogmatic tone, have been highly and deserv-
edly praised.

Lawrence, D[avid] H[erbert] (1885–1930) English
novelist, poet and short-story writer. Brought up in a
poor mining community in Nottingham, he attended
university there with the aid of a scholarship. His
novels, e.g. *Sons and Lovers* (1913), *The Rainbow*
(1915) and *Lady Chatterly's Lover* (1928), caused much
controversy for their frank treatment of sex, the last
book not being published in its full four-letter form
until 1960, when it was the subject of an unsuccessful
prosecution for obscenity. Opinions about Lawrence's
novels are sharply divided: his stirringly eloquent
attack on the damage done to human relations by
industrial society, his desire for a closer union between
man and nature, most movingly expressed in his
poems, e.g. *Birds, Beasts and Flowers* (1923), and for
sexual honesty have been widely praised, but others
are repelled by his CARLYLE-like worship of elemental
forces and exaltation of the darker impulses within us.
His dialogue can often be wildly (but unintentionally)
comic in his novels, a fault not evident in his collection
of short stories, e.g. *The Prussian Officer* (1914). Lawrence and his wife Frieda spent most of their married
life outside England, and he wrote several fine travel
books, notably *Etruscan Places* (1932).

Lawrence, Jacob (1917–) American painter. He
trained at FEDERAL ART PROJECTS classes and was an
important figure in highlighting social problems
drawn out of Black culture in the 1930s. Major works

include the 60 paintings in a series entitled *The Migration of the Negro* (1940–41).

Lawrence, Sir Thomas (1769–1830) English painter, mainly self-taught. He established his reputation at the age of 20 with a commissioned portrait of *Queen Charlotte* (1789), and quickly became the leading portraitist of his time. He succeeded REYNOLDS as King's Painter in 1792. A notable achievement is the series of 24 full-length portraits of the military leaders after the battle of Waterloo (1818). His work rises out of 18th-century traditions but with a fluidity and sparkle that anticipates the ROMANTICISM of the 19th century.

Lawrence, T[homas] E[dward] (1888–1935) English soldier, scholar and writer, known as "Lawrence of Arabia" for his role as a leader of irregular Arab forces in the war against the Turks (1916–18). His masterpiece is *Seven Pillars of Wisdom* (1926), which blends reminiscences of the war with an account of his spiritual growth. Opinions of Lawrence's character vary dramatically, from Winston Churchill's "one of the greatest beings alive in our time," to Lawrence DURRELL's "disgusting little thing." *See also* RATTIGAN.

Lear, Edward (1912–88) English poet and painter. An accomplished watercolourist (he gave drawing lessons to Queen Victoria), he travelled widely and published accounts of his travels, e.g. *Illustrated Excursions in Italy* (1846), but he is particularly noted for his ingenious and amusing nonsense verse, especially in limerick form, e.g. *Book of Nonsense* (1846) and *Botany and Alphabets* (1871) which includes "The Owl and the Pussycat."

Leavis, F[rank] R[aymond] (1895–1978) English literary critic, who, with his wife Q[ueenie] D. Leavis, made a major impact on literary criticism from the early 1930s on, through such works as *New Bearings in English Poetry* (1932) and *The Great Tradition* (1948).

Their critical journal *Scrutiny* (1932–53) lambasted the modern age of mass culture and advertising, which they saw as destructive of the true "organic" culture of Old England. The Leavises promoted the close "practical" study of the texts of a severely limited group of authors, principally Jane AUSTEN, George ELIOT, Henry JAMES, Joseph CONRAD, and, latterly, Charles DICKENS, as charts for a moral "serious" way of living. Unfortunately, they argued their case in a vicious, intolerant and egoistic manner that tended to negate their case for the humanizing influence of great literature.

Lebrun, Charles (1619–90) French painter. He trained with Simon VOUET and worked in POUSSIN's studio in Rome. Returning to Paris in 1646, he established himself in decorative murals doing vigorous and grandiose illusionistic paintings, such as the ceiling of the gallery at the Hotel Lambert. He was a fine draughtsman and portraitist, and was court painter to Louis XIV from 1661. He was responsible for much of the decor of Versailles, including the Galérie des Glaces (1679–84) and the Great Staircase (1671–8), since destroyed. In 1663 he became director of the Gobelins factory and designed the famous tapestry *Louis XIV visiting the Gobelins* (1663–75). He was also director of the Academy of Art, and established the basis of a powerful academic tradition, devolved from the CLASSICISM of Poussin, the theory of which he published in a treatise in 1698.

Le Carré, John [pseud. of David John Cornwell] (1931–) English novelist. Le Carré's novels are sombre anti-romantic narratives of Cold War espionage, and usually have as their chief protagonist a disillusioned, cynical spy, e.g. *The Spy Who Came in from the Cold* (1963) and *Smiley's People* (1980). Many of his novels have been filmed.

Léger, Fernand (1881–1955) French painter. His early works were strongly influenced by CUBISM and he was a member of the SECTION D'OR group from 1910 to 1914. His early paintings and most of his figurative works involve simplifications of form and structure resulting in static, rather tubular figure forms, as in *Nude in the Forest* (1909–10). He subsequently began to introduce mechanical forms and reflective metallic surfaces into his work, e.g. *Contrasting Forms* (1913, one of a series), and in-creasingly derived his imagery from the machine. Later works are again more figurative and monumental, as in his large-scale paintings, *The Builders* (1950) and *The Great Parade* (1954).

Le Guin, Ursula K[roeber] (1929–) American novelist and short-story writer, who is regarded as one of the leading 20th-century science fiction and fantasy authors. Her works include the "Hainish" or "Hain" series of novels, e.g. *The Left Hand of Darkness* (1969), an exploration of human sexuality through alien eyes, and *The Dispossessd* (1974), an intriguing study of political systems. Her "Earthsea" trilogy for children, *A Wizard of Earthsea* (1968), *The Tombs of Atuan* (1971) and *The Farthest Shore* (1972), has become a modern classic.

Lehmann, Rosamond [Nina] (1901–90) English novelist. Her best-known novels are *A Note in Music* (1930), which caused controversy in its open treatment of homosexuality, *The Weather in the Streets* (1936), more frank sex plus an abortion, and *The Ballad and the Source* (1944), a study of adult sexuality seen through the eyes of an innocent child, that is generally regarded as her masterpiece.

Lehmbruck, Wilhelm (1881–1919) German sculptor and illustrator who studied at Düsseldorf and Paris. He was greatly influenced by RODIN's EXPRESSIONISM, although his own work contains elements of the classical smoothness of MAILLOL and the graceful, stylized distortions of Gothic sculpture, e.g. *Kneeling Woman* (1911). Along with BARLACH, he played an influential role in the revival of sculpture in Germany at the beginning of the 20th century.

Lely, Sir Peter [Pieter van der Faes] (1618–80) Dutch-born English painter who trained at Haarlem and moved to England *c*.1643. His early works are landscapes and historical paintings, but he soon turned to portrait painting, in which he was greatly influenced by van DYCK. He lacked van Dyck's flair for elegance, and his approach was generally more superficial, but he set a trend for society portrait styles, which continued for nearly a century. He painted most of the court of Charles II, e.g. the two series *The Windsor Beauties* and *Maids of Honour*. He was knighted in 1680.

Lem, Stanislaw (1921–) Polish novelist, critic and scientist. Lem's critically acclaimed science fiction novels include *Cyberiad* (1967) and *Solaris* (1961). The latter novel, in which the crew of a space station circling a planet covered by a sentient ocean experience what they take to be hallucinations caused by the ocean, was made into a remarkable film by the Russian director Andrei Tarkovsky in 1972. The image of the ocean, and the crew's difficulties in communicating with it, serves as an extended metaphor for communication between man and God, a theme central to many Slav writers' fictions.

Le Nain, Antoine (*c*.1588–1648), **Louis** (*c*.1593–1648) and **Matthieu** (1607–77) French painters. Brothers from Laon, they established a studio in Paris from *c*.1630, and were founder members of the Academy. The fact that they all signed their works without initials has created an element of uncertainty in attributing which to whom, but it is generally accepted that Louis was the most important of the three, creating simple and dignified genre paintings of peasant life, e.g. *The Peasant's Meal* (1642). Of the other two brothers, Antoine painted small works and miniatures, e.g. *The Little Singers*, and Matthieu painted portraits and larger pictures, e.g. *The Guardroom* (1643). All three collaborated on religious paintings.

Lennox, Charlotte (1720–1804) American-born English novelist and dramatist. Her best-known work is the novel *The Female Quixote* (1752), a comedy modelled on CERVANTES' great novel, that was very popular in its day. Her work was praised by both FIELDING and her friend Dr JOHNSON, the latter crowning her with laurel at a BLUESTOCKING party to celebrate the publication of her first novel, *Harriot Stuart* (1751).

Leonardo da Vinci (1452–1519) Florentine painter, draughtsman, engineer, musician and thinker; the outstanding genius of his time, and of many others. He trained in the studio of VERROCCHIO, where he probably painted the left-hand angel in Verrocchio's *Baptism of Christ* (c.1472). Verrocchio was reputedly impressed to the extent that he gave up painting. Leonardo was a painstaking worker and evolved a technique of thin glazes of oil paint to build up an image of extraordinary translucence and detail, e.g. the far distance landscapes in *The Annunciation* . His use of this technique was to prove disastrous for the mural of *The Last Supper* (1489) in the refectory of San Maria del Grazie, Milan, which began to deteriorate within his own lifetime. He was also ambitious in his compositions, although somewhat dilatory in their execution, so that many of his works remained unfinished, e.g. *The Adoration of the Magi* (commissioned 1881, not completed). In 1483 he wrote recommending himself to Duke Sforza of Milan as an engineer and a musician. While in Milan he painted the two versions of *The Virgin of the Rocks*, which demonstrate the subtle modelling of light and shade between figures and background, known as *sfumato*. This represented a remarkable departure from the RENAISSANCE art stress on strong lighting and outline. Leonardo's works had a profound influence on the art of RAPHAEL and PERUGINO. He also began the Sforza Monument, an equestrian statue for which he only completed the horse, which was later destroyed. Leonardo left Milan in 1499 and travelled between Florence and Rome, where he painted the *Mona Lisa* (*c*.1505) for Giulio de' MEDICI. He also composed the beautiful cartoon of *The Virgin and St Anne* (1504–6), which he exhibited as a work of art in its own right. He was always more interested in devising the composition of a work, in developing character and gesture, than in completion; his creative ingenuity was always pursuing some new idea. With Leonardo originates the view of the artist as a creative thinker and not merely a skilled artisan. In 1516 he was invited to France by King Francis I, and he remained there until his death. His later years were devoted to scientific studies, and he completed no more major paintings, although his drawings for other projects were prolific and beautiful. Leonardo's influence on art and science in his own and succeeding generations was colossal and vitrually unmatched up to the present day.

Lermontov, Mikhail Yurievich (1814–41) Russian novelist and poet. His works include a verse play, *Masquerade* (1842), and several very fine poems, e.g. "The Novice," "The Demon" and "A Wish," the last reflecting his interest in things Scottish (he was of Scottish, "Learmont," descent). He was exiled to the Caucasus after writing a poem on Pushkin's death in 1837; allowed to return to St Petersburg, he was then re-exiled after fighting a duel. His masterpiece is his novel *A Hero of our Time* (1840), a brilliant study of a disaffected, Byronic young aristocrat (like many Russians of the time, Lermontov was fascinated by BYRON's life and work). Like Pushkin, his life ended prematurely in a duel.

Lessing, Doris [May] (1919–) English novelist and short-story writer. Her novels include the *Children of Violence* quintet, beginning with *Martha Quest* (1952) and ending with *The Five-Gated City* (1969). Her most famous work is the seminal feminist novel, *The Golden Notebook* (1962). She has also written science fiction novels, e.g. *Briefing for a Descent into Hell* (1971). *The Good Terrorist* (1985), a stunning account of the self-deception involved in political fanaticism, marked a new and intriguing departure in her work.

Lessing, Gotthold Ephraim (1729–81) German dramatist and critic. His plays include three important tragedies, *Miss Sara Sampson* (1755), an adaptation of LILLO's *The London Merchant; Emilia Galotti* (1772), a study of sexual obsession and oppression; and *Nathan the Wise* (1779), a remarkable plea for religious tolerance (the central character is modelled on Lessing's friend, the Jewish philosopher Moses Mendelssohn, grandfather of Felix Mendelssohn). Lessing's critical work is of great significance in the development of German ROMANTICISM, particularly his defence of SHAKESPEARE against the NEOCLASSICAL theorists of France. Lessing remains one of the most interesting and attractive personalities of German literature.

Levi, Primo (1919–87) Italian novelist, short-story writer and poet. His most famous work is his autobiographical trilogy, *If This is a Man* (1947), *The Truce* (1958) and *The Periodic Table* (1975). Levi was a survivor of Auschwitz, and his deeply moving writings on the subject, e.g. the first volume of his autobiography, are among the key texts of the 20th century. His *The*

Drowned and the Saved was published posthumously in 1988.

Levi-Strauss, Claude *see* **Structuralism**.

Lewis, C[live] S[taples] (1898–1963) English novelist and critic. His works include *The Allegory of Love* (1936), an important study of medieval literature; works of (conservative) Christian apologetics, e.g. *The Problem of Pain* (1940); and three science fiction novels, e.g. *Out of the Silent Planet* (1938). He is best remembered for his enchanting "Narnia" stories for children, e.g. *The Lion, the Witch and the Wardrobe* (1950), and for a "spiritual" autobiography, *Surprised by Joy* (1955), both of which have been successfully dramatized for television and theatre.

Lewis, Norman (1914–) English novelist and travel writer. His travel books include two modern classics of the genre, *A Dragon Apparent* (1952) on Vietnam, and his book on Burma, *Golden Earth* (1952). His novels include *A Small War Made to Order* (1966), a chilling study of the Bay of Pigs invasion of Cuba, and *The Sicilian Specialist* (1975), a thinly fictionalized account of President Kennedy's assassination, which was reputedly withdrawn from sale in several American cities following a Mafia ban on the book. Lewis regards as his main achievement the exposure of the genocidal campaign that has been waged against Brazilian Indians ("Genocide in Brazil" in *A View of the World*, 1986). He is one of our finest living writers.

Lewis, Sinclair (1885–1951) American novelist. His work is particularly noted for its satirical view of the self-righteous Philistinism of small-town American life. His best-known novels are *Main Street* (1920), a study of the monotonous life within a mid-West town appropriately called Gopher Prairie, *Babbitt* (1922), a searching and disturbing depiction of an average man's rebellion and consequent submission to conformity (the name "Babbitt" has come to denote the average, conformist, "don't make waves" man), and *Elmer Gantry* (1927), a still unsurpassed exposé of the dark, hypocritical side of American evangelism. Other notable novels include *Dodsworth* (1929) and *It Can't Happen Here* (1935). Lewis became the first American to win the Nobel Prize for literature in 1930.

Lewis, [Percy] Wyndham (1882–1957) English painter, novelist and critic. He was a leader of the short-lived Vorticist movement and major contributor and editor of the two issues of its magazine, *Blast* (1914), in which he advocated a departure from traditional Victorian values. His use of violent colour and severe angularity in his paintings is reminiscent of Italian FUTURISM. Using reiterated forms suggestive of the machine age, he created some of the earliest virtually abstract works, e.g. *Workshop* (1914). Later works include some outstanding portraits, notably that of *T.S. Eliot* (1938).

His best-known fictional work is the novel *Apes of God* (1930), a withering satire on his intellectual contemporaries. Lewis was very much a singular figure described by AUDEN as "that lonely old volcano of the right."

Lewitt, Sol (1928–) American sculptor whose work centres on the infinite variety of combinations of simple geometric forms. He developed series of arrangements of two- and three-dimensional images and grid projections in monochrome, e.g. *Open Modular Cube* (1966). Later pieces included the three primary colours also.

Leyden, Lucas van (1494–1533) Dutch painter and engraver. He was a child prodigy, producing mature, accomplished works from the age of 14, e.g. *Mohammed and the Murdered Monk* (1508). He was greatly influenced by DÜRER, but his subject matter is more diverse and the quality of his prolific output less consistent although often outstanding in originality. He had a large and widespread influence on other painters. Other notable works include *The Game of Chess* (*c*.1510), *The Card Players* (*c*.1516) and the *Last Judgment* triptych (1526–27), which was his masterpiece.

Lichtenstein, Roy (1923–) American painter, graphic artist and sculptor. He initially worked in commercial art, and his early paintings are in the ABSTRACT EXPRESSIONIST tradition, but he is best known as a protagonist of Pop Art. He draws his imagery from comic strip magazines, blowing up single frames and reproducing the enlarged dot matrix by hand, e.g. *Whaam!* (1963) and *As I Opened Fire* (1963).

Liebermann, Max (1847–1935) German painter and graphic artist. He studied in Berlin and Weimar, and came under the influence of the BARBIZON SCHOOL while travelling in France and Holland. He was influential in promoting new Impressionist ideas in German art, and was a founder of the Berlin SEZESSION in 1898. He was also president of the Berlin Academy from 1922 to 1933. Although his work was declared degenerate by the Nazis, he finally came to represent the formal traditionalism that artists, such as those of Die BRÜCKE, later reacted against.

Lillo, George (1693–1739) English dramatist. He wrote seven plays, the most important of which is *The London Merchant*, or *The History of George Barnwell* (1731), a DOMESTIC TRAGEDY which had great influence throughout Europe, most notably on Gotthold LESSING, whose adaptation had great success in Germany (Diderot was also much influenced by the work).

Limbourg, Jean, Paul and **Herman** (all *fl*. 1400–1416) Dutch illuminators. They worked on Biblical texts for Philip, Duke of Burgundy, until his death in 1404. They then went into the service of his brother Jean, Duke of Berry, for whom they produced the *Belles*

Heures (*c*.1408). A second manuscript, *Les Très Riches Heures*, which was unfinished at the time of their deaths, represents the major work of their career. It is an outstanding example of the INTERNATIONAL GOTHIC style, and surpasses contemporary accomplishments in its complex composition and landscape detail.

Lipchitz, Jaques (1891–1973) Russian sculptor. He originally trained as an engineer before settling in Paris in 1909, when he began to study art. His early work is concerned with the three-dimensional potential CUBIST ideas, based on interlocking planes, e.g. *Head* (1915). Later works are more linear and surrealist in approach, but he returned to his Cubist principles after settling in the US in 1941. Notable works include *Sacrifice* (1948).

Lippi, Filippino (1457–1504) Florentine painter, son of Filippo LIPPI. He trained in BOTTICELLI's studio, where he became an excellent draughtsman. His style is bolder and more vigorous than that of Botticelli, as in his first important painting *The Vision of St Bernard* (*c*.1480). His most outstanding works are his frescoes, in particular *The Life of St Thomas Aquinas* (1488–93) for Santa Maria sopra Minerva in Rome, and *The Lives of Saints Philip and John* (1495–1502) in Santa Maria Novella, Florence.

Lippi, Fra Filippo (*c*.1406–69) Florentine painter. He took up painting under the influence of MASACCIO, who had decorated the Brancacci Chapel in the Carmine monastery where Filippo was a monk. He later forsook his vows in order to marry the mother of his son, Filppino LIPPI. Early works reveal the influence of Masaccio, although without the same strength of form or light, e.g. *Annunciation*. However, his style gradually became more lyrical and fluid, investing his paintings with a certain wistful melancholy and naive charm, e.g. *Adoration in the Wood*. He was one of the first to explore and develop the *Madonna and Child* theme, and most of his work was innovative both in style and subject.

Li Shizheng *see* **Duoduo.**

literary ballad *see* **ballad.**

Llosa, Mario Vargas *see* **Vargas Llosa, Mario.**

Lodge, David (1935–) English novelist and critic. His best-known novels are the highly entertaining satires on academic life, *Changing Places* (1975) and *Small World* (1984). His novel *Nice Work* (1988) is a remarkable hybrid of the academic novel with the 19th-century "condition of England" tradition, and contains many shrewd (and very funny) observations on modern British life.

Lombardo, Pietro (*c*.1435–1515) Venetian sculptor, father of **Tullio** (*c*.1455–1532) and **Antonio** (d.1516), with whom he ran a family workshop producing decorations and monuments for chapels in Venice, Padua and Treviso. Pietro executed the monument to *Doge Pietro Mocenigo* (*c*.1476–81) and was also the architect for the Church of Santa Maria dei Miracoli in Venice. Tullio's style is more fluid and sensual, e.g. the *Adam* from the *Vendramin* Monument (1439). Antonio's work is less well documented, but he collaborated with his brother on a number of commissions, notably *St Anthony's Shrine* (*c*.1500).

London, Jack (1876–1916) American novelist and short-story writer. Born in San Francisco, he led an adventurous early life as a sailor, tramp and goldminer, before becoming a writer. His best-known works are the bloodily Darwinian dog stories *The Call of the Wild* (1903) and *White Fang* (1906); a documentary account of life in the London slums, *The People of the Abyss* (1903); and *The Iron Heel* (1908), a prophetic novel about future totalitarianism. London described himself as a socialist, but his "blond beast" heroes and their ideals have more in common with Nazi thinking than with modern democratic socialism. His rarely read novel *The Mutiny of the "Elsinore"* (1914), for example, is an unsavoury fable about white racial supremacy.

Longfellow, Henry Wadsworth (1807–82) American poet. Several of his poems, e.g. "The Wreck of the Hesperus," "The Village Blacksmith" and "Excelsior!" were among the most popular poems of the 19th century. His narrative poems on American legends and folk tales, e.g. *Evangeline* (1849) and *The Song of Hiawatha* (1858), were also extremely popular. *Hiawatha*, thanks to its hypnotic unrymed rhythms, "By the shore of Gitche Gumme,/By the shining Big-Sea-Water," became one of the most-parodied poems of all time (e.g. by CARROLL). Several of Longfellow's phrases, e.g. "Ships that pass in the night" (*Tales of a Wayside Inn*, 1874), have become firmly embedded in the English language.

Lorca, Federigo Garcia (1899–1936) Spanish poet and dramatist. His dramatic masterpiece in his trilogy of tragedies on the frustrated and oppressed life of Spanish women, *Blood Wedding* (1939), *Yerma* (1934) and *The House of Bernarda Alba* (1936). His poetry was heavily influenced by the SURREALIST MOVEMENT, e.g. in *Poet in New York* (1940). His gypsy songs, especially *Romancero Gitano*, "Gipsy Ballads" (1928, 1935) are still highly popular in Spain. Lorca was killed by Fascist forces near the beginning of the Spanish Civil War. *See also* BOWLES.

Lorenzetti, Ambrogio, and **Pietro** (both *fl.* 1320–48) Sienese painters and brothers, they probably trained under DUCCIO, although they developed a style that shows the influence of GIOTTO in the fullness of form and the depth of perspective in their works. Typical of Pietro's works are the early polyptych altarpiece *The*

Virgin and Child with Saints (1320) and the later *Birth of the Virgin* (c.1342). Ambrogio was particularly skilled in his use of perspective, as in his most important work, the fresco series on *Good and Bad Government* (1338–9) for the Palazzo Pubblico in Siena.

Lotto, Lorenzo (c.1480–1556) Venetian painter and contemporary of TITIAN and GIORGIONE, he probably trained in the studio of Giovanni BELLINI, who influenced his early works. His career was idiosyncratic and his successes inconsistent, His best works are probably his portraits, which have a disturbing quality of intensity and unusual modes of colour and composition, e.g. *Young Man in his Study* (c.1528). Other notable works include *The Crucifixion* (1531). In later life his eyesight deteriorated and he spent his last years in the monastery at Loreto as a lay brother.

Louis, Morris (1912–62) American painter. His early influences include CUBISM and EXPRESSIONISM, but in 1954 he saw *Mountains and Sea* by Helen FRANKENTHALER, and pioneered techniques in colour stain painting. This method of pouring thin washes of colour on to unprimed, or even unstretched, canvas afforded him a means of avoiding the gestural marks and surface textures of expressionist painting. His major works were series paintings, notably the *Veil* series, e.g. *Vav* (1960), and the *Unfurled* series, e.g. *Alphaphi* (1961).

Lovelace, Richard *see* **Cavalier Poets**.

Lowell, Amy (1874–1925) American poet and critic. She became an enthusiastic member of the IMAGIST school of poetry after visiting England in 1913, where she met and befriended Ezra POUND who was to coin the term 'Amy-gism" ("When I get through with that girl she'll think she was born in free verse"). She described her verse as "unrhymed cadence" and became a very popular figure on the American lecture circuit. Her volumes of poetry include *Sword Blades and Poppy Seed* (1914) and *Men, Women and Ghosts* (1916). Her critical works include *Tendencies in Modern American Poetry* (1917).

Lowell, James Russell (1819–91) American poet, essayist and diplomat. His best-known work, inspired by his fervent abolitionism, is contained in the *Biglow Papers* (1848, 1867). His verse is written in "Yankee" dialect, and includes crushing satires against the pro-slavery lobby: "It's wal enough agin a king / To dror resolves an' triggers, / But libbaty's a kind o' thing / Thet don't agree with niggers."

Lowell, Robert [Traill Spence] (1917–77) American poet. Lowell's verse is intensely personal, with an occasionally impenetrable private symbolism. Notable volumes include his first, *Land of Unlikeness* (1944), and *Life Studies* (1959) and *Near the Ocean* (1967). He was a conscientious objector during World War II, and played an active role in opposing the Vietnam war.

Lowry, L[aurence] S[tephen] (1887–1976) English painter from Salford, near Manchester. His main employment was as a clerk for a property company, and he trained at art classes only intermittently between 1905 and 1925. He evolved a highly idiosyncratic painting style, mainly of urban industrial environments populated by matchstick-style figures. His paintings convey an intense atmosphere of human loneliness and alienation. Although he had an important exhibition in the Reid-Lefevre Gallery, London, in 1939, his work only achieved wider recognition in the Arts Council Retrospective Exhibition of 1966. A major retrospective was held at the Royal Academy in 1976. Critical opinion of his stature is widely divergent.

Lowry, [Clarence] Malcolm (1909–57) English novelist and poet. Lowry's novels, e.g. *Ultramarine* (1933) and *Under the Volcano* (1947), often feature thinly veiled accounts of incidents from his own adventurous life. Alcoholism is a major theme in his much revised work. His *Selected Poems* appeared in 1962.

Luks, George Benjamin (1867–1933) American painter and graphic artist. He studied at the Pennsylvania Academy and became a member of The EIGHT and the ASHCAN SCHOOL under the influence of Robert HENRI. His style is flamboyant and vigorous, and his subject matter is concerned with social and urban realism. Much of his work reveals his indebtedness to Henri and also to MANET. Notable among his paintings is *The Wrestlers* (1905).

Lurie, Alison (1926–) American novelist, noted for her witty, ironic satires centred on the middle-class liberal way of life. Typical examples are *Love and Friendship* (1962), *Imaginary Friends* (1967) and *The War Between the Tates* (1974).

Lyly, John (*c.*1554–1606) English dramatist and prose romance writer. His romances, *Euphues, the Anatomy of Wit* (1579) and *Euphues and his England* (1580), are for the most part now unreadable, but were highly popular in Elizabethan times and had some influence on the development of the English novel. The romances consist mainly of conversations and observations on love, in language that came to be described as "Euphusitic," a style characterized by an exaggerated use of antithesis and alliteration.

M

Mabuse, Jean de *see* **Gossaert, Jan**

Macaulay, [Dame] Rose (1881–1958) English novelist, essayist and travel writer. Her post-World War I novels, e.g. *Dangerous Ages* (1921), are witty social satires that were very popular in their day. She underwent a spiritual conversion to Higher Anglicanism in the late 1940s, an experience reflected in what is held to be her best novel, *The Towers of Trebizond* (1956).

Macaulay, Thomas Babington (1800–59) English essayist and historian. Macaulay's writings were very popular with the "middlebrow" reading public of Victorian times, reflecting as they do, e.g. in *Essays Critical and Historical* (1834), a view of human society as a steady movement from barbarism to the triumph of the enlightened 19th-century middle classes. This view steadily lost ground from the 1880s onwards, when Macaulay's tone came to be seen as insufferably smug. He was created Baron Macaulay in 1857.

McCarthy, Mary (1912–89) American novelist, short-story writer and critic. Her most famous novel is *The Group* (1963), the narrative of which deals with the lives and careers of a group of upper-middle class female university students, and which created a mild stir in its open, matter-of-fact account of female sexuality. *See also* Edmund WILSON.

McCullers, Carson (1917–67) American novelist and short-story writer. Her works include *The Heart is a*

Lonely Hunter (1940), *Reflections in a Golden Eye* (1941), and the short-story collection *The Ballad of the Sad Cafe* (1951). Her central characters are usually loners and misfits, living in what she called "spiritual isolation."

MacDiarmid, Hugh [pseud. of Christopher Murray Grieve] (1892–1978) Scottish poet and critic. He was expelled from the Scottish Nationalist Party in the 1930s for Communist sympathies, and shortly afterwards from the Communist Party for Nationalist sympathies. His masterpiece is *A Drunk Man Looks at the Thistle* (1926), a triumphant allegory of awakening Scottish consciousness that inspired many Scottish writers of the 1920s and 1930s. More broadly influential was his *First Hymn to Lenin* (1931), the first great leftist poem of the decade. His scathing epigram on the dilettante revolutionism of AUDEN, etc, "Epitaph on British Leftish Poetry, 1930–40," remains one of the best short political poems of the 1930s.

Macdonald, George (1824–1905) Scottish novelist and poet, remembered chiefly for his children's stories, *At the Back of the North Wind* (1871) and *The Princess and the Goblin* (1872), and for two adult fantasy novels, *Phantastes* (1858) and *Lilith* (1895). His work has had a marked influence on many 20th-century fantasy writers, notably C. S. LEWIS, who regarded him as an important allegorical writer.

Macdonald-Wright, Stanton (1890–1973) American painter who was a co-founder of SYNCHROMISM, a movement in colour abstraction along similar lines to ORPHISM. Macdonald-Wright's paintings tended to have a representational motif, e.g *Sunrise Synchromy in Violet* (1918). In 1919 he settled in California where he taught art and experimented in colour film. After 1937 he became interested in Zen and travelled annually to Japan. His later Synchromist paintings indicate the influence of oriental art.

MacGonagall, William (*c*.1830–*c*.1902) Scottish poet, renowned for his memorably awful doggerel verse. His poems are uniformly bad: the lines do not scan, and the subject matter, frequently a disaster of some kind, is loaded with bathos. A typical example of his work is "The Tay Bridge Disaster," which commemorates the collapse of the railway bridge over the River Tay in 1879: "Beautiful railway bridge of the silv'ry Tay/Alas, I am very sorry to say . . ." His poems were published posthumously in *Poetic Gems* (1934) and *More Poetic Gems* (1963). A curious feature of his verse is that it is virtually impossible to produce convincing imitations of it.

Machen, Arthur [Llewellyn] (1863–1947) Welsh writer of supernatural and horror stories. Representative collections include *The Great God Pan* (1894) and the nasty *The Three Imposters* (1895).

Machiavelli, Niccolò (1469–1527) Italian statesman and political theorist. His treatise on the art of ruling, *The Prince* (1513), takes a somewhat dim view of human nature, seeing humanity as essentially corrupt and therefore best ruled by whatever method ensures the stability of the state, even if the method is merciless cruelty. Machiavelli's treatise caused outrage, especially in its suggestion that the ruler should maintain a reputation for being virtuous while indulging in treachery and brutality, and his name came to be virtually synonymous in Elizabethan drama with that of the devil (he appears in the prologue to Marlowe's *Jew of Malta*, 1592). Machiavelli's comedy *Mandragola (The Mandrake, c.*1518), is a notably licentious piece.

Macke, August (1887–1914) German painter and founder member of Der BLAUE REITER. His early influences include FAUVISM and CUBISM, e.g. *Church in Bonn*

(1911). He exhibited with Der Blaue Reiter in 1911. Subsequent works are coloured by the influences of ORPHISM, e.g. *Walk on the Bridge* (1911), and by the powerful atmospheric light of North Africa. Macke's works had a powerful influence on Paul KLEE.

Mackenzie, Sir [Edward Montagu] Compton (1883–1972) English novelist. His best-known novels are *Sinister Street* (1914), a semi-autobiographical account of a privileged young man's life at Oxford University and in London's slums, and his series of very popular comic novels set in the Scottish Western Isles, e.g. *Whisky Galore* (1947) and *Rockets Galore* (1957). He also wrote two memorable novels on homosexual relationships, *Extraordinary Women* (1928) and *Thin Ice* (1956), and his Scottish nationalist sympathies surface in his six-volume *Four Winds of Love* (1937–45).

Mackenzie, Henry (1745–1831) Scottish lawyer and novelist. His most famous work is the extraordinarily weepy novel *The Man of Feeling* (1771), the hero of which is a sort of 18th-century "new man" who bursts into tears at every onslaught on his emotions. An edition published by Henry Morley in London in 1886 gives a useful index of the different varieties of tears in the book. Mackenzie also wrote *The Man of the World* (1773) and the epistolary *Julia de Roubigne* (1777), and was on the committee that investigated MACPHERSON's "Ossian" hoax.

Mackintosh, Charles Rennie *see* **Art Nouveau**.

Maclean, Sorley [Somhairle Macgill-Eain] (1911–) Scottish Gaelic poet, who is widely regarded as one of the leading Scottish poets of the 20th century. Influenced by English poetry and by Celtic literature, he has reinstated Gaelic as a poetic language, and his own translations into English, e.g. *Spring Tide and Neap Tide* (1977) from his Gaelic *Reothairt is Contraigh*, have brought his work to a wider readership.

Macleish, Archibald (1892–1982) American poet and dramatist. He was one of the "lost generation" (*see* HEMINGWAY) of American poets in 1920s Paris, and the fashionable disillusionment of the period is reflected in *The Pot of Earth* (1925). Subsequent volumes of poetry include *Conquistador* (1932), *Frescoes for Mr Rockefeller's City* (1933) and *New Found Land* (1930), all of which follow the leftwing trend of the 1930s.

Macleod, Fiona [pseud. of William Sharp] (1855–1905) Scottish writer of Celtic fantasy tales set in the Scottish Western Isles. An operatic version of his eerie "faery" play *The Immortal Hour* (1900), set to music by the socialist composer, Rutland Boughton, enjoyed great popularity in the 1920s. The identity of "Fiona Macleod" was kept secret during Sharp's lifetime (Sharp would wear a dress while writing in the Fiona persona).

McLuhan, Marshall *see* **Structuralism**.

MacNeice, [Frederick] Louis (1907–63) Irish poet and classical scholar. He was one of the leading "AUDEN generation" poets. Representative 1930s collections include *Letters From Iceland* (1937 written in collaboration with Auden) and *Autumn Journal* (1938). His later poems, e.g. *Solstices* (1961), are suffused with a less optimistic view of life. His translations of the *Agamemnon* (1936) from AESCHYLUS' *Oresteia* and of GOETHE's *Faust* (1951) are still highly regarded.

Macpherson, James (1736–96) Scottish poet. His supposed translations of early Scottish Gaelic verse, *Fragments of Ancient Poetry* (1760), *Fingal* (1762) and *Temora* (1763), the latter two allegedly by an ancient bard called Ossian, achieved extraordinary popularity. GOETHE quoted from them in *The Sorrows of Young Werther*, and Napoleon slept with the poems under his pillow. Macpherson certainly used some ancient Gaelic poetry as the basis for the poems, but they are unquestionably largely his own creation. AUDEN claimed that Macpherson's Ossianic verse is the forerunner of advertising prose.

McTaggart, William (1835–1910) Scottish painter, sometimes referred to as the Scottish Impressionist, although his magnificent sky- and seascapes are closer to the ideas and aspirations of CONSTABLE in their depiction of changing light and cloud movement. He is renowned for having painted mainly out of doors and in all weathers. His works are freely and powerfully painted, conveying the breathtaking shock of strong winds and stormy seas and skies.

Maes, Nicolaes (1634–93) Dutch painter from Dordrecht. He studied with REMBRANDT, and his early genre works show the deep influence of his teacher in his rich palette of reds and browns and in contrasts of light and shade, e.g. *The Listening Maid* (1656). After the mid-1660s his style changed; he painted portraits more in the style of van DYCK, and his palette became cooler and greyer. He moved to Amsterdam in 1673, where he became a successful society portraitist. His work had a strong influence on succeeding generations of portrait painters.

maestà The Italian word for "majesty," used in art to denote a depiction of the Virgin and Child enthroned in majesty and surrounded by angels or saints.

magic realism a term devised in the 1920s to describe the work of a group of German painters, part of the *Neue Sachlichkeit* ("new objectivity") group, whose work exhibited a disquieting blend of surreal fantasy with matter-of-fact representationalism. In literature, the term is often applied with particular reference to the work of certain South American novelists, notably Mario VARGAS LLOSA and Gabriel Garcia MARQUEZ, whose work combines deadpan description of the everyday world with (often equally deadpan) excursions into

fantasy. Some European novelists have been characterized as "magic realists," e.g. CALVINO and RUSHDIE.
The techniques of magic realism have a long ancestry;
CHESTERTON's novel *The Man Who Was Thursday* is a
notable early 20th-century example, and there are
clear links with the Gothic Novel. By 1991, there were
signs that the form was losing its avant-garde appeal.
The cult TV series of 1990, *Twin Peaks*, provides a
useful example of the degeneration of the form in its
knowingly dissonant double act between the wacky
FBI agent (surreal) and the hick sheriff (soap
character).

Magritte, René (1898–1967) Belgian painter. His early
styles included IMPRESSIONISM and CUBISM, but he
became interested in SURREALISM after seeing *Song of
Love* (1922) by de CHIRICO. He was involved with the
production of the DADAist publication *Oesophage,* and
painted his first Surrealist works, e.g *The Menaced
Assassin* (1926), from about 1925. He had links with
the French Surrealists, including BRETON and DALI
while living near Paris between 1927 and 1930.

Mahfouz, Naguib (*c.*1911–) Egyptian novelist and
short-story writer. Now long established as the most
important modern Arab novelist, his novels include the
controversial and allegorical *Awlad Haritna* (1959),
which was initially banned in Egypt for its treatment
of Islam, and *Miramar* (1967), the action of which is
set against a daring exposé of the sordid reality of
Nasserite socialism. He was awarded the NOBEL PRIZE
for literature in 1988.

Mailer, Norman (1923–) American novelist and essayist. His first novel, *The Naked and the Dead* (1948),
based on his experiences in World War II, was highly
successful. Subsequent novels include *The Deer Park*
(1955), the semi-autobiographical *An American Dream*
(1966) and *Ancient Evenings* (1983), an enormous work

set in Ancient Egypt. His nonfiction works include *The Executioner's Song* (1977), a gruesome CAPOTE-style "factional" study of a murderer.

Maillol, Aristide (1861–1944) French sculptor, designer and painter. He initially worked in tapestry design and was a succesful painter, but took up sculpture when his eyesight began to deteriorate. He is best remembered for his sculptures of the female nude in the classical and dignified style of Greek and Roman sculpture, e.g. *The Mediterranean* (*c*.1901). His sculptural works were highly influential.

Malamud, Bernard (1914–) American novelist and short-story writer. His best-known work is *The Fixer* (1967), a tragic tale of anti-Semitism in Czarist Russia. Other works include the novels *The Natural* (1952) *The Assistant* (1957), *Dublin's Lives* (1979) and the short-story collection *The Magic Barrel* (1958).

Malevich, Kasimir Severinovich (1878–1935) Russian painter of Polish origins, his early works, such as *The Knife Grinder* (1912), combine the influences of CUBISM and FUTURISM. From around 1915 he pioneered SUPREMATIST ideas of purely abstract art, sometimes anticipating the Minimalist art of the 1960s, e.g. *Black Square* (1915) and the series *White on White* (*c*.1918). From 1919 he taught at the Vitebsk School of Art, where he championed Suprematist theories over those of CONSTRUCTIVISM. His later works revert to an earlier interest in genre themes, and he produced some notable portraits of his friends and family.

Mallarmé, Stephane (1842–98) French SYMBOLIST poet. His impressionistic FREE-VERSE works include *the Afternoon of a Faun* (1876), which was set to suitably sensuous music by Claude Debussy. His literary theorizing, e.g. in *Verse and Prose* (1893), had a strong influence on the development of the Symbolist movement.

Malory, Sir Thomas (*fl.* 15th century) Translator, largely from French sources, of *Le Morte d'Arthur* (printed by Caxton, 1485), a collection of Arthurian legends (*see* ARTHUR). The work includes several episodes, e.g. the quest for the Holy Grail, that have been recycled by generations of authors, e.g. TENNYSON and T. H. WHITE. The author has been traditionally identified with a rather violently inclined Warwickshire knight of that name, but the attribution is doubtful.

Mamet, David (1947–) American dramatist. Mamet's plays, e.g. *American Buffalo* (1977) and *House of Games* (1985), are engrossing and highly ingenious studies of bluff and double-cross among American low-life characters. *House of Games* was filmed in 1987 and directed by Mamet. He is regarded by many critics as one of the most talented modern American dramatists.

Mandelstam, Osip (1891–1938) Russian poet, associated with AKHMATOVA in the Acmeist group. The collections published in his lifetime are *Stone* (1913), *Tristia* (1925) and *Poems* (1928). In 1934 he read a satirical poem about Stalin to a group of friends, and within a few days was sent into exile with his wife, Nadezhda. He died in Siberia, probably of typhoid. Nadezhda's two books describing her husband's life and work, *Hope Against Hope* (1971) and *Hope Abandoned* (1974), contain much fascinating detail about the Acmeist poets, and are among the great books of the century, affirming as they do the resilience of the human spirit.

Mandeville, Sir John (*c.*14th century) Supposed English author of *The Travels of Sir John Mandeville*, an eventful and thoroughly mendacious travel book that has charmed countless readers since its first appearance in the 14th century. The work is ostensibly an account of the author's travels in the Holy Lane, but is actually a gathering together of various unlikely traveller's tales from Africa to India, e.g. of a race of people with no heads but eyes on their shoulders. The influence of the book was widespread (there are references to it in SHAKESPEARE's work, for example).

Manet, Edouard (1832–83) French painter. He derived much of his inspiration from the Old Masters and from the Spanish painters VELAZQUEZ and RIBERA. He established early success at the Salon with *The Guitarist* (1861). Subsequent paintings, however, such as *Le Déjeuner sur l'Herbe* (1863) and *Olympia* (1863), caused outrage due to his direct approach and fresh, painterly style. The public could not accept his use of contemporary figures and settings, and the critics objected to the direct, bold lighting that reduced midtone modelling of the figures. The subjects derive from older paintings: GIORGIONE's *Concert Champêtre* and TITIAN's *Venus d'Urbino*. Manet was by no means a willing leader of the avant-garde, and although his pupils and associates, such as DEGAS and MORISOT, were IMPRESSIONISTS, he himself never exhibited with them. They did encourage him to paint out of doors, and his later works have a lighter, freer atmosphere, e.g. *Argenteuil* (1874). He sketched much of the subject matter of his late paintings, e.g. *Bar aux Folies Bergères* (1881) in Parisian cafés. His paintings won increasing acceptance, and he was awarded the Légion d'Honneur in 1881. His work had a widespread and profound influence on 20th-century painting.

Mann, Thomas (1875–1955) German novelist, critic and essayist. His chief preoccupation was the role of the artist and the purpose of artistic creation in modern society. Representative works include the novella *Death in Venice* (1912), and the novels *The Magic Mountain* (1930), a parable of European cultural disintegration set in a sanatorium; *Mario and the Magician* (1930), an antifascist allegory; *Lotte in Weimar* (1939), based on an incident in the life of his hero GOETHE; and

The Confessions of the Confidence Trickster Felix Krull (1954), a masterly PICARESQUE comedy. He was awarded the NOBEL PRIZE for literature in 1929 and fled Nazi Germany in 1933. He is now universally recognized as one of the great novelists.

Mannerism An exaggerated and often artificial sense of style found in Italian art between *c*.1520 and 1600, i.e. between the High RENAISSANCE and BAROQUE periods. It represents a reaction against the balanced forms and perspectives of Renaissance art and is characterized by uncomfortably posed, elongated figures and contorted facial expressions. Harsh colours and unusual modes of perspective were also used to striking effect. The major artists of the period, e.g. PONTORMO and Giovanni BOLOGNA, were able to create emotional responses of greater power and sophistication, and they paved the way for the development of Baroque art.

Mansfield, Katherine [pseud. of Kathleen Mansfield Beauchamp] (1888–1923) New-Zealand born English short-story writer. She is widely recognized as one of the masters of the short-story form, and is frequently compared with CHEKHOV. The story collections are *In a German Pension* (1911), *Bliss* (1920), *The Garden Party* (1922), *The Dove's Nest* (1923) and *Something Childish* (1924). She married Middleton Murry in 1918; they had a rather strained friendship with D. H. LAWRENCE and his wife.

Mantegna, Andrea (*c*.1430–1506) Italian painter and prominent figure of the early RENAISSANCE, who was the brother-in-law of Giovanni BELLINI. A proficient draughtsman, skilled in the use of perspective, he used his knowledge of classical antiquity in his frescoes for the Eremetani church in Padua (1448–57), since mainly destroyed. One of his major works that made full use of illusionistic perspective was the decor for the bridal chamber of the Ducal Palace in Mantua. It depicts groups of visitors to the palace, along with court figures, in a setting that seems to extend the space of the room and open out the ceiling to the sky. His mastery of foreshortening is fully expressed in the *trompe l'oeil* figures looking down from a ceiling balcony. Among his late works are the masterpieces depicting the *Triumph of Caesar* (1486–94), nine canvases commissioned by Francesco Gonzago. Mantegna also produced engravings of his works, which earned him widespread popularity and influenced the art of Bellini and DÉRER. He was greatly revered in his own lifetime, and his stature in art history remains undiminished.

Maratti, Carlo (1625–1713) Italian painter. He trained with SACCHI, and became a proficient portrait painter, e.g. *Pope Clement IX* (1667–9). His best works were influenced by the calm, classical tradition of RAPHAEL, in contrast to the Baroque dynamism of his contemporaries. He established an early successful career with works such as *The Adoration of the Shepherds* and *Madonna and Child* (c.1695). Due to his successes, his work was much imitated, and his achievements subsequently declined as his paintings became less distinguishable from those of his followers.

Marc, Franz (1880–1916) German EXPRESSIONIST painter, one of the leading members of Der BLAUE REITER. He studied in Munich and was in Paris from 1903 to 1906; early influences include IMPRESSIONISM and the works of van GOGH. From 1908 he began making small animal figures in bronze, and developed a personally symbolic colour system in his works, e.g. *The Blue Horse* (1911). Along with KANDINSKY, he formed the New Artists Association in 1910, and then der Blaue Reiter in 1911. Later works, influenced by DELAUNAY and CUBISM, are more abstract although still powerfully symbolic, e.g. *Fighting Forms* (1913). Marc was killed fighting in World War I.

Marinetti, Filipo *see* **Futurism**.

Marlowe, Christopher (1564–93) English dramatist and poet. He was one of the first English dramatists to use blank verse to great dramatic and poetic effect in his plays, the most famous of which are *Tamburlaine the Great* (1590) and his masterpiece *Doctor Faustus* (1604). He also wrote some very fine classically inspired poetry, e.g. *Hero and Leander*, published posthumously in 1598, and the superb lyric "Come Live with me, and Be My Love." He was probably an atheist (see KYD), and was also probably a secret agent in the employ of the Elizabethan government at one stage. He was killed in a tavern brawl. SHAKESPEARE paid him a fine tribute in *As You Like It*: "Dead Shepherd, now I find thy saw of might: / 'Who ever lov'd that lov'd not at first sight?' "

Marquez, Gabriel Garcia (1928–) Colombian novelist. His masterpiece is *One Hundred Years of Solitude* (1967), a vivid narrative of the lives of a family in a decaying, provincial village. Marquez is generally regarded as the greatest practitioner of MAGIC REALISM. His novel, *The General in his Labyrinth* (1990), a fictionalized biography of Simon Bolivar, the hero of Latin American independence, seemed to many critics to mark a new departure in his work in its sombre, realistic approach to its subject.

Marquis, Don[ald Robert Perry] (1878–1937) American newspaper columnist, author of several books, e.g. *archys life of mehitabel* [sic] (1934), narrated by a cockroach, Archy, often featuring an alley cat called Mehitabel, and with a minor cast drawn from all parts of the animal kingdom. The poems (written in lower case as Archy cannot use the shift keys) display a rare combination of sharp wit and knockabout humour, with flashes of remarkable lyricism. Marquis remains one of the most underrated American poets.

Marsh, Reginald (1898–1954) American painter. He worked as an illustrator for *Harper's Bazaar* and *The New Yorker* and painted seriously from about 1923. He painted the tawdry, downbeat side of city life in the Depression of the 1930s, contrasting it with the contentment of the rich. His work was therefore in the social-realist tradition, and suggests the influence of German NEUE SACHLICHKEIT. Typical works include *The Park Bench* (1933) and *Pip and Flip* (1932).

Marvell, Andrew (1621–78) English poet. A (passive) supporter of Parliament during the English Civil War, Marvell became member of parliament for Hull in 1659, a position he held until his death. His verse satires were much enjoyed by the wits of the day, even by those whose vices were attacked. His "Last Instructions to a Painter," for example, a coldly brilliant assault on the moral and political corruption of the court, was particularly liked by Charles II. His strange, METAPHYSICAL poems, e.g. "The Garden" and "Upon Appleton House," display an enormous talent for symbolism and metaphor, and are now very highly regarded. His poem of 1650 celebrating Cromwell's suppression of the Irish Rebellion, "An Horatian Ode upon Cromwell's Return from Ireland," remains one of the great political poems of all times, in its cool, restrained appreciation of Cromwell's stature.

Marx, Karl (1818–83) German philosopher. His theories on class struggle dominated 20th-century political thought from the Bolshevik Revolution of 1917 to the collapse of the Communist regimes in Eastern Europe in 1989–90. *Das Kapital*, his study of the economics of capitalism, appeared in 1867; subsequent volumes, edited by **Friedrich Engels** (1820–95), appeared in 1885 and 1895. *Das Kapital* is the most unread and unreadable influential book of all time. Marx himself seems to have been bored stiff by it. His literary criticism, however, which is scattered throughout his writing, is often intensely interesting and provocative, his favourite writers being AESCHYLUS, SHAKESPEARE and GOETHE. HEINE was a friend, and he very much admired BALZAC. *Marxist Literary Criticism* is the application of Marx and Engels' theories to literature, a process that reached its lowest depths in the 1930s doctrine of "socialist realism," and its accompanying feeble theorizing. The preference of Marx and Engels for Balzac over ZOLA, and Engels' advice to the English novelist Margaret Harkness that propaganda novels don't work, raises issues that socialist realism simply ignored.

Masaccio [Tommaso di Ser Giovanni di Mone] (1401–c.1428) Florentine painter, a key figure of the early RENAISSANCE. His earliest dated work, the San Giovenale triptych (1422), portrays *The Madonna and Child with Saints,* painted with revolutionary realism. The figures and the throne are solidly modelled, with all the weight and authority of a sculpture, revealing Masaccio's indebtedness to DONATELLO. Masaccio is properly the heir to GIOTTO in his rejection of Gothic elegance and decorative detail, and his development of perspective is informed by the architecture of BRUNELLESCHI. His most important surviving masterpieces are the Pisa polyptych (1426), the Brancacci Chapel frescoes, particularly those on *The Life of St Peter*, in Santa Maria del Carmine, Florence, and the *Trinity* fresco (c.1428) in Santa Maria Novella, Florence.

Masefield, John [**Edward**] (1878–1967) English poet. His *Salt-Water Ballads* (1902) includes his best-known poem, "I must go down to the sea again." Many of his later poems, e.g. *The Everlasting Mercy* (1911), caused much scandal with their frank treatment of such themes as rural brutality and incest. His poetic reputation, once very large, shrank rapidly after his appointment as POET LAUREATE in 1930.

Masolino da Panicale (c.1383–1447) Florentine painter. He trained under GHIBERTI and was influenced by GENTILE DA FABRIANO. His early work is in the fluid, elegant style of INTERNATIONAL GOTHIC, as in the idealized and decorative *Madonna and Child* (1423). Subsequent works, such as *The Crucifixion* from the San Clemente frescoes (1428–31) in Rome, were influenced by the solid, sculptural painting style of MASACCIO; Masolino collaborated with him on the frescoes for the Brancacci Chapel of Santa Maria del Carmine in Florence (c.1425–8). Later works revert to a more Gothic style of decorative line, although he maintained a sense of pictorial space and perspective.

Masson, André (1896–1987) French painter, one of the circle of SURREALISTS that included BRETON, MIRÉ and ERNST. He established techniques of "automatic" linear drawings based on the expression of the subconcious. Paintings were developed incorporating pigments, sand and adhesive. He broke away from the Surrealist group in the late 1920s, and his later works have a mythological symbolism with imagery derived from Spanish bullfights or from nature, e.g. *Meditations on an Oak Leaf* (1942).

Master of Flemalle, *see* **Campin, Robert.**

Matisse, Henri (1869–1954) French painter who studied law before beginning art classes in 1892. Early influences include the NEOIMPRESSIONISM of SIGNAC. At the Salon d'Automne in 1905 he exhibited, along with DERAIN and VLAMINCK, the fresh, brightly coloured works that earned them the soubriquet "Fauves" (*see* FAUVISTS). He continued to paint more abstract and decorative works, emphasizing the flat picture plane rather than spatial depth and volume, e.g. *Joie* *de Vivre* (1906). Subsequent works were more austere and formal, e.g. *Bathers by a River* (1916–17) although he gradually developed a more naturalistic style in his series of *Odalisques* (1920s). Despite serious illness, his late works are joyful and brightly coloured. He made use of cut-outs and COLLAGE in simple compositions , e.g. *Escargot.* Notable sculptures include *Back I-IV* (1909–30), and he designed the Chapel of the Rosary at Vence (1949–51), including ceramic tiles and vestments, as a gift for the nuns who cared for him during his illness.

Matsuo Basho *see* **Basho**.

Maugham, W[illiam] Somerset (1874–1965) English novelist, dramatist and short-story writer. His first novel was *Liza of Lambeth* (1897), based on his experiences as a doctor working in the London slums. His best-known novels are *Of Human Bondage* (1915), which is another semi-autobiographical work, *The Moon and Sixpence* (1919), based on the life of the painter Paul Gauguin, and the satirical comedy *Cakes and Ale* (1930). Several of his plays, e.g. *The Circle* (1921) and *The Constant Wife* (1926), both of which examine the typical Maugham themes of hypocrisy and infidelity, were very successful. His masterpiece is often said to be the short story "Rain," in *The Trembling of a Leaf* (1921), which describes the love of a sexually repressed missionary for a prostitute. Maugham was a British secret agent during World War I, and his experiences form the basis of his enthralling spy novel *Ashenden* (1928).

Maurer, Alfred Henry (1868–1932) American painter. His early paintings are naturalistic in the IMPRESSIONIST style, but from 1908 he began to experiment more under the influence of FAUVISM, and his late works show an interest in CUBISM. He exhibited in the ARMORY SHOW of 1913. His potential was somewhat stifled by the conservatism of his father, who was a lithographer. Maurer committed suicide shortly after his father's death. Typical works include *Still Life with Fish* (1927–8).

Mauve, Anton (1838–88) Dutch painter, prominent leader of The Hague School. He painted small, delicately lit landscapes which show the influence of COROT and MILLET. His work was popular, and he was admired by his nephew van GOGH, whom he encouraged to paint. His work is well represented in Dutch collections and abroad, e.g. *Scheveningen* (1874).

Mayakovsky, Vladimir *see* **Futurism**.

Medici Italian family, political rulers of Florence in the 15th century and dukes of Tuscany from the 16th century to 1737. They were important patrons of the arts throughout their dynasty. Artists who came under their patronage at various times included DONATELLO, BRUNELLESCHI, Fra ANGELICO, Fra Filippo LIPPI and his son Filippino, MICHELANGELO, VERROCCHIO, RAPHAEL, VASARI and BOLOGNA. Cosimo I de' Medici [Cosimo the Elder] began the great art collection now in the Uffizi, Florence.

medium A material used in art, e.g. oil in painting, pencil in drawing, or bronze in sculpture. The term is also used to denote a method, e.g. painting as opposed to sculpture.

melodrama A form of drama, so named from the Greek for "song" plus "drama", that seems to have arisen in 18th-century France and that contained elements of music, spectacle, sensational incidents and sentimentalism (see SENTIMENTAL COMEDY). The form reached its peak in the popular theatre of 19th-century England, when quite spectacular stage effects often accompanied the action, and villains became blacker than black in their persecution of pure heroes and heroines. A typical example of the form is *The Miller and*

his Men (1813) by Isaac Pocock (1782–1835), a Gothic
melodrama with splendid bandits, virtuous and faithful young lovers, battles, a wild ravine, and an explod-
ing bridge at the climax. *See also* DOMESTIC TRAGEDY.

Melville, Herman (1819–91) American novelist, short-
story writer and poet. His early experiences as a sailor,
including service on a whaler, imprisonment for
mutiny, and captivity among cannibals, are reflected
in his early novels, e.g. *Typee* (1846) and *Omoo* (1847).
His masterpiece, and one of the greatest of all novels,
is *Moby Dick* (1851), a complex and symbolic narrative
in which Captain Ahab leads his whaling crew in a
doomed quest for the white whale that bit off his leg.
Other notable works include the satirical romance
Pierre, or the Ambiguities (1852), the magnificent story
"Bartleby the Scrivener," which is about a clerk who
lives and eventually dies by the phrase "I would prefer
not to," and his great short novel *Billy Budd, Foretop-
man*, published posthumously in 1924. This last work,
a tale of innocence destroyed by evil, was turned into a
popular opera by Benjamin Britten in 1951. Melville
died poor and neglected, but is now regarded as a great
writer.

Memling *or* **Memlinc, Hans** (*c*.1430/40–1494) German-
born Dutch painter, probably a pupil of Rogier van der
WEYDEN. His works are influenced by his master in
terms of subject and composition, but they have a
calmer, more serene quality in contrast to van der
Weyden's emotional intensity. He was a prolific and
popular artist and carried on a successful career as a
portraitist. Notable works include *Tommaso Portinari
and his Wife* (*c*.1468).

Menander (*c*.342–*c*.292BC) Greek dramatist, whose
"new comedies" (*see* COMEDY) were known only from
small fragments and through adaptations by the
Roman dramatists Terence and Plautus until the 20th

century. A complete play, *The Misanthropist*, was discovered in Egypt in 1957.

Mengs, Anton Raffael (1728–79) German painter prominent in the NEOCLASSICAL movement. He was taught by his father and achieved success with his portraits, becoming court painter from 1745. In 1761 he was invited to Spain, where his portraits and ceilings for the royal palaces were preferred to those of his rival, TIEPOLO. With the exception of the Parnassus ceiling painting in the Villa Albani in Rome, his portraits were more noteworthy than his frescoes. He expounded his theories in *Considerations on Beauty and Taste in Painting* (1672).

Meredith, George (1828–1909) English novelist and poet. His novels, e.g. *The Ordeal of Richard Feverel* (1859) and *The Egoist* (1879), are complex studies of human relationships in which the woman's perspective is often the most sympathetically represented. Meredith's strange, intricate dialogue and narration is quite unique. His sonnet sequence *Modern Love* (1862), virtually a novel in verse form, is an intriguing and innovative study of the dissolution of a marriage.

Metaphysical painting An art movement begun in Italy in 1917 by CARRÉ and de CHIRICO. They sought to portray the world of the subconscious by presenting real objects in incongruous juxtaposition, as in their *Metaphysical Interiors* and *Muses* series (1917). Carré abandoned the movement after a very short time, and by the early 1920s both artists had developed other interests. Although short-lived, the movement did have some influence on other artists of the time.

Metaphysical poetry A poetry movement of the 17th century, noted for intense feeling, extended metaphor and striking, elaborate imagery, often with a mystical element. DONNE is regarded as the first important Metaphysical poet. Other notable poets described as

Metaphysical include CRASHAW, COWLEY, HERBERT, TRAHERNE and VAUGHAN.

method acting *see* **Stanislavsky, Konstantin**.

Meyerhold, Vsevolod (1874–1940) Russian theatrical producer and director. By the time the Bolsheviks came to power in 1917, Meyerhold was recognized as the most prominent exponent of avant-garde ideas and productions on the Russian stage. Among the plays he produced at this Meyerhold Theatre were those of Mayakovsky (*see* FUTURISM). His productions (which were strongly influential on BRECHT) cheerfully abandoned traditional conventions, such as the sanctity of the proscenium arch, and broke plays up into episodic segments. Stage sets were determinedly *Constructivist*, i.e. they used technological artefacts derived from industrial processes to emphasize the kinetic, active nature of the stage (in large part, this was a development from Russian Futurism). Actors were encouraged to think of themselves as "biomechanisms," and to study circus acrobatics and the conventions of COMMEDIA DELL'ARTE. Meyerhold's ideas inevitably proved intolerable to the Soviet cultural commissars of Socialist REALISM and he was executed in 1940. *See also* STANISLAVSKY.

Meynell, Alice *see* **Thompson, Francis**.

Michelangelo Buonarotti (1475–1564) Florentine painter, sculptor, draughtsman, architect and poet, an outstanding figure in art history and influential genius of the Italian RENAISSANCE. He trained in Florence with GHIRLANDAIO. Lorenzo the Magnificent [de' MEDICI] was one of his early patrons. In Rome from 1496–1501 he established his reputation with the sculptures *Bacchus* (1496–7) and *Pietà* (1499). The fresco of *The Battle of Cascina*, commissioned in 1501 for the Palazzo Vecchio, was not completed, but before returning to Rome he executed the powerful sculpture of *David* (1501–4) for the Florentine Council. From 1505 Pope Julius II was his patron, and it was he who commissioned the ceiling paintings for the Sistine Chapel (1508–12), Michelangelo's great and lasting achievement. The upper part of the ceiling contains images from the book of Genesis, lower down are the prophets and sybils, and the lunettes and spandrels portray characters from the ancestry of Christ and the Virgin. The *Last Judgment* fresco (1536–41) on the altar wall was a much later addition and reflects the pessimism of the artist and a post-Reformation obsession with wrath and punishment. The intervening time was spent working in the Medici Chapel, San Lorenzo, on the tombs of Lorenzo and Giuliano de' Medici. Much of his later life was taken up with the rebuilding of St Peter's, but notable later works include the unfinished *Rondanini Pieté* and a series of drawings of the Holy family and the Crucifixion for Vittorio Colonna. Michelangelo's art inspired and affected his contemporaries and subsequent generations of painters with incalculable effects up to the present day.

Middleton, Thomas (*c*.1570–1627) English dramatist. His two powerful tragedies, *The Changeling* (1622) and *Women Beware Women* (1627), are now highly regarded. His other works include the satirical comedy *A Trick to Catch the Old One* (1608) and a political satire, *A Game at Chesse* (1624). The latter play almost resulted in himself and the actors being imprisoned. He collaborated with many other dramatists, e.g. DEKKER.

Millais, Sir John Everett (1829–96) English painter. A child prodigy, he studied at the Royal Academy Schools where he met Holman HUNT and, along with ROSSETTI, they founded the PRE-RAPHAELITE BROTHERHOOD. They embraced a philosophy of truth to nature and attention to detail, chosing themes that embodied strongly poetic or moral sentiment. The results often involved posed, studio tableaux in clashing colours, and the Pre-Raphaelites were unpopular with the critics until championed by John RUSKIN, whose wife Millais later married. Millais gradually achieved success and later abandoned his Pre-Raphaelite style. He became President of the Royal Academy in 1896 and painted the portraits of many prominent politcal figures, including *Gladstone* and *Carlyle*. Other notable works are *Bubbles* (1886) and *The Boyhood of Raleigh* (1870).

Millay, Edna St Vincent (1892–1950) American poet. Her early collections, e.g. *Renascence and Other Poems* (1917) and *A Few Figs from Thistles* (1920), established her reputation as a daring, Bohemian-style New Woman, a real-life example of the fictional "liberated" females who were appearing in the novels and drama of the period.

Miller, Arthur (1915–) American dramatist. His well-constructed tragedies include three classics of the American stage: *Death of a Salesman* (1949), which describes the destruction of a travelling salesman by the false values of everyday society, *The Crucible* (1952), in which the Salem witchcraft trials are used to comment on Cold-War McCarthyism, and *A View from the Bridge* (1955), a curious yet successful combination of naturalism with the conventions of Greek drama. He married Marilyn Monroe in 1955 (they divorced in 1961), and wrote the screenplay for her last film *The Misfits* (1961).

Miller, Henry (1891–1980) American novelist, notorious for his graphic descriptions of his numerous sexual experiences in such works as *Tropic of Cancer* (1931) and *Tropic of Capricorn* (1939). He was a strong influence on the BEAT GENERATION and on other writers (see DURRELL). The best examination of his work is in ORWELL's essay "Inside the Whale."

Milles, Carl (1875–1955) Swedish sculptor who studied in Paris and Munich and was influenced by RODIN. He experimented with various styles, which he incorporated in his work. He was professor of the academy at Stockholm and also taught in the US. Notable works include the Peace Monument (1936) and the Orpheus Fountain (1930–36).

Millet, Jean-François (1814–75) French painter who studied at Cherbourg before winning a scholarship in 1837 to train in Paris. He earned his living by portraiture and exhibited his first major genre painting, *The Winnower*, at the Salon in 1848. He lived at BARBIZON from 1849, and his pastoral scenes developed a strong sense of realism. In 1850 he exhibited *The Sower* along with works by COURBET at the Salon, and he was labelled a social-realist although his works had no political motive. From the 1860s he painted more direct landscapes.

Milne, A[lan] A[lexander] (1882–1956) English writer and dramatist. His children's books, e.g. *When We Were Very Young* (1924), *Winnie-the-Pooh* (1926) and *The House at Pooh Corner* (1928), are much loved classics of children's literature.

Milton, John (1608–74) English poet. One of the most formidably learned of all English poets, Milton had a European-wide reputation by his late twenties. His early poems, e.g. the magnificent elegy *Lycidas* (1637), are steeped in the humanist tradition which looked to classical literature for ethical principles and modes of expression, and to Scripture and the Christian tradition for faith. He supported Parliament during the Civil War and wrote tracts attacking royalty and episcopacy. His most famous prose work is the tract *Areopagitica* (1644), a rousing defence of the liberty of free speech. His masterpiece is the great epic poem on the Fall of Man, *Paradise Lost* (1667–74). Other notable works include the verse drama *Samson Agonistes* (1671), i.e. "Samson at the Games," in which the blind hero is clearly to be identified with Milton himself (he was completely blind by 1651). Some of his sonnets, e.g. "On His Blindness," are among the greatest ever written. Robert GRAVES' novel *Wife to Mr Milton* (1942), is an intriguing study of one obsessive genius by another.

Miró, Joan (1893–1983) Spanish painter, sculptor and designer. His early works were influenced by DADA, CUBISM and Catalan art. *Catalan Landscape* (1923) marks the beginning of his SURREALIST style. From the late 1920s, his works are characterized by simplified, brightly coloured forms, free-floating against a plain background; a dream world more whimsically abstract and humorous than the works of his contemporaries, DALI and MAGRITTE. Notable among his works are the *Sun Wall* and *Moon Wall* murals (1958) for the UNESCO building in Paris, and his *Constellation* series (1940). His sculptural works were highly inventive and linked to the imagery of his paintings.

Mishima, Yukio (1925–70) Japanese novelist and short-story writer. His work, e.g. the novel *The Temple of the Golden Pavilion* (1956), is dominated by the themes of homosexuality, beauty and death. The opening words of the epigraph to his *Confessions of a Mask* (1949), from DOSTOEVSKY's *The Brothers Karamazov* sum up his central concern: "Beauty is a terrible and awful thing!" (WILDE was another European influence on him). He committed suicide in public while exhorting his followers to perform a military coup. A good introduction to the man and his work is Paul Schrader's film of 1985, *Mishima*.

Mitchell, James Leslie *see* **Gibbon, Lewis Grassic**.

mobile *see* **Calder, Alexander**.

Modigliani, Amadeo (1884–1920) Italian painter and

sculptor. His early training was in Florence and Naples, but from 1906 he lived and worked mainly in Paris, and little of his Italian work has survived. Influenced by BRANCUSI, he took up sculpture and created naive, powerful figures and heads inspired by AFRICAN and primitive art, e.g. *Head* (*c*.1911–12). His paintings, mainly portraits, were influenced by CÉZANNE and PICASSO, e.g. *Jeanne Hebuterne* (1919), and reached a peak of simplification of form and refinement of line and colour in the last decade of his life.

Moholy-Nagy, Laszlo (1895–1946) Hungarian-born painter and sculptor. He trained in Hungary and was initially influenced by CUBISM. In 1920 he moved to Berlin and was subsequently inspired by CONSTRUCTIVISM. In 1922 he exhibited metal sculptures in his first one-man show. Later pieces involve the use of transparent sheeting and film to organize space. From 1923 he was head of metalwork at the BAUHAUS and began to experiment with film and with light-sensitive paintings, or "photograms." He left the Bauhaus in 1928 and worked in Paris, Amsterdam and London as a photographer and designer. He lived in Chicago from 1937 and directed the New Bauhaus, later the Institute of Design, until his death. His importance lies in his pioneering experimentation and in his influence as a teacher. He published his treatise, *The New Vision*, in 1946 and *Vision in Motion* was published posthumously later the same year.

Molière [pseud. of Jean-Baptiste Poquelin] (1622–73) French dramatist. Molière's great comedies are as popular now as when they were first performed; only SHAKESPEARE's plays have been performed more widely. Some examples of the plays are: *Tartuffe* (1664), a crushing satire on religious hypocrisy; *The Misanthrope* (1666), a study of a cynic in love; and

The Imaginary Invalid (1673), a hilarious depiction of hypochondria and quack medicine.

Mondrian, Piet (1872–1944) Dutch painter. A leading member of De STIJL, his early works contain SYMBOLIST and EXPRESSIONIST styles until 1911 when he moved to Paris and was influenced by CUBISM. His work gradually became more abstract, and his interest in horizontal and vertical lines became evident in his *Pier and Ocean* series (from 1913). He advanced his theories on Neoplasticism in the De Stijl magazine and developed the strict geometry of his paintings. His best remembered and most typical works are white and primary colour rectangles bounded by solidly rigid black lines, e.g. *Composition in Yellow and Blue* (1929). Mondrian's ordered and harmonious compositional structure was the antithesis of Expressionism. From 1940 he lived in New York, and other notable works include *Broadway Boogie Woogie* (1942–3) and the unfinished *Victory Boogie Woogie*.

Monet, Claude Oscar (1840–1926) French IMPRESSIONIST painter, whose *Impression: Sunrise* (1872) gave its name to the movement. He came from Le Havre, where his teacher, BOUDIN, encouraged him in outdoor painting. From 1862 to 1863 he studied in Paris, where he met RENOIR and SISLEY, and together they began the direct studies of nature and changing light that was to characterize their works. MANET was an early influence on Monet, but Monet was more interested in experiment with light and colour, e.g. *Women in a Garden* (1867). In London with PISSARRO in 1870–71 he admired the works of TURNER and CONSTABLE and did a series of paintings of the Thames. Returning to France, he lived for a time at Argenteuil before settling at Giverny. From the 1890s, he concentrated on series paintings of places or objects at different seasons or times of day, recording the effects of changing light and shifting colours, e.g. *Haystacks* (1891) and *Rouen Cathedral* (1894). His paintings from later life, as his eyesight failed him, include the *Waterlilies* series (1899–1926). These are large vibrant canvases in which the subject is so secondary to the light effects that the forms are difficult to distinguish and become almost unintentionally abstracted.

monochrome A drawing or painting executed in one colour only. *See also* GRISAILLE.

Montaéés, Juan Martinez (1568–1694) Spanish sculptor. He lived and worked in Seville, where he carved and painted wooden statues of great dignity and grace. He ran a busy workshop and influenced both his own pupils, e.g. VELAZQUEZ and ZURBARÉN. His best-known masterpiece is the *Christ of Clemency* (1603–6), which is intensely moving in its poignant realism.

montage A technique similar to COLLAGE, where the images used are photographic.

Montagu, Mrs Elizabeth (1720–1800) English author and BLUESTOCKING, whose *Essay on the Writings and Genius of Shakespeare* (1769), a reply to VOLTAIRE's daft criticisms of SHAKESPEARE's work, was highly acclaimed by her contemporaries (her friend Dr JOHNSON, however, was not impressed, declaring that Voltaire's arguments were not worth responding to).

Montaigne, Michel Eyquem de (1553–92) French essayist. His essays first appeared in 1580. His achievement was to establish the essay as a literary form; his fascinating self-examination of his reflections on incidents in his life and on his favourite (usually Stoic) authors, has had a wide and lasting influence. His motto was "What do I Know?," with tolerance and anti-dogmatic scepticism being the dominant theme in his work. The essays were translated into English by John FLORIO in 1603, and SHAKESPEARE used this translation as one of the sources for *The Tempest* (1611).

Moore, Brian (1921–) Irish-born Canadian novelist.
Moore's highly praised novels place him in the first
rank of modern writers. The novels range in setting
from a Jesuit mission in 17th-century Canada in *Black
Robe* (1985), to 1980s Eastern Europe in *The Colour of
Blood* (1987), and, as in these two and *Catholics* (1972)
frequently involve Roman Catholic doctrine and practice. *The Lonely Passion of Judith Hearne* (1955) and *I
am Mary Dunne* (1968) have been hailed as being
among the most penetrating analyses of the female
psyche by any author. Moore also has a quite extraordinary gift for blending supernatural events with
the commonplace patterns of everyday life, as in the
astonishing novel *Cold Heaven* (1983), in which a
woman is haunted by visions of the Virgin Mary.

Moore, George [Augustus] (1852–1933) Irish novelist.
His novels, e.g. *Esther Waters* (1894) and *The Brook
Kerith* (1916), were heavily influenced by BALZAC and
ZOLA and other French NATURALIST and REALIST novelists. His first novel, *A Modern Lover* (1883), is a fairly
typical example of his risqué novels of modern life. He
was a friend of YEATS, and played a leading role in the
founding of the ABBEY THEATRE.

Moore, Henry (1898–1987) English sculptor. He studied at Leeds School of Art and at the Royal Academy
and during the 1930s was involved in the same avant-
garde circles as Ben NICHOLSON and Barbara HEP-
WORTH. He was responsible for reviving the popularity
of direct carving methods, disliking the accepted
methods of modelling and casting pieces of sculpture.
AFRICAN and Mexican art had a profound influence on
his works, in which mass and solidity take precedence
over surface texture and detail, e.g. *Reclining Figure*
(1929). Despite the abstract form of much of his work,
the exploration of human relationships is evident in
pieces such as *Two Forms* (1934). The latent energy

and enormous presence of his sculptures became predominant as essentials were pared away. He explored the idea of pierced and hollowed masses, and the relationships of figures to landscape, e.g. *Reclining Figure* (1938). As a sculptor and draughtsman he was distinguished with awards from the art world and the civic world alike. Other notable works include his drawings from London Underground station shelters when he was a war artist during World War II.

Moore, Marianne [Craig] (1887–1972) American poet, noted for sophisticated and witty verse. T. S. ELIOT wrote the introduction to her *Selected Poems* (1935). Her description of poetry, in the poem "Poetry," as "imaginary gardens with real toads in them," is the best known of her teasing, oblique observations.

Moore, Thomas (1779–1852) Irish poet. His *Irish Melodies* (1807–34), songs of his own composition set to traditional Irish airs, achieved great popularity and are still loved and sung. Some of the best known are "Believe me, if all those Endearing Youth Charms," "The Harp that once through Tara's Halls," and "The Last Rose of Summer." His *Lalla Rookh* (1817), a series of oriental tales in verse, also enjoyed great popularity. He was a friend of BYRON, who praised him extravagantly. Byron gave Moore his unpublished *Memoirs*, which were subsequently bought and burned by their publisher John MURRAY, because of their sexually explicit content.

More, Hannah (1745–1833) English writer, who became one of the most prominent and popular members of the BLUESTOCKING circle gravitating around Dr JOHNSON, a world captured in her good-natured poem *Bas Bleu* (1786). Her works include tragedies, one of which, *Percy* (1777), was produced by her friend David GARRICK (earning her over £750), and many poems. The greater part of her output, however, consisted of "improving" works directed at reforming the morals and domestic economy of the poor, e.g. the monthly tracts published in 1795–8 under the title of *The Cheap Repository*, and the didactic novel *Coelebs in Search of a Wife* (1809). (Ten editions of the latter were sold in one year.) She was also concerned with reforming the morals of the upper classes, e.g. *Thoughts on the Importance of the Manners of the Great to General Society* (1788), a work which, after the French Revolution, was much pondered upon by writers and policy formers of all parties in Britain. More was in fact a sharply witty and tough-minded writer. She made a lot of money from her writing, gave generously to charity, and died leaving £30,000 to various causes.

More, Henry (1614–87) English philosopher, who became the leading light of a small group of Anglican divines known as the *Cambridge Platonists* (*see* PLATO, NEOPLATONISM). The writings and teachings of all the Cambridge Platonists can be cloudy and contradictory, but may be summarized as: (a) a rejection of dogmatism, e.g. of Calvin's strictures on man's sinful nature, and of materialism, especially that of Hobbes; (b) the compatibility of reason with Christianity in an essentially harmonious universe; (c) the fundamental unity of truth and goodness; (d) the necessity for combining reason, Christian faith and the writings of great pagan philosophers such as Plato, in the quest to explain the true, orderly nature of God's creation. The Cambridge Platonists were much influenced by Humanist thinkers such as Erasmus (*see* Thomas MORE), and by the tolerant, learned writings of the great Anglican divine HOOKER. More's works include *Psychozoia Platonica* (1642) and *Divine Dialogues* (1668). Other notable members of the group were Benjamin Whichcote (1609–83) and Ralph Cudworth (1617–88).

More, Sir Thomas (1478–1535) English statesman and

Roman Catholic saint. He was Henry VIII's Lord Chancellor, and his refusal to recognize the annulment of Henry's marriage to Catherine of Aragon and declaration of supremacy over the Church of England led to his execution for treason. More was widely recognized as an honourable man, and his execution revulsed moderate Catholic and Protestant opinion throughout Europe. More's greatest work is his fantasy of a supposedly ideally organized state, *Utopia* (1516). More's close friend, the great humanist Erasmus, supervized the printing of *Utopia* (the word means "no place"). The work spawned a host of imitations throughout the centuries but the impact of 20th-century totalitarianism has lessened enthusiams for the form. Aldous HUXLEY's *Island* (1962) is a modern example of a Utopian novel; the same author's *Brave New World* (1932) is an example of its opposite, a "dystopia" or "bad place." More was canonized in 1935, and has always been admired for his firm principles and love of justice. His involvement in heresy trials, however, and his dispute with Tyndale (*see* AUTHORIZED VERSION) show a less attractive side of his character.

Morgan, Edwin George (1920–) Scottish poet and translator, best known for his witty, experimental verse, e.g. the much anthologized "The First Men on Mercury," and for his poems on Scottish life, e.g. *Glasgow Sonnets* (1972).

Morisot, Berthe (1841–95) French painter. She was a pupil of COROT and also of MANET, whose brother she married. She was instrumental in encouraging Manet to paint outdoors and to experimnent with IMPRESSIONIST colours. She exhibited in all but one of the Impressionist shows and had 13 paintings at the London Impressionist Exhibition of 1905. Typical works include *The Cradle* (1873) and *Jeune Femme au Bal* (1880).

Morris, William (1834–96) English designer, poet, writer, artist and craftsman. Morris was a social reformer who believed that people would be enabled to do better work if they had beautiful surroundings, and to this end he was instrumental in founding the ARTS AND CRAFTS MOVEMENT. He drew his inspiration from the medieval guild systems of the Middle Ages, convinced that utility and art were inseparable. He formed a manufacturing and decorating company producing wallpapers, fabrics and artefacts, and also started the Kelmscott Press to produce a better quality of books in a range of typefaces. The artist BURNE-JONES was one of several who worked for the company, and Morris's own elegant style in some ways anticipated ART NOUVEAU.

Morris' best-known prose romance, *New from Nowhere* (1891), is a Utopian (*see* THOMAS MORE) fantasy about a future socialist commonwealth of England. His other prose fictional works are mostly sagas of ancient northern Europe, e.g. *The House of the Wolfings* (1889), and are a curious blend of gore and sentiment. His best-known poem, *The Earthly Paradise* (1868–70), is a long, Norse-inspired saga in which a group of stranded Vikings recount stories at tedious length.

Moses, Grandma [Mary Anne Robertson] (1860–1961) American painter. She was entirely self-taught and was discovered by the collector L. J. Calder through a small exhibition of paintings and embroideries in her local drugstore. The simplistic directness of her style and her bright, uncomplicated colours soon won her popularity and success. She had a one-man show at the age of 80 in New York in 1940, and her 100th birthday was declared a state holiday. Her works are a romantic and unsophisticated record of country life in her native New York State.

Mosley, [Sir] Nicholas [3rd Baron Ravensdale] (1923–) English novelist. His early novels, e.g. *Accident* (1964, filmed by Joseph Losey in 1967) and *Impossible Object* (1968), were highly acclaimed in their day, but interest in Mosley's work declined due to a growing critical distaste for anyone labelled, as he was, as an "experimental" English writer. His novel *Hopeful Monsters* (1990), however, a wide-ranging study of the dilemmas of modern life, reinstated his reputation as a highly distinctive and gifted author. Mosley's father was the British fascist leader Sir Oswald Mosley, of whom he wrote a damning two-volume biography, *Rules of the Game* (1982) and *Beyond the Pale* (1983).

Motherwell, Robert (1915–) American painter. Originally a graduate in philosophy and an aesthetics theorist, he took up painting professionally in 1941. Influences include PICASSO and MATISSE, although his work is mainly in the ABSTRACT EXPRESSIONIST tradition. He experimented with COLLAGE and with colour staining, developing his compositions with black or white lines. Notable works include the series *Elegies to the Spanish Republic* begun in 1949. He also wrote a great deal on art and artists and produced a series of publications entitled *The Documents of Modern Art* (from 1944).

Mucha, Alfons (1860–1939) Czech painter, designer and graphic artist famous for his ART NOUVEAU posters for the actress Sarah Bernhardt in the 1890s in Paris. In Prague he designed the decor for the burgomaster's room in the municipal hall, windows for the Cathedral, and his country's first banknotes and stamps. Part of his *Slav Epic* (1910s-20s) paintings were shown in the US but are now stored in Czechoslovakia.

Muggeridge, Malcolm [Thomas] (1903–90) English journalist. He was Moscow correspondent for the

Guardian (1930–33), an experience which resulted in complete disillusion with Communism. He published a semi-autobiographical novel about his experiences in the USSR, *Winter in Moscow* (1934), a remarkably clear-eyed view of the horror of the Soviet Union, which is spoiled for modern readers by some unpleasant anti-Semitic passages. By 1940, when he published his creepily entertaining review of the decade, *The Thirties*, he had become a noted cynic, disliked by both left and right. His friend ORWELL's review of *The Thirties*, "brilliant but depressing," pointed out that the trouble with Muggeridge was not that he was wrong in seeing the 20th century as a "cesspool full of barbed wire," but that he seemed to enjoy it. Muggeridge served in World War II as a spy, most notably in Africa, where his nearest colleague was Graham GREENE, and in Paris at the end, where he did his best to help P. G. WODEHOUSE, whom most British people then regarded as a traitor. Muggeridge eventually became a nondenomenational Christian, then, under the influence of Mother Theresa, a Roman Catholic. He produced two superb volumes of autobiography, *The Green Stick* (1972) and *The Infernal Grove* (1973), collectively titled *Chronicles of Wasted Time*.

Muir, Edwin (1887–1959) Scottish poet, translator and critic. He and his wife **Willa** (1890–1970) produced what are still the standard English translations of KAFKA's novels in the 1930s. His volumes of poetry include *The Labyrinth* (1949) and *One Foot in Eden* (1956). His best poems, e.g. "A Child Dying," are powerfully elegiac in tone. His essays, collected in *Essays in Literature and Society* (1949), are still highly regarded.

Munch, Edvard (1860–1944) Norwegian painter. He studied in Oslo and was influenced by IMPRESSIONIST and SYMBOLIST works during visits to France in the

1880s. GAUGUIN's use of colour was particularly influential in the development of his emotional expressionism. Much of Munch's painting reflects a morbid obsession with sickness and isolation. The imagery is like a recurring nightmare, angst-ridden and violent in its distortion of line and powerful contrasts of blacks and reds. His best-known work, *The Scream* (1893), is typical of his most creative period. After recovering from a nervous breakdown in 1908, Munch's works take on a brighter more optimistic atmosphere. He carried out a series of murals for Oslo University and left most of his works to the city of Oslo, where it is housed in the Munch Museum.

Munro, Alice (1931–) Canadian novelist and short-story writer. Her stories, e.g. *Dance of the Happy Shades* (1968) and *Something I've Been Meaning to Tell You* (1974), are set in the fictional town of Jubilee, Ontario. The typical Munro story features a sensitive young girl's reactions to the petty struggles of small-town life.

Munro, Hector Hugh *see* **Saki**.

Murdoch, Dame Iris (1919–) Irish-born English novelist. Her novels are often described as intellectual sex comedies, with complex symbolism and a strong dash of the macabre. The novels include *A Severed Head* (1961), *The Sea, the Sea* (1978) and *The Book and the Brotherhood* (1987).

Murillo, Bartolomé Esteban (1618–82) Spanish painter from Seville whose early works were influenced by his older contemporary ZURBARÉN. He established his own reputation with a painting cycle for the Seville Franciscan Monastery in 1645 to 1646 and became the first director of the academy in Seville in 1660. He painted religious and genre scenes popular for their pretty sentimentality; soft draperies and misty backgrounds gave an appealing quality to his work. His reputation was high during the 18th century but declined thereafter. Large selections of his work are in the Prado, Madrid, and the Museo de Belles Artes, Seville.

Murray, John (1778–1843) English publisher whose authors included Jane AUSTEN, Thomas MOORE, BYRON, CRABBE and COLERIDGE. Despite Byron's alleged misquotation of the Bible, "Now Barabbas was a publisher," to Murray, he was renowned for his hospitality and generous assistance to authors, and his premises became a common meeting ground for many of the literary figures of the day. Murray was also a shrewd businessman; the basis for his prosperity was the burgeoning middle-class market for books in the Regency period. His edition of Byron's *The Corsair* (1814) sold over 10,000 copies on the first day of publication; he paid Byron around £20,000 for his works (and burned his *Memoirs*; *see* Thomas MOORE).

Musil, Robert [Elder von] (1880–1942) Austrian novelist and dramatist. His masterpiece is his huge unfinished novel, published in English as *The Man Without Qualities* (1953–60), a psychological study, in the EXISTENTIALIST manner, of a purposeless drifter in pre-1914 Vienna. Musil was a qualified engineer and also studied philosophy and psychology, and adopted an "empirical, scientific" approach to his characters and their decaying milieu. *The Man Without Qualities* is widely regarded as required reading for anyone interested in early 20th-century German and Central European intellectual currents.

N

Nabis A group of painters working in France in the 1890s. Principal members of the group were SERUSIER and VUILLARD. Influenced by the works and ideas of GAUGUIN and by oriental art, they worked in flat areas of strong colour, avoiding direct representation in favour of a symbolic approach of mystical revelation.

Nabokov, Vladimir (1899–1977) Russian-born American novelist and short-story writer. Nabokov and his family left Russia in 1919, following the 1917 Bolshevik revolution. After studying in England, Nabokov lived in Berlin and Paris, writing several novels in Russian, including *Despair* (1926). After settling in the US in 1940, he wrote and published in English. His most famous novel is one of his slightest, *Lolita* (1955), in which a middle-aged lecturer falls obsessively in love with a nymphet. Novels such as *Bend Sinister* (1947) and *Pale Fire* (1962) are better examples of his marvellous gift for narrative and sharp, ironic wit.

Naipaul, V[idiadhar] S[urajprasad] (1932–) Trinidad-born English novelist and travel writer. His family were of Indian (Brahmin) ancestry. He settled in England in the mid-1950s, and began writing novels set in Trinidad. His fourth novel, *A House for Mr Biswas* (1961), a humanely ironic semi-autobiographical study of Trinidad, established him as an important writer. His travel writing is also of the highest quality. He is a sharp observer of the various modes of oppression and exploitation, whether native or colonial, and (as with Norman LEWIS) his experiences can result in a novel, e.g. *A Bend in the River* (1979), a disturbing portrait of postcolonial Africa, or a travel book, e.g. *An Area of Darkness* (1964), a deeply pessimistic study of India. His brother, **Shiva Naipaul** (1932–85), was also a noted travel writer.

naive art Works by untrained artists whose style is noted for its innocence and simplicity. Scenes are often depicted literally, with little attention to formal perspective and with an intuitive rather than studied use of pictorial space, composition and colour. Naive painters have existed in various countries throughout the 20th century, independently of contemporary trends or movements in art, and their works are often fresh and invigorating by comparison. Notable naive painters include "Douanier" ROUSSEAU and Grandma MOSES.

Nanni di Banco (d.1421) Florentine sculptor. He was taught by his father, and the bulk of his work was commissioned for Florence Cathedral and the Or San Michele. He was greatly influenced by the ANTIQUE and by his contemporary DONATELLO, although the large number of his undated works makes the extent of his own innovations difficult to trace. Early works, e.g. *St Luke* (1408–13), show a graceful, elongated fullness of form that suggests the influence of Gothic art, while his mature masterpiece, *The Assumption*, combines the natural force and vigour of a Donatello sculpture with ideal Antique proportions.

Narayan, R[asipuram] K[rishnaswami] (1906–) Indian novelist who writes in English. Most of his gentle, witty fiction, e.g. *The World of Nagaraj* (1990), is set in a fictional Indian town called Malgudi (based on Mysore, where he lives), yet his appeal is worldwide. Graham GREENE recommended his first novel, *Swami and Friends* (1935), for publication.

Nashe, Thomas (1567–1601) English writer of pamphlets and tracts on various subjects, which were usually satirical and often contain barbs directed at his many literary and religious enemies. He was particularly virulent against the Puritans, and was heavily involved in the so-called "Martin Marprelate" pamphlet war. He also wrote poems, plays, and a striking PICARESQUE NOVEL, *The Unfortunate Traveller* (1594).

Nash, Ogden [Frederick] (1902–71) An American humorous poet. His fiendishly clever and quite unique irregular verse, as in *You Can't Get There from Here* (1957), was originally published in *The New Yorker* magazine (for which he worked) and has achieved lasting popularity.

Nash, Paul (1889–1946) English painter and illustrator. He was an official war artist in both World Wars and founded the avant-garde group Unit One in 1933. Essentially a landscape artist, his works are enhanced by an empathy with the land that helps to express the horror and devastation he witnessed in war, e.g. *We Are Making a New World* (1918). The influences of SURREALIST art and the works of de CHIRICO are evident in works such as *Monster Field* (1939). A major painting from World War II is *Totes Meer* (1940–41). Nash also carried out a number of exceptional book illustrations, in particular the 12 woodcut pictures of the story of creation from the Book of Genesis, commissioned by the Nonesuch Press, and the drawings for *Urn Burial* by Sir Thomas BROWNE.

Naturalism A term deriving from the late-19th French literary movement of the same name, denoting fiction characterized by close observation and documentation of everyday life, with a strong emphasis on the influence of the material world on individual behaviour. Naturalistic novels therefore tended to adopt a very deterministic approach to life and fiction, and most

practitioners of the form would have described themselves as socialists or social Darwinists. The leading
exponent of the school was ZOLA. (Some followers of
Zola were reputed to have written novels in which the
dialogue was a scrupulous reproduction of everyday
speech heard on the street; few of their works seem to
have survived.) The influence of the school on writers
in English was patchy; there are strong elements of
naturalism in George MOORE and Arnold BENNETT.
(Virginia WOOLF's rather severe strictures on Bennett,
in *The Common Reader* (1925), encapsulate the standard English highbrow response to the school. Many
American writers, however, e.g. DREISER, were
strongly influenced by the Naturalist doctrines. *See
also* MARX; *compare* REALISM.

Navarrete, Juan Fernández (1526–79) Spanish painter from Navarre, who studied in Italy, possibly under
TITIAN, and from 1568 was court painter to Philip II
of Spain. Out of the naturalistic Spanish tradition he
evolved a unique style reflecting the monumental her-
oism of his Italian training. His works for Philip II in
the Escorial are still in situ, and of the 36 paintings
commissioned in 1576 for the Escorial Church, he completed eight before he died. His later works, notably
The Burial of St Lawrence (1579), anticipate CARAVAG-
GIO's effects of chiaroscuro.

Nazarenes An art movement based on the Brotherhood
of St Luke formed in Vienna in 1809. It involved painters of German and Austrian origins, who worked
mainly in Italy. Inspired by the medieval guild systems, they worked cooperatively with a common goal
of reviving Christian art. Influences included German
medieval art and Italian RENAISSANCE painting.
Notable among their works are the frescoes of the *Life
of St Joseph* (1816–17) for the Casa Bartholdy in Rome,

which are now housed in Berlin. A leading member of the group was CORNELIUS.

Neoclassicism A term denoting any movement in the Arts emphasizing the virtues of imitating the style and precepts of the great classical writers and artists (Neoclassicist principles in literature derive mostly from the writings of ARISTOTLE – principally the *Poetics* – and some observations by the Augustan Roman poets, VIRGIL and HORACE). The hallmarks of Neoclassicism are traditionally defined as balance, moderation, attention to formal rules – such as the dramatic *Unities*, in which time and space is strictly ordered around a sequential plot with a beginning, middle and end – avoidance of emotional display and distrust of enthusiasm, and the assumption that human nature has changed little, if at all, since Classical times. Neoclassicism is frequently contrasted with ROMANTICISM, and, interestingly, the strongest period of Neoclassicism in art and architecture is contemporary with the peak period of Romanticism, the late 18th and early 19th centuries (*see* GOETHE). (A less savoury aspect of Neoclassicism was identified by the art historian Kenneth Clark, when he observed that although not all Neoclassical art was totalitarian, much if not all of totalitarian art was Neoclassical.

In literature, neoclassicism is generally held to have begun with Petrarch in the mid-14th century. The greatest neoclassical English poets are DRYDEN and POPE; the greatest neoclassical English critic is sometimes said to be Dr Johnson, but Johnson's espousal of neoclassical virtues was heavily qualified, particularly in response to French criticism of Shakespeare as virtually a "literary savage." Neoclassicism had been a powerful influence on French literature of the 17th century, particularly in drama (see CORNEILLE,

RACINE), but has never won wide acceptance among writers in English, not even in the 18th century.

In art and architecture Neoclassicism was the dominant style in Europe in the late 18th and early 19th centuries. It followed on from, and was essentially a reaction against, BAROQUE and ROCOCO styles. Classical forms were employed to express the reasoned enlightenment of the age, and Neoclassical painters, such as CANOVA and DAVID adhered to the Classical principles of order, symmetry and calm. At the same time, they felt free to embrace ROMANTIC themes, and much of David's work in particular is charged with emotion in a tensely controlled form. *See also* CLASSICISM.

Neoimpressionism A scientific and logical development of IMPRESSIONISM pioneered by the pointillist painters SEURAT, SIGNAC and PISSARRO. The brokenly applied brushwork of MONET and RENOIR was extended and refined to a system of dots of pure colour, applied according to scientific principles, with the intention of creating an image of greater purity and luminosity than had hitherto been achieved.

Neoplatonism A synthesis of Platonic (*see* PLATO) and mystical concepts that originated in the Greek-speaking Mediterranean world of the 3rd century. **Plotinus** (*c*.205–*c*.270) was the main figure behind the synthesis. His ideas, such as the notion of a world soul and the perception of the poet as an inspired prophet who sees the real world behind the shadowy illusions of the material world, have been influential on many English writers, notably SHELLEY (*see also* Henry MORE). The metaphysical thrillers of Charles WILLIAMS are modern examples of the Christian Neoplatonist tradition in fiction.

Neruda, Jan (1834–91) Czech writer. His plays and prose, e.g. *Tales of the Little Quarter* (1878), are highly regarded, as are his lyrical poems, e.g. *Ballads and Romances* (1883). He had been described as a late Romantic writer, an early Realist, and as a Classicist. However labelled, he is one of Czechoslavakia's greatest writers.

Neruda, Pablo [pseud. of Ricardo Neftali Reyes] (1904–73) Chilean poet and diplomat, noted both for his highly political (socialist) verse and for highly personal, cryptic lyrics. He was awarded the NOBEL PRIZE for literature in 1971.

Nerval, Gerard de (1808–55) French writer, whose life and work, in roughly equal proportions, influenced both the Symbolist and Surrealist movements. His fantastic short stories, e.g. *Tales and Drolleries* (1852), were particularly influential, and his poem "El Desdichado" is quoted by T. S. ELIOT in *The Waste Land*. His eccentricities, such as taking his pet lobster for a walk on a lead, were developed to the point of mannerism.

Nesbit, E[dith] (1858–1924) English writer of children's books such as *The Treasure Seekers* (1899), which went against the patronizingly moralistic tradition in children's literature of the time. Her books are still very popular, and several, e.g. *The Railway Children* (1906), have been filmed.

Neue Sachlichkeit A German term meaning "new objectivity," it was originally the title of an exhibition of postwar figurative art planned in 1923 by Gustave Hartlaub, director of the Mannheim Kunsthalle. It then came to represent any art concerned with objective representation of real life; such works were the opposition movement to EXPRESSIONIST subjectivity. Artists associated with the term include BECKMANN, DIX, and GROSZ.

Nevelson, Louise (1899–) Russian-born American sculptor, who trained in Munich and settled in the US from 1905. Typical of her works are her large-scale

ASSEMBLAGES created out of shallow boxes filled with found wooden objects and sprayed with black, white or gold paint, e.g. A*n American Tribute to the British People (Gold Wall)* (1959).

Nevinson, Christopher Richard Wynne (1889–1946) English painter. He published the English Futurist manifesto, *Vital English Art* (1914), along with the poet Marinetti. Although a leading figure in British FUTURISM, his work was also influenced by the Vorticist Wyndham LEWIS, as in *Returning to the Trenches* (1915). Later works, such as *Twentieth Century*, are more traditional in approach.

Newbery, John (1713–67) English publisher, who became the first publisher to specialize in selling books written for children, usually "improving" works such as *Goody Two Shoes* (1766), which was written partly by him and possibly with GOLDSMITH. He was a friend of many writers, and Goldsmith based the character of the bookseller in *The Village of Wakefield* on him.

Newbolt, Sir Henry [John] (1862–1938) English poet, whose patriotic naval poems, e.g. "Drake's Drum," were extremely popular at the turn of the century and still crop up in anthologies.

new comedy *see* **comedy**.

Newman, Barnett (1905–70) American painter. He trained at the Art Students' League and was a pioneer of ABSTRACT EXPRESSIONISM along with ROTHKO and MOTHERWELL. Typical of his own style is *Onement* (1948), a monochromatic COLOUR FIELD painting with a single vertical stripe of lighter colour in the centre. His use of very large-scale canvases, sometimes irregularly shaped, greatly influenced other abstract expressionist painters.

Newman, Cardinal John Henry (1801–90) English theologian, whose spirited defence of his faith, *Apo-*

logia pro vita sua (1864), created a deep impression on believers and nonbelievers alike.

Nibelungenlied An anonymous medieval German epic recounting the hero Siegfried's capture of a hoard of gold belonging to a race of dwarfs (the Nibelungs). The epic forms the basis for Wagner's great opera cycle, *The Ring of the Nibelungs*, and was influential on TOLKIEN's *Lord of the Rings*.

Nicholson, Ben (1894–1982) English artist who studied briefly at the Slade School of Art but was otherwise largely self-taught. Early works developed from his own interpretation of CUBIST principles and were mainly figurative, e.g. *Fireworks* (1929) and *At The Chat Botte* (1932). From 1933 he began low-relief plaster carvings in a geometrically abstract style, e.g. *White Relief* (1935). He was also a member of the avantgarde circle of artists that included Henry MOORE, Paul NASH and Barbara HEPWORTH, to whom he was married (1932–51). After World War II he acquired an international reputation, winning numerous prizes and awards for works that throughout his versatile career had a stamp of consistent good taste. Notable later works include *Carnac. Red and Brown* (1966) and *Tuscan Relief* (1967).

Nicolson, Sir Harold [George] (1886–1968) English diplomat, essayist and literary critic. He married Vita SACKVILLE-WEST in 1913. His *Diaries and Letters 1930–1962*, published in three volumes in 1966, 1967 and 1968, are a fascinating record of the political, social and literary world of his day. The comic/sinister figure of Sir Ralph Brompton in Evelyn WAUGH's *Sword of Honour* trilogy is modelled partly on Harold Nicolson.

Nietzsche, Friedrich Wilhelm (1844–1900) German philosopher and poet, whose works, e.g. *Thus Spake Zarathustra* (1866) and *Beyond Good and Evil* (1886), were highly critical of traditional morality and Christianity ("slave morality") and proclaimed the advent of the superman, the "splendid blond beast." He has been very influential on many 20th-century writers, e.g. D. H. LAWRENCE, MANN, SARTRE and SHAW. He was claimed by the Nazis to be one of their spiritual fathers, but Nietzsche, who despised anti-Semitism, would probably have rejected this paternity claim.

nihilism A philosophical movement originating in mid-19th century Russia that rejected all established authority and values. The revolutionary Bazarov in TURGENEY's *Fathers and Sons* is the first significant fictional portrait of a nihilist. Much of DOSTOEVSKY's work, e.g. *The Possessed*, is concerned with exposing the essential shallowness and banality of nihilism. Nihilist characters crop up frequently in English fiction of the late 19th and early 20th century, e.g. in Joseph CONRAD's *The Secret Agent*.

Nin, Anais (1903–77) French-born American novelist and essayist. She is best known for her seven volumes of diaries (1966–80) depicting life among the literary coteries of Paris and New York from the 1930s.

No *see* **Noh.**

Nobel prize Any of the annual awards endowed by the Swedish chemist Alfred Nobel (1833–96) (apparently in penance for his invention of dynamite) for significant contributions in the fields of chemistry, physics, literature, medicine or physiology, and peace, with economics added later. Winners of the Nobel prize for literature include KIPLING (1907), YEATS (1923), SHAW (1925), T. S. ELIOT (1948), PASTERNAK (1958), HEMINGWAY (1954) and BECKETT (1969). British reaction to the announcement of the award each year has mostly consisted of parochial irritation that Graham GREENE has once again not been awarded it, but some unreadable foreigner has. Most recipients of the literature prize have in fact been distinguished writers. The standard reference work (in three volumes covering the years 1901–26, 1927–61, 1962–87) on the Nobel prizewinners is *The Nobel Prize Winners: Literature* (1990), published by the Salem Press. The devaluation of the Nobel peace prize in the 1980s, however, with its award to the likes of Henry Kissinger, has contributed to a parallel lowering of the esteem of its award in literature.

Noguchi, Isamu (1904–) American sculptor who was brought up in Japan and returned to the US in 1917. He trained with BRANCUSI in Paris, and his early works involve highly polished sheet-metal abstractions. He was also influenced by oriental art in his ceramic and brush drawing works. He won commissions for works as diverse as a *Play Mountain* (1933) for New York City Parks and a Japanese Garden for UNESCO in Paris. While working on the FEDERAL ARTS PROJECT he did a sculptured mural, *History of Mexico* (1935), in Mexico City. Other notable works include *Bridge Sculpture* for Peace Park, Hiroshima. A retrospective exhibition of his work was held at the Whitney Museum of American Art in 1968.

Noguchi, Yone [Jiro] (1875–1947] Japanese poet and essayist who wrote in both Japanese and English, e.g. *Selected Poems* (1921). His works are regarded as forming an important bridge between Japanese and Western culture.

Noh *or* **No** A form of highly stylized drama originating in 14th-century Japan. The typical Noh play is short, slow-paced, draws heavily on classical Japanese symbolism, and usually involves song, dance, mime and intricately detailed costume.

Nolan, Sir Sidney (1917–92) Australian painter. He took up painting at the age of 21 and was almost completely self-taught. Early works are mainly abstract, but he established his reputation with SURREAL figurative works based on themes from Australian history and legend. He worked in a fluid, painterly style, often using unusual surfaces, e.g. glass, which enhanced the liquid translucency of his brushwork. Notable works include the series on Ned Kelly begun in 1946, e.g. *Kelly at Glenrowan* (1955). He also did cover illustrations for the books of his friend, the novelist Patrick White.

Nolde, Emil (1867–1956) German painter. Born Emil Hansen, he changed his name to that of his home town in 1904. Originally trained as a woodcarver, he studied painting in Munich and in Paris, settling in Berlin in 1906. He was briefly a member of Die BRÜCKE, but maintained an essentially individual style of EXPRESSIONISM. His works are inspired by deep religious feeling and mysticism, his imagery influenced by tribal art, all expressed through violent distortion and clashing colours. Notable among his works are *Dance around the Golden Calf* (1910) and *Masks and Dahlias* (1919). He was classed as a degenerate by the Nazis, and his later works include "unpainted paintings," small watercolours that he painted in secret.

Norris, [Benjamin] Frank[lin] (1870–1902) American novelist, heavily influenced by ZOLA. He became one of the chief American naturalistic novelists in works such as *McTeague* (1899), and his unfinished trilogy attacking American capitalism, the first two of which, *The Octopus* (1901) and *The Pit* (1903), are polemical assaults on the railroad and wheat industries.

North, Sir Thomas (*c*.1535–*c*.1601) English author. His translations of works such as Plutarch's *Lives* (1579) exerted a strong influence on Elizabethan writers, notably SHAKESPEARE, who seems to have largely derived his knowledge of ancient history from North's works.

Nostradamus [Michel de Notredame] (1503–66) French astrologer and physician. He published two books of cryptic prophecies in rhymed quatrains, called *Centuries* (1555–8), which enjoyed a huge vogue throughout Europe and were first published in English in 1672. His work has no literary merit.

Novalis [Friedrich Leopold von Hardenberg] (1772–1801) German poet and novelist, who was called the "Prophet of ROMANTICISM" in Germany. He wrote two novels, both unfinished, the best known of which is *Heinrich von Ofterdingen* (1802), which involves a symbolic quest for a "blue flower." He also wrote mystical and love poetry, e.g. *Hymns to the Night* (1800), a series of laments on the death of his fiancée. He died of consumption.

novel A sustained fictional prose narrative. Although most of the essential characteristics of the form can be found in ancient texts, such as the Greek Romances of the 3rd century, and in the works of writers of the Roman world, such as APULIEUS and PETRONIUS, the novel as the term is generally understood, with complex characterization and multilayered strands of plot and character development, is essentially a creation of 18th-century writers in English, particularly DEFOE, RICHARDSON and FIELDING.

Like all generalizations about the novel, however, the foregoing is at best only a grouping of partial truths; Petronius' *Satyricon* is a fine novel by any standards, and CERVANTES' *Don Quixote* is one of the very finest.

In the early years of the 19th century, the dual tradition of the novel – adventure in the great world outside, and exploration of personality – reached striking new levels in the novels of Sr Walter SCOTT and Jane AUSTEN respectively, with the latter setting standards of characterization that have rarely been matched. In the course of the 19th century, writers throughout Europe and America, e.g. DICKENS, STENDHAL, George ELIOT, TOLSTOY, DOSTOYEVSKY, BALZAC, MELVILLE and Henry JAMES, developed the novel into a highly sophisticated vehicle for exploring human consciousness. The 20th century has seen many adaptations of the traditional form of the novel, from the use of the stream of consciousness (*see* William JAMES) technique by JOYCE and WOOLF, to the MAGIC REALISM of South American writers such as MARQUEZ, with such oddities as the so-called "antinovels" of writers such as ROBBE-GRILLET occurring along the way. Finally, it is worth noting Gore VIDAL's observation that the fact that a modern novelist can work with greater freedom of expression, and in a wider variety of forms, than earlier novelists, does not necessarily mean that the modern novelist has anything more profound to say.

Some quotes: a novel is "some work in which the most thorough knowledge of human nature, the happiest delineation of its varieties, the liveliest effusions of wit and humour are conveyed to the world in the best chosen language" (Jane AUSTEN); "A good novels tells us the truth about its hero; but a bad novel tells us the truth about its author" (CHESTERTON); "Yes – oh dear, yes – the novel tells us a story" (FORSTER); "A novel is a mirror walking down a main road" (STENDHAL). *See also* MARX, NASHE, NOVELLA, PICARESQUE NOVEL, GOTHIC NOVEL, CAMPUS NOVEL.

novella A short version of the NOVEL; a tale usually leading up to some point, and often, in early versions of the form such as the tales in BOCCACCIO's *Decameron*, of a satirical or scabrous nature.

Noyes, Alfred (1880–1958) English poet. His work, e.g. the epic poem *Drake* (1908), is representative of the once-common bluff, hearty, out-of-doors and patriotic tradition within English verse. Like NEWBOLT and AUSTIN, he was happiest when writing manly verses about sailors.

nursery rhyme A (usually traditional) short verse or song for children. Many nursery rhymes, e.g. "Ring a Ring a Roses" (which refers to the Great Plague) have their roots in ancient and occasionally unsavoury events.

O

Oates, Joyce Carol (1938–) American novelist and poet. Her novels are naturalistic in form with strong elements of symbolism (as in ZOLA), linking the American way of life with violence and destructive emotions. Her novels include *A Garden of Earthly Delights* (1967), the title taken from a painting by Hieronymous Bosch, with whom she has much in common, and *A Bloodsmoor Romance* (1982).

objet trouvé *see* **found object**.

O'Brien, Edna (1932–) Irish novelist and short-story writer. Her first three novels, describing the lives of provincial Irish girls in Dublin and London, form a trilogy that is still regarded as her best work: these are *The Country Girls* (1960), *The Lonely Girl* (1962) and *Girls in their Married Bliss* (1963). Subsequent novels include *A Pagan Place* (1971) and *Night* (1972), as well as several screenplays.

O'Brien, Flann [pseud. of Brian O'Nolan *or* O Nuallain] (1911–66) Irish novelist and journalist. His regular column in the *Irish Times*, "Cruiskeen Lawn," written under the name Myles na Gopaleen, established him as one of the major Irish satirists, ridiculing the clichés of Irish life. A collection of the articles was published in 1968 as *The Best of Myles*. His reputation outside Ireland has risen sharply since his death, and he is now regarded as a comic writer of genius. His novels include *The Dalkey Archive* (1964), in which James

JOYCE (who admired O'Brien's work) is discovered to be alive and a writer of pious tracts.

O'Casey, Sean (1880–1964) Irish dramatist. His three early plays, *The Shadow of a Gunman* (1923), *Juno and the Paycock* (1924) and *The Plough and the Stars* (1926), caused great controversy in Ireland by focusing, not altogether approvingly, on the outburst of patriotism which followed the 1916 Easter Rising (the first production of *The Plough and the Stars* was disrupted by outraged Irish nationalists). His later plays, e.g. *The Silver Tassie* (1928), belong more to the world of experimental Expressionist drama and were less controversial (and less popular).

O'Connor, Frank [pseud. of Michael Francis O'Donovan] (1903–66) Irish short-story writer and critic. He is best known for his affectionate but sharply observed portraits of Irish life in such short-story collections as *Bones of Contention* (1936) and *Domestic Relations* (1957).

O'Connor, [Mary] Flannery (1925–64) American novelist and short-story writer. Her main theme is religious fanaticism in the Southern US States, where life is portrayed as veering grotesquely from tragedy to comedy. Her masterpiece is *Wise Blood* (1952), a novel about a young religious fanatic and his misconceptions, which was made into an equally fine film by John Huston.

odalisque A term in art for a painting of a reclining female nude figure often wearing the baggy trousers of a Middle Eastern female slave. MATISSE painted a series of odalisques.

Odets, Clifford (1906–63) American dramatist. A committed socialist, his masterpiece is *Waiting for Lefty* (1935), a play about a taxi-drivers' strike which ends in a mass meeting (in which the audience is invited to participate) calling for a strike.

oeuvre The French word for "work," used in art to denote the total output of an artist.

O'Faolain, Sean (1900–1991) Irish novelist and short-story writer. Like Frank O'CONNOR, his stories focus on the constricting patterns of provincial Irish life, but from a more edgily critical perspective. His *Collected Stories* were published in 1981. His vigorous campaign against censorship and narrow-mindedness is a prominent theme in his autobiography *Vive-Moi!* (1964).

O'Flaherty, Liam (1897–1984) Irish novelist and short-story writer. His novels include *The Informer* (1925), and collections of short stories, e.g. *Spring Sowing* (1948).

O'Hara, John [Henry] (1905–70) American novelist and short-story writer. His tough, satirical works on "sophisticated" American life, e.g. the novels *Butterfield 8* (1935) and *Pal Joey* (1940), were very popular in the 1930s and 1940s.

oil paint A paint made by mixing colour pigments with oil (generally linseed oil) to produce a slow-drying, malleable sticky substance. Oil paint has been the dominant medium in European art since the 15th century because of the range of effects that can be produced.

O'Keefe, Georgia (1887–1986) American painter. Her early works are inspired by the Texan landscape, but most of her art concerns precisionist abstraction of observed forms, often using the technique of isolating one detail in close-up. Her work was exhibited from 1918 at the 291 Gallery owned by the American photographer **Alfred Stieglitz** (1864–1946), whom she married in 1924. Later abstractions suggest empty landscapes and city scenes, or organic forms, e.g. *Black Iris* (1926).

old comedy *see* **comedy**.

Oldenburg, Claes (1929–) Swedish-born American

sculptor, one of the originators of pop art. He won popular acclaim with *Dual Hamburger* (1962), which formed part of a display of giant foodstuffs and other objects on sale at his shop, "The Store," in New York. He challenged the accepted nature of things with wit and humour, creating "soft" hardware objects and playing with scale and texture.

Olitzki, Jules (1922–) Russian-born American painter who studied in New York and Paris. His early works are in a thick impasto style, but from 1960 he began to experiment with colour staining and with spray-gun techniques. Throughout his work there is a common thread of interest in the edges of the canvas, where most of the pictorial imagery and gestural significance of his work occurs. A typical work is *Pink Alert* (1966).

O'Neill, Eugene [Gladstone] (1885–1923) American dramatist. His plays of the early 1920s, e.g. *Beyond the Horizon* (1920), *The Emperor Jones* (1921) and *Desire Under the Elms* (1924), established him as one of America's finest dramatists. His greatest plays are *Mourning Becomes Electra* (1931), a tragedy based on AESCHYLUS's *Oresteia* trilogy transposed to the American South in the aftermath of the Civil War, *The Iceman Cometh* (1946), a tragicomedy set in the Bowery, and the semi-autobiographical *Long Day's Journey into Night* (1940–1), a gloomy study of family breakdown which is often regarded as his masterpiece. He was awarded the Nobel prize for literature in 1936.

Op Art *or* **Optical Art** An ABSTRACT ART that uses precise, hard-edged patterns in strong colours that dazzle the viewer and make the image appear to move. The principal artists in this field are VASARÉLY and the British painter **Bridget Riley** (1931–), who for a while worked solely in black and white.

Orcagna [Andrea di Cione] (*fl.*1343–68) Florentine painter, sculptor and architect. His masterpiece and only certain dated work is the altarpiece, *The Redeemer with the Madonna and Saints* (1354–7), in the Church of Santa Maria Novella. Its vivid colours and shallow picture plane reflect a more Byzantine style than the naturalism of GIOTTO, although the figures are solidly modelled in a Gothic vein. His sculptures adorn the Tabernacle in the Or San Michele, and other important works attributed to him include the remains of *The Triumph of Death*, *Last Judgment* and *Hell* frescoes in Santa Croce. His brothers, **Nardo** (*fl.* 1346–65) and **Jacopo** (*fl.* 1365–98) also worked in the family studio.

Orley, Bernard van (*c.*1488–1541) Netherlandish painter and designer, known as "RAPHAEL of the Netherlands" because of the influence of the art of Raphael on his work. He was also influenced to an extent by DÜRER, whom he met in 1520. He painted portraits at the court of the Regent, Margaret of Austria, where he was official court painter. Notable works include *The Ordeal and Patience of Job* (1521). He also designed tapestries and stained glass.

Orozco, José Clemente (1883–1949) Mexican painter. He trained in architectural drawing but after the loss of his left hand and eye in an accident he taught himself painting. He worked as a cartoonist for various publications, including *La Vanguardia*. He admired the work of MICHELANGELO, and his early paintings are also influenced by POSTIMPRESSIONISM. He was comissioned to paint a large number of murals and frescoes, of which *An Epic of American Civilization* (1932–4) is a notable example. His mature work reveals an interest in the geometric abstractions of LÉGER, and his last masterpiece is the emotive and powerful *Hidalgo and Castillo* (1949).

Orpen, Sir William (1878–1931) Irish-born English painter, a friend and contemporary of Augustus JOHN.

He established himself as a successful society portraitist in the fashion of SARGENT, although his own costume self-portraits and his group portraits are generally works of better quality and insight. Some of his most outstanding work was done as an official war artist in World War I, e.g. *The Signing of the Peace Treaty at Versailles* (1919–20) and *Dead Germans in a Trench.*

Orphism *or* **Orphic Cubism** A brief but influential art movement developed out of CUBIST principles by the artists DELAUNAY, LÉGER, PICABIA, DUCHAMP and KUPKA. Their aim was to move away from the objectivity of Cubism towards a more lyrical and colourful art. The artists were influenced in part by Italian FUTURISM, and typical works use juxtaposed forms and strong colours. The term Orphism was coined by the French poet Guillaume Apollinaire in 1912, and the movement had a deep influence on the German Expressionists MACKE and MARC, and on SYNCHROMISM.

Orton, Joe [John] (1933–67) English dramatist. His first play, *Entertaining Mr Sloane* (1964), a black comedy in which a businessman and his sister compete for the favours of a young villain, was a surprise hit on the London stage. His two other best-known works, *Loot* (1966) and the posthumously performed *What the Butler Saw* (1969), are, like the first, cleverly constructed dramas focusing on sexual depravity and social corruption. Orton was murdered by his lover.

Orwell, George [pseud. of Eric Arthur Blair] (1903–50) Indian-born English novelist and essayist. Brought up in the upper-middle class and educated at Eton, Orwell became a socialist in the 1920s. His first published work was a documentary work, *Down and Out in Paris and London* (1933), which describes his often gruesome experiences as a tramp. His other two great nonfiction works are *The Road to Wigan Pier* (1937), a passionate, coldly angry study of poverty in the North of England, and *Homage to Catalonia* (1939), an account of experiences fighting for the Republican Government in the Spanish Civil War. The latter book caused great offence to many of Orwell's socialist friends for its strong condemnation of Communist treachery and brutality. His first published novel, *Burmese Days* (1934), was based on his experiences as a colonial police officer in Burma. His two greatest novels have become classics of world literature: *Animal Farm* (1945), a grim allegory of the history of the Soviet Union in which farm animals create a revolutionary state that goes horribly wrong; and *Nineteen Eighty-Four* (1949), an even more grim picture of a future totalitarian world. Orwell is also recognized as one of the greatest English essayists; his *Collected Essays, Journalism and Letters* were published in four volumes in 1968.

Osborne, John [James] (1929–) English dramatist. His first play, *Look Back in Anger* (1956), the hero of which is an irascible and frustrated young working-class man, was an immediate and influential success on the British stage. No one was quite sure what the hero was angry about (see ANGRY YOUNG MEN), but whatever it was, it was felt to be significant. The best known of his later plays are *The Entertainer* (1957), in which a seedy music-hall comedian long past his best (played by Laurence Olivier) represents the decadent spirit of post-imperial Britain, and *Luther* (1961), an intriguing psychological study of Martin Luther. Like his friend AMIS, Osborne moved sharply to the right politically in the 1960s, and became increasingly notorious for his bad-tempered invective against anything that smacked of permissiveness or the loosening of society's ties.

Ossian *see* **Macpherson, James**.

Otway, Thomas (1652–85) English dramatist, remembered chiefly for one work, the great tragedy *Venice Preserved* (1682), a penetrating study of treason and loyalty.

Ouwater, Albert van *see* **Bouts, Dieric**.

Ovid [Publius Ovidius Naso] (43BC–c.17AD) Roman poet. His sensual, witty love poems have always been admired, but his long narrative poem *Metamorphoses*, which describes myths in which characters change their forms, is of much greater significance. It was used as a source book for Greek and Roman mythology by many Renaissance writers, e.g. MARLOWE and SHAKESPEARE.

Oz, Amos (1939–) Israeli novelist, essayist and short-story writer. Regarded as one of the most important Israeli writers, his novels include *My Michael* (1968), *To Know a Woman* (1990) and *The Third Condition* (1991). Oz's work shows a deep and humane concern for what Israel's struggle for existence is doing to the soul of the Israeli nation.

P

Pacheco, Francisco (1564–1654) Spanish painter, poet and writer from Seville. He was the teacher of VELAZQUEZ, who later became his son-in-law. His most important contribution to Spanish art history is his book, *The Art of Painting* (1649), and his finest work is *The Immaculate Conception* (*c.*1621).

Pacher, Michael (*fl.c.*1645–98) Austrian painter and sculptor. He worked in an advanced style of the Late Gothic tradition, given the full modelling and lively gesture of his figures within the carved tracery confines of their Gothic architecture settings. A sound knowledge of the works of MANTEGNA is evident in his sensitive use of space. His masterpiece is the *Wolfgang Altarpiece* (1481), and another notable work is *The Four Doctors of the Church* (*c.*1483).

Paine, Thomas (1737–1809) English-born American political theorist and pamphleteer. He travelled to America in 1774, where he wrote the highly influential pamphlet *Common Sense* (1776), which argued for American independence. The pamphlet's lucid, expertly argued prose was recognized by George Washington as being a sigificant contribution to the Revolution. Paine returned to England in 1787 and published a defence of democratic principles, *The Rights of Man* (1791–2), in reply to Edmund Burke's *Reflections on the Revolution in France*. In danger of arrest (he was apparently warned to escape by BLAKE), he moved to

France where he was welcomed as a revolutionary hero and was elected to the National Convention. He sided with the moderates, was imprisoned by Robespierre's faction and released after 11 months, having narrowly escaped execution. He returned to America in 1802, where he alienated most of his old allies by publishing the deist work, *The Age of Reason* (1793), a no-holds-barred attack on Christian revelation. BYRON was one of the many former allies who now detested Paine; he wrote a vitriolic epigram of COBBETT's return from America with Paine's bones.

Palmer, Samuel (1805–81) English painter and engraver. He painted pastoral landscapes, and *A Hilly Scene* (c.1826) is typical of his most intensely creative period, which was spent at Shoreham in Kent. He was acquainted with BLAKE, who deeply influenced the visionary mysticism of his work

Paolo, Veneziano (*fl.* 1321–62) Venetian painter who executed a number of important state commissions, including the cover for the Pala d'Oro in the Church of San Marco (1345). His large polyptych altarpieces have a strong Byzantine feel for colour and decoration. His sons **Luca** and **Giovanni** were also painters, the former collaborating with him on the Pala d'Oro.

Paolozzi, Eduardo (1924–) Scottish sculptor and printmaker of Italian parentage. Major influences on his work include DADA and SURREALISM. He questioned the accepted values of art in his *Bunk* series of COL-LAGES. Sculptural images of figures and animals were created from found pieces of machinery and cast in bronze, e.g. *St Sebastian No 2* (1957). Later works, such as *The City of the Circle and the Square* (1963–66), embrace some of the lighthearted elements of Pop Art.

Paret y Alcazar, Luis (1746–99) Spanish painter of versatile talent, who painted historical, mythical and religious scenes as well as landscapes and still lifes.

His Rococo genre paintings have a lasting charm that recalls the works of FRAGONARD. He was one of the outstanding artists of his time, surpassed only by GOYA. The Prado, Madrid, houses a good selection of his work.

Parker, Dorothy [Rothschild] (1893–1960) American journalist, poet and short-story writer, noted especially for her dry wit and sharply ironic epigrams and satires, many of which were first published in the *New Yorker* magazine.

Parmigianino [Girolamo Francesco Maria Mazzola] (1503–40) Italian MANNERIST painter and etcher of precocious talent. His early works were influenced to an extent by CORREGGIO, and he was familiar with the works of RAPHAEL and DÜRER. His religious compositions are subtle, elegant and gracefully elongated, while his portraits are more directly realistic. An early masterpiece is *The Vision of St Jerome* (1526–7), and his best-known mature piece is *The Madonna of the Long Neck* (c.1535). His works were widely known through engravings and through his own innovative use of the etching medium. He had a profound influence on French Mannerist painting.

Pasmore, Victor (1908–) English painter. His early landscapes were influenced by WHISTLER, and he was a founding member of the Euston Road School in 1937. During the 1930s he was interested in objective abstraction, and he later experimented with COLLAGE before finding his niche in CONSTRUCTIVISM. The bulk of his mature work is strictly geometric abstraction, although he later incorporated more organic forms. Typical works include *Evening, Hammersmith* (1943) and *Triangular Motif in Pink and Yellow* (1949).

pastel A paint medium of powdered colour mixed with gum arabic to form a hard stick. When applied to paper, the colour adheres to the surface. Pastel was used to great effect by CHARDIN and, particularly, DEGAS.

Pasternak, Boris (1890–1960) Russian poet, novelist and translator. His third poetry collection, *My Sister, Life* (1922), established him as a highly original and passionate lyric poet. He published a "political" poem in 1927, *The Year 1905*, but his heart was clearly not in it. Like his friends AKHMATOVA and MANDELSTAM, his position became increasingly dangerous under a regime that demanded safe verse praising its achievements. Pasternak turned to translation as a safe and honourable way of earning a living, and his translation of SHAKESPEARE's works is still highly valued. His great novel *Dr Zhivago* was first published in Italy in 1958. He was awarded the NOBEL PRIZE for literature in that year, but was forced to decline acceptance by the Soviet authorities, who subjected him to a hate campaign until his death. All his works are now freely published in the USSR, where he is ranked as one of Russia's greatest writers.

pastoral Any piece of literature celebrating the country way of life. The first pastoral poems of any significance are those of **Theocritus** (*c*.310–*c*.250BC), a Greek poet whose work established the standard frame of the form: shepherds and shepherdesses (none of whom seems to do any actual work) singing to one another of their loves in a world of peace and plenty, in which the sun always shines. Death, however, is occasionally present in the form of a shepherd lamenting the death of a friend (SHAKESPEARE's "Dead shepherd" couplet – *see* MARLOWE – is a moving, later example of this convention being used as a tribute). Theocritus' form was used by VIRGIL in his *Eclogues*, so establishing a tradition that lasted for centuries. Later practitioners of the form include PETRARCH, MILTON and SHELLEY. William EMPSOM's *Some Versions of Pastoral* (1935) is a notable (and highly entertaining) study of the form and its variations.

Pater, Walter [Horatio] (1839–84) English essayist and critic, noted especially for his flowery, ornate prose style, described by Oscar WILDE as "the holy writ of beauty." His essay on Leonardo da Vinci in *Studies in the History of the Renaissance* (1873) includes his famous description of the Mona Lisa, "older than the rocks among whom she sits." Pater was a strong influence on the AESTHETIC MOVEMENT: Max BEERBOHM, however, described his prose as lifeless, laid out like "a corpse for inspection."

Paton, Alan [Stewart] (1903–88) South African novelist. His best-known work is *Cry the Beloved Country* (1965), a moving study of the hideous consequences of South Africa's race laws.

Paz, Octavio (1914–) Mexican poet and critic. His collections of poems include *The Violent Season* (1958) and *Configurations* (1971). His other works include two important reflections on Mexican cultural identity and society, *The Labyrinth of Solitude* (1950), and *Eagle or Sun* (1990). Like ORWELL, Paz became a strong opponent of the totalitarian ideologies of both left and right while in Spain during the Civil War, and has been a fearless champion of the rights of the individual against what Orwell called the "smelly little orthodoxies." His poem "Nocturne of San Idelfenso" describes poetry as the bridge between history and truth. He was awarded the NOBEL PRIZE for literature in 1990.

Peacock, Thomas Love (1785–1866) English novelist, essayist and poet. His highly entertaining satirical novels consist mostly of ingeniously witty dialogue between characters modelled on Peacock's friends and contemporaries, e.g. BYRON, COLERIDGE and SHELLEY. The novels include *Headlong Hall (1816), Nightmare*

Abbey (1818), *Crotchet Castle* (1831) and *Gryll Grange* (1860–61).

Peake, Mervyn [Laurence] (1911–68) English artist, novelist and poet. His best-known literary work is the "Gormenghast" trilogy, which is widely held to constitute one of the great fantasy worlds in modern fiction. The novels are *Titus Groan* (1946), *Gormenghast* (1950) and *Titus Alone* (1959). Peake was an official war artist during World War II, and his visit to Belsen concentration camp in 1945 profoundly affected him.

Peale, Charles Willson (1741–1827) American painter. He trained in London under WEST, and from 1775 he lived in Philadelphia where he painted portraits in the NEOCLASSICAL tradition. Famous works include *The Exhumation of the Mastodon* (1806) and *Staircase Group* (1795). Of his 17 children, five became artists, the three most important being **Raphaelle** (1774–1825), who was a gifted still life painter, his best-known work being *After the Bath* (1823); **Rembrandt** (1778–1860), who was a portrait painter like his father; and **Titian Ramsay** (1799–1885), who was a painter of natural history.

pencil A mixture of graphite and clay in stick form and covered by a hard casing. The greater the clay element, the harder is the pencil. Graphite replaced lead as the principal component in the 16th century. Until the end of the 18th century, the word "pencil" also denoted a fine brush.

Peploe, Samuel John (1871–1935) Scottish painter, who was influenced by CUBISM and the works of CÉZANNE. Richness of colour, fairly formal structure and free brushwork are the hallmarks of Peploe's works. He mainly painted still lifes of flowers, although the subject was always secondary to his painterly style. He also painted series of landscapes of the island of Iona.

Pepys, Samuel (1633–1703) English diarist and

Admiralty official. His diary (written in code) was first published in 1825. The full uncensored version was published in 11 volumes, 1970–83, and contains much fascinating detail of life in 17th-century London. *See also* EVELYN.

Percy, Thomas *see* **Ballad**.

Perelman, S[idney] J[oseph] (1904–79) American humorist. He wrote the sceenplays for some of the Marx Brothers' films, and published several collections of articles under such Marxist titles as *The Road to Milltown; or, Under the Spreading Atrophy* (1957).

perspective In art, the representation of a three-dimensional view in a two-dimensional space by establishing a vanishing point in the distance at which parallel lines converge, the objects or figures in the distance being smaller and closer together than objects or figures nearer the viewer. Perspective is demonstrated in the works of GIOTTO, and its rules were formulated by ALBERTI in *De Pictura* (1435), but by the 20th century these were being abandoned by artists.

Perugino, Pietro [Pietro Vannucci] (*c.*1445–1523) Italian painter, possibly a contemporary of LEONARDO DA VINCI in VERROCCHIO's studio in Florence. He took his name from his native Perugia, where he mainly worked. He painted *The Giving of the Keys to St Peter* fresco (*c.*1481) in the Sistine Chapel, Rome, and also produced portraits and altarpieces in the course of his career. A peaceful serenity pervades his work, as in the gentle and graceful *Virgin and Child*. RAPHAEL was influenced by him, and indeed may have been his pupil, and he was also a source of inspiration for the PRE-RAPHAELITES.

Petrarch [Francesco Petrarca] (1304–74) Italian lyric poet and humanist. His love poems are sonnets, madrigals and songs in praise of a woman he called "Laura" (whose true identity is unknown), and were strongly influential on Tudor and Elizabethan writers and poets, notably WYATT. His work popularized the sonnet form, subsequently used to great effect by people as diverse as Michelangelo and SHAKESPEARE. Petrarch is regarded as the first major poet of the Renaissance.

Petronius [Gaius Petronius Arbiter] (d. c.66AD) Roman courtier and satirist. His great satirical novel, the *Satyricon*, gives a unique and vivid portrait of the seamy side of Roman life; salacious, funny, and occasionally deeply moving, the work is an important landmark in Western literature. The "Trimalchio's banquet" scene in the book gave T. S. ELIOT the epigraph for *The Waste Land*. Petronius was ordered to commit suicide by Emperor Nero.

Pevsner, Antoine (1886–1962) Russian-born French painter and sculptor, and leading CONSTRUCTIVIST artist. He studied at Kiev and St Petersburg, and was influenced by CUBISM. Together with his brother NAUM GABO, he worked in Oslo during World War II, returning to teach in Russia in 1917. They published their *Realistic Manifesto* in 1920 but disagreed with the utilitarian approach of TATLIN and RODCHENKO and moved to Berlin in 1922–3. Pevsner settled in Paris from 1924, where he founded the Abstaction-Creation group. Notable works include *Torso* (1924–6) and *Development Column* (1942).

Philips, Katherine (1631–64) English poet. Her work was much admired by her contemporaries, e.g. COWLEY and DRYDEN, among whom she was known as the "Matchless Orinda." The name "Orinda" seems to have been chosen by herself in a social and literary group of "Antenors," "Rosanias," etc, which seems to have been a precursor of the 18th-century BLUESTOCKINGS, but not much is known about the group. Her collected poems were issued posthumously in 1667.

Piaget, Jean *see* **Structuralism**.

Picabia, Francis (1879–1953) French painter. His
early works are in an IMPRESSIONIST style but, influenced by DUCHAMP, he took a more avant-garde direction from 1912 and was involved with the SECTION D'OR
group. Notable works include *I see again in memory
my dear Udnie* (1914), which shows the influence of
Duchamp. He also collaborated with Alfred Stieglitz
(*see* O'KEEFE). His works and writings were highly
influential.

picaresque novel A type of NOVEL in which the hero
(very rarely, the heroine – Defoe's *Molly Flanders* is
the best-known example in English) undergoes an episodic series of adventures. The term derives from the
Spanish *picaro*, a rogue of trickster. Many examples
appear in 16th-century Spanish literature, when the
genre first established itself, but picaresque novels
have been appearing since the very earliest days of the
novel; both Petronius' *Satyricon* and Apulieus' *Golden
Ass* may be classed as Picaresque novels. The first
major English example is Thomas NASHE's lurid *The
Unfortunate Traveller*, which appeared in the 1590s
along with other, lesser examples. Several great novels
of the 18th and 19th centuries, e.g. Smollett's *Roderick
Random*, Fielding's *Tom Jones* and Dickens' *Pickwick
Papers*, have picaresque elements, but inhabit an
entirely different emotional and moral world from that
of the earlier examples of the genre. Thus, Tom Jones
will have a characteristically picaresque sexual esca-
pade with Molly Seagrim, but will not abandon her to
the mob, as his scabrous fictional predecessors would
cheerfully have done.

Picasso, Pablo (1881–1973) Spanish painter, sculptor,
designer and illustrator. The son of a drawing teacher,
he showed an early precocious talent in works such as
The Girl with Bare Feet (1895). Of his "Blue" and
"Rose" periods in the early 1900s, typical works include

Child Holding a Dove (1903) and *Family of Saltimban-
ques* (1905). AFRICAN tribal art and the works of CÉZ-
ANNE directed the development of his "Negro" period
from 1907–9. In 1906–7 he painted *Les Demoiselles
d'Avignon,* which was to herald CUBISM and represents
a major turning point in modern art. From 1910 to 1916
he worked closely with Georges BRAQUE, developing
synthetic and analytic forms of Cubism and experimenting with COLLAGE techniques. A further development is represented by the painting *Guernica* (1937), a
tensely emotional expression of the artist's horror at
the bombing of the Basque capital by German planes
during the Spanish Civil War. While much of his later
painting was powerfully expressive, his sculptural
pieces, including *Baboon and Young* (1951) are noted
for their wit and humour.

Piero della Francesca (*c.*1416–92) Italian early
RENAISSANCE painter from Borgo San Sepolcro, who
was in Florence in 1439 working on frescoes in San
Egidio for DOMENICO VENEZIANO. While there he was
deeply influenced by the works of MASACCIO, who
inspired the monumental grandeur of his subsequent
works, e.g. *The Compassionate Madonna* (1445). From
*c.*1460 he was at the court of Federico da Montefeltro
of Urbino, and during this time he painted some of his
finest masterpieces, including *The History of the True
Cross* frescoes (*c.*1452–64), *The Resurrection* (*c.*1460)
and portraits of Federico da Montefeltro and his wife.
Another notable masterpiece is his last major work,
The Madonna and Saints with Federigo da Montefeltro
(*c.*1475). In later years he gave up painting, possibly
due to failing eyesight, and concentrated on theoretical
works on perspective and mathematics. He had a
strong influence on the works of PERUGINO and SIGNOR-
ELLI.

Piero di Cosimo (1462–1521) Florentine painter. He

trained with Cosimo ROSELLI, from whom he took his name. He was an interesting and unusual character whose development is difficult to establish due to his large number of undated works. He painted mainly scenes featuring mythological creatures and figures and depicting animals in a sympathetic manner. Notable works include *Cephalus and Procris* and *Mythological Subject*. ANDREA DEL SARTO was his pupil.

pieté The Italian word for "pity," used in art to denote a painting or sculpture of the body of the dead Christ being supported by the Virgin, often with other mourning figures.

Pigalle, Jean-Baptiste (1714–85) French sculptor. He studied in Rome and established his reputation with the marble sculpture of Mercury (1744), which is outstanding in its lively naturalism. Notable monumental works include the tomb for Maurice of Saxony (begun 1753). A technically accomplished and naturally versatile artist, he also painted brilliant portraits, including *Self Portrait* (1780) and *Voltaire* (1770–76), and his skill extended to genre scenes of great charm, e.g. *Child with a Birdcage* (1750).

Pilon, Germain (1527–90) French sculptor. His early works are decorative in the MANNERIST style, as in his figures of the Graces for the monument to King Henry II (1560). A much more moving naturalism is expressed in the tomb of the king and his queen, Catherine de' MEDICI, at St Denis (1563–70). Succeeding generations of French sculptors were much influenced by Pilon's early naturalist style, although his later works were more emotionally personal and had less of a following, e.g. *The Virgin of Piety* (c.1585).

Pindar (c.522–c.443BC) Greek lyric poet, noted for his odes (based on the choral odes of Greek drama) celebrating victories in the Greek games, e.g. at Olympia. His carefully constructed and elaborate poems became influential in late 17th-century England (through COWLEY's works), where he was (mistakenly) seen as a much freer, less restrained poet than HORACE. KIPLING's marvellous spoof Horatian ode "A Translation" (in *A Diversity of Creatures*, 1917) has Horace saying: "Me, in whose breast no flame hath burned / Lifelong, save that by Pindar lit . . ."

Pinter, Harold (1930–) English dramatist. The adjective "Pinteresque" to describe dialogue derives from his use of halting, menacing dialogue punctuated by sinister pauses. *The Birthday Party* (1958), *The Caretaker* (1960) and *No Man's Land* (1975) are the most performed of Pinter's plays, which are usually characterized as belonging to the tradition of the Theatre of the ABSURD. He has also written several screenplays, notably that for John FOWLES' novel *The French Lieutenant's Woman*.

Piper, John (1903–92) English painter, writer and designer and a leading abstract painter of the 1930s. By the 1940s he had given up abstraction in favour of a more traditionally subjective style. He expounded his theories in *British Romantic Artists* (1942), and was an official war artist from 1940–42, when he recorded outstanding images of the devastation of bombing. He has also designed stained glass for Liverpool Metropolitan and Coventry Cathedrals.

Pirandello, Luigi (1867–1936) Italian dramatist, short-story writer and novelist. His two best-known plays are *Six Characters in Search of an Author* (1921) and *Henry IV* (1922), both of which are very influential experimental plays with fragmented action and characterization, and feature relentless questioning of theatrical conventions, such as the barrier between performers and audience. He was awarded the NOBEL PRIZE for literature in 1934.

Piranesi, Giovanni Battista (1720–78) Italian artist.

Born in Venice, he settled in Rome in 1740 and established his reputation with etchings of architectural views. These are impressive in their scale and grandeur, and his other engraved works, notably the *Carceri d'Invenzione*, also involve an astonishing degree of inventive imagery. He designed the Church of Santa Maria del Priorato in Rome and was extremely influential among NEOCLASSICAL architects.

Pisanello [Antonio Pisano] (*c.*1395–1455/6) Italian painter. He worked in Rome and Venice on frescoes, since destroyed, in collaboration with GENTILE DA FABRIANO who influenced his INTERNATIONAL GOTHIC style. His decorative and detailed works are rich in colour and texture. Excellent draughtsmanship is evident in carefully observed drawings of birds and animals and in the accuracy of his portraits. Notable works include the fresco, *St George and the Princess* (*c.*1435), and the painting, *The Vision of St Eustace*.

Pisano, Giovanni (*fl. c.*1265–1314) Pisan sculptor, one of the leading Italian sculptors of his time. His works are expressive and elegant in the Gothic tradition. Most notable are his high-relief facades for the Cathedral at Siena (1248–96) and the baptistry at Pisa (*c.*1295). Other important works include the statue of the Madonna at the Arena Chapel in Padua. His father **Nicola** (*fl. c.*1258–84) was also a sculptor, famous for the pulpits in the Baptistry at Pisa (1260) and the Cathedral at Siena (1265–8). These are majestic and powerful in innovation and execution, with high-relief figures and architectural forms inspired by classical antiquity.

Pissarro, Camille (1830–1903) West Indian-born French IMPRESSIONIST painter. He moved to Paris in 1855 where he studied with COROT and later met MONET. He was in London from 1870 to 1871 and was influenced by the works of CONSTABLE and TURNER, as in *Lower Norwood, Snow Scene* (1870). He helped organize and exhibited in all eight Impressionist exhibitions, a typical work being *Red Roofs* (1887). During the mid-1880s he experimented with pointillism (*see* NEOIMPRESSIONISM) but later resumed a freer style of brushwork and a less vivid palette. His eldest son, **Lucien** (1863–1744), also experimented with pointillism and was influenced by the English ARTS AND CRAFTS MOVEMENT before establishing his Neo-impressionist style. Notable works include *Rue Ste Victoire, Winter Sunshine* (1890).

Plath, Sylvia (1932–63) American poet and novelist. She married Ted HUGHES in 1956, and settled in England in 1959. She published only two books in her lifetime: a volume of poems, *Colossus* (1960), and a semi-autobiographical novel, *The Bell Jar* (1963). She died by her own hand. Her posthumous collection of poems, *Ariel* (1965), which has many fine lyrics describing her personal problems, has been much admired. Following her sad end, Plath became the subject of a rather creepy elevation to cult status.

Plato (*c*.427–*c*.347BC) Greek philosopher, who is regarded as the main founder of Western philosophy. Taught by SOCRATES, Plato was in turn ARISTOTLE's tutor. His *Theory of Forms*, in which the objects as we perceive them are distinguished from the idea of the objects, has had a strong influence on many writers, e.g. DONNE, WORDSWORTH, and, most of all, SHELLEY (*see also* NEOPLATONISM). The term *Platonic love* has been derived from Plato's works to denote a selfless non-physical love for another, although Plato's interest in young men was certainly not non-physical. Plato's speculations are contained in dialogue form in several works, notably the *Symposium* and *Phaedo*, and in *The Republic*, the last being an examination of the principles of good government.

Plautus, Titus Maccius (*c*.254–*c*.184BC) Roman dramatist. His COMEDIES were adaptations of lost Greek originals (*see* MENANDER). He wrote about 130 plays, of which 20 are extant, featuring such stock characters as the wise servant who knows more than his master (WODEHOUSE's Jeeves is a distant descendant). It was through the plays of Plautus and TERENCE that succeeding dramatists inherited the classical comic tradition, and many of his plots, adaptations themselves, have been adapted by others (SHAKESPEARE's *Comedy of Errors* is a version of a Plautus play).

plein air The French term for "open air," used of paintings that have been produced out of doors and not in a studio. *Plein air* painting was particularly popular with the BARBIZON SCHOOL and became a central tenet of IMPRESSIONISM.

Plotinus *see* **Neoplatonism**.

Pocock, Isaac *see* **melodrama**.

Poe, Edgar Allan (1809–49) American short-story writer, poet and critic. His macabre, highly Gothic horror stories, e.g. *Tales of the Grotesque and Arabesque* (1839), are studies in pathological obsession with a strong element of sadism, and feature themes such as premature burial and necrophilia. The best of the stories, e.g. "The Masque of the Red Death," have retained their power, as have the best of his poems, e.g. "The Raven." His detective stories, e.g. "The Murders in the Rue Morgue," are very good (and influential) early examples of the form.

poet laureate A poet appointed to a court or other formal institution. In Britain, the post is held for life and the poet laureate is expected, although not forced, to write a poem to commemorate important events. Ben JONSON held the post unofficially, being succeeded by DAVENANT. The first official poet laureate was

DRYDEN, who was also the first to lose the post before his death, in the upheaval surrounding the "Glorious Revolution." Dryden's successor in 1689 was SHADWELL. TATE held the office from 1692–1715 and Nicholas ROWE 1715–18. **Laurence Eusden** (1688–1730) succeeded in 1718, more for political reasons than for poetic ones. He is better known for being mentioned in POPE's *Dunciad* for his drinking habits than for any skill as a poet. His successor in 1730, the actor and dramatist **Colley Cibber** (1671–1757), also became a target of the *The Dunciad*, Pope personifying him as "Dullness" in the final edition. The appointment in 1757 of the dramatist **William Whitehead** (1715–85) also attracted satirical comment, in the face of which he remained calm, a course he recommended in *A Charge to the Poets* (1762). WARTON held the post from 1785 to 1790, and **Henry James Pye** (1745–1813) from 1790 to 1813. The reputation of the post revived a little with the appointment of SOUTHEY in 1813 and considerably with WORDSWORTH (1843–50) and TENNYSON (1850–92) but suffered a setback with the appointment of AUSTIN in 1896. The 20th-century holders of the post were BRIDGES (1913–30), MASEFIELD (1930–67), DAY-LEWIS (1968–72), BETJEMAN (1972–84), and Ted HUGHES (1984–).

pointillism *see* **Neo-Impressionism**.

Pollaiuolo, Antonio del (1431–98) Florentine artist who ran a workshop with his brother **Piero** (1441–96). They continued the traditions of CASTAGNO and Filippo LIPPI, both of whom influenced their work. Although they collaborated on many works, including *The Martyrdom of St Sebastian* (1745), Antonio's superior talent is evident in his outstanding pen drawings. Their designs for the tombs of Pope Sixtus IV (1484–95) and Pope Innocent VIII (1492–8) had a strong influence on the works of BERNINI, CANOVA and MICHELANGELO.

Pollock, Jackson (1912–56) American painter. A major figure in ABSTRACT EXPRESSIONIST painting, his early influences include American Indian art. In the late 1930s he worked on the FEDERAL ARTS PROJECT and explored mythical and SURREALIST imagery, e.g. *Guardians of the Secret* (1943). From the 1940s he developed a more abstract and painterly style, creating the works for which he is best remembered, in which the paint is poured and splattered over a canvas on the floor, e.g. *Echo, Number 25, 1951* and *Blue Poles* (1953). His style was uniquely innovative and influential over a whole generation of abstract painters.

polyptych A painting, usually an ALTARPIECE, consisting of two or more paintings within a decorative frame. *See also* DIPTYCH, TRIPTYCH.

Pontormo [Jacopo Carucci] (1494–1557) Italian painter who took his name from his native village in Tuscany. He trained under PIERO DI COSIMO and may have studied with LEONARDO prior to entering the workshop of ANDREA DEL SARTO in 1512. He established his MANNERIST style with *Joseph in Egypt* (c.1515) and worked for the MEDICI family from 1520–21. His works are characterized by vivid colours and a graceful dynamism conveying a strong spiritual feeling and sense of grandeur. Influences include MICHELANGELO and DÜRER, and a notable work is *The Deposition* (c.1526–8).

Pop Art A realistic art style that uses techniques and subjects from commercial art, comic strips, posters, etc. The most notable exponents include LICHTENSTEIN, OLDENBURG, and RAUSCHENBERG.

Pope, Alexander (1688–1744) English poet. His poetry is generally divided into three (rather arbitrary) periods; an early period in which he made his name as a poet with, especially, the *Essay on Criticism* (1711), a poetic manifesto of NEOCLASSICAL principles, the nature poems such as *Windsor Forest* (1713), a mock-heroic love poem, *The Rape of the Lock* (1714), designed to reunite two feuding upper-class Roman Catholic families (Pope was himself a Catholic); a middle period in which his translations of HOMER's *Iliad* (1720) and *Odyssey* (1725–6) and his edition of SHAKESPEARE (1725) made him rich; a third period spent at Twickenham (outside London) where he completed his great satire on his contemporaries, *The Dunciad* (1728), and philosophical poems such as *An Essay on Man* (1733–4). Pope's reputation suffered a partial eclipse during the 19th century (although BYRON vigorously defended his verse). However, his mastery of the rhymed couplet, his deadly satirical powers and gift for sustaining a metaphor, place him as one of the most important English poets. *See also* ADDISON.

portraiture The art of painting, drawing or sculpting the likeness of someone, either the face, the figure to the waist, or the whole person. Portraits vary from the idealized or romanticized to the realistic.

poster paint *see* **gouache**.

Postimpressionism A blanket term used to describe the works of artists in the late 19th century, who rejected IMPRESSIONISM. It was not a movement in itself, and most of the artists it refers to worked in widely divergent and independent styles. They include BRAQUE, PICASSO, CÉZANNE, GAUGUIN, van GOGH and MATISSE. The name was originated by the English art critic **Roger Fry** (1866–1934), an enthusiastic supporter of modern art, who organized the first London exhibition of Postimpressionist painters in 1912.

Poststructuralism *see* **Structuralism**.

Pound, Ezra [Weston Loomis] (1885–1972) American poet, editor, translator and critic. Notable poetry volumes include *Quia Pauper Amaris* (1919), *Hugh Selwyn Mauberley* (1920) and the unfinished sequence of poems entitled *Cantos* (1925–70). Pound gave generous support to T. S. ELIOT, JOYCE, ROSENBERG and HEMINGWAY, and many others. He lived in Italy from 1925, where he became a supporter of Italian fascism and broadcast propaganda against the Allies during World War II. He was committed to a US mental asylum after the war until 1958, when he returned to Italy. *See* IMAGISM.

Poussin, Nicolas (1594–1655) French painter. He studied the ANTIQUE in Rome and was influenced by TITIAN and VERONESE, e.g. *The Poet's Inspiration* (*c*.1628). During the 1630s he developed a more CLASSICAL style and was commissioned to decorate the Grande Salle of the Louvre, but his preference was for easel paintings rather than large-scale decorative works. He was a painstaking worker, completing paintings from numerous drawings and from specially created miniature sets with wax figures. *The Holy Family on the Steps* (1648) marks his achievement of a pure, harmonious classical order. Through his works in figure composition and landscape, he exerted a huge influence and set the standard in painting for almost the next two centuries.

Powell, Anthony [Dymoke] (1905–) English novelist, noted particularly for his sequence of 12 novels entitled *A Dance to the Music of Time*, beginning with *A Question of Upbringing* (1951) and ending with *Hearing Secret Harmonies* (1975). The sequence is a large canvas (the title is from a Poussin painting) of British cultural, social and political life from the 1930s to the 1970s.

Powys, J[ohn] C[owper] (1872–1963) English novelist, essayist and poet. His novels include *Wolf Solent* (1929), *Weymouth Sands* (1934) and his masterpiece,

A Glastonbury Romance (1932), in which the ancient spiritual world of the town of Glastonbury (a centre of Arthurian, Christian and pagan legend) is entwined with the everyday lives of the novel's characters. His brother **T[heodore] F[rancis] Powys** (1875–1953) also wrote novels and stories in the same West Country setting, the most notable of which is the remarkable fantasy novel *Mr Weston's Good Wine* (1927), in which God descends upon an English village in the form of a vintner selling the wines of love and death (the title taken from Jane AUSTEN's *Emma*). Another brother, **Llewellyn Powys** (1884–1939), was a journalist and essayist, whose *Skin for Skin* (1925) is an account of his fight against tuberculosis and contains periods of West Country idyll when the disease abated.

Pre-Raphaelite Brotherhood A movement founded in 1848 by Holman HUNT, MILLAIS and ROSSETTI, who wanted to raise standards in British art. They drew their imagery from medieval legends and literature in an attempt to provide an escape from industrial materialism. They sought to recreate the innocence of Italian painting before RAPHAEL, and were influenced by the works of the NAZARENES. They had a large following, partly due to the support of the critic John RUSKIN, which included BURNE-JONES and William MORRIS. The movement broke up in 1853.

Priestley, J[ohn] B[oynton] (1891–1984) English novelist and dramatist. His huge output includes the novels *The Good Companions* (1929) and *Angel Pavement* (1930), the plays *Time and the Conways* (1937) and the much staged mystery *An Inspector Calls* (1947). His uplifting radio broadcasts during World War II made him one of the best-known literary figures during the 1940s.

primary colours The colours red, blue and yellow, which in painting cannot be produced by mixing other colours. Primary colours are mixed to make orange (red and yellow), purple (red and blue) and green (blue and yellow), which are the secondary colours.

Prior, Matthew (1664–1721) English poet, diplomat and spy. His first important work, *The Hind and Panther Transvers'd* (1687), was a satire on Dryden's defence of Roman Catholicism. Much of Prior's subsequent life was spent immersed in the murky waters of political intrigue and espionage, and earned him a year in jail. The best of his poems are light, mock-serious lyrics such as "Jinny the Just" and "Henry and Emma." Addison described him as a master of the "easy way of writing," i.e. of epigrammatic, everyday expression.

Pritchett, Sir V[ictor] S[awdon] (1900–) English short-story writer, novelist, essayist and critic. He is best known for his excellent short stories, a collected edition of which was published in 1983. His critical works, e.g. *The Living Novel* (1946), have been highly praised for their shrewd insights into the creative process.

Proust, Marcel (1871–1922) French novelist, essayist and critic, known principally for his long semi-autobiographical novel in seven sections, *A la recherche du temps perdu* (1913–27). The book was first translated into English as *Remembrance of Things Past* (1922–31) by Charles Scott-Moncrieff (1889–1930) and consists of *Swann's Way, Within a Budding Grove, The Guermantes' Way, Cities of the Plain, The Captive, The Sweet Cheat Gone*, and *Time Regained*. The novel provides a fascinating picture of the narrator Marcel's often convoluted relationships and artistic vocation in upper-class French society. By subjecting a mass of detail to an analytical eye and by using a circular form for the novel, Proust broke new ground in conveying the complexity of life and time and the importance of memory, and had a great influence on 20th-century novelists, e.g. Virginia WOOLF.

Pryce-Jones, David (1936–) English novelist, biographer and travel writer. His work includes the novels *Owls and Satyrs* (1960); his nonfiction work includes *Paris in the Third Reich* (1981) and a controversial and pessimistic study of Arab culture, *The Closed Circle* (1989).

Psalmanazar, George (*c.*1679–1763) French-born English literary hoaxer. Little is known for certain of his origins; he arrived in London in 1703, claiming to be a "Formosan," for which country he invented a language and to which published a travel guide. After years as a hack writer, he eventually (in 1728) renounced his imposture and became, strangely enough, a much respected literary figure. Dr JOHNSON called him "the best man he ever knew."

Pushkin, Alexander (1799–1837) Russian poet, novelist and dramatist. Widely regarded as Russia's greatest poet, the best known of his works are the historical tragedy *Boris Gudonov* (1825), the verse novel *Eugene Onegin* (1823–31) and the macabre short story "The Queen of Spades." His life was brought to a premature end in a duel.

Puvis de Chavannes (1824–98) French painter. He trained under DELACROIX and established his reputation as a decorative mural painter working in oils rather than fresco. His chaste, timeless allegorical works, such as *The Inspiring Muses* (1893–5), were extremely popular and highly influential. *The Poor Fisherman* (1881) is typical of his SYMBOLIST style.

Pye, Henry James *see* **poet laureate.**

Pym, Barbara (1913–80) English novelist, whose works are gently satirical, occasionally melancholic, comedies of middle-class life, with clergyman and/or university dons frequently involved in a foreground

dominated by an ironically observant (unmarried)
lady. Representative examples are *Excellent Women*
(1952), *Less than Angels* (1955), *A Glass of Blessings*
(1958) and *Quartet in Autumn* (1977). She was a friend
of Philip LARKIN, who admired her work greatly.

Pynchon, Thomas (1937–) American novelist, whose
huge and complex books employ black humour to portray his vision of humanity's struggle against technology. His best-known novels are *V* (1963) and *Grav-
ity's Rainbow* (1973).

Q

Quarton [Charonton], Enguerrand (*c*.1410–66) French medieval painter. Only two of his authenticated works have survived: *The Virgin of Mercy* (1452) and *The Coronation of the Virgin* (1454). The *Avignon Pieté* has also been attributed to him. His works are characterized by strong light and powerful draughtsmanship, richly illuminated.

quattrocento An Italian term that refers to 15th-century Italian art, often used descriptively of the early RENAISSANCE period.

Queirolo, Francesco (1704–62) Italian sculptor. He worked in Rome and Naples and was influenced by BERNINI. The intricacy of his work is evident in his *Allegory of Deception Unmasked* (1750s) which is of outstandingly high quality.

Quellin, Artus I (1609–68) Flemish sculptor. He studied in Rome and established his reputation as a CLASSICAL sculptor in his decoration of Amsterdam Town Hall (1650–64). He also carried out commissions for portraits and religious sculptures, e.g. *St Peter* (1658). His cousin, **Artus II** (1625–1700), sculpted in a more BAROQUE style, as in *God the Father* (1682), and his nephew, **Artus III** [Arnold Quellin] (1653–86), who settled in England in 1678, won an important commission for the tomb of Thomas Thynne (1682).

Quercia, Jacopo della [Jacopo di Pietro d'Angelo] (*c*. 1375–1438) Italian sculptor from Siena, a contemporary of GHIBERTI and DONATELLO. He competed unsuccessfully for the commission for the Baptistry doors of Florence Cathedral in 1401, but went on to create the tomb of Ilaria del Carretto (*c*.1406) in Lucca. This demonstrates an odd mixture of styles, which are more successfully reconciled in a later work, the Fonte Gaia (1409–19) in Siena. His last major commission was for the relief scenes of *Genesis* and *The Birth of Christ* at San Petronio in Bologna, the energetic directness and strength of which were admired by MICHELANGELO.

Quidor, John (1801–81) American painter. He was influenced by Netherlandish painting and by the English satirists HOGARTH and ROWLANDSON. He drew his imagery from literary sources, e.g. *The Return of Rip van Winkle* (1829), but his lively and humorous genre paintings were generally unappreciated, and he was obliged to earn his living as a sign painter.

R

Rabelais, François (*c.*1494–*c.*1553) French physician and satirist, noted for his huge, rambling prose fantasy *Gargantua and Pantagruel* (1553–62), which includes many fascinating insights into the intellectual currents of the age. The adjective "Rabelaisian" is used to denote language that is healthily and robustly bawdy; however, as ORWELL pointed out, there is little that is healthy about the grossly anti-female content of *Gargantua and Pantagruel*, even by late medieval standards.

Racine, Jean (1639–99) French dramatist, regarded as the finest of the French tragedians. Several of his plays, e.g. *Andromache* (1667) and *Phaedra* (1677) have been performed in English translations from the late 17th century onwards, but the only productions that have achieved any real popularity on the British and American stage are those that have parted quite radically from Racine's strict NEOCLASSICAL principles. The full impact of Racine's powerfully restrained language can only be appreciated in the original French.

Radcliffe, Mrs Ann (1764–1823) English novelist, whose GOTHIC NOVELS, e.g. *A Sicilian Romance* (1790) and *The Mysteries of Udolpho* (1794), were very popular in their day, but are now largely remembered as part-sources for Jane AUSTEN's wonderful satire on the Gothic novel, *Northanger Abbey*.

Raeburn, Sir Henry (1756–1823) Scottish painter. He

was in London from 1784, where he met Joshua REYN-OLDS, then visited Italy before settling in Edinburgh in 1787. He established himself as a society portraitist and held a position in Scotland similar to that of Reynolds in England. He worked directly on to the canvas without preliminary studies or sketches, in a bold, original style. This occasionally resulted in a somewhat flashy superficiality, but still retained a freshness that suited the character of his sitters, e.g. *The MacNab* (*c.*1803–13). Another notable work is the delightfully unusual *Reverend Robert Walker skating* (*c.*1784).

Raine, Kathleen [Jessel] (1908–) Anglo-Scottish poet and critic, whose work reflects her life-long mystical vision of the world (Blake and Neoplatonism are the major concerns of her critical work). Her works include *Collected Poems* (1981), and three autobiographical volumes, *Farewell Happy Fields* (1973), *The Land Unknown* (1975) and *The Lion's Mouth* (1977).

Ramsay, Allan (1713–84) Scottish painter. The son of Allan Ramsay the poet, he studied in London, Naples and Rome, settling in London in 1737. His graceful female portraits, e.g. *Rosamund Sargent* (1749), and his tasteful cosmopolitan air established his popularity. Later works, influenced by French pastellists and a second visit to Rome (1754–7), were lighter and more delicate, culminating in the masterpiece, *The Artist's Wife* (*c.*1755). He ranked alongside his contemporary, REYNOLDS, and his work forms a link between that of HOGARTH and GAINSBOROUGH. His last major works were the coronation portraits of *George III* and *Queen Charlotte* (1761–2). He gave up painting after an accident in 1773.

Ransome, Arthur (1884–1967) English novelist and journalist. Ransome's first popular success was as a popularizer of Russian folk tales, with his *Old Peter's Russian Tales* (1916), and he subsequently became an authority on (and propagandist for) the Bolshevik Revolution, and one of British journalism's best-known foreign correspondents (he married Trotsky's ex-secretary in 1924). He is best remembered, however, for his classic children's adventure novels, the first three of which were *Swallows and Amazons* (1930), *Swallowdale* (1931) and *Peter Duck* (1932). Nine more children's bestsellers were to follow. (His publisher only reluctantly accepted *Swallows and Amazons*, being much more interested in his fishing essays, *Rod and Line*, 1929).

Ransom, John Crowe (1888–1974) American poet and critic. His poetic output, e.g. *Poems about God* (1919) and *Two Gentlemen in Bonds* (1926), was small but is highly regarded, as are his literary studies, *God without Thunder* (1930) and *The New Criticism* (1941).

Raphael [Raffaello Sanzio] (1483–1520) Italian painter from Urbino, a leading figure of the High RENAISSANCE. He is thought to have studied under PERUGINO, and he was deeply influenced by the works of MICHELANGELO and LEONARDO during a visit to Florence *c*.1504. By the age of 25, he had established enough of a reputation to be summoned to Rome by Pope Julius II, where he painted the *School of Athens* fresco (*c*.1509). He spent the rest of his career in Rome, where he enjoyed huge success and was in such great demand that from *c*.1515 much of his work was carried out by assistants, most notably **Giulio Romano** (*c*.1492–1546), who went on to be one of the major exponents of MANNERISM. Raphael's adaptability and openness to influence, combined with his own self-assurance, helped him achieve the harmony and balance that was to characterize High Renaissance art. His fully human portrayals of the Madonna and the Holy Family are imbued with a deep religious feeling as he combined Christian ideals with the grace and grandeur of classical antiquity. He had a strong influence on TITIAN and was emulated by succeeding generations of painters well into modern times.

Rattigan, Sir Terence [Mervyn] (1911–77) English dramatist. Many of his plays, e.g. the comedy *French Without Tears* (1936), and the melodramas of middle-class hypocrisy and crisis, *The Browning Version* (1948) and *The Deep Blue Sea* (1952), having become firm repertory favourites. Another notable play is *Ross* (1960), a psychological study of T. E. LAWRENCE during his life in semi-hiding as an RAF aircraftsman. The new wave of dramatists of the 1950s and 1960s (primarily the ANGRY YOUNG MEN), tended to denigrate Rattigan's plays, describing them as middle-class and trivial. More recent critical opinion regards Rattigan as a sensitive explorer of regions or spiritual aridity.

Rauschenberg, Robert (1925–) American artist. He trained at Black Mountain College under ALBERS, who influenced his early style. From *c*.1954 he began to experiment with "combine-paintings," in which he applied paint to ordinary objects, e.g. *Bed* (1955). His best-known work in this style is *Monogram* (1959), in which a stuffed goat with a tyre around its middle is splattered with paint after the manner of the abstract expressionists. His works form a link between the introversion of ABSTRACT EXPRESSIONISM and the worldly celebration of pop art. A continuing interest in the relationship between everyday objects and created images is expressed in his screenprints and collages of the 1960s. *Jammers* (1975–6) is typical of his more recent innovative experiments.

Ray, Man (1890–1976) American artist. He studied in New York and founded the DADA group there, along with DUCHAMP and PICABIA. He experimented with SURREALISM and photography, developing the "rayograph," a photographic image created by placing objects directly on to a light-sensitive plate. From 1921–40 he worked in Paris and did some film-making, e.g. *L'Etoile de Mer* (1928).

Realism In literature, a true and faithful representation of reality in fiction. Once defined, discussion of the term usually breaks down into personal prejudices of various kinds. The process of distinguishing the term from NATURALISM is particularly fraught; any artist must select from the chaos of life in order to create, and in the process of choosing must impose some personal, even if banal, vision on the world, and in the process either convince the reader that the world portrayed is a real one, or fail. In the last analysis, there is only good writing and bad writing. Sometimes the process of conviction occurs *despite* the author's intervention; thus George ELIOT, often described as the first great Realist of English fiction, begins a chapter of *Middlemarch* with the words "Destiny stands by sarcastic, our fate in her hands." The action of the novel in fact contradicts this snooty deterministic pronouncement rather well. BALZAC is regarded as the founding father of literary realism in the novel (*see* MARX).

In art, Realism is taken to be in general, the objective representation of scenes. The term is used particularly of the 19th-century French painters, e.g. DAUMIER and COURBET, who broke away from CLASSICISM and ROMANTICISM.

The genre of *socialist realism*, which GORKY helped to create (*see also* DEUS EX MACHINA, NEOCLASSICISM), bears no relation to Realism; the term usually denotes any form of fiction, within a socialist dictatorship, that is written to serve the interests of the ruling clique of that state by lauding the achievements of "the socialist paradise where there is no more pain or suffering, where happy people under the guidance of wise leaders construct a new life and harshly chastize their enemies" (Igor Golomstock, *Totalitarian Art* 1990). *See also* FUTURISM, MAGIC REALISM.

Redon, Odilon (1840–1916) French painter and lithographer. He influenced the SURREALIST MOVEMENT with his dreamlike images drawn from the works of Edgar Allan Poe and Baudelaire. His pastel drawings of flowers and his portraits make use of intense, translucent colour, e.g. *Silence*. His writings were published in letters and diaries during the 1920s.

Redpath, Anne (1895–1965) Scottish painter, who studied in Edinburgh and worked in France from 1919 to 1934. Scenes from the Mediterranean coast, villages and church interiors are vigorously painted in thick impasto and rich joyful colour. The still life *Pinks* (1947) is a representative work.

Redskins and Palefaces A distinction between authors who write about outdoor, manly topics such as men at war (Redskins), and those who write about the problems and relationships of indoors, "cultivated" people. The distinction was formulated by an American academic, Leslie Fielder, and works easily in terms of much American literature, e.g. Hemingway is as obviously a Redskin as Henry JAMES is a Paleface. The distinction is less helpful elsewhere.

Reinhardt, Ad[olf] (1913–67) American painter. He studied in New York and was a member of the American Abstract Artists from 1947. He experimented with ABSTRACT EXPRESSIONISM and studied oriental art during the 1940s. In the 1950s, however, he assumed a more formal style of hard-edged abstraction, and eventually achieved an almost minimalist approach in his *Black Paintings* (1960–62) in which a square canvas is divided into nine equal, barely distinguishable black squares.

relief A sculptural form that is not freestanding. The

three-dimensional shape is either carved, e.g. in stone, wood, ivory, etc, or built up, as in metal, etc. Relief sculpture can be *low relief* (*basso relievo* or *bas-relief*), where the depth of the pattern is less than half; *medium relief* (*mezzo relievo*), where the depth is roughly half; or *high relief* (*alto relievo*), where practically all the medium has been removed. The extremely low-relief technique of *stiacciato*, "drawing in marble," was devised by DONATELLO.

Rembrandt Harmensz, van Rijn (1606–69) Dutch painter, draughtsman and etcher from Leyden. He trained in Amsterdam, where he developed a CARAVAGGesque style, as in *The Stoning of St Stephen* (1625). He established his reputation as a portraitist with *The Anatomy Lesson of Dr Tulp* (1632) and was subsequently in great demand, painting more than 40 commissions in the next two years. In 1634 he married Saskia van Uylenburgh, and painted the confident *Self Portrait with Saskia*. He reached the peak of his BAROQUE style in 1636 with *The Blinding of Samson*, and later works are less dramatic, although more spiritually and psychologically perceptive, e.g. *Supper at Emmaus*. His series of self portraits painted over a period of about 40 years reveals the growing insight and depth paralleled in other works. Youthful exuberance and flamboyant style gives way to patience, compassion and essential simplicity. The drama of early works is replaced by a profound, compelling intensity. As a result, he was less favoured as a society portraitist, and his genius went unappreciated except by a few perceptive clients, e.g. *Jan Six* (1654). Rembrandt died alone and in poverty, having outlived his wife, his son Titus, and his mistress Hendrikje Stoffels. He was not mourned nationally, and it was to be another 50 years before his unique genius and indubitable influence were recognized.

Renaissance In literature, the revival of the arts that occurred in Europe in the 14th–16th centuries, as a result of the rediscovery of the writing of the great classical writers, notably the works of PLATO and ARISTOTLE. In the case of the latter, the "rediscovery" occurred in terms of reinterpretation; instead of taking the texts of Aristotle as literal, unchallengable authority, as medieval scholars had tended to do, the new thinkers, such as Francis BACON (the father of modern scientific method) approached written authority with a new, sceptical eye. The Renaissance period in England is usually given as 1500–1660, i.e. from the visit of Erasmus (*see* Thomas MORE) in 1599 to the RESTORATION.

In art, the early Renaissance was established in Italy with the works of GIOTTO, in a spectacular move away from Gothic conventions and ideals. The sculptors PISANO and DONATELLO emulated Greek and Roman sculpture in an expression of the new humanist and aesthetic values of the "age of reason." The movement reached a peak between 1500 and 1520 with the works of LEONARDO DA VINCI, MICHELANGELO and RAPHAEL. The Northern Renaissance took place as ideas spread to Germany, the Netherlands and the rest of Europe during the early 16th century.

Reni, Guido (1575–1642) Italian painter and engraver from Bologna. After training at the CARRACCI Academy he made several visits to Rome, where he established himself as a leading BAROQUE artist and a rival of CARAVAGGIO with the ceiling fresco *Aurora* (1613–14). He ran a highly productive studio in Bologna, producing mainly religious paintings that maintained their popularity throughout the 17th and 18th centuries. He was an important and influential figure whose works were much imitated.

Renoir, Pierre Auguste (1841–1919) French

IMPRESSIONIST painter. He trained in Paris, where he met MONET and SISLEY and began to paint out of doors. He exhibited in the first three Impressionist exhibitions and thereafter pursued his own version of Impressionism, giving more value to perspective, solidity of form and preliminary sketches, e.g. *The Bathers* (c.1884–7). Other notable works include *Mme Carpentier and her Children* (1876) and *Moulin de la Galette* (1876).

representational art *see* **figurative art**.

reredos *see* **altarpiece**.

Restoration (1) The re-establishment of the British monarchy in 1660, following the return to England of Charles II in that year. (2) The period of Charles II's reign (1660–85). The characteristics of Restoration literature are wit, salaciousness, and religious and philosophical questioning. Some typical Restoration literary figures include ROCHESTER, DRYDEN, ETHEREGE, CONGREVE, WYCHERLEY, PEPYS, BUNYAN, HOBBES, MARVELL, FARQUHAR (*see also* WESLEY, MILTON). **Restoration comedy**, *see* **comedy of manners**.

retable *see* **altarpiece**.

revenge tragedy A form of TRAGEDY that appeared in the late Elizabethan period, heavily influenced by the bloodthirsty language and plots of SENECA's plays, in which revenge, often for the death of a son or father, is the prime motive. Thomas KYD's *The Spanish Tragedy* (1588–9) is the earliest example, *Hamlet* (1602) the greatest. MARLOWE's *The Jew of Malta* (1592) and TOURNEUR's *The Revenger's Tragedy* (1607) are two other notable examples (*see* JACOBEAN TRAGEDY).

Reyes, Ricardo Neftalí *see* **Neruda, Pablo**.

Reynolds, Sir Joshua (1723–92) English painter and art theorist. He trained in London and worked as a portraitist in his native Devon. He visited Italy in 1950–52 and developed his theories on the Grand

Manner from his studies of RENAISSANCE and BAROQUE painting and CLASSICAL sculpture. On his return to London he began to organize his sitters in the poses of classical sculpture, e.g. *Commodore Keppel* (1753). As first president of the Royal Academy, he set high standards in portraiture and history painting, and as a versatile and prolific painter, he enhanced the reputation of English art.

Ribera, Jusepe *or* **José de** *called* **"Lo Spagnoletto"** (1591–1652) Spanish painter, engraver and draughtsman. He spent nearly all his career in Italy, where he was influenced by the works of CARAVAGGIO. Notable works include *The Martyrdom of St Bartholomew* (*c*.1630) and *The Clubfooted Boy* (1642). Later works are painted with a lighter palette, and their broadly painted, rich colours convey a deepening sense of spirituality, e.g. *The Mystic Marriage of St Catherine* (1648). He was a major influence on Spanish and Italian painting.

Richardson, Dorothy [Miller] (1873–1957) English novelist, noted for her "stream of consciousness" (*see* William JAMES) narrative technique or "interior monologue," as she called it, which anticipated JOYCE's use of the technique in *Ulysses* (the device was not really new; similar effects can be found in, e.g. DICKENS). Her work enjoyed a considerable revival in the 1970s. Her best-known work is the semi-autobiographical *Pilgrimage* sequence of novels, e.g. *Pointed Roofs* (1915) and (posthumously) *March Moonlight* (1967).

Richardson, Samuel (1689–1761) English novelist. All his novels were written in epistolary form, and all were highly popular. The first was *Pamela; or Virtue Rewarded* (1740), in which a servant girl achieves an upwardly mobile marriage by resisting seduction (the work was savagely attacked by Fielding in *Shamela* for its dubious morality). Richardson subsequently published *Clarissa Harlowe* (1747–8) and *Sir Charles Grandison* (1753–4). Fielding was not the only contemporary to feel unease at the moral ambiguity of Richardson's work, or the tendentious verbosity of much of the prose. However, Fielding's sister Sarah (also a novelist) and Dr JOHNSON were convinced of Richardson's superiority to all novelists for his insight into human (especially female) character, and for his portrayal of the darker aspects of human behaviour.

Riding, Laura Jackson *see* **Graves, Robert**.

Rilke, Rainer Maria (1875–1926) German poet. His lyrical, mystical poems, in such volumes as *Duino Elegies* (1922) and *Sonnets to Orpheus* (1923), are regarded as being amongst the finest religious verse published this century.

Rimbaud, Arthur (1854–91) French poet. An early SYMBOLIST, he stopped writing poetry at the age of 19 after a torrid affair with VERLAINE, described in *Une Saison en enfer* (*A Season in Hell*) (1873). Some of the pieces in his collection of hallucinatory, vivid prose poems, *Les Illuminations* (1884), were set to music by Benjamin Britten.

Riopelle, Jean Paul (1923–) Canadian abstract painter and sculptor. He founded Les Automatistes along with BORDUAS in Canada, but settled in Paris from 1946. Early works are lyrical in style, but he gradually developed an interest in surface texture, possibly influenced by POLLOCK, e.g. *Knight Watch* (1953). His interest in texture is also represented in his sculptural works.

Rivera, Diego (1886–1957) Mexican painter. He studied in Mexico and Madrid, and worked in Paris from 1911. His early influences include CUBISM, but on returning to Mexico in 1922 he developed a style derived from Mexican and Aztec art. A leading muralist, he carried out commissions for public buildings in

Mexico, and later in San Francisco and New York. Notable works include mosaics for the Mexico City National Stadium.

Rivers, Larry (1923–) American artist. He originally trained as a musician and began painting in 1945. Influences include ABSTRACT EXPRESSIONISM and IMPRESSIONISM, from which he developed a painterly, figurative style. He was associated with the younger generation of the New York School. Notable works include *Washington crossing the Delaware* (1953).

Robbe-Grillet, Alain (1922–) French novelist, whose works, e.g. *Topology of a Phantom City* (1975), and the screenplay *Last Year in Marienbad* (filmed 1961), are regarded as "new novels" or "antinovels," or, more simply, as unreadable novels. His work has not achieved a great deal of popularity, not even in France.

Robinson, Edwin Arlington (1869–1935) American poet. His early poems are mostly concerned with New England small-town characters, e.g. *The Children of the Night* (1897). His later verse includes a trilogy on the Arthurian legend, *Merlin* (1917), *Lancelot* (1920) and *Tristram* (1927).

Rochester, John Wilmot, 2nd Earl of (1647–80) English poet. Renowned (and feared) for his savage wit and supposedly limitless depths of depravity, his verse is among the most sexually explicit in English (or any language). A representative (and very fine) poem is his "Satyr Against Mankind" (1675), with its memorable image of man as, in death, "a reasoning engine" huddled in dirt. Graham GREENE's *Lord Rochester's Monkey* (1974) is the best introduction to the man and his work.

Rocky Mountain School *see* **Bierstadt, Albert**.

Rococo A style in art following on from BAROQUE and even more exaggerated in terms of embellishments and mannered flourishes. It became established around the beginning of the 18th century and spread throughout Europe, lasting up until the advent of NEOCLASSICISM in the 1760s. The main exponents of the style were FRAGONARD, WATTEAU, and BOUCHER in France and, to a lesser extent, TIEPOLO in Italy and HOGARTH in England. It continued in some areas to the end of the century, particularly in church decoration.

Rodchenko, Alexander Mikhailovich (1891–1956) Russian artist. His early works were influenced by MALEVICH, but he soon developed a more rigorous approach of "nonobjectivism." A typical work of this period is *Black on Black* (1918). He subsequently worked in a CONSTRUCTIVIST style, concentrating on line and also producing some delicate hanging sculptures in a similar vein. From 1922 he followed the utilitarian approach of TATLIN, experimenting with photomontage and designing textiles and posters.

Rodin, Auguste (1840–1917) French sculptor. He suffered considerable setbacks in his early career, including three rejections from the Ecole des Beaux Arts. He came to prominence in a whirlwind of controversy over *The Age of Bronze* (1875–6), a male nude figure that he was accused of having cast from life. The vitality of the piece was in fact inspired by the works of DONATELLO and MICHELANGELO, which Rodin had studied during a visit to Italy in 1875. It was bought by the state, who commissioned *The Gates of Hell,* a bronze door for a planned museum of art. It was never completed, although the project occupied most of the rest of his career. Figures for the door, enlarged into independent pieces, include some of his most famous works, *The Thinker*, *The Kiss* and *Adam and Eve*. The rough realism of Rodin's modelling and its intense ROMANTICISM were too radical for the commissioners of the monument to Balzac in 1897, but from 1900 on he won increasing recognition. He was responsible for reviving sculpture as an independent art form rather than as an embellishment or decoration for buildings and monuments. His influence was huge, particularly with the sculptors BOURDELLE and MAILLOL.

Rolle, Richard *see* **Julian of Norwich, Dame**.

Romanticism A term denoting any movement in the arts which emphasizes feeling and content as opposed to form and order. The Romantic Movement can be roughly dated from the late 18th century to the early 19th century, although the contrast between the need to express emotion and the desirability of following artistic rules dates back as far as the great Athenian dramatists (e.g. the contrast between AESCHYLUS and SOPHOCLES). Other distinctive features of the Romantic Movement are: the supremacy of individual over collective judgment; a "progressive" faith in the reformability and essential goodness of humanity; the supremacy of "natural" and "organic" virtues over society's artifical construction. The extent and meaning of Romanticism in 18th-century English literature is still a matter of hot debate. It is certainly true that elements of what we call Romanticism can be found in poets such as COWPER and SMART, and even in Dr JOHNSON's writings, but the first great works of Romantic literature are BLAKE's works of the 1790s and WORDSWORTH and COLERIDGE's *Lyrical Ballads* (1798). Debate on the merits or demerits of Romanticism tends to be conducted in aphoristic terms, e.g. GOETHE's dictum (in rejection of his early Romantic principles) that "Classicism is health, Romanticism disease." Other prominent Romantic poets are BYRON, SHELLEY, KEATS, HEINE and SCOTT. *Compare* NEO-CLASSICISM.

In art, the movement dates from the late 18th until the mid-19th century. It was a reaction to the balanced harmony and order of CLASSICISM, and identified with the Romantic writers of the age. In response to increasing industrialization, Romantic painters viewed nature from a nostalgic point of view, imbuing landscapes with powerful emotions, often in a melancholic or melodramatic way. Notable Romantic artists include FUSELI, GOYA, DELACROIX, GÉRICAULT, FRIEDRICH, RUNGE, CONSTABLE, TURNER and the visionary Blake.

Rosenberg, Isaac (1890–1918) English poet and artist. His family were emigré Romanian Jews who settled in London's East End. By 1914 he had established a reputation as a promising poet; his first collection, *Night and Day* (1912), was praised by Pound. He enlisted in the British Army in 1914, and was killed in action in 1916. His war poems have a more objective tone than those of contemporaries such as OWEN and SASSOON, although they are no less grim (e.g. "Dead Man's Dump"). His *Collected Poems* were published in 1937.

Rosenstock, Samuel *see* **Tzara, Tristan**.

Rosetti, Dante Gabriel (1828–82) English painter and poet. He studied at the Royal Academy, and was a founding member of the PRE-RAPHAELITE BROTHERHOOD. He worked with BURNE-JONES and William MORRIS on murals for Oxford University Union. His paintings draw on medieval literature and legend for inspiration. His favourite models included his wife, Elizabeth Siddal, e.g. in *Beata Beatrix* (1864) and Jane Morris, the wife of William Morris. His works had an influence on SYMBOLISM.

Rosselli, Cosimo (1439–1507) Florentine painter. He worked on a fresco series for the Sistine Chapel in the Vatican. His own work was pedantic and uninspired but he had the gift of teaching others and ran an important workshop. His pupils included PIERO di COSIMO and Fra BARTOLOMMEO.

Rossetti, Christina Georgina (1830–94) English poet, noted for her reflective, occasionally melancholic religious poems. She also wrote verses for children, and the remarkable verse fairy story *Goblin Market* (1882). Her brother, **Dante Gabriel Rossetti** (1828–82), was both a poet and an artist. With the painters Millais and Holman Hunt, he founded the Pre-Raphaelite Brotherhood school of painting. His most famous poems are "The Blessed Damozel" (1850) and the fine sonnet sequence "The House of Life," the complete version of which is in *Ballads and Sonnets* (1881).

Rostand, Edmond (1868–1918) French dramatist and poet. His best-known work is his verse drama *Cyrano de Bergerac* (1897). *See* CYRANO DE BERGERAC.

Roth, Philip (1933–) American novelist and short-story writer. Much of his fiction is concerned with the problems (often sexual) of Jewish family life, e.g. the novella *Goodbye Columbus* (1959) and his hymn to masturbation, *Portnoy's Complaint* (1969). His novel *Deception* (1990) is intriguing semi-autobiographical work.

Rothko, Mark (1903–70) Latvian-born American painter, a leading figure of the New York School and a pioneer of COLOUR FIELD PAINTING. Early influences included SURREALISM, but from the 1950s he worked in an individual style of ABSTRACT EXPRESSIONISM, creating huge canvases overlaid with soft rectangular areas of colour, e.g. *Black on Maroon* and *Red on Maroon* (1958–9).

Rouault, Georges (1871–1958) French painter. He trained first as a stained glass designer before studying painting along with MATISSE. He joined the FAUVISTS in 1904, and while he made the same use of bright colours, his style was more influenced by his early training, many of his paintings resembling stained glass windows. His subject matter was concerned with human frailty, depicted in images of judges, prostitutes and sad clowns e.g. *Little Olympia* (1906). *Christ Mocked* (c.1932) is typical of his religious painting.

Rousseau, Henri Julien *called* **"Le Douanier"** (1844–1910) French painter. He worked in the Paris Toll Office, which earned him his soubriquet, and took up painting when he retired in 1885. He exhibited at the Salon des Independants (1886–9, 1901–10) and came into contact with PISSARRO, GAUGUIN and PICASSO in the course of his career. His NAIVE style was unaffected, however, and he continued to defy conventions of colour and perspective in his exotic imaginary landscapes and painted dreams, e.g. *The Dream* (1910).

Rousseau, Jean-Jacques (1712–78) French philosopher. His most notable fictional works are the novels *Julie, or the New Heloise* (1761) and *Emile* (1762), the former describing a highly improbably virtuous *menage à trois*, the latter being a didactic work on how to educate children (whom he saw as naturally good). These works and others, notably the political tract *The Social Contract* (1762), which begins with the famous statement "Man is born free, and is everywhere in chains," were profoundly influential on the intellectual ferment which resulted in the French Revolution (*see also* VOLTAIRE). His very frank 12 volumes of autobiography, *Confessions*, were published posthumously in 1781–8 and set a fashion for this style of reminiscence.

Rousseau, [Pierre Etienne] Théodore (1812–67) French landscape painter. He painted directly from nature and gained early success with *Forest of Compiègne* (1834), which was bought by the Duc d'Orléans. Over the next decade, however, he was consistently rejected by the Salon, and he became known as "*Le Grand Refusé*." He later became leader of the BARBIZON SCHOOL and exhibited again from 1849. Rousseau's work varied in quality and was always controversial.

Rowe Nicholas (1674–1718) English dramatist and poet, his best-known plays being *Tamerlane* (1702) and *Jane Shore* (1714), the latter written for the actress Sarah Siddons. His translation of the Roman poet Lucan's *Pharalia* (1718) was much admired by Dr JOHNSON, and he also produced an important edition of SHAKESPEARE. He was POET LAUREATE from 1715 until his death.

Rowlandson, Thomas (1756–1827) English caricaturist and printmaker. He studied at the Royal Academy Schools and in Paris, returning to London in 1777. He worked as a portraitist for a time, then began his famous watercolour caricatures and book illustrations. His popular series of engravings included *The Comforts of Bath* (1798) and *The Tour of Dr Syntax in search of the Picturesque* (1812, 1820 and 1821).

Rubens, Sir Peter Paul (1577–1640) Flemish painter and diplomat. He went to Italy in 1600, studying the works of TITIAN and VERONESE in Venice before entering the service of the Duke of Mantua. During a diplomatic visit to Madrid he painted numerous court portraits and historical scenes. On his return, he began copying famous works of Italian art for the Duke, and his own paintings of this period reflect the influence of the Italian RENAISSANCE. He returned to Antwerp in 1609, and became court painter to the Spanish viceroys, Albert and Isabella. He was already famous when he painted his masterpiece, the triptych *Descent from the Cross* (1611–14). In the 1620s he painted scenes from her life for Marie de' MEDICI in France. In 1628 he was again in Madrid, where he met VELAZQUEZ and painted five portraits of Philip IV of Spain. In 1629 he was envoyed to Britain to negotiate peace with Charles I, and while there he painted *Peace and War*. His last work was *The Crucifixion of St Peter*, and he died in Antwerp. A humanist, he was a man of erudition and culture, and his immense energy and exuberance is reflected in the quality of his work.

Ruisdael, Jacob van (*c*.1628–82) Dutch landscape painter. He joined the Haarlem painters' guild in 1648 and moved to Amsterdam *c*.1655. His atmospheric landscapes and seascapes are among the most outstanding of the time, anticipating the intuitive perceptions of CONSTABLE. He was never held in great regard by his contemporaries, but gained appreciation in modern times.

Runge, Philipp Otto (1777–1810) German Romantic painter. He studied in Copenhagen and then moved back to Germany, where he met FRIEDRICH and GOETHE. His linear style and allegorical subjects were influenced by BLAKE and FLAXMAN, e.g. *The Four Phases of Day* (1808–9).

Runyon, [Alfred] Damon (1884–1946) American short-story writer, noted for his humorous, racy short stories about New York low life and the seamier side of Broadway, e.g. *Guys and Dolls* (1931).

Rushdie, Salman (1947–) Indian-born British novelist. Regarded as one of the leading young British novelists, his first major success was *Midnight's Children* (1981), a fantasy on post-independence India seen through the eyes of children born at midnight on Independence Day, 1947. After the publication of his *The Satanic Verses* (1988), Ayatollah Khomeini of Iran pronounced a death sentence for blasphemy on the author. The offence caused by the book was (and is) primarily the assertion that parts of the Koran are of Satanic origin, and led to a worldwide debate on free speech and censorship.

Ruskin, John (1819–1900) English writer, artist and influential art critic. He came to prominence with his book *Modern Painters* (1843) in which he championed the works of TURNER. This and subsequent writings eventually totalled 39 volumes through which he virtually dictated Victorian taste in art for over half a century. His works include *Modern Painters* (1843–60), *The Seven Lamps of Architecture* (1849), *The Stones of Venice* (1851–3), *Unto this Last* (1860) and *Sesame and Lilies* (1865, 1871). Ruskin was an enthusiast for Gothic art, and supported the PRE-RAPHAELITE BROTHERHOOD, of which he was a member, being himself a prolific and talented artist. Like his friend CARLYLE, he was a strong critic of the values and ugliness of industrial England. His personal life was not happy. He was educated by tutors before entering Oxford University; his marriage was annulled, and his wife married his friend MILLAIS. During the 1870s he began to lose his reason, and he lost a notorious libel case against WHISTLER in 1878. His writings and philosophies had a profound influence on the ARTS AND CRAFTS MOVEMENT.

Russell, Morgan (1886–1953) American painter, who also studied sculpture with MATISSE. In 1913 he co-founded with MACDONALD-WRIGHT the abstract SYNCHROMISM movement, although he did not completely renounce more representational works.

Russian Futurism *see* **Futurism**.

Ruysdael, Salomon (1600–1670) Dutch landscape painter and the uncle, and possibly the teacher of, Jacob van RUISDAEL. His early influences include Elias van de VELDE, and his works of the 1630s are lyrical in style, but he gradually developed a fresher palette, e.g. *River Scene* (1644). His son, **Jacob Salomonsz van Ruysdael** (*c*.1629–81) was also a painter.

Ryder, Albert Pinkham (1847–1917) American painter. He was reclusive and largely self-taught, and his works have an intense, mystical quality. He was influenced by the Romantic writers, Poe in particular, and painted haunting, macabre pieces, e.g. *The Race Track,* in a bold impasto style.

S

Sacchi, Andrea (1599–1661) Italian painter who was influenced by RAPHAEL, and worked in a strong CLASSICAL style. The ceiling fresco *Divine Wisdom* (1629–33), while not his best work, illustrates his preference for simplicity of composition, involving few figures. His masterpiece is the *Vision of St Romuald* (c.1631).

Sackville-West, Vita [Hon. Victoria Mary] (1892–1962) English poet and novelist, best known for her novels *The Edwardians* (1930) and *All Passion Spent* (1931), and her long pastoral poem *The Land* (1926). Her *Collected Poems* were published in 1933, and she also wrote books on her travels with her husband, the diplomat Sir Harold NICOLSON, and on gardening. Her many female lovers included Virginia WOOLF, who used her as the model for the reincarnated hero/heroine Orlando in the novel of the same name. Her unconventional marriage was described by her son, Nigel Nicolson, in *Portrait of a Marriage* (1973).

sacra conversazione The Italian term for "holy conversation," in art denoting a painting in one panel of the Virgin and Child with saints.

Sade, Marquis de (1740–1814) French soldier and novelist. He was condemned to death in 1772 for acts of extreme depravity, escaped, was recaptured and spent most of the rest of his life in prison. His highly licentious works include several novels, of which the least difficult to read is *Justine* (1791). The term "sadism" derives from the dominant theme in his life and work, the desire to inflict pain in the pursuit of (usually sexual) pleasure. He was released from prison during the French Revolution and was appointed a judge, but was soon back in prison for being too lenient in sentencing. (His main contribution to the Revolution was a memorably evil speech in praise of Marat's blood lust.) He died insane.

Saint-Gaudens, Augustus (1848–1907) American sculptor of French extraction, born in Ireland. He studied in Paris and Rome, where he was influenced by RENAISSANCE sculpture. On his return to the US he established himself as a leading sculptor with the monument to Admiral Farragut (1878–81). His finest work is the Adams Memorial (1891).

Saki [pseud. of Hector Hugh Munro] (1870–1916) Burmese-born Scottish short-story writer, noted for his satirical short stories, e.g. *The Chronicles of Clovis* (1911) and *Beasts and Super-Beasts* (1914). The stories are wickedly funny, often have a macabre or supernatural slant, and are studded with aphorisms, e.g. "It's the Early Christian that gets the fattest lion." His finest story is "Sredni Vashtar," in which a young boy's ferret, which he worships as a god, answers his prayers by killing his cruel aunt. Saki was killed in the trenches during World War I, shot by a sniper. His last words were "Put out that light."

Salinger, J[erome] D[avid] (1919–) American novelist and short-story writer, best known for his highly successful novel of adolescence, *The Catcher in the Rye* (1951). The close Werther-like (*see* GOETHE) identification of many readers with the young narrator's distrust of the adult world has been widely commented upon. A curious feature of the book's appeal is its strong influence on many disturbed young males, such as John Lennon's killer. An equally curious feature of the author is his extreme reluctance to give interviews, which has given rise on occasions to rumours of his death.

salon The French word for "room," which now also denotes an art exhibition (from the Salon d'Apollon in the Louvre in Paris). In the 19th century, the Salon was the annual exhibition of the Académie française, whose powerful and conventional jury increasingly refused to show the work of innovative artists. In 1863 Napoleon III ordered that there be an exhibition of artists' work rejected by the Salon, the *Salon des Refusés*. In 1881 administration of the Salon was taken over by the Société des Artistes Français.

Sandburg, Carl August (1878–1967) American poet. His WHITMAN-influenced poems, e.g. *Chicago Poems* (1916) and *Smoke and Steel* (1920), celebrate the lives of ordinary people. He also wrote a six-volume life of Abraham Lincoln (1926–39).

Sappho (b. *c.*650BC) Greek poet. The Greeks regarded her as one of the greatest of all lyric poets, but only tantalizingly short fragments of her poetry have survived, e.g. her magical little hymn to the Evening Star.

Sargent, John Singer (1856–1925) American painter born in Florence. He trained in Paris and caused outrage with the portrait of *Mme X* (1884), which was considered too openly erotic. He settled in London in 1885, where he established himself as a society portraitist. He was a flattering painter of virtuoso technique and enjoyed immense popularity throughout his career. He also painted outstanding watercolour landscapes and murals.

Sartre, Jean-Paul (1905–80) French philosopher, novelist and dramatist. His attempts at combining EXISTENTIALIST philosophy, which places humanity in a largely meaningless universe in which human actions count for little, with Marxist political philosophy, which sees humanity as progressing to an ever brighter future, are now only of interest as period pieces. His novels, however, particularly *Nausea* (1938) and the *Roads to Freedom* trilogy (1945–9) are highly readable. Several of his plays, e.g. *The Flies* (1943) and *Huis clos* (1944, in English *No Exit*), which features the famous line, "Hell is other people," are frequently performed. In 1964 he was awarded the NOBEL PRIZE for literature, but declined to accept it. *See* BEAUVOIR

Sassetta [Stefano di Giovanni] (*c.*1392–1450) Italian painter. He trained in his native Siena, but quickly absorbed the influences of INTERNATIONAL GOTHIC and early RENAISSANCE styles, as in *Madonna of the Snow* (1432). His masterpiece is the *St Francis in Ecstacy* from the St Francis altarpiece (1437–44) created for the Borgo Sansepolcro.

Sassoon, Siegfried [Lorraine] (1886–1967) English poet and novelist, whose grimly realistic poems have established him as one of the two major poets, with OWEN, of World War I. He was awarded the Military Cross during the war, and achieved notoriety by organizing a public protest against the war and throwing his medal away. Two notable collections of the poems are *Counter-Attack* (1918) and *Satirical Poems* (1926). His semi-autobiographical trilogy of novels, *Memoirs of a Fox-Hunting Man* (1928), *Memoirs of an Infantry Officer* (1930) and *Sherston's Progress* (1936), describes the progress of a young man from sports-loving boyhood through the horrors of trench warfare.

Saussure, Ferdinand de *see* **Structuralism**.

Schiele, Egon (1890–1918) Austrian painter and draughtsman. He met KLIMT while studying in Vienna, and was influenced by ART NOUVEAU, from which he developed his own linear style of EXPRESSIONISM. He caused a scandal with his erotically posed nudes, for which he was arrested in 1912, and some of his works were destroyed. His paintings reveal the influence of Klimt's abstractions, e.g. *The Artist's Mother sleeping* (1911).

Schongauer, Martin (*c.*1450–91) German painter and engraver from Colmar. His finest extant work is the *Madonna of the Rose Garden* altarpiece (1437), which indicates the influence of Flemish art, and he was probably familiar with the works of Rogier van der WEYDEN. In engraving he created new standards in subtlety of modelling and delicacy of line, which, combined with a rich imagination, provided a source of inspiration for engravers throughout Europe, including the young DÜRER. A typical example is *The Temptation of St Anthony* (*c.*1470).

school In art, a group of artists who hold similar principles and work in a similar style. In art history, it also denotes that a painting has been executed by a pupil or assistant.

Schotz, Benno (1889–1983) Estonian-born Scottish sculptor. His bronze portraits and figure compositions were cast from freely executed models in clay and other media, and have a strong, tactile surface texture. He is well represented in Glasgow, where he lived from 1912, and elsewhere.

Schreiner, Olive (1855–1920) South African novelist, remembered chiefly for one work (published under the pseudonym of "Ralph Iron"), *The Story of an African Farm* (1883). The work, which has a lovingly described background based on Schreiner's own childhood on a South African farm, has a "New Woman" heroine who defies convention by refusing to marry the lover by whom she has a baby.

Schwitters, Kurt (1887–1948) German painter, sculptor and poet. He studied in Dresden, and his early works are abstract in style. He initiated the Hanover group of DADAists in 1919. He is mainly remembered for *Mertz*, the invented name for his relief COLLAGES and sculptural constructions created from junk materials. From 1920 he began constructing his *Mertzbau*, or large junk constructions, which completely filled his house in Hanover. It was destroyed during World War II. His final *Mertzbau*, unfinished when he died, was constructed at Ambleside in England and is now in the Hatton Gallery, Newcastle-upon-Tyne. *Mertz* was also taken as the name of a Dadaist magazine launched by Schwitters in the 1920s.

Sciascia, Leonardo (1921–1989) Italian novelist, short-story writer and essayist. Sciascia's work, whether fictional or non-fictional, is concerned with the endemic public corruption at the heart of Italian society. Sciascia was born and raised in Sicily, where he developed a strong sense of injustice at the immorality of any political system working to oppress the poor and preserve social injustice. He was no ordinary polemicist, but a highly gifted and original writer, with a rare talent for exposing self-delusion and hypocrisy. Notable examples of his work include *Sicilian Uncles* (1958), *Candido* (1977) and *The Moro Affair* (1978).

Scott, Sir Walter (1771–1832) Scottish novelist and poet. His early, highly romantic narrative poems, set in the Scottish past, e.g. *Marmion* (1808), *The Lady of the Lake* (1810) and *The Lord of the Isles* (1815), established his popularity with both the reading public and the literary world, BYRON being particularly generous in his praise. His historical novels (a genre he refined and made into an art form), particularly *Waverley* (1814), *The Heart of Midlothian* (1818) and *Ivanoe* (1819), were enormously popular and influential, and spawned a host of imitators, e.g. Fenimore COOPER. Scott's re-creation (or invention) of Scottish Highland culture, e.g. making the kilt respectable and glorifying the Highland virtues of courage and loyalty, was also of enormous influence, and inspired similar undertakings throughout all Europe. Mark TWAIN claimed that Scott's novels were an indirect cause of the American Civil War by creating the myth of the noble, warlike gentleman, an ideal that many Southern men aspired to.

Scott, William Bell (1811–90) Scottish painter and poet who trained as an engraver with his father, **Robert Scott** (1777–1841). William showed paintings at the Royal Scottish Academy from 1834 and at the Royal Academy from 1842. His first volume of poetry was published in 1938. In 1843 he became head of the Government School of Design at Newcastle-upon-Tyne. He was acquainted with ROSSETTI and RUSKIN, and his paintings reveal a PRE-RAPHAELITE influence. Some of his best works are contemporary scenes of the North East, e.g. *Iron and Coal*, which was part of a series (from 1855) of history paintings for Wallington Hall, Northumberland. His brother **David Scott** (1806–49) was also a painter, and they were both proficient illustrators.

Sebastiano del Piombo [Sebastiano Veneziano] (*c*.1485–1547) Italian painter, influenced by BELLINI and GIOGIONE in his early works, of which *Salomé* (1510) is a typical example. He moved to Rome in 1511, where he met RAPHAEL and worked with MICHELANGELO, who helped him design his masterpiece, *The Raising of Lazarus* (1517–19). The rest of his major work was in portraiture, e.g. *Clement VII* (1526). In 1523 he became Keeper of the Seals to Pope Clement VII, which earned him his nickname "del Piombo."

secondary colours *see* **primary colours**.

Section d'Or A group of painters in France who associated between 1912 and 1914 and whose aim was to hold group exhibitions and to encourage debate of their aesthetic ideals. They admired the works of CÉZANNE and were concerned with harmony and proportion of composition. They also drew inspiration from FUTURISM. Painters involved with the group included the DUCHAMP brothers, LÉGER, KUPKA and PICABIA.

Sedley, Sir Charles (1639–1701) English poet and dramatist. He was a friend of both DRYDEN and ROCHESTER, and, like the latter, was involved in many sordid incidents; he was once fined for indecent exposure, but reformed to some extent when the roof fell in on him during a tennis match (with ETHEREGE). His three plays are the tragedy *Antony and Cleopatra* (1677) and two comedies, *The Mulberry Garden* (1668) and *Bellamira* (1687). His lyrics include the magical "Love still has something of the sea" and several other very fine poems, collected in the posthumously issued *Miscellaneous Works* (1702).

Segal, George (1924–) American sculptor. He was initially a painter in the ABSTRACT EXPRESSIONIST tradition, and was influenced by KAPROW to take up sculpture. He is best known for his plaster figures, cast from life and usually unpainted, placed like frozen ghosts in realistic settings, e.g. *Cinema* (1963).

Seghers, Hercules Pietersz (*c*.1589–*c*.1635) Dutch painter and engraver from Haarlem. He trained in Amsterdam and worked in Utrecht and The Hague. He was an innovative landscape painter, imbuing small canvases with a sense of immense scope and drama. His etchings were of an outstanding quality, and he did experimental prints on various fabrics and tinted papers. He was admired by REMBRANDT, who owned several of his works, but fell into neglect towards the end of his life and was only rediscovered by the art world in 1871.

Semiotics *see* **Structuralism**.

Seneca [Lucius Anneus Seneca] (*c*.4BC–65AD) Roman dramatist and Stoic philosopher. The violent rhetoric of his verse tragedies (which often have a supernatural content) was very influential on Elizabethan dramatists such as SHAKESPEARE, although the plays were probably meant for private readings rather than public performance. T. S. ELIOT's essays "Shakespeare and the Stoicism of Seneca" and "Seneca in Elizabethan Translation," in *Elizabethan Essays* (1934), provide valuable insights into Seneca's philosophy and influence. Like PETRONIUS, he was ordered to commit suicide by Emperor Nero.

sentimental comedy A form of English COMEDY that arose in the early 18th century, focusing on the problems of middle-class characters. The plays always end happily and feature strongly contrasting good and bad characters and high emotional peaks. The form was developed by Richard STEELE in a conscious reaction to the excesses of Restoration comedy (*see* COMEDY OF MANNERS). Examples include Steele's *The Tender Husband* (1705) and, notably, *The Conscious Lovers* (1722). The form led on to MELODRAMA (*see also* DOMESTIC TRAGEDY).

Serusier, Paul (1863–1927) French painter and founding member of the NABIS group. He was influenced by GAUGUIN in his symbolic use of colour, e.g. *The Talisman* (1888). He entered the Benedictine school of religious painting at Beuron, Germany, in 1897, and published his theories on colour and proportion in his *ABC of Painting* (1921).

Seurat, Georges (1859–91) French painter and leading figure of NEOIMPRESSIONISM. He studied at the Ecole des Beaux Arts and developed the system of Pointillism, based on the theories of DELACROIX and recent scientific discoveries about colour. The pointillist painting is composed of tiny areas of pure colour, arranged so as to merge together and present an image of great luminosity when viewed from a distance. It depends on scientific precision and meticulous brushwork and represents a radical departure from the free, intuitive brushwork of the Impressionists. Important works include *La Grande Jatte* (1884–6), *The Parade* (1887–8) and *The Circus* (unfinished when he died in 1891). He was also an outstanding draughtsman and had a great influence on contemporary and succeeding generations of painters.

Sezession The German word for "secession," adopted as a name in the 1890s by groups of painters in Austria and Germany when they broke away from official academies to work and exhibit in contemporary styles, e.g. IMPRESSIONISM. In Germany, the first German Sezession was in Munich in 1892, followed by the Berlin Sezession of 1899, led by BECKMANN and LIEBERMANN, which in turn in 1910 repudiated the works of Die BRÜCKE, which resulted in the latter group forming the Neue Sezession. In Austria, the Vienna Sezession was organized by KLIMT in 1897.

sfumato *see* **Leonardo da Vinci**.

Shadwell, Thomas (*c.* 1642–92) English dramatist and poet. In the best of his 17 plays, the comedies, he gives a lively and often satirical account of contemporary life, e.g. *The Virtuoso* (1676). In 1682 he quarrelled with DRYDEN, his political opponent (Shadwell was a "true-blue" Whig), and from then until after the "Glorious Revolution" of 1688 his plays were not produced on the London stage. He replaced Dryden as POET LAUREATE in 1689.

Shakespeare, William (1564–1616) English dramatist and poet. He was born and brought up in Stratford-upon-Avon, where he attended the local grammar school. He married Anne Hathaway in 1582, and they had three children by 1585 (his last surviving descendant, a granddaughter, died in 1670). Nothing is known for certain of the circumstances of his move to London and entry into the theatrical world, but in 1592 there appeared a reference to him in a pamphlet by Robert GREENE. Shakespeare's plays are generally divided into three groups. The first group (late 1580s–c.1594) consists of histories, e.g. the *Henry VI* trilogy, early comedies such as *The Two Gentlemen of Verona, The Comedy of Errors* and *Love's Labour's Lost*, and the tragedy *Romeo and Juliet*. The second group (c.1595–c.1599) includes histories such as *King John, Henry IV* Parts I and II, and *Henry V*, the comedies *A Midsummer Night's Dream, Much Ado About Nothing* and *As You Like It*, and the tragedy *Julius Caesar*. The third group (c.1600–c.1612) includes the great tragedies *Hamlet, Othello, King Lear, Macbeth, Antony and Cleopatra, Coriolanus* and *Timon of Athens*, the so-called "dark comedies," *Troilus and Cressida, All's Well That Ends Well*, and *Measure for Measure*, and tragicomedies such as *The Winter's Tale* and *The Tempest*. (The plays are unquestionably by Shakespeare and not, as some argue, by BACON.) Shakespeare's other major works are the narrative poems *Venus and Adonis* (1593) and *The Rape of Lucrece* (1594), and the magnificent *Sonnets*, which are known to have been in private circulation in London in 1598 before being published, possibly not with his approval, in 1609. The sonnets feature a romantic triangle between the poet (Shakespeare), a dark lady (identity unknown) and a beautiful young nobleman (possibly the Earl of Southampton). Speculation about the background to the sonnets has been intense, and occasionally manic (AUDEN doubted the sanity of anyone who had a theory concerning them). Shakespeare's status as the greatest of all dramatists and poets has only rarely been challenged in modern times. The works have been translated into every major language, and are among the greatest products of Western culture. *See also* FLETCHER.

Sharp, William *see* **Macleod, Fiona**.

Shaw, George Bernard (1856–1950) Anglo-Irish dramatist and critic. He began his literary career as a drama, literary and music critic in the 1880s, and after a false start in novel-writing (he wrote five) began writing plays in the 1890s. His treatise *The Quintessence of Ibsenism* (1891) sets out his belief in the new "IBSENite" drama of social realism (and also in socialism). The plays, e.g. *Man and Superman* (1903), *Major Barbara* (1905), *Pygmalion* (1913, which later became the musical *My Fair Lady*) and *Back to Methuselah*, bear the hallmarks of a failed novelist, with fussily detailed stage directions about the characters' motivations, colour of eyes, etc., but have proved very successful, thanks largely to Shaw's mastery of bright, witty dialogue, and ability to persuade the watcher or reader of the plays that he or she is ranged with the author against the boors and bores. Shaw seems to have genuinely believed that he was a greater dramatist than SHAKESPEARE. He adopted the role of "intellectual maverick," delighting all sections of society with his wit, and became something of a national institution in Britain. Like many intellectuals, he longed for a "great man" to put his "rational, commonsense" ideas into practice, and wrote admiringly of both Hitler and Stalin (like Hitler, he was a vegetarian who hated cruelty to animals, yet was capable of monstrous intellectual callousness; his praise of Stalin's prison camps has to be read to be believed). YEATS described him as an atheist, "haunted by the mystery he flouts." He was awarded the NOBEL PRIZE for literature in 1925.

Shelley, Mary Wollstonecraft (1797–1851) English novelist. The daughter of two prominent social reformers, William Godwin and Mary Wollstonecraft, she eloped with SHELLEY in 1814 and married him in 1816 after his wife died. Her masterpiece is *Frank-*

enstein, or the Modern Prometheus (1818), a GOTHIC fantasy that has been hailed as the first science fiction novel. There have been innumerable (usually very loose) stage and film adaptions of the novel, which arose out of an agreement between Shelley, BYRON and herself to write supernatural tales.

Shelley, Percy Bysshe (1792–1822) English poet. His extraordinary talent for creating public scandal got off to a flying start at Oxford University, where he was expelled for co-writing a tract called *The Necessity of Atheism* (1811), in which year he married Harriet Westwood. Two years later, his poem *Queen Mab* was published, which celebrated a future republican millennium of free love and vegetarianism. In 1814, he eloped with Mary Godwin (see Mary Wollstonecraft SHELLEY) and her fifteen-year-old step-sister. Harriet committed suicide in 1816, in which year he married Mary. Shelley and his entourage moved to Italy in 1818, where he drowned in 1822. His poems are among the greatest of English ROMANTIC poetry. The highlights are: *The Revolt of Islam* (1817); *Prometheus Unbound* (1820); *Adonais* (1821), his elegy on the death of KEATS; and several of the finest poems in the language, notably *Ode to the West Wind* and *To a Skylark* (both 1820). His essay *A Defence of Poetry* (1821, published 1840) finishes with the defiant assertion that "poets are the unacknowledged legislators of the world." His last great (unfinished) poem, *The Triumph of Life* (1824), is a very bleak work (the title is profoundly ironic). *See also* SOCRATES, BYRON.

Sheridan, Richard Brinsley (1751–1816) Irish dramatist and politician, noted for his superb comedies of manners, *The Rivals* (1775) and *School for Scandal* (1777), both of which are firm repertory favourites. His other major play is *The Critic* (1779), an extremely funny burlesque which mercilessly satirizes the conventions of tragedy and the (seemingly eternal) sleazy aspects of theatrical production.

Shizheng, Li *see* **Duoduo**.

Sholokhov, Mikhail [Alexandrovich] (1905–84) Russian novelist. Sholokhov's *And Quiet Flows the Don* (issued in 4 volumes, 1928–40), which presents a panorama of Don Cossack life before and during the Bolshevik Revolution, has been hailed as a masterpiece by many critics. There have been persistent rumours that the work is not entirely his own (it has been suggested that Sholokhov stole the basis of the book from a manuscript by a dead White Army officer). He was awarded the NOBEL PRIZE for literature in 1965.

Sickert, Walter Richard (1860–1942) German-born English painter of Danish extraction. He studied with WHISTLER and was influenced by him and by DEGAS, whom he met in 1885. In 1905 he established a studio in London, which became a focal point for young English painters. His subject matter is concerned with the sordid realities of urban life, as in his best-known work, *Ennui* (*c*.1913).

Sidney, Sir Philip (1554–86) English poet, soldier and courtier. His works include *Arcadia* (1590), the first major English pastoral poem; the sonnet sequence *Astrophel and Stella* (1591), which inspired a host of imitations; and *A Defence of Poetry* (1595), a spirited defence of English as a medium for writing great poetry. His death in action against the Spaniards in the Netherlands was followed by a host of tributes from his many admirers throughout Europe. *See* BALLAD.

Signac, Paul (1863–1935) French painter. Along with SEURAT he was a pioneer of pointillist techniques, and he exhibited some of his works at the last IMPRESSION-IST Exhibition in 1886. He published his theories on the scientific application of colour in *From Delacroix to Neoimpressionism* (1899). He later developed a freer style and brighter palette, which influenced the works of MATISSE.

Signorelli, Luca (*fl.*1470–1523) Italian painter, possibly taught by PIERO DELLA FRANCESCA, whose influence can be seen in *Madonna and Child* and *Flagellation* (*c.*1480). The drama of *Mother and Child with Saints* (1484) also shows the influence of the POLLAIUOLI. From 1484 he worked on some of the frescoes for the Sistine Chapel and later painted his masterpiece, *The Last Judgment* fresco cycle in Orvieto Cathedral (1499–1502). He was an outstanding draughtsman, his depictions of the male nude being particularly noteworthy.

Simon, [Marvin] Neil (1927–) American dramatist. His very popular (New-York based) comedies of manners include *Barefoot in the Park* (1963) and *The Odd Couple* (1965). More recent works, e.g. *Brighton Beach Memoirs*, have an autobiographical element while retaining their wit and humour.

Simone Martini (*c.*1285–1344) Italian painter from Siena, who succeeded DUCCIO as the leading figure in Sienese painting. Early works include the *Maesté* fresco (1315), for the Siena Town Hall, and *St Louis* (1317). The graceful, linear style and rich decor of his mature works reveal the influence of French Gothic art, as in *Christ Reproved by His Parents* (1342). Other notable works include the frescoes of *Guidoriccio da Fogliano* (1328) and the *Annunciation* (1333).

Sinclair, Upton [Beall] (1878–1968) American novelist. The best-known works of his huge fictional output are *The Jungle* (1906), which features a no-holds-barred account of the Chicago meat trade, and resulted in legislation against the horrors described in the book, and the "Lanny Budd" sequence of political novels, e.g. *World's End* (1940) and *The Return of Lanny Budd* (1953).

Singer, Isaac Bashevis (1904–91) Polish-born American Yiddish short-story writer and novelist. He emigrated from Poland to the US in 1935. Much of his fiction deals with the now vanished world of Polish Judaism, e.g. *The Magician of Lublin* (1960). He was awarded the NOBEL PRIZE for literature in 1978.

Sisley, Alfred (1839–99) French painter of English extraction. Early works reveal an admiration for COROT, but he came under the influence of the Impressionists RENOIR and MONET while studying in Paris. He painted mainly peaceful landscapes, carefully composed and sensitively coloured in a pointillist manner, e.g. *Floods at Marly* (1876).

Sitwell, Dame Edith Louisa (1887–1964) English poet and critic. She and her brothers, **Sir Osbert Sitwell** (1892–1969) and **Sacheverell Sitwell** (1897–1988), were ardent proponents of modernism in the arts, and worked quite hard at attracting controversy. Edith Sitwell's works include *Facade*, an "entertainment" consisting of jazz-influenced abstract verses, which was first performed in 1923 with music by William Walton, and several fine elegaic poems, e.g. "Still Falls the Rain" (on the "total war" of World War II). The essential work on the Sitwells is Sir Osbert's six-volume autobiography, from *Left Hand, Right Hand* (1945) to *Tales my Father Taught me* (1962), which also provides a remarkable portrait of upper-class English life in the 20th century.

sketch A preliminary drawing made by an artist to establish points of composition, scale, etc.

Sloan, John (1871–1951) American painter and, along with Robert HENRI, a founding member of THE EIGHT. Trained at the Pennsylvania Academy of Fine Arts, he painted in the American Realist tradition, depicting the back-street life of New York in a warm-hearted and unpretentious style, e.g. *Hairdresser's Window* (1907).

Smart, Christopher (1722–71) English poet. His best-known works are his great, highly idiosyncratic religious poems *A Song to David* (1763) and *Jubilate Agno* (unpublished until 1939), a wonderfully original celebration of God's creation written while Smart was confined in a lunatic asylum (1759–63). The most quoted lines from the poem are those describing his cat Jeoffrey. Dr JOHNSON (another cat lover) was an admirer of Smart's piety if not his poetry, and his strange, beguiling verse has only gained full recognition in this century.

Smart, Elizabeth (1913–86) Canadian author of two short novels, *By Grand Central Station I sat Down and Wept* (1945) and *The Assumption of the Rogues and Rascals* (1978). The first book, a lush, rhapsodic study of desire, was inspired by Smart's love for the poet George BARKER. She fell in love with him through reading his poetry, pursued him ("I must marry a poet") and had four children by him (Barker remained married to someone else). Her journal for 1933–40 was published in 1991 under the title *Necessary Secrets*.

Smith, David (1906–65) American sculptor. His early work experience in a car factory facilitated his technique of cutting and welding metal. Early influences include PICASSO, but from around 1940 he developed his own style with a strong emphasis on surface texture. *Australia* (1951) is typical of his open structuring at this period. Mature works are more concerned with volume, notably his stainless steel *Cubi* series (from the late 1950s), and almost all his pieces explore the relationship of sculpture to its setting.

Smith, Stevie [Florence Margaret] (1902–71) English poet and novelist. Her graceful, melancholic, and occasionally fiercely funny verse has been much admired, especially the superb collection *Not Waving but Drowning* (1957). She also wrote three novels,

Novel on Yellow Paper (1936), *Over the Frontier* (1938) and *The Holiday* (1949), in a style likened by some to that of Gertrude STEIN.

Smollett, Tobias [George] (1721–71) Scottish novelist. He served in the Royal Navy as a ship's surgeon and took part in an attack upon a Spanish port in the West Indies. In the early 1740s, he set up a surgical practice in London. His PICARESQUE NOVELS, of which the most important are *The Adventures of Roderick Random* (1748), *The Adventures of Peregrine Pickle* (1751), and his masterpiece *The Expedition of Humphrey Clinker* (1771), are cleverly plotted satirical works rich in characterization, which achieved lasting popularity. His works have had a strong influence on many other authors, notably DICKENS.

socialist realism *see* **Realism**.

social realism A form of realism, in which an artist's political viewpoint (usually on the left) affects the content of his work. It is not the same as socialist realism (*see* REALISM), the name given to official art in the Soviet Union, which was intended to glorify the achievements of the Communist Party.

Socrates (469–399BC) Greek philosopher, the tutor of PLATO. The sources of Socrates' teachings are many and widely varied, but it is Plato's Socrates, a somewhat maddening genius with a gift for answering questions with another question, who has come down to posterity in Plato's "Socratic dialogues," e.g. *Protagoras*. The central theme in Socrates' thinking is a quest for truth through rigorous self-examination: "the unexamined life is not worth living" (Plato, *Apology*). Shelley paid him a very high compliment in *The Triumph of Life*, describing Socrates and Jesus as the only two humans to break free from the murderous wheel of life. Socrates was forced to commit suicide by the

Athenians for supposedly corrupting youths through teaching them "impiety."

Solzhenitsyn, Alexander [Isayevich] (1918–) Russian novelist and historian. His novella *One Day in the Life of Ivan Denisovich* (1962), based on his experiences in a Soviet labour camp, created a sensation when published in the USSR during a brief thaw in cultural restrictions. His subsequent novels, *The First Circle* and *Cancer Ward*, were too critical of Soviet life for the authorities' liking, and were published abroad in 1968, as was his study of the history and organization of the labour camp system, *The Gulag Archipelago* (1973–5). He was awarded the NOBEL PRIZE for literature in 1970, was deported from the USSR in 1974, and settled in Vermont. In a remarkable development in September 1990, the Soviet Communist Youth League newspaper published a long article by Solzhenitsyn entitled "How We are to Rebuild Russia," calling for a return to pre-Bolshevik, Christian Slavic values. His Soviet citizenship has been restored.

Sophocles (*c*.496–406BC) Greek dramatist. Seven of his *c*.120 plays are extant. He was the most popular of the three great Athenian tragedians (the others being AESCHYLUS and EURIPEDES). The reasons for his popularity still hold good for audiences: his characters are plausible, have recognizable human failings, and their tragic situations have a strong element of pathos. His plays have been very influential on many writers, e.g. on MILTON, SHELLEY and ARNOLD (who mentions him in "Dover Beach"). *Oedipus Rex* and *Oedipus at Colonus* have had a powerful influence on modern thought through the theories of FREUD. *Antigone*, in which Oedipus' daughter Antigone decides to obey divine law in burying her brother rather than the law of the state which forbids his burial, has acquired strong resonances in the context of 20th-century totalitarianism. *See also* ANOUILH.

Southey, Robert (1774–1843) English poet. He was closely associated with WORDSWORTH and COLERIDGE, but only a few of his large output of poems are still regarded as having much merit. He was POET LAUREATE from 1813, and was heavily satirized by BYRON (particularly in *Don Juan*), for his abandonment of revolutionary principles.

Soutine, Chaim (1893–1943) Lithuanian-born French artist who studied at Vilna and at the Ecole des Beaux-Arts in Paris. His influences include EXPRESSIONIST works, particularly those of KOKOSHKA. He painted in a vivid impasto style, mainly landscapes and portraits of great psychological depth, e.g. *The Old Actress* (1924). He influenced the painter Francis BACON.

Soyinka, Wole (1934–) Nigerian poet, novelist, dramatist and critic. He worked in London in the late 1950s, where three of his plays, *The Swamp Dwellers, The Lion and the Jewel* and *The Invention*, were produced in 1958–9. He supported the Biafran side in the Nigerian Civil War, and was imprisoned by the Nigerian Government for nine months; *The Man Died: Prison Memoirs* (1972) describes his experiences in prison. His early works, e.g. the novel *The Interpreters* (1965), are more optimistic about the future of postcolonial Africa than his later novels and poems. He was awarded the NOBEL PRIZE for literature in 1986.

Spark, Muriel [Sarah] (1918–) Scottish novelist. She became a Roman Catholic in 1954, and her conversion forms the basis of her first novel, *The Comforters* (1957). Graham GREENE had given her £20 a month to give up publishing hack-work – described with brutal accuracy in *A Far Cry from Kensington* (1988) – to concentrate on writing novels; she wrote six in four years. Her novels are usually comic and satirical, with a strong element of the fantastic or supernatural, as in *Memento Mori* (1958) and *The Ballad of Peckham Rye* (1960). Her novel *Symposium* (1990) begins with an epigraph from Plato stating that "the genius of comedy is the same with that of tragedy," and this is a key to much of her work. She sees evil as a form of moral blindness, a self-destructive self-love. The problem of the nature of God and his tormented creation also appears in her novels, e.g. *The Only Problem* (1984). Her best-known novel is *The Prime of Miss Jean Brodie* (1961), a tragicomedy in which an eccentric teacher is gradually brought to face the consequences of her self-deluding domination over "her" schoolgirls.

Spencer, Sir Stanley (1891–1959) English painter, who trained at the Slade School of Art. He remained uninfluenced by contemporary art trends and developed his own eccentric idiom, based on personal beliefs and expressed in a precise, simplified style. He painted mainly Biblical themes, transposed into a modern context drawn from his native Berkshire, e.g. *Resurrection, Cookham* (1923–7). Other notable works include the mural cycle for the Sandham Memorial Chapel, Burghclere (1926–32).

Spender, Sir Stephen [Harold] (1909–) English poet and critic. He was a close associate of AUDEN, and one of the most prominent of the left-wing "Auden generation" poets of the 1930s. His poem "The Pylons" in *Poems* (1933) resulted in the derisive label of "Pylon poets" being applied to Spender and other leftwing poets who celebrated the industrial era and the coming triumph of the industrial working class. His critical work, *The Destructive Element* (1935), is a useful guide to the thought processes of the politically committed writers of the 1930s. He abandoned communism in the 1950s. A few of his poems, e.g. "I think continually of those who are truly great," have become anthology standards.

Spenser, Edmund (*c.* 1552–99) English poet, noted particularly for his huge allegorical poem *The Faerie Queene* (1590–6), which describes the adventures of 12 knights (who represent 12 virtues). Many of the adventures begin at the court of Gloriana, the Faerie Queene (an idealized version of Elizabeth I; she does not appear in the poem, however). Despite determined efforts by many critics to persuade the general public of the work's readability, it remains one of the Great Unread among English classics. Many poets have been influenced by it, notably MILTON and KEATS. Others share LANDOR's view, in "To Wordsworth," that "Thee gentle Spenser fondly led, / But me he mostly sent to bed."

stabile *see* **Calder, Alexander**.

Staël, Nicolas de (1914–55) Russian-born French painter. Born in St Petersburg, he trained at the Academy of Fine Arts in Brussels and settled in France from 1937. BRAQUE influenced his early style, and from the 1940s he used rectangular patches of colour to depict volume and texture in an abstract manner. Later paintings were more representational and quieter in tone. *The Roofs* (1952) is typical of his best work.

Stanislavsky, Konstantin (1863–1938) Russian director and actor, who was co-founder of the Moscow Art Theatre in 1897. Stanislavsky made his name as a director of CHEKHOV's plays, although the latter was not always convinced by Stanislavsky's emotion-saturated, highly detailed approach to production, which often involved a fanatically NATURALISTIC attention to stage sets and sound effects. Chekhov's main objection was that the subtlety and delicate ambiguity of his plays tended to get lost along the way.

Stanislavsky's influence on the training of actors

through his theory of acting has been immense. The actor is to immerse himself in the "inner life" of the character he is playing, and, using the insights gained in this study, convey to the audience the hidden reality behind the words. His theory is contained in such works as *An Actor Prepares* (1929) and *Building a Character* (1950). His theories were adopted and adapted by the American director **Lee Strasberg** (1901–82), whose **method** style of acting achieved world fame (or notoriety) through pupils such as James Dean and Marlon Brando. *See also* MEYERHOLD.

Steele, Sir Richard (1672–1729) Anglo-Irish essayist and dramatist. He was a close associate of ADDISON, with whom he was chief contributor to *The Tatler* (1709–11) and *The Spectator* (1711–12). His plays, which were determinedly moral, Christian responses to the excesses of Restoration dramatists such as WYCHERLEY and ETHEREGE, were, apart from *The Conscious Lovers* (1722), not terribly successful on the stage, but had lasting influence on the course of 18th-century SENTIMENTAL drama. He was a good man, and was much liked by his contemporaries.

Steen, Jan (1626–79) Dutch painter, who studied in Haarlem and The Hague. He painted genre scenes of domestic and social life with good humour and insight, and enjoyed great popularity. He had a prolific output, and his works varied in subject and in quality. A typical piece is *The Egg Dance* (c.1675).

Stein, Gertrude (1874–1946) American author. She settled in Paris 1902, where her home became a focal point for "modernist" writers and artists. HEMINGWAY and Sherwood ANDERSON were among the many writers she encouraged. Her phrase "a lost generation" to describe the post-World War I generation of American poets and artists, was used by Hemingway as the epigraph to *The Sun Also Rises* (1926). Her own best-known work is her autobiography, which she eccentrically presented as the work of her life-long companion Alice B. Toklas, *The Autobiography of Alice B.Toklas* (1933). Stein's highly distinctive narrative technique, with its disregard for standard punctuation, makes her prose instantly recognizable. Her works on literary theory include *Composition as Exploration* (1926).

Steinbeck, John [Ernst] (1902–68) American novelist, who achieved great success with his novels about America's rural poor, e.g. *Of Mice and Men* (1937) and *Grapes of Wrath* (1939). Like quite a few other American novelists of his generation, Steinbeck took a rather deterministic, "biological" view of human nature, and his literary reputation is not as high as it once was. He was awarded the NOBEL PRIZE for literature in 1962.

Stella, Frank (1936–) American painter. His earliest works are ABSTRACT EXPRESSIONIST, but from 1959 he developed tightly controlled symmetrical patterns of black stripes, as in *Jill* (1963). In later works he experimented with shaped canvases and bright colours, and during the 1970s developed these themes by using supporting structures splattered with paint and glitter, e.g. *Guadalupe Island* (1979).

Stendhal [pseud. of Henri Beyle] (1788–1842) French novelist and critic, noted for his great mastery of character analysis in such historical novels as *The Red and the Black* (1830) and *The Charterhouse of Parma* (1839). He was a firm supporter of SHAKESPEARE and the ROMANTIC view of life and culture generally, as his *Racine and Shakespeare* pamphlets of 1823 and 1835 demonstrate.

Sterne, Laurence (1713–68) Irish-born English novelist. He was ordained as an Anglican clergyman in 1738, and his learned, witty and offbeat sermons at York became very popular. His wildly eccentric "novel" *The Life and Opinions of Tristram Shandy* (1759–67) created a sensation in the 1760s. The work, with its deliberately disordered narrative (the Preface appears in Volume III), lack of plot, practical jokes on the reader and mordant sense of humour, remains one of the most unclassifiable works of fiction ever published. Sterne also published *A Sentimental Journey through France and Italy* (1768), another odd "novel" recounting the adventures of Parson Yorick on holiday (he gets as far as Lyon). Interest in Sterne's two peculiar books seems to have declined rapidly after his death. By 1776, Dr JOHNSON was observing: "Nothing odd will do long. *Tristram Shandy* did not last," but they are now established as engagingly idiosyncratic classics of English prose.

Stevens, Wallace (1878–1955) American poet, whose elegant, enigmatic poems have gained increasing recognition since his death. Collections include *Harmonium* (1923), *The Man with the Blue Guitar* (1937) and *Collected Poems* (1954). He also published a book of essays, *The Necessary Angel* (1951). Further poems, essays and plays were published posthumously in 1957, *Opus Posthumous* (1957).

Stevenson, Robert Louis (1850–94) Scottish novelist, poet and essayist. He trained in Edinburgh as an advocate, but had decided by his early twenties that his true vocation was to be a writer. He was encouraged in his writing by HENLEY, with whom he co-wrote a number of plays, notably *Deacon Brodie* (1880). By the time his first important fictional work, the classic tale of piracy and adventure, *Treasure Island* (1883), had been published, Stevenson had established himself as an author of note with his essays, poems, and two travel books, *Travels with a Donkey in the Cevennes* (1879), and *The Silverado Squatters* (1883). His masterpiece is a work that has become part of world myth, *The Strange Case of Dr Jekyll and Mr Hyde* (1886), a strange and disturbing story of dual personality and the clash between good and evil. His other works include his Scottish romances, e.g. *Kidnapped* (1886) and *The Master of Ballantrae* (1889), and his great, sombre unfinished work, *Weir of Hermiston* (1896). He settled in Samoa, where he died. The Samoan nickname for him was "Tusitala," i.e. "The Storyteller."

Stewart, J[ohn] I[nnes] M[ackintosh] (1906–) Scottish novelist and critic. Under the pseudonym of **Michael Innes**, he has published around 30 detective novels starring Inspector John Appleby, a cultured, erudite individual whose sometimes fiendishly complex but always enjoyable adventures include *Death at the President's Lodging* (1936), *Hamlet's Revenge* (1937) and *Lament for a Maker* (1938). Under his own name, he has published several notable works of criticism, most notably *Eight Modern Writers* (1963), a superb and entertaining study of HARDY, Henry JAMES, SHAW, CONRAD, KIPLING, YEATS, JOYCE and D. H. LAWRENCE.

Stewart, [Lady] Mary [Florence Elinor] (1916–) English novelist. She has written several popular thrillers, e.g. *Madam, Will You Walk* (1955) and *Thunder on the Right* (1957). Her masterpiece, however, is her excellent retelling of the Arthurian legend, a trilogy consisting of *The Crystal Cave* (1970). *The Hollow Hills* (1973) and *The Last Enchantment* (1979). She has also written several children's adventure stories, e.g. *The Little Broomstick* (1971) and *A Walk in Wolf Wood* (1980).

stiacciato *see* **relief**.

Stieglitz, Alfred *see* **O'Keefe, Georgia**.

Stijl, De A group of Dutch artists, founded to spread the theories of DOESBURG and MONDRIAN on ABSTRACT ART, principally through the *De Stijl* magazine, which was edited by Doesburg and published 1917–28. The group rejected the representational in art, believing that art's object was to convey harmony and order, achieved by the use of straight lines and geometrical shapes in primary colours or black and white. Their ideas had great influence, particularly on the BAUHAUS, on architecture and on commercial art.

still life A genre of painting depicting inanimate objects such as fruit, flowers, etc, begun by Dutch artists seeking secular commissions after the Reformation and the loss of Church patronage. Within the genre, the *vanitas* still life contains objects symbolic of the transcience of life, e.g. skulls, hour-glasses, etc, while others contain religious symbols, such as bread and wine. In the 18th century, CHARDIN gave new life to the form, and in the 19th century CÉZANNE's use of it in his experiments with structure was very influential on the CUBISTS.

Stoker, Bram [Abraham] (1847–1912) Irish novelist and short-story writer who is noted primarily for one work, the novel *Dracula* (1897), which has been filmed many times and remains one of the classic horror stories of all times.

Stoppard, Tom (1937–) Czech-born British dramatist. His plays have been very successful on the stage, due to their sharp, witty wordplay and dialogue, and fast, cleverly plotted action. Examples include *Rosencrantz and Guildenstern are Dead* (1966), *The Real Inspector Hound* (1968), *Jumpers* (1972), *Every Good Boy Deserves Favour* (1977) and *The Real Thing* (1982). Stoppard's willingness to engage with complex intellectual and political issues, and to challenge totalitarianism of the left as well as that of the right, combined with his undoubted talents as a writer, has given him a special status in modern drama. *See also* TZARA.

Stowe, Mrs Harriet Elizabeth Beecher (1811–96) American novelist. She wrote several novels, but the one she is remembered for is the anti-slavery novel

Uncle Tom's Cabin, or, Life Among the Lowly (1852).
The novel, and its succeeding dramatization, created a
sensation in the US and Europe, and has been
described as one of the significant events leading up to
the Civil War. The novel has been criticized for being
over-sentimental and melodramatic, and patronizing
to black people ("Uncle Toms"), but it was written for a
particular purpose, to expose the horrors of slavery,
and this it did remarkably well. It remains a compelling and readable work.

Strasberg, Lee *see* **Stanislavsky, Konstantin**.

stream of consciousness *see* **James, William**.

Strindberg, Johan August (1849–1912) Swedish
dramatist and novelist. His unremittingly bleak plays,
in which the strongest element is a pathological fear
and hatred of women, are powerful, highly innovative
works that have had a strong influence on many 20th-
century dramatists, notably O'NEILL. The plays
include *Miss Julie* (1888), *The Dance of Death* (1901),
A Dream Play (1902) and *The Ghost Sonata* (1907).

Structuralism (in literary criticism) A critical
approach to literature in which the text being studied
is viewed as a "cultural product" that cannot be "read"
in isolation, and in which the text is held to absorb
its meaning from the interconnected web of linguistic
codes and symbols of which it is but a part. The process
of studying the codes, etc., and their relation to each
other, is called *Semiotics*. A Structuralist approach to
the novels of Fennimore COOPER, for example, would
include recognition of the linguistic and cultural conventions underlying the author's use of language, with
particular reference to the significance of both the
"Noble Savage" myth in Western culture and the
emerging frontier myth in American culture. The
heroic persona of the Deerslayer, and his portrayal as a
transient figure between the mythic world of primitive

America and the swelling wave of modern civilization, results in a creative tension ripe for hours of happy exploration and parallel (e.g. with John Ford's film *The Man Who Shot Liberty Valance*).

Figures associated with the development of Structuralist theory are the Canadian critic **Marshall McLuhan** (1911–80), whose studies of mass culture and communication include *The Gutenberg Galaxy* (1962) and *The Medium is the Message* (1967); the linguist **Ferdinand de Saussure** (1857–1913); the anthropologist **Claude Levi-Strauss** (1908–); the critic **Roland Barthes** (1915–80); and the psychoanalyst **Jacques Lacan** (1901–81). Structuralism is thus an approach drawing on a wide range of disciplines, with some critics, e.g. followers of Lacan, focusing on the play between unconscious and conscious concepts, while others, e.g. followers of Saussure, will focus on the linguistic relativism that emerges between the *signifier* (the spoken word) and the *signified* (the mind's concept of the word). **Deconstruction**, a concept developed by the French philosopher **Jacques Derrida** (1930–), is a term for the process or "strategy" of examining the elements (signs) of language in isolation from other elements, thus exposing the contradictions inherent within language. This approach is also called **Poststructuralism**.

The psychologist **Jean Piaget** (1896–1980) usefully defines structure as composed of wholeness, transformation and self-regulation (*Structuralism*, 1971). Thus, HOMER's *Iliad*, for example, (a) is a work with a unity of structure conforming to the conventions of epic poetic form; (b) includes recognizable "types" of characters who appear in other such works, e.g. warriors, who may also behave in ways outside the expected form, as when the young Achilles hides himself amongst women dressed as a girl; (c) can alter its meaning according to external factors, e.g. the reader's understanding of the characters' behaviour can vary at different times, as fresh experiences alter the reader's perception.

The Structuralist approach can, perhaps surprisingly, be rewarding and even fun for the general reader, and some of its aspects are hardly new; it has long been recognized, for example, that reading a great novel such as TOLSTOY's *Anna Karenina* can be an entirely different experience at different stages of one's life. It is sometimes asserted by critics hostile to Structuralism and its progeny that the approach is essentially a spiritually barren one, an enmeshment in "ways of reading" that gets in the way of understanding rather than being an aid to appreciation. This is certainly true of some Structuralists, but is also true of some non-Structuralists. (For a sane discussion of Structuralist theory, and such issues as the "lucidity" debate, i.e. the weird and elitist argument that literary theory should not be accessible to the general reader, *see* Frank Kermode's collection of essays, *The Uses of Error*, (1991.)

Stuart, Gilbert (1775–1828) American painter, who studied with WEST in London and travelled widely in Great Britain and the US before settling there permanently 1792. He was one of the foremost portrait painters of his time, working in a distinctive painterly style, and capturing the character of his sitters with conviction. He is best known for his many portraits of George Washington, categorized into three basic types, one of which, the *"Athenaeum"* (1796), is featured on the US one-dollar banknote.

Stubbs, George (1724–1806) English painter and engraver, best known for his paintings of horses, of which he had an outstanding anatomical knowledge. He published his *Anatomy of the Horse* (1766) with his own engraved illustrations, beautifully and accurately depicted. The book established his reputation as a horse painter, and he won numerous commissions for portraits of horses, often portrayed with their owners. His works are also distinguished by masterly composition and atmospheric rendition of landscape. *Mares and Foals by a River* (1763–8) and *Horses attacked by a Lion* (1770) give an idea of the range and scope of his works.

study A drawing or painting of a detail for use in a larger finished work.

Suckling, Sir John (1609–41) English poet and dramatist. Suckling is classed as one of the finest of the CAVALIER POETS. The best known of his lyrics is the charming "Ballad upon a Wedding," which often appears in a discreetly bowdlerized version (the "Dick" addressed in the poem is Richard Lovelace). Most of his works are included in the posthumous collection *Fragmenta Aura* (1646). He was reputed to be the best card-player and bowler in England, and may have invented the game of cribbage.

Suprematism A Russian art movement based on principles of nonobjectivity. It was begun by Casimir MALEVICH in 1913, and evolved on a parallel with CONSTRUCTIVISM. *White on White* by Malevich is typical of the work of the movement. The influence of Suprematism spread through the BAUHAUS to Europe and the US.

Surrealism An avant-garde art movement of the 1920s and 1930s in France, which grew out of DADA and was inspired by the dream theories of Sigmund FREUD and by the literature and poetry of RIMBAUD and BAUDELAIRE.

Surrealism took from Dadaism a love for the juxtaposition of incongruous images, the purpose of which in the Surrealist view was to express the workings of the unconscious mind. The term "Surrealism" had been coined by the poet Guillauime APOLLINAIRE, but the movement really got going with the publication of the poet **André Breton**'s (1896–1966) first *Surrealist Manifesto* in 1924. According to Breton (who was much influenced by Freud), the "higher reality" could only be achieved in art by freeing the mind from the lower world of superficial rationality. *See also* ARTAUD.

In art, its influences include the works of de CHIRICO. There were two main trends: automatism, or free association, was explored in the works of MIRÓ, ERNST and MASSON, who sought deliberately to avoid conscious control by using techniques of spontaneity to express the subconscious. The world of dreams was the source of inspiration for the incongruously juxtaposed, often bizarre, but precisely painted imagery of DALI, and MAGRITTE.

Surrey, Earl of [Henry Howard] (*c.*1517–47) English poet, soldier and courtier. His translations of parts of VIRGIL's *Aeneid*, printed posthumously in a miscellaneous collection, *Tottel's Miscellany* (1557), are notable for being the first (printed) blank verse in English. He was also among the first English poets to use the sonnet form (and was strongly influenced by PETRARCH). Wyatt's version of the form, the so-called "English sonnet," is the form used by Shakespeare in his sonnets. Surrey's brave, unruly life ended in his execution for treason.

Surtees, Robert Smith (1803–64) English sports journalist, creator of a remarkable series of novels mainly concerned with the sporting life of the foxhunting grocer, Mr Jorrocks, e.g. *Jorrock's Jaunts and Jollies* (1838) and *Handley Cross* (1843). His fictions are boisterous, rowdy celebrations of the hunting life: "all time is lost wot is not spent in 'unting . . . it's the sport of kings, the image of war without its guilt" (*Handley Cross*), and are highly addictive. Surtees wrote eight novels in all; his complete oeuvre is being issued in a long-term project by the Surtees Society.

Sutherland, Graham (1903–80) English artist, who trained as an engraver and whose early works are influenced by PALMER. He began painting landscapes in the 1930s, using vivid colours to depict effects of light, and highlighting features of a scene, as in *Entrance to a Lane* (1939). He was an official war artist during World War II and afterwards was commissioned for the *Crucifixion* (1946) at St Matthew's Church, Northampton. He went on to produce some outstanding portraits, notably *Somerset Maugham* (1949) and *Winston Churchill* (1954). The latter was never liked by Sir Winston and was later destroyed by Lady Churchill. Another outstanding work is the tapestry *Christ in Glory* (1962).

Swift, Jonathan (1667–1745) Anglo-Irish divine, poet and satirist. His first important satirical works, published in 1704, were *The Battle of the Books*, a defence of the merits of classical literature against the claims of the moderns, and *A Tale of a Tub* (which also includes digressions on the ancient/modern debate), a satire on religious extremism, with particular emphasis on the excesses of Roman Catholicism, with Calvinism coming a close second and Lutheranism (close to Swift's own position) getting off fairly lightly. In politics, Swift started out with Whiggish sympathies (he was friendly with two notable Whig propagandists, ADDISON and STEELE), but soon became a staunch Tory, closely associated with such Tory wits as POPE. He was appointed Dean of St Patrick's Cathedral in Dublin in 1713, and over the course of his life published several tracts defending the rights of the Irish poor against their overlords, the most notable being *A Modest Proposal* (1729), in which he argues with merciless wit that the children of the poor should be fattened to feed the rich. His masterpiece, and one of the greatest satires ever written, is *Gulliver's Travels* (1726), which culminates in Gulliver's voyage to the Houyhnhnms ("whin-ims"), intelligent horses whose nobility is contrasted with the degraded brutality of mankind. It is sometimes said that Swift's work was intended to satirize mankind but ended up being a harmless children's book. This view is only tenable if one regards heavily BOWDLERized versions of the book as valid. Swift died leaving money to found a hospital for imbeciles; he was much mourned by the Irish people. His own epitaph (in Latin) describes him as lying "Where fierce (or savage) indignation can no longer tear his heart."

Swinburne, Algernon [Charles] (1837–1909) English poet and critic, noted for his sensuous verse, accurately described by himself as having a "tendency" to a "dulcet and luscious form of verbosity." His poems, e.g. *Poems and Ballads* (1866), created a public scandal not just for their sexuality, heavily tinged with undertones of depravity (he had read SADE), but for the author's clear dislike of Christianity ("Thou hast conquered, O Pale Galilean") and sympathy for paganism. In later years, he lived in respectable retirement with his friend, Theodore Watts-Dunton, at The Pines, Putney, where Max BEERBOHM visited them and later wrote a cruelly funny essay on the pair.

Symbolism In literature, a French poetry movement of the late 19th century that rejected the dictates of both REALISM and NATURALISM by seeking to express a state of mind by a process of suggestion rather than by attempting to portray "objective reality." As MALLARMÉ put it, "not the thing, but the effect produced." Other prominent poets associated with Symbolism include VERLAINE, RIMBAUD and VALÉRY. The movement has strong links with the world of Impressionist composers, such as Claude Debussy. Poets outside the

French-speaking world who were influenced by Symbolism include T. S. ELIOT, POUND, RILKE, and, notably, YEATS, whose superb epigram "Three Movements" serves as an epitaph both for the movement and for his own involvement with it. Several important plays of the late 19th century, e.g. CHEKHOV's *The Seagull* (1895) and IBSEN's *The Master Builder* (1896), also display the influence of Symbolism.

In art, also in late 19th-century France, Symbolism represented a response to the intrinsically visual work of the IMPRESSIONISTS and fell into two distinct trends: REDON and PUVIS DE CHAVANNES were inspired by the images of Symbolist Literature; GAUGUIN, van GOGH and the NABIS explored the symbolic use of colour and line to express emotion.

Synchromism An art movement originating in the US in 1913 with the works of RUSSELL and MACDONALD-WRIGHT. They were concerned with the balanced arrangement of pure colour, or "colours together," as in Russell's *Synchromy in Orange: to Form* (1914). The movement influenced a number of American painters.

Synge, [Edmund] John Millington (1871–1909) Irish dramatist, whose plays of Irish peasant life (written at YEATS' suggestion) were performed at the ABBEY THEATRE in Dublin. The first two (both one-acters) were *In the Shadow of the Glen* (1903), a dour "comedy" about infidelity, and *Riders to the Sea* (1904), a superb little tragedy about a mother and the death of her last son. A comedy, *The Well of the Saints*, followed in 1905, and after that his masterpiece, the highly controversial comedy *The Playboy of the Western World* (1907). A riot broke out at the latter's première, when the word "shifts," i.e. female undergarments, was used. (The play was claimed by its detractors to be a vicious slur on the virtuous Irish peasantry.) Synge's language is not really an authentic rendering of peasant speech, as he claimed; it is an artificial language, but no less charming for that in its occasionally haunting lyricism. Yeats described Synge as having a heart like his race, "passionate and simple."

T

Taeuber, Sophie *see* **Arp, Jean**.

Tarkington, [Newton] Booth (1869–1946) American novelist and dramatist, remembered chiefly for his novel of Midwest life *The Magnificent Ambersons* (1918), which was made into a major film by Oscar Welles in 1942.

Tate, [John Orley] Allen (1899–1979) American poet and critic. A "regional patriot," he supported the concept of a local sense of identity against the corrupting abstract notion of "America." His *Collected Poems* was published in 1977.

Tate, Nahum (1652–1715) English poet and dramatist, whose notorious version of SHAKESPEARE's *King Lear* gave the play a happy ending (Cordelia and Edgar become lovers). Dr JOHNSON, who could not bear to re-read the closing scenes of the play, gave qualified approval to Tate's version for the stage. Shakespeare's original ending was not restored until the early 19th century. Tate's other main claim to fame is his metrical version of the psalms, written with **Nicholas Brady** (1659–1726). Many of their versions of the psalms, e.g. "While shepherds watched their flocks by night," remain popular standards. Tate became POET LAUREATE in 1692 and was one of the many poetasters satirized by POPE in *The Dunciad*.

Tatlin, Vladimir (1885–1953) Russian painter and designer. He studied in Moscow, and his early CON-

STRUCTIVIST sculptures were influenced by the works of PICASSO, e.g *Painting Reliefs* (1913). His commission for a *Monument to the Third International* was, unfortunately, never executed. During the 1920s he began designing utilitarian objects and theatre sets, and these gradually conformed more and more to officially approved trends in socialist realism.

Taylor, Jeremy (1613–67) English bishop and theologian. His prose has been highly praised by many critics, notably T. S. ELIOT and COLERIDGE, for its daring and colourful use of imagery and metaphor, combined with a talent for expressing complex issues in a simple way. He was also a believer in religious toleration, in the moderate high Anglican tradition (*see also* Lancelot ANDREWES). His works include *The Rule and Exercises of Holy Living* (1650) and *The Rule and Exercises of Holy Dying* (1651).

tempera A paint medium made by mixing colour pigments with egg. It was much used until the 15th century and the development of OIL PAINT.

Tennyson, Alfred Lord [1st Baron Tennyson] (1809–92) English poet. He first came to public notice with *Poems, Chiefly Lyrical* (1830). Subsequent volumes, e.g. *Poems* (1833), established him as a highly skilled and popular poet. He was appointed poet laureate in succession to WORDSWORTH in 1850, the year in which he published his great elegy for his dead friend A. H. Hallam, *In Memoriam*. Tennyson became a much respected public figure; several of his poems, e.g. "Locksley Hall" (1842) and "Locksley Hall Revisited" (1886) being regarded by many of his contemporaries as oracular statements on the Spirit of the Age. (He himself felt that he was a great poet with nothing much of consequence to say about anything.) His literary reputation sank somewhat in the late 19th century, but he is now universally regarded as a great poet.

Terborch *or* **Terburg, Gerard** (*c.*1617–81) Dutch painter, who studied with his father and in Haarlem. He travelled to Italy, England and Germany, where he painted a group portrait at the *Peace Congress of Munster* (1648). From 1654 he settled at Deventer, where he passed the rest of his career painting refined and sophisticated genre scenes and society portraits, e.g. *A Young Man* (*c.*1663).

Terbrugghen, Hendrick (1588–1629) Dutch painter. He trained in Utrecht and travelled in Italy, where he was influenced by the works of CARAVAGGIO. Works such as *The Liberation of St Peter* (1629) and *The Flute Player* (1621) influenced the painters FABRITIUS and VERMEER.

Terence [Publius Terentius Afer] (*c.*190–159BC) Roman dramatist. He wrote six plays, all of which are extant and, like those of PLAUTUS, are adaptations of Greek "New Comedy" originals (*see* MENANDER, COMEDY). Terence's works are less coarse than those of Plautus, and the characters have more depth.

Thackeray, William Makepeace (1811–63) Indian-born English novelist and essayist, noted particularly for the witty social satire of both his novels and his nonfiction works, e.g. *The Book of Snobs* (1846–7), a wickedly funny description of the different varieties of British snobbery. His masterpiece is *Vanity Fair* (1847–8), a decidedly nonmoralistic tale of the opportunistic "antiheroine" Becky Sharp, set during the Napoleonic wars. His other main fictional works are the novels *Pendennis* (1850) and *Henry Esmond* (1852). His American lecture tours (1851–3, 1955–6) were very popular.

Theocritus *see* **Pastoral**.

Thomas, Dylan [Marlais] (1914–53) Welsh poet. He worked as a journalist in Wales before moving to London in 1934, in which year his book of poems *18*

Poems appeared. He rapidly acquired a reputation as a hard drinking, boisterous pub poet, which, combined with his exuberant, florid and occasionally obscure verse, created a lived-up-to persona which ultimately led to his death (in New York). His own recordings of his work are superb. His first collected edition, *Collected Poems* (1952), sold over 30,000 copies in its first year. His best-known single work is *Under Milk Wood* (1954), a radio drama in poetic prose that is regarded as a milestone in broadcasting.

Thomas, [Philip] Edward (1878–1917) English poet. He began his literary career by writing books on rural Britain, e.g. *Beautiful Wales* (1905), and various journalistic pieces. He met Robert Frost in 1913, who encouraged him to write poetry. He enlisted in 1915 and was killed in action before the publication of his *Poems* (1917). His best-known poem is "Adlestrop," which typifies the quietly reflective nature of much of his work.

Thomas, R[onald] S[tuart] (1913–) Welsh poet and Anglican priest, who is regarded by many critics as one of the foremost religious poets of modern times. His poems, e.g. *The Stones of the Field* (1946) and *An Acre of Land* (1952), display a Crabbe-like, deep concern for the bleak and often spiritually barren way of life of the poor of rural Wales.

Thompson, Flora [Jane] (1876–1947) English author, noted for her autobiographical trilogy *Lark Rise* (1939), *Over to Candleford* (1941) and *Candleford Green* (1943), issued in one volume as *Lark Rise to Candleford* (1943). The trilogy gives a valuable picture of the vanished pre-World War I life of the rural poor in England. A curious feature of modern editions of the work is that they are often packaged and publicized in such a way as to suggest that the world the book depicts is one of comfort, cosiness and stability, which is far from the case.

Thompson, Francis (1859–1907) English poet. Rescued from opium addiction by the poet and fellow Roman Catholic **Alice Meynell** (1847–1922), Thompson produced three volumes of poetry in the 1890s, *Poems* (1893), *Sister Songs* (1895) and *New Poems* (1897). The best known of his poems, e.g. "The Hound of Heaven" and "In No Strange Land," are intensely spiritual, with elaborate imagery.

Thompson, Jim, (1906–76) American novelist. His grim crime novels are solidly in the tradition of seedy American determinism, and feature the usual stock characters of no-hopers, whores, psychotics and freaks (he has been dubbed "the dimestore Dostoevsky," not to be confused with "the poor man's Dostoevsky," Nelson ALGREN). Thompson's novels have a firm cult following (especially in France), and there have been many film adaptations, most notably of *The Getaway* (1959, filmed 1972) and *The Grifters* (1963, filmed 1990). Thompson wrote the screenplays for *Paths of Glory* (1957) and *The Killing* (1956), and made one screen appearance himself, in the 1975 version of Chandler's *Farewell, my Lovely*.

Thomson, James (1700–1748) Scottish poet and dramatist. His once very popular tragedies, e.g. *Sophonisba* (1730), are tediously rhetorical works that are no longer performed, or even read much. His most famous poems are *The Seasons* (1726–30) and *The Castle of Indolence* (1748). His work was admired by the ROMANTIC poets, e.g. WORDSWORTH, who saw him as a true nature poet struggling free from the fetters of 18th-century poetic diction.

Thomson, James (1834–82) Scottish poet, chiefly remembered for his poem "City of Dreadful Night" (1874), a long, nightmarish vision of a decaying city, through which runs a River of Suicides. The city is presided over by a personification of melancholy, and is inhabited by wandering, suffering souls. Thomson died an alcoholic.

Thoreau, Henry David (1817–62) American philosopher (and friend of EMERSON), whose advocacy of self-sufficiency and passive resistance to tyrannical government has been very influential, Gandhi being his most notable admirer. The best known of his books is *Walden, or Life in the Woods* (1854), which describes his two-year retreat to live in a cabin in the woods. He was an aphorist of genius, e.g. "The mass of men lead lives of quiet desperation."

Thorvaldsen, Bertel (1770–1844) Danish sculptor. The son of an Icelandic woodcarver, he trained at Copenhagen and settled in Rome from 1796. He drew his inspiration from ANTIQUE sculpture, and his work is austerely classical. He achieved fame with the statue of *Jason with the Golden Fleece* (1802–3) and enjoyed a successful career. He ranks alongside CANOVA and FLAXMAN as an outstanding sculptor of the NEOCLASSICAL period.

Thurber, James [Grover] (1894–1961) American humorist, cartoonist and essayist. As with Dorothy PARKER, much of his work first appeared in the *New Yorker*, including his most famous story, "The Secret Life of Walter Mitty," in which a typical Thurber-style mousy little man, who is dominated by his wife, has fantasies in which he features in various heroic roles, e.g. as a fighter pilot. The Thurber world is one where such men stumble through minefields of everyday banality and absurdity, coming home at the end of the day to women even more fearful and incomprehensible than the objects outside. Representative works include *My Life and Hard Times* (1933) and Thurber Country (1953).

Tiepolo, Giambattista (1696–1770) Italian artist, the greatest decorative fresco painter of the ROCOCO period. From 1737 he was doing fresco cycles characterized by a light, ethereal chiaroscuro, presenting a subtly atmospheric celestial vision. His greatest work is the decor for the Archbishop's Palace in Würtzburg, including the fresco *The Marriage of Frederick Barbarossa and Beatrice of Burgundy* (1751). From 1762 he worked for Charles III of Spain, and there painted some outstanding religious works for the Royal Chapel, some of which remained unfinished at his death. The preparatory sketches are in the Courtnauld Collection, London. His sons **Lorenzo** (1736–c.1776) and **Domenico** (1727–1804) were also painters and assistants to their father. Of the two, Domenico was the more talented and achieved success working mainly in his father's style.

Tiffany, Louis Comfort *see* **Art Nouveau**.

Tintoretto, Jacopo [Jacopo Robusti] (1518–94) Venetian painter, the son of a dyer, or *tintore*, from whom he took his name. He absorbed the lessons of TITIAN in his use of colour and was inspired by the drawing of MICHELANGELO, as in *The Miracle of the Slave* (1548). The synthesis of these great influences resulted in a dynamic, highly imaginative style of painting, which was to evolve into the MANNERIST tradition and pave the way for the BAROQUE. As his mature style developed, he experimented with the effects of lighting and highlighting, and with a heightened sense of space and perspective, e.g. *The Finding of the Body of St Mark*. From 1564 he worked on the decor of the Scuola di San Rocco, painting scenes from the life of Christ, including a striking *Crucifixion*. One of his last and finest paintings is *The Last Supper* (1592–4). Of his seven children, three became painters: **Domenico**

(1562–1635), **Marco** (1561–1637) and **Marietta** (*c*.1556–90), who was known as "La Tintoretta."

Tissot, James [Jaques Joseph] (1836–1902) French painter and engraver. He trained in Paris and was influenced by DEGAS. He moved to London after 1871 and achieved success with his polished scenes of Victorian society, e.g. *The Last Evening* (1893), which reveal the influence of MANET and WHISTLER. He spent the last 20 years of his life visiting Palestine and painted *c*.300 watercolours on the life of Christ.

Titian [Tiziano Vecelli] (*c*.1490–1576) Venetian painter, one of the greatest figures in world art. He studied under Giovanni BELLINI and was influenced by him and by GIOGIONE, to whom he was an assistant. After the death of Giorgione, many of whose works he completed, Titain was unrivalled in Venice for about 60 years. He achieved fame with *The Assumption of the Virgin* (1516–17), equal in power and grandeur to the best of Rome's talents, but surpassing all in its richness of colour. His subsequent commissions for the Duke of Ferrara include the masterpiece *Bacchus and Ariadne* (1523). From 1530 he was patronized (and in 1533 ennobled) by the Holy Roman Emperor Charles V, portrayed on horseback in *Charles V at Méhlberg* (1548). Philip II of Spain succeeded his father as Titian's patron. His commissions for mythical subjects resulted in the development of Titian's *Poesies*, paintings of earthy sensuality and glowing harmony of colour, e.g. *Bacchanal* and *The Rape of Europa* (1562). A delicate poignancy pervades the works of his last years, from *The Fall of Man* (*c*.1570) and *Christ Crowned with Thorns* (*c*.1590) to *Madonna Suckling the Child* (1570–6) and culminating in the beautiful, unfinished *Pietà* (1576). In the course of his career, he painted almost every kind of picture and fully explored the potential of oil paint in his free and revolutionary techniques. His influence on succeeding generations of painters is incalculable.

Tolkien, J[ohn] R[onald] R[euel] (1892–1973) South African-born British fantasy writer and scholar. Tolkien is probably the most influential (and bestselling) fantasy writer of all time. The success of his stories, and the cult that grew around them, seems to have somewhat bemused Tolkien, who trained as a philologist and had acquired a deep knowledge of myth and the structures of language by the mid-1930s, when he published his paper "Beowulf: the Monsters and the Critics" (1936). The works on which his fame rests are *The Hobbit* (1937), and the remarkable three-volume quest romance *The Lord of the Rings* (1954–5). He was a friend of C. S. LEWIS and Charles WILLIAMS, with whom he formed an informal little group of mythmakers called the "Inklings."

Tolstoy, Count Leo [Lev Nikolayevich Tolstoy] (1828–1910) Russian novelist, dramatist, short-story writer and philosopher. Born into the Russian aristocracy, Tolstoy lived the normal dissolute life of a young aristocrat, joined the army in the Caucasus, and commanded a battery at Sevastopol during the Crimean war. His autobiographical trilogy *Childhood* (1852), *Boyhood* (1854) and *Youth* (1857) is one of the most remarkable autobiographies ever published by a young man. By the time he had settled at Yasnaya Polyana, he had established a reputation as a writer of great talent, and had embarked upon the spiritual self-questioning that resulted in some of the greatest works of fiction ever produced. Two of his novels, in particular, are frequently described as the greatest of all novels. The first of these, *War and Peace* (1863–9), is a panoramic epic of the Napoleonic invasion of Russia, in which the muddled Pierre Bezuhov represents the author's own spiritual and moral confusion. The second is *Anna Karenina* (1875–7), a tragic tale of adulterous love which raises profound questions about personal and social morality. Tolstoy's remorseless examination of how a Christian should live, and such principles as his belief that the "normal" married situation, in which an experienced man is wed to a "pure" female, is profoundly immoral, led to his excommunication in 1901. His version of Christian pacificism (virtually an anarchist position) came to be called "Tolstoyanism," and influenced many modern thinkers, notably Gandhi.

tondo The Italian word for "round," used in art to denote a circular picture or sculpture.

Toulouse-Lautrec, Henri [Marie Raymond] de (1864–1901) French painter and lithographer. The son of a wealthy aristocrat, ill health in childhood and a subsequent accident, in which both legs were broken, stunted his growth. He trained in Paris, where he met van GOGH and was influenced by the works of DEGAS. His subjects were café clientele, prostitutes and cabaret performers in and around Montmartre, where he lived and worked, e.g. *In the Parlour at the Rue des Moulins* (1894). He is best known for his lithographs and posters advertising cafes and entertainers, such as Aristide Brouant and Yvette Guilbert. Much of his flattened linear style was influenced by Japanese prints.

Tourneur, Cyril (*c.*1575–1626) English dramatist. He was the author of *The Atheist's Tragedy* (1628), and possibly also the author of one of the greatest examples of the REVENGE TRAGEDY genre, *The Revenger's Tragedy* (1607), a highly bloodthirsty piece with cold, brilliantly malevolent dialogue.

tragedy A form of drama in which a hero or heroine comes to a bad end. The cause of the protagonist's failure can be either a personal flaw or a circumstance beyond his or her control, or both. (The origin of the term, which means "goat song," is obscure, but possibly derives from the sacrifice of goats in Dionysian fertility rituals.) The earliest tragedies known, those by AESCHYLUS, SOPHOCLES and EURIPIDES, are still among the greatest. The first critical study of the form is in ARISTOTLE's *Poetics*, where Aristotle defines tragedy as an imitation (*mimesis*) of a serious, complete action on a grand scale, "grand" meaning a momentous action involving highly placed characters in society. The protagonist will make an "error of judgment" – the word for this, *hamartia*, has often been rendered, a bit misleadingly, as "tragic flaw" – but the protagonist's main fault is as often the result of having to undertake a certain action at a certain time, as in any character defect; thus, in Sophocles' *Antigone*, the heroine is in the position of having to choose between divine and human law. The protagonist is usually a good person, but not perfect, and progresses from happiness to misery. Another important concept in the *Poetics* is that of *catharsis*, the "purging" (or purification, cleansing) of the emotions of pity and fear aroused in the spectators by the play.

The great tradition of the Greek tragedians was filtered through the plays of SENECA to the dramatists of the RENAISSANCE, although Renaissance tragedies, such as those of SHAKESPEARE, differ significantly from those of the past. The interplay in Shakespeare's tragedies between the heroic and the ironic or comic commonplace worlds, e.g. the banter between the rustic clown and Cleopatra at the end of *Antony and Cleopatra*, is profoundly foreign to the world of the *Poetics*, just as the pagan, multideistic and fate-haunted world of the Greeks was ultimately alien to Renaissance dramatists brought up in the Christian tradition.

Several 20th-century dramatists, e.g. Arthur MILLER

and Eugene O'Neill, have tried, with debatable results, to adapt the form of Athenian tragedy to the modern stage. The most that can be said for such adaptations is that they may result in effects similar to those of the originals. Miller, for example, in *Death of a Salesman*, locates the cause of Willy Loman's fall in a social (capitalist) directive to compete for victory in the American Dream rather than in blind fate. However, the fact that such dramas invariably have as subtext the notion that *this state of affairs is reformable*, and the equally invariable ironic presentation of the protagonists such as Loman as "losers of history," rather than as victims of forces as permanent as they are merciless, puts such plays as *Death of a Salesman* at a further remove from the Athenian drama than, say, *King Lear*, with its bleak vision of a fallen world in which bloody tyranny is an everpresent threat.

See also DOMESTIC TRAGEDY, HEROIC TRAGEDY, JACOBEAN TRAGEDY, REVENGE TRAGEDY.

Tragicomedy *see* COMEDY.

Traherne, Thomas (1637–74) English poet and author of religious meditations. He was ordained into the Anglican Church in 1660, and was renowned for living "a devout life," according to the normally uncharitable antiquary, Anthony Wood. The manuscript of his *Centuries of Meditations*, which includes many beautiful mystical passages, was discovered on a London bookstall in 1896, and published in 1908.

Traven, B. [pseud. of Albert Otto Max Feige] (*c.*1882–1969) German-born American novelist. Traven's origins and career are shrouded in an artfully constructed obscurity. He was described by his biographer Will Wyatt (in *The Man who was B. Traven*, 1980) as "one of the most mysterious figures of the twentieth century." Traven wrote approximately 12 adventure novels, of which the best known are *The Death Ship* (1925) and *The Treasure of the Sierra Madre* (1934).

trecento The Italian term for the 14th century.

Trevor, William [William Trevor Cox] (1928–) Irish novelist and short-story writer. His highly regarded fiction, often set in rural Ireland or on the down-at-heel fringes of English middle-class life, includes the novels *The Old Boys* (1964) and *Fools of Fortune* (1983); short-story collections include *Angels at the Ritz* (1975) and *Beyond the Pale* (1981).

Trilling, Lionel (1905–75) American critic. His collection of essays, *The Liberal Imagination* (1950), was very influential in its concern for locating literary criticism as something central to Western, liberal culture. He was much influenced by FREUD in his later work, which includes close and highly perceptive analysis of the creative imagination. His short book *Sincerity and Authenticity* (1972) is one of the key postwar critical works.

triptych A painting, usually an ALTARPIECE, consisting of three hinged parts, the outer two folding over the middle section. *See also* DIPTYCH, POLYPTYCH.

Trollope, Anthony (1815–82) English novelist, whose more than 50 books have a wide and devoted following (a thriving Trollope Society exists). His mother, **Frances Trollope** (1780–1863), was herself a prolific author, whose most notable work is a bad-tempered (and very successful) study of American life, *Domestic Manners of the Americans* (1832). Trollope wrote two main novel sequences: the "Barsetshire" novels ("Barsetshire" is an imaginary West Country county where the home life is very different from that of Thomas Hardy's "Wessex"), which focus on the trials and tribulations of the provincial lives of the gentry, clergy and middle classes, e.g. *Barchester Towers* (1857) and *The Last Chronicle of Barset* (1867), and the "Palliser" novels of political life, e.g. *Can You Forgive Her?* (1864) and *Phineas Finn* (1869). Each sequence includes characters who reappear in the action of succeeding novels, thus building up an evolving panorama of English life that has fascinated generations of readers. Trollope was also a highly industrious civil servant, with a formidable Victorian appetite for life and work. Nathaniel HAWTHORNE described him as 'just as English as beef-steak."

Trumbull, John (1756–1843) American painter. He studied under WEST in London and was influenced by him and by COPLEY, as in the famous *Death of General Warren at the Battle of Bunker Hill* (1786). He painted many scenes from the American War of Independence, also landscapes and some notable portraits of George Washington.

Tupper, Martin Farquhar (1810–89) English poet, whose monotonous and rhythmically plodding versified maxims were immensely popular in both Britain and the US, particularly *Proverbial Philosophy* (1838–42). By the 1890s, he had become a standard target for parodists such as GILBERT, and editions of his work were issued with tongue-in-cheek commendations. (It should be pointed out that much of his work, although rambling and sententious, is wholly admirable in content, e.g. his attacks on cruelty to animals.) He also invented some rather strange devices which never quite caught on, e.g. safety horseshoes.

Tura, Cosimo (*c.*1431–95) Italian painter, who studied in Padua and established the School of Ferrara in 1452. His highly individual style was characterized by tortured forms and harsh colouring, creating scenes of tense emotion. This powerful atmosphere is enhanced by an enigmatic use of architectural detail. Notable works include *Pieté* and *St Jerome*.

Turgenev, Ivan Sergeyevich (1818–83) Russian

novelist, short-story writer and dramatist. His great novels, e.g. *A Nest of Gentlefolk* (1859), *On the Eve* (1860), and his masterpiece *Fathers and Sons* (1862), explore such major issues of Russian life as serfdom and the question of revolutionary change through the lives, thoughts and actions of his characters, particularly those of the intelligentsia. Unlike his great contemporaries TOLSTOY and DOSTOEVSKY, Turgenev looked to Western culture for help in solving Russia's problems, and was friendly with many Western authors, e.g. DICKENS and George ELIOT. The greatest of his plays is *A Month in the Country* (1850).

Turner, Joseph Mallord William (1775–1851) English painter. Of precocious talent, he exhibited his first work at the Royal Academy at the age of 15. He collaborated on a series of architectural studies in watercolour, and from 1796 began painting in oils under the influence of CLAUDE and WILSON. In 1802 he visited Paris, where the works of TITIAN and POUSSIN at the Louvre inspired his developing personal style, as in *The Shipwreck* (1805). He visited Italy in 1819 and thereafter became more interested in gradations of shifting light and atmosphere, and bolder in his application of brilliant colours, e.g. *The Bay of Baiae, with Apollo and the Sybil* (1823). He made a second visit to Italy in 1829, and the works of the next two decades represent his finest period. Paintings such as *The Burning of the Houses of Parliament* (1834), *The Fighting Temeraire* (1839), *The Sun of Venice going to Sea* (1843) and *Rain, Steam and Speed* (1844) might have been painted with the very elements they depict, and they were described at the time by CONSTABLE as "airy visions painted with tinted steam." Turner's innovations were not approved by the critics, but he had a supportive patron in Lord Egremont of Petworth, and an influential champion in John RUSKIN, who defended him in *Modern Painters* (1843). He became reclusive in old age, and died in lodgings in Chelsea, London, under the assumed name of Booth. He left nearly 20,000 watercolours and drawings and 300 oil paintings to the nation.

Twain, Mark [pseud. of Samuel Langhorne Clemens] (1835–1910) American novelist, short-story writer and humorist. After training as a printer, he became a Mississippi river pilot, taking his pseudonym from the depth-sounding call meaning "by the mark two fathoms." His two most famous books, *The Adventures of Tom Sawyer* (1876) and (his masterpiece) *The Adventures of Huckleberry Finn* (1884), have become world classics of children's literature, despite the fact that the latter work includes much that is quite grim and indeed shocking, e.g. the brutal tarring and feathering of the two shysters, the King and the Duke. *Huckleberry Finn* is perhaps the greatest of all American novels; outwardly simple and entertaining, but with complex undercurrents (Huck's river journey down the Mississippi with Jim, the escaped slave, and Huck's innocent compassion, humour and growing consciousness, have haunted American literature since the book's publication). Twain's other works include a satirical travel book, *The Innocents Abroad* (1869); an autobiographical account of his experiences in Nevada, self-explanatorily titled *Roughing It* (1872); and several dark little misanthropic fables, e.g. *The Man that Corrupted Hadleyburg* (1900). *See also* SCOTT.

Twombly, Cy (1929–) American painter. He studied in Boston, New York and The Black Mountain College before settling in Rome in 1957. He established a distinctive gestural technique based on graffiti and children's art, e.g. *Untitled* (1968). His ideas are informed by SURREALIST automatism, and he owes a certain debt to KLEE and to RAUSCHENBERG.

Tworkov, Jack (1900–1982) Polish-born American painter whose early works were influenced by CÉZANNE. In the 1930s he worked on the FEDERAL ARTS PROJECT and met DE KOONING, who was to influence his later ABSTRACT EXPRESSIONIST style. A typical work of the 1950s is *Duo I* (1956).

Tyndale, William *see* **Authorized Version**.

Tzara, Tristan [pseud. of Samuel Rosenstock] (1896–1963) Romanian-born French poet and essayist. He was one of the founders of DADA at the Cabaret Voltaire in Zürich, 1916 (*see* Tom STOPPARD's play of *Travesties*, 1974, for a brilliantly funny presentation of the birth of Dada; James JOYCE and Lenin also appear). The word "Dada," from the French children's word for "hobbyhorse," was apparently taken at random from a dictionary. The Dada movement rejected rationality, sense and order; its most notable principles were irreverence and incongruity, its impetus deriving from the mad background of World War I and the influence of NIHILISM. In the *Seven Dada Manifestoes*, Tzara argued for the reduction of poetry to meaningless jumbles of words, and, in Paris, staged some deliberately shambolic theatrical events. Dada waned in Paris in the early 1920s, becoming gradually supplanted by SURREALISM, which movement Tzara happily joined. Tzara's best-known volume of poetry is *Approximate Man* (1931).

U

Uccello, Paolo (*c*.1396–1475) Florentine painter, who trained with GHIBERTI and worked on mosaics in Venice (1425–31). His earliest dated work is the fresco of *Sir John Hawkwood* (1436), and his use of a double viewpoint indicates an interest in perspective that was to dominate all his work. In *The Flood* fresco (*c*.1455) he uses a similar device of two vanishing points to powerfully dramatic effect. Uccello combined RENAISSANCE ideas concerning spatial composition with a Gothic sense of decorative detail in his most famous work, *The Battle of San Romano* (1455), which was painted for the MEDICI Palace. This combination of styles is synthesized to a masterly degree in some of his later works, including *The Night Hunt* (*c*. 1465–9), which is also one of the first paintings on canvas to be painted in Italy.

Unities *see* **Neoclassicism**.

Updike, John (1932–) American novelist, short-story writer and poet. His best-known work is the "Rabbit" sequence, i.e. *Rabbit, Run* (1960), *Rabbit Redux* (1971), *Rabbit is Rich* (1981), and *Rabbit at Rest* (1990), which describes the troubles and relationships of a middle American (Harry Angstrom, "Rabbit") in his progress through the changing fabric of American society in the 1960s, 1970s and 1980s. Updike's other works include the novels *The Centaur* (1963) and *The Coup* (1979), and short-story collections, e.g. *Pigeon Feathers and Other Stories* (1979).

Utopian novel *see* **More, Sir Thomas**.

Utrecht School A movement in Dutch art begun by HONTHORST, , TERBRUGGHEN and **Dirck van Baburen** (*c*.1595–1624), who were in Rome between 1610 and 1620 and were strongly influenced by CARAVAGGIO, whose style they took back to the Netherlands, thus influencing in turn such northern masters as VERMEER and REMBRANDT.

Utrillo, Maurice (1883–1955) French painter. He was largely self-taught, encouraged to paint by his mother, the painter **Suzanne Valadon** (1867–1938), and by his adoptive father, the writer Miguel Utrillo. He painted the Parisian streets around Montmartre, e.g. *La Place du Tertre* (*c*.1910) in richly subtle colours and thick impasto. A victim of alcoholism and drug addiction, he was frequently convalescent in nursing homes, but despite this his output was prolific and his paintings much sought after. His palette brightened in his later works, but paintings from his "white period" (1908–14) represent the peak of his popular achievements.

V

Valéry, Paul (1871–1945) French poet and critic associated with the SYMBOLIST MOVEMENT. Volumes of his poetry include *The Young Fate* (1917) and *Graveyard by the Sea* (1920). He published five collections of essays on literature and aesthetics, all called *Variety* (1922–44).

Vanbrugh, Sir John (1664–1726) English dramatist and architect, noted for his witty comedies, e.g. *The Relapse* (1696), *The Provok'd Wife* (1697), and *The Confederacy* (1705). He was also an architect of note, the most famous of his buildings being Blenheim Palace.

Van der Post, Sir Laurens (1906–) South African novelist, travel writer and mystic. His works are strongly influenced by JUNG and display a strong sympathy for the "primitive" peoples of the world, particularly the African Bushmen. His fiction includes the novels *The Seed and the Sower* (1963), *The Hunter and the Whale* (1967) and *A Story Like the Wind* (the first of these, based on his experiences as a prisoner of war of the Japanese, was filmed as *Merry Christmas, Mr Lawrence*). His travel books include two African classics, *Venture to the Interior* (1952) and *The Lost World of the Kalahari* (1958). In the mid-1980s he acquired a good deal of public notice as the Prince of Wales' reputed "guru."

van Gogh, Vincent *see* **Gogh, Vincent van**.

Vargas Llosa, [Jorge] Mario [Pedro] (1936–) Peruvian novelist. His novels include *The Time of the Hero* (1966), a satire on Peruvian society centred on Llosa's former military academy (which burned the book publicly), the historical novel *The War of the End of the World* (1984), and *The Storyteller* (1990), a powerful fable on power and the rights of the Peruvian Indians. Vargas Llosa's fiction, with its often radical restructuring of time, space and even character identity within the narrative, has some affinities with MAGIC REALISM and the work of his friend MARQUEZ. His brave and passionate opposition to the murderous policies of the Maoist *Sendero Luminoso* party in Peru and espousal of democratic right-wing policies (he ran for President in 1990) has earned him many enemies on both the left and right. The themes of dictatorship and of Utopian terrorism are central to his work, and both of these themes are incarnated in Vargas Llosa's main enemy, the infamous *Sendero* leader, Professor Guzman, who, in a magically realist situation, may be alive or may have been dead for years.

Vasarély, Victor (1908–) Hungarian-born French painter. He trained in Budapest under MOHOLY-NAGY, and in 1930 moved to Paris where he began working in graphic design. During the 1930s he produced the black and white semi-abstract paintings *Zebras* and *Harlequins*. In the late 1940s his works became completely abstract, and he later became a leading exponent of Op Art, with works such as *Timbres II* (1966). He published his ideas in *Yellow Manifesto* (1955).

Vasari, Giorgio (1511–74) Italian painter, writer and architect from Arezzo, famous as the chronicler of the RENAISSANCE period in Italian art. The first edition of his *Lives of the Most Eminent Painters, Sculptors and Architects* was published in 1550 and revised and enlarged in 1568. In it he traces the revival of ancient

Roman aesthetic values and the development of art from GIOTTO and PISANO to MICHELANGELO, coining the term *Rinascente*, or Renaissance. It remains a source of prime importance for modern art historians. As a painter he trained under ANDREA DEL SARTO and worked in Rome on decorations for the Vatican and the Cancelleria. He emulated Michelangelo in his MANNERIST style, evidenced in the decor for the Palazzo Vecchio in Florence (from 1563). In architecture, his finest work is the Uffizi in Florence (from 1560), which, appropriately, now houses many of Italy's finest art treasures.

Vaughan, Henry (1621–95) Welsh poet, best known for his collection of mystical religious verse, *Silex Scintillans* (1650, 1655). Several of his poems, like those of HERBERT, have startlingly vivid opening lines, e.g. "They are all gone into the world of light," or "I saw Eternity the other night."

Vega Carpio, Lope de (1562–1635) Spanish poet and dramatist. His eventful life included service in the Spanish Armada in 1588, and, near the end of his life, in the Spanish Inquisition. He reputedly wrote around 1,500 plays, of which a few hundred survive.

Velazquez *or* **Velésquez, Diego Roderiguez de Silva y** (1599–1660), Spanish painter, the greatest master to come out of Spain. He trained in Seville with PACHECO from 1613 and married Pacheco's daughter in 1618, the year he set up his own studio. His earliest paintings were *bodegones*, a type of genre painting peculiar to Spain, consisting largely of domestic scenes, e.g. *An Old Woman Cooking Eggs* (1618). From 1623 he was court painter to Philip IV at Madrid, painting portraits and some historical events. In 1628 RUBENS visited Madrid, and on his advice Velazquez travelled to Italy, where he was deeply influenced by the works of TITIAN and TINTORETTO. A lighter palette and freer brushwork are evident in his subsequent works. It was on a second visit to Italy that he painted his best single portrait, of *Pope Innocent X* (1650). He also painted one of the most remarkable history paintings, the moving *Surrender of Breda* (1634–5). Notable among his court portraits are *Infante Baltasar Carlos on Horseback* (1635–6), several of the Infantas, Margarita and Maria Theresa, and the full-length portraits of *Philip IV* (c.1632) and the young queen *Anne Maria of Austria* (1552). His most complex and best-known work is *Las Meninas* (1656), a fine example of his realist style. Overall, his works are distinguished by their unflattering truth to nature, combined with an integrity and respect for the individual, resulting in an overwhelmingly direct character analysis

Velde, Henri Clemens van de (1863–1957) Belgian painter, architect and designer. He studied in Paris, and his early works are in a NEOIMPRESSIONIST style. From 1893 he was interested in architecture and interior design, influenced by the works of Willaim MORRIS and the ARTS AND CRAFTS MOVEMENT. In 1906 he initiated the Deutscher Werkbund along with his pupil, Walter Gropius (*see* BAUHAUS), and became a Director of the Weimar School of Arts and Crafts. He designed furniture and ornaments in the ART NOUVEAU style, and his building designs disseminated the ideas of Charles Rennie Mackintosh.

Vergil *see* **Virgil.**

Verlaine, Paul (1844–96) French poet, regarded with his lover RIMBAUD as an early SYMBOLIST. The affair ended when Verlaine shot and wounded Rimbaud, spending two years in prison for the deed. Collections of Verlaine's verse include *Saturnian Poems* (1866), the religious poems of *Wisdom* (1881) and *Romances Without Words* (1874). His memoir *Accurse Poets* includes studies of contemporaries such as Rimbaud and MALLARMÉ.

Vermeer, Jan *or* **Johannes** (1632–75) Dutch painter. The son of a Delft art dealer, he may have studied under FABRITIUS, but little of his work is documented and the chronology of his development is uncertain. One of his accepted early works is *Christ in the House of Mary and Martha* (c.1654). He is best remembered for his small-scale intimate interior scenes, carefully composed and lit, usually by daylight through a window, e.g. *Girl Reading*. Portraits and interiors make up the bulk of his oeuvre, but he left two paintings of the town of Delft: *A Street in Delft* and *A View of Delft*. The latter is notable for its tonal verity and quiet intensity. His business, inherited from his father, failed to support his wife and 11 children, whom he left bankrupt when he died. His full significance as a painter was only recognized in the 19th century, although his works were not unpopular in his day.

Verne, Jules (1828–1905) French novelist, whose innovative fantasy novels, e.g. *Voyage to the Centre of the Earth* (1864) and *20,000 Leagues Under the Sea* (1969), are regarded as the earliest great science fiction novels of the modern era.

Veronese, Paolo [Paolo Caliari] (1528–88) Italian painter born in Verona, one of the outstanding decorative painters of his time. He was indebted to the influence of TITIAN, who encouraged him to settle in Venice in 1553. In the same year he won his first major commission for frescoes on the Doge's Palace, and from 1555 to 1558 he worked in San Sebastiano in Venice on scenes from the *Book of Esther*. He decorated the Villa Maser at Treviso c.1561 and was back at the Doge's Palace from 1575 to 1582. A technical virtuoso, he created scenes of grandeur or anecdotal playfulness with equal confidence. Sumptuous fabrics and sensual figures adorn his magnificent architectural settings and landscapes. The secular quality of his religious paintings, e.g. *The Marriage at Cana* (1562–3) and *The Last Supper* (1573), brought down the wrath of the Inquisition, before whose tribunal he was called to defend his works. As a result, *The Last Supper* was renamed *Feast in the House of Levi*. Veronese's work embodies the last representations of Renaissance ideals.

Verrocchio, Andrea del [Andrea di Cione] (1435–88) Florentine sculptor and painter. Possibly a pupil of DONATELLO, he originally trained as a goldsmith. His earliest important commission was for the sculpture *The Doubting of Thomas* (1465), a beautifully detailed piece. It was followed by his refined *David* (c.1475), which rivalled the work of Donatello, as did Verrocchio's masterpiece, the equestrian statue *Bartolommeo Colleoni* (1481–90). Few paintings can be attributed to Verrochio with any certainty, although he ran a large and busy workshop. *The Baptism of Christ* (c.1472) is one that owes its fame to the contribution of his celebrated pupil, LEONARDO DA VINCI.

Vidal, Gore (1925–) American novelist, dramatist and critic. His American historical fiction constitutes an unofficial and waspishly entertaining alternative history of the US and its leaders and customs, e.g. *Burr* (1973) and *1876* (1976). His other work includes a comedy of sexual identity, *Myra Breckinridge* (1968), and several important essay collections, e.g. *The Second American Revolution* (1982) and *Armageddon* (1987).

Villiers, George [2nd Duke of Buckingham] (1606–67) English poet, dramatist and courtier. The son of one of James I's catamites, Villiers became one of the most notorious rakes and political intriguers of his day. He was satirized by DRYDEN in *Absalom and Achitophel*

(1681), where he features as "Zimri," and was the central figure of a loosely connected group of wits (including ROCHESTER, WYCHERLEY and SAMUEL BUTLER (1613–80). Villiers produced, in the manner of his time, several vicious and funny poems, but his main claim to literary fame is his superb send-up of the conventions of the HEROIC TRAGEDY genre, *The Rehearsal* (1672; written in collaboration with, among others, Butler), which mercilessly satirizes Dryden and other dramatists specializing in the genre. The play was updated by Sheridan as *The Critic* (1779). Villiers' sordid death in "the worst inn's worst room" is described in POPE's *Moral Essays*.

Villon, François (c.1431–1463?) French poet. The little that is known of his life indicates a violent, unstable personality. He graduated from the University of Paris, became involved with a criminal gang and killed a priest, being eventually pardoned for the murder. He was banished from Paris in 1463, and nothing is known of him after this date. Two main collections of his work survive: *Le Lais* or *Little Testament*, and *Testament* or *Great Testament*. The latter includes the remarkable "Ballad of Ladies of Long Ago," with its haunting refrain, *"Mais où sont les neiges d'antan?"* ("But where are the snows of yesteryear?"). A curious feature of this poem (and of much of Villon's work) is the poet's ability to present the exalted (Joan of Arc) in conjunction with the common (Bertha of the Big Foot) without creating a bathetic or ridiculous effect.

Villon, Jacques [Gaston Duchamp] (1875–1963) French painter, brother of Marcel DUCHAMP and Raymond DUCHAMP-VILLON. He studied in Paris and exhibited at the Salon d'Automne from 1904. From 1911 he worked in a CUBIST style, exhibiting alongside LÉGER and others with whom he formed the SECTION D'OR group. He also had works in the ARMORY SHOW of 1913.

Later works explore both representational and abstract themes.

Vingt, Les A group of 20 Belgian painters, including ENSOR, who exhibited together in Brussels for ten years from 1884. Their exhibitions also included works by innovative French painters, e.g. SEURAT, GAUGUIN, CÉZANNE *and* van GOGH.

Virgil *or* **Vergil** [Publius Vergilius Maro] (70–19BC)Roman poet. His works include the *Eclogues* or *Bucolics*, ten pastoral poems; the *Georgics*, poems on agricultural subjects that also celebrate the rural way of life; and his masterpiece, the *Aeneid*, an epic poem in 12 books that charts the progress of the Trojan hero Aeneas from the fall of Troy to the founding of the Roman state. He was a friend of HORACE, and one of the most influential poets of all time.

Vlaminck, Maurice de (1876–1958) French FAUVIST painter, who was influenced in his vigorous approach by the works of van GOGH. He worked alongside DERAIN, and they exhibited together with MATISSE at the famous Salon exhibition of 1905. His painting *The Bridge at Chatou* (1906) is a representative work of the period.

Voltaire [pseud. of François Marie Arouet] (1694–1778) French philosopher, poet, historian, dramatist, essayist and novelist. He is regarded as one of the most important of the French so-called "Age of Enlightenment" philosophers. His most influential single work is the *Philosophical Letters* (1734, inspired by British and American conceptions of liberty), a collection of very witty, acerbic attacks on the tyranny of the *ancien régime* of France. Voltaire's war cry was "Ecrasez l'infame" ("Crush the abuses") of religious, political and intellectual despotism, and his writings, with those of ROUSSEAU (with whom he disputed bitterly), are often described as the main intellectual roots of the French

Revolution. His other works include several plays and poems, and the remarkable novel *Candide* (1759), which, like Dr JOHNSON's *Rasselas*, takes a markedly unoptimistic view of human capacity for rational modification of society, concluding with the famous observation that "we must cultivate our garden." Voltaire's most famous (attributed) statement of principle is "I disapprove of what you say, but I will defend to the death your right to say it."

Vonnegut, Kurt (1922–) American novelist, essayist and short-story writer. Vonnegut's gloomy science fiction fables include *The Sirens of Titan* (1959), *Cat's Cradle* (1963) and *Slaughterhouse-Five* (1969). This last novel, in which the hero Billy Pilgrim travels back and forth in time and place, has a grim base in the reality of the firebombing of Dresden, which Vonnegut experienced on the ground as a prisoner of war, and is generally regarded as his masterpiece. The recurring phrase in the book, "So it goes," sums up the author's despairing attitude to humanity's folly. The hack science-fiction writer "Kilgore Trout," who appears in many of Vonnegut's works, serves as a fictional alter ego for the author, who was not amused when another science-fiction writer, Philip José Farmer, wrote and published a Kilgore Trout novel (*Venus on the Half Shell*, 1975).

Vorticism A short-lived English Cubist art movement devised by Wyndham LEWIS, who also edited the two issues of its magazine *Blast* (1914, 1915). *See* FUTURISM.

Vouet, Simon (1590–1649) French painter. He was in Italy from 1613–27, and his early works are in the style of CARAVAGGIO. He later adopted a BAROQUE style modified by Bolognese CLASSICISM, as in *The Appearance of the Virgin to St Bruno* (c.1626). He returned to France as court painter to Louis XIII in 1627 and achieved great popular success, establishing a large studio where he taught the major painters of the next generation, including LEBRUN.

Vuillard, Edouard (1868–1940) French painter. A contemporary of BONNARD, he was influenced by Gauguin and by Japanese art in his flattened planes and decorative style. *Mother and Sister of the Artist* (c.1893) is typical of his most important work in its sensitive application of colour and lighting. Later works are more naturalistic.

W

Walcott, Derek [Anton] (1930–) St Lucian-born West Indian poet and dramatist, who has lived most of his life in Trinidad. Volumes of his poetry include *In a Green Night: Poems 1948–60* (1962) and *Omeros* (1990), a marvellous reworking, in a Caribbean setting, of themes from HOMER's *Odyssey* and *Iliad* and DANTE's *Divine Comedy*. Walcott's plays, e.g. *The Dream on Monkey Mountain and Other Plays* (1971), draw on Creole traditions and imagery, and are highly regarded. He was awarded the NOBEL PRIZE for literature in 1992.

Walpole, Horace [4th Earl of Oxford] (1717–97) English author, noted for his vast correspondence, and for his fascination with the "Gothic." His gossipy (rather feline) letters, which have many often highly entertaining anecdotes about his friends and contemporaries, provide an invaluable guide to the manners and interests of the 18th century. His novel, *The Castle of Otranto* (1764), the first major GOTHIC NOVEL, which is crammed with supernatural incidents and violently emotional rhetoric, set high and rarely exceeded standards for succeeding examples of the genre (fearing ridicule, Walpole had it issued pseudonymously, claiming that it was a translation from medieval Italian). He transformed his house, Strawberry Hill, into a Gothic pseudo-castle that attracted admiration and ridicule in about equal amounts.

Walpole, Sir Hugh (1884–1941) English novelist. His best-known work is a sequence of historical novels set in Northwest England, the *Herries Chronicle*, i.e. *Rogue Herries* (1930), *Judith Paris* (1931), *The Fortress* (1932) and *Vanessa* (1933).

Walton, Izaak (1593–1683) English author, best known for his hugely popular work *The Compleat Angler* (1653, revised 1655, 1676), which is both a treatise on the art of angling and a celebration of the quiet life. The work has been in countless editions since the 17th century. The word "compleat" in the title has also been endlessly reused in imitation of Walton's classic, e.g. *The Compleat Cakemaker*.

Ward, Mrs Humphrey [Mary Augustus Ward] (1851–1920) English novelist. The best known of her many novels is *Robert Ellsmere* (1880), a study of religious commitment that inspired much public debate. She was very highly thought of by her contemporaries throughout Europe (TOLSTOY called her the "English Tolstoy"). Matthew ARNOLD was her uncle.

Warhol, Andy (*c.*1928–87) American painter, designer and film-maker of Czech parentage, best known as a pioneer of POP ART. He studied at the Carnegie Institute of Technology and worked as a commercial artist before setting up his studio, "The Factory," in the 1960s. He exhibited his first stencilled and silk-screened pieces from 1962, e.g. *Green Coca-Cola Bottles* (1962) and the famous *Campbell's Soup* reproduction, the enduring image of Pop Art. He created multiple image screenprints of famous figures, such as *Marilyn Monroe*, *Elvis Presley* and *Mao Tse Tung*. He made several films, experimenting with long, silent shots filmed from a fixed viewpoint e.g. *Sleep* (1963), which lasted six hours. He also managed the rock band, The Velvet Underground.

Warren, Robert Penn (1905–) American poet, novelist and critic. The best known of his novels is *All the King's Men* (1946), which charts the progress of a demagogic politician (based on Governor Huey Long of Louisiana) in the Southern US. Collections of his poetry include *Brother to Dragons* (1953) and *Now and Then* (1979).

Warton, Thomas (1728–90) English poet, who was professor of poetry at Oxford University (1757–67) and POET LAUREATE (1785–90). A prolific poet, his work shows the influence of MILTON, whose early poems he edited (1785). He was a friend of Dr JOHNSON, but is best known for his *History of English Poetry* (1774–81), the first such work of any depth and important for its collection of works by early poets such as CHAUCER, SPENSER and DANTE.

watercolour A paint medium of colour pigments mixed with water-soluble gum arabic. When moistened with water, a watercolour paint produces a transparent colour that is applied to paper, usually white, the paper showing through the paint.

Watteau, Jean-Antoine (1684–1721) French painter, an outstanding exponent of the ROCOCO, whose early influences included Flemish art. He moved to Paris from Valenciennes in 1702 and worked at the Opera as a scene painter before entering the studio of the decorative painter Audran in 1707. He achieved success with *Embarkation for Cythera* (1717) and was accepted as a member of the Academy. Influenced by the works of GIORGIONE and RUBENS, he painted his *Fêtes Gallantes*. Idyllic pastoral scenes of great sensuality, they portray aristocratic figures in court dress or masquerade, sensitively drawn and coloured. Their Rococo atmosphere of frivolity is tinged with a wistful sense of transient pleasure, and the artist himself was already suffering from the consumption that caused his premature death. His final work, *Enseigne de Gersaint*

(1721), was drawn from nature and more classically composed, suggesting the potential of a new realism in his work. His many admirers and imitators failed to achieve his delicacy of colour and sensitivity of composition.

Waugh, Evelyn [Arthur St John] (1903–66) English novelist. His first novels, e.g. *Decline and Fall* (1928), *Vile Bodies* (1930) and *A Handful of Dust* (1934), are brilliant satires featuring, in the main, the brittle, bittersweet pleasures of the postwar "Bright Young Things" generation of the young upper classes of Britain. He was received into the Roman Catholic Church in 1930, his conversion giving a sharper, less frivolous edge to his satire. His experiences (largely farcical) as a war correspondent during the Italian invasion of Abyssinia form the basis of his novel *Scoop* (1938), which is still regarded as the definitive (and funniest) satire on war reporting. He served in World War II with the Royal Marines, taking leave to write his best-known novel *Brideshead Revisited* (1945), in which a young Englishman becomes involved with an aristocratic Roman Catholic family. The novel, which includes some biting satire but also displays a growing spiritual concern, achieved immense popularity. Towards the end of the war, Waugh was posted to Yugoslavia to join his equally eccentric friend Randolph Churchill (Winston Churchill's son) with the Communist partisans. Waugh's experiences there resulted in his masterpiece, the *Sword of Honour* trilogy, i.e. *Men at Arms* (1952), *Officers and Gentlemen* (1955) and *Unconditional Surrender* (1961). As in all Waugh's work, the trilogy is shot through with a cruel, dark humour (which is also at his own expense: *Unconditional Surrender* includes a merciless parody of *Brideshead Revisited*), but the sombre, spiritually questioning element is stronger. Two other notable Waugh novels are *The Loved One* (1948), a satire on Californian burial practices, and an astonishing autobiographical novel, *The Ordeal of Gilbert Penfold* (1957). *See also* ACTON, CONNOLLY.

Webster, John (*c.*1578–*c.*1632) English dramatist, noted for two very powerful tragedies, *The White Devil* (*c.*1609–12) and *The Duchess of Malfi* (*c.*1613). Webster's command of the chilly rhetoric of JACOBEAN TRAGEDY is unrivalled by any other contemporary specialists in that narrow, malevolent genre. T. S. ELIOT praised Webster highly, and describes him in his poem "Whispers of Immortality" as "much possessed by death."

Weldon, Fay (1933–) English novelist. Her novels, which belong with the feminist "consciousness-raising" fictions that began to emerge in the 1970s, include *Female Friends* (1975) and *The Cloning of Joanna May* (1989), the latter being a typical example of the genre in its often leaden satire and paranoid atmosphere. Since the *fatwa* on Salman RUSHDIE came into force in 1989, Weldon has campaigned vigorously on his behalf.

Wells, H[erbert] G[eorge] (1866–1946) English novelist and short-story writer. His science fiction works include several undisputed classics of the genre, e.g. *The Time Machine* (1895), *The Island of Dr Moreau* (1896), *The War of the Worlds* (1898) and *The Shape of Things to Come* (1933). His novels on contemporary themes generally address their subject matter from a "progressive" standpoint (Wells was a leading propagandist, with SHAW and others, for Fabian socialism), e.g. *Ann Veronica* (1909), and sometimes have a comic element mixed in with the mildish social satire, e.g. *Love and Mr Lewisham* (1900), *Kipps* (1905) and *The History of Mr Polly* (1910). He was also a short-story writer of rare genius, e.g. *The Country of the Blind and Other Stories* (1910). His last treatise on political and social issues, *Mind at the End of its Tether* (1945), displays a quite stark pessimism about the human future. It should be noted that, like almost all his early "progressive" contemporaries (e.g. Jack LONDON), Wells' work, as in *When the Sleeper Awakes* (1899), occasionally includes a brutal form of racism in which Blacks are portrayed as subhumans, whereas Christian novelists and thinkers (e.g. Harriet Beecher STOWE, Lord Shaftesbury) saw them as fellow humans, as indeed (but to a less emphatic degree) did many non-, or barely, Christian rightwingers, such as KIPLING and Rider HAGGARD. Wells, to do him credit, became aware of such disquieting paradoxes of "rational progressiveness." *See also* Dame Rebecca WEST.

Wesley, Samuel (1662–1735) English poet and divine, noted mainly for fathering the founder of Methodism, his fifteenth child John Wesley (1703–91; *see* Richard GRAVES). Another of his children, Charles Wesley (1707–88), wrote many very fine hymns, e.g. "Jesu, Lover of my soul." Samuel Wesley's other works include a now unreadable and huge epic poem on the life of Christ. His earlier collection of poems, however, *Maggots* (1685), deserves to be better known. This extraordinary (even for a 17th-century divine) volume includes several scabrously funny poems. A characteristic specimen is "The Beggar and Poet," in which the beggar's words appear in Gothic type.

West, Benjamin (1738–1820) American painter, who studied in Philadelphia and Rome before settling in London in 1763. He was patronized by George III, and his studio was a focal point for American art students in London. In his great innovative work, *The Death of General Wolfe* (1770), he defied traditions in history painting by depicting his characters in contemporary dress. The precedent was soon copied by COPLEY and other American history painters. His early NEOCLASSI-

CAL style gradually gave way to ROMANTIC themes, e.g. *Saul and the Witch of Endor* (1777) and *Death on a Pale Horse* (1802). He became President of the Royal Academy in 1792.

West, Dame Rebecca [pseud. of Cecily Isabel Fairfield] (1892–1983) Anglo-Irish novelist and journalist, whose novels are regarded as classics of feminist writing for their sharp, fierce wit (H. G. WELLS, who was her lover, nicknamed her "Panther"). The novels, which include *The Return of the Soldier* (1918) and *The Birds Fall Down* (1966), have never lacked for admirers, and her status as a writer has steadily risen. She reported on the Nuremberg Trials after World War II in *The Meaning of Treason* (1947), which she revised in 1964 to include postwar treason trials. Her son by H. G. Wells, **Anthony [Panther] West** (1914–87) was also a novelist, who moved to the US. Following his mother's death, he wrote a bitter account of his relationship with her in *H. G. Wells: Aspects of a Life* (1984).

West, Nathanael [pseud. of Nathan Weinstein] (1903–40) American novelist. His macabre novels have as their main theme the souring of the American dream, e.g. *Miss Lonelyhearts* (1933) and *The Day of the Locust* (1939).

Weyden, Rogier van der (*c*.1399–1464) Flemish painter. No signed works by him survive, and his career has been established through documentation in other contemporary sources. He is thought to have trained under Robert CAMPIN, and was influenced by him and by van EYCK. A notable early painting is *The Deposition* (*c*.1435), and his finest work is the *Last Judgment* altarpiece (*c*.1450). His outstanding achievement and the distinguishing quality of his work lies in his ability to convey drama and emotion. Later works, e.g. *The Adoration of the Magi* from the Columba altarpiece, are characterized by the sense of peaceful serenity that marks his portrait work.

Wharton, Edith [Newbold Jones] (1862–1937) American novelist and short-story writer. Much of her fiction deals with the ironies and tragedies of New York social life, e.g. *The House of Mirth* (1905) and, notably, *The Age of Innocence* (1920). Another well-known work is her (very uncharacteristic) short novel of poverty and vengeance on a New England farm, *Ethan Frome* (1911). Her other novels include *The Custom of the Country* (1913) and *Hudson River Bracketed* (1929). Short-story collections include *Crucial Instances* (1901) and *Ghosts* (1937).

Whichcote, Benjamin *see* **More, Henry**.

Whistler, James Abbot McNeill (1843–1903) American painter. He studied in Paris, and his early works are Realist in style. He settled in London from 1859 and was influenced by the PRE-RAPHAELITE movement, and by Japanese art. He became famous as a portraitist, with works such as *Arrangement in Grey and Black*, a portrait of the artist's mother. He explored the idea of colour harmony in his paintings, and often gave his works musical titles, such as *Chelsea: Nocturne in Blue and Green* (c.1870) and *Old Battersea Bridge: Nocturne in Blue and Gold*. His Thames paintings transformed the riverside docks and warehouses into images of misty beauty, but his exhibition at the Grosvenor Gallery in 1877 aroused the acid criticism of RUSKIN. The result was a notorious lawsuit that initiated the mental breakdown of Ruskin and bankrupted the victor, Whistler, who was awarded only a penny in damages. He published his collected writings, *The Gentle Art of Making Enemies* in 1890.

White, Patrick [Victor Martindale] (1912–90) English-born Australian novelist. His historical novels, e.g. *The Tree of Man* (1955) and *Voss* (1957), are set in the Australian outback, and describe the suffering and struggles of those settlers and explorers of the wilderness. A central concern of White's is to show how men react to extreme situations, in which they grow or fail spiritually. Other novels include *Riders in the Chariot* (1961) and *The Vivisector* (1970). He was awarded the NOBEL PRIZE for literature in 1973.

White, T[erence] H[anbury] (1906–64) English novelist, whose trilogy on the Arthurian legends, published in one volume as *The Once and Future King* (1958), is the most popular and entertaining of the modern versions of the ARTHUR myth. The first volume of the trilogy, *The Sword in the Stone* (1937), is regarded as a classic of children's literature.

Whitehead, William *see* **poet laureate**.

Whitman, Walt[er] (1819–92) American poet. His collection, *Leaves of Grass*, was first published in 1855; eight subsequent revised and enlarged editions appeared throughout his life, and the book is regarded as the most important single volume of poems in American literature. Its significance lies primarily in Whitman's celebration of America as the land of liberty and democracy, with a concurrent celebration of the poet himself, his sexuality, and the great, honest world of nature. He was a fervent admirer of EMERSON, and was in his turn highly influential on a great many American poets. Ezra POUND said of him, "He *is* America." Whitman's comment on himself should also be noted: "Do I contradict myself? / Very well then I contradict myself, / I am large, I contain multitudes" ("Song of Myself"). His other poems include "O Captain! My Captain!" (1865), commemorating the death of Abraham Lincoln, and a superb elegy, also for Abraham Lincoln, "When Lilacs Last in the Dooryard Bloom'd" (1867).

Whittier, John Greenleaf (1807–92) American poet.

Whittier's strong Quaker principles pervade his work, which, like WHITMAN's, celebrates the common people of America. His verse was enormously popular, and his antislavery poems, e.g. *Voices of Freedom* (1846), contributed significantly to the abolitionist cause. Other volumes include *Legends of New England in Prose and Verse* (1831), *Songs of Labor* (1850) and *Snow-Bound* (1866).

Wilcox, Ella Wheeler (1850–1919) American poet, whose prolifically produced verses, in collection *Poems of Passion* (1883), were enormously popular in their day. Her appeal was due to a blend of sentimentalism and everyday "common sense," exemplified in her best-known lines "Laugh and the world laughs with you;/ Weep, and you weep alone" ("Solitude").

Wilde, Oscar [Fingal O'Flahertie Wills] (1854–1900) Irish dramatist, poet, essayist and wit. He first came to public notice in the late 1870s as a prominent member of the AESTHETIC MOVEMENT, and lived gaily up to the "Bunthorne" image of an aesthete presented in GIL-BERT and Sullivan's comic opera *Patience*. After the publication of his *Poems* (1881), he made a lecture tour of the US. The tour was highly successful, and Wilde became a household name. In 1888 he published a volume of fairy stories for children, *The Happy Prince and Other Tales* (1888), with his only novel, *The Picture of Dorian Gray*, following in 1890. The first of his great comedies, *Lady Windermere's Fan*, appeared in 1892. The succeeding plays, *A Woman of No Importance* (1893), *An Ideal Husband* (1895) and *The Importance of Being Earnest* (1895), established him as the most important dramatist of the age. The plays are still very popular, with their superbly witty dialogue and flashes of biting satire. His other works include several important essays, e.g. "The Decay of Lying" and "The Critic as Artist." He was jailed for homosexuality from 1895 to 1897, and during his imprisonment wrote *De Profundis*, a bitter apologia addressed to **Lord Alfred Douglas** (1870–1945), the English poet whose relationship with Wilde had led to his imprisonment. It was published in part in 1905 by Douglas. After his release, Wilde fled to France, where he wrote *The Ballad of Reading Gaol* (1898), an account of his experience there. He died in poverty in Paris. YEATS' *Autobiographies* includes a remarkable portrait of Wilde.

Wilder, Thornton [Niven] (1897–1975) American novelist and dramatist. His best-known novel is *The Bridge of San Luis Rey* (1927), a historical novel set in 18th-century Peru. His plays include *Our Town* (1938), *The Merchant of Yonkers* (1938, later remade into the musical *Hello, Dolly* in 1963) and *The Skin of our Teeth* (1942). Wilder's fiction is, for the most part, an optimistic celebration of the lives of ordinary people.

Wilkie, Sir David (1785–1841) Scottish painter, who studied in Edinburgh and settled in London from 1805. He achieved popularity with his genre paintings, which were small in scale and depicted rural festivities and domestic scenes with wit and humour. His *Chelsea Pensioners reading the Gazette of the Battle of Waterloo* (1822) was an immediate success when shown at the Royal Academy. Later works, influenced by the Old Masters, were more serious in subject and grander in approach, e.g. *John Knox preaching before the Lords of the Congregation*. He was also a successful portraitist and etcher. In 1840 he travelled to the Middle East to research material for his Biblical paintings, but he died on the return voyage.

Williams, Charles (1886–1945) poet, novelist and critic, whose highly individual supernatural thrillers, e.g. *War in Heaven* (1930), *Descent into Hell* (1937) and *All Hallows Eve* (1944) have a devoted following. The novels are written from a Christian standpoint, and feature odd and chilling clashes between the forces of good and evil. *See also* TOLKIEN, NEOPLATONISM.

Williams, Tennessee [pseud. of Thomas Lanier Williams] (1911–83) American dramatist. His plays, lurid melodramas about sexual and social frustration in the Deep South, include *The Glass Menagerie* (1944), *A Streetcar Named Desire* (1947),*Cat on a Hot Tin Roof* (1955) and *The Night of the Iguana* (1962). Other publications include a short novel, *The Roman Spring of Mrs Stone* (1950), volumes of poems, and his *Memoirs* (1975). The best introduction to Williams's life and work is Gore VIDAL's splendidly bitchy essay, "Tennessee Williams: Someone to Laugh at the Squares with" (in *Armageddon*, 1987).

Williams, William Carlos (1883–1963) American poet, novelist and short-story writer. His early volumes of poems, *Poems* (1909) and *The Tempers* (1913), belong to the Imagist school (he was a friend of IMAGISM's American godfather Ezra POUND). Later volumes, e.g. *Pictures from Breughel* (1963), use the idioms of everyday speech and concentrate on everyday objects. His most famous poem is "The Red Wheelbarrow," an eight-line minimalist work, half of which is "so much depends / upon / a red wheel / barrow."

Wilmot, John *see* **Rochester, 2nd Earl of**.

Wilson, Colin [Henry] (1931–) English novelist and critic, whose study of EXISTENTIALIST writers, e.g. CAMUS and SARTRE, *The Outsider* (1956), received extraordinary praise from the critics on publication. The work appeared in the same week as OSBORNE's *Look Back in Anger*, resulting in both writers being classified as ANGRY YOUNG MEN. Subsequent volumes received a much more muted welcome, and Wilson's work began to be savaged by the very critics who had earlier hailed him as a great writer. As has been pointed out, the most unnerving aspect of the affair was the virtual unanimity of the critical establishment, first one way, then the other. Wilson's critical reputation remains low; his very many nonfiction works, e.g. *A Criminal History of Mankind* (1984), show signs of being under-researched, and his novels, e.g. *Ritual in the Dark* (1960), are pot-boiling studies of alienated "Outsiders" with heavy doses of sex and violence that are of little interest. As a popularizer of major writers, however, Wilson's influence has been both very wide and largely unrecognized.

Wilson, Edmund (1895–1972) American critic, poet and dramatist. Wilson's main critical work is *Axel's Castle* (1931), an influential study of such SYMBOLIST writers as W. B. YEATS. His other principal works are *To the Finland Station* (1940), a history of European socialism, and *The Wound and the Bow* (1941), a collection of Freud-inspired studies (MARX and FREUD were the two main influences on him). Another fine work is his *Patriotic Gore: Studies in the Literature of the American Civil War* (1962), a very useful and much quarried study of the writers of the period. His third wife was Mary McCARTHY.

Wilson, Harriette (1786–1846) English author and courtesan. Her *Memoirs of Harriette Wilson* (1825) created a public scandal by naming and discussing her various "protectors," associates and acquaintances, many of whom were among the most prominent men of the day. The work is not a totally reliable narrative: advance publicity for each edition of the work was designed to extort hush money from those due to be named, the Duke of Wellington responding famously with "Publish and be damned." The book is written in a lively, restless prose that often modulates into captivating pastiches of contemporary prose styles; for example, her meeting with BYRON is described in a suitably "sentimental" manner. The opening sentence of the book is itself a small masterpiece: "I shall not say why and how I became, at the age of fifteen, the mistress of the Earl of Craven."

Wilson, Richard (1713–82) Welsh painter and founding member of the Royal Academy. His early works are portraits, e.g. *Admiral Thomas Smith* (c.1745). After visiting Italy from 1750 to 1757, he took up landscape painting, influenced by the works of CLAUDE LORRAINE. His classically composed paintings are enhanced by a lyrical freedom of style, e.g. *View of Rome from the Villa Madama* (1753). Some of his finest works were achieved when he applied this style to the landscape of his native Wales, e.g. *Snowdon from Llyn Nantil* (c.1770).

Wilson, Sir Angus (1913–91) South African-born English novelist and short-story writer. Long regarded as one of the finest 20th-century English writers, his fictions are sharply observed satires within a wide variety of social settings, and often have a macabre ending. The major novels are *Hemlock and After* (1952), *Anglo-Saxon Attitudes* (1956), *The Old Men at the Zoo* (1961) and *No Laughing Matter* (1967). The *Collected Stories* were published in 1987. He is regarded by many critics as the main heir of the great Victorian writers. *See also* ANGRY YOUNG MEN.

wit "What oft was thought but ne'er so well expressed" (POPE, *An Essay on Criticism*). The term has had many meanings and shades of meanings down through the years, and can denote either the thing itself or a notable practitioner of it. The main shifts of meaning to bear in mind are: (a) Elizabethan usage, meaning intelligence or wisdom; (b) early 17th-century usage, meaning ingenious thought, "fancy," and original figures of speech, as in DONNE's verse and METAPHYSICAL POETRY; (c) the period relevant to Pope's definition, roughly from the mid-17th century to the last half of the 18th, which is discussed below; (d) 19th-century to modern times usage, meaning an amusing, perhaps surprising observation, usually involving paradox.

Wit as defined by Pope must be distinguished from what we now regard as humour: wit can be malicious, humour is benevolent amusement. SWIFT is witty, ADDISON and STEELE, who set the pattern for the future, are both witty and humorous. Wits tended to congregate in groups of like-minded intellectuals sharing similar political, social and religious views, e.g. the debauched circle around George VILLIERS, 2nd Duke of Buckingham, which included ROCHESTER, SEDLEY and WYCHERLEY, or the Tory quasi-Jacobite circles around Pope and Swift.

By the late half of the 18th century, the term largely ceased to be used to describe intellectual groups, implying as it did either heartless frivolity or political faction. Intellectual groupings became looser, although certainly no less formidable: a literary gathering in 1780 London, for example, could include figures as diverse as SHERIDAN, Dr JOHNSON, BURKE and Edward GIBBON, all of whom could be described as sharp-witted heavyweight thinkers and controversialists, although not "wits" in the previous sense of the term.

Wodehouse, Sir P[elham] G[renville] (1881–1975) English novelist and short-story writer, who became a US citizen in 1955. He wrote amiable accounts of aristocratic life, featuring such characters as Lord Emsworth and the Empress of Blandings (a prize pig), but his most famous creations are Bertie Wooster, a giddy young upper-middle-class man who spends his large amount of spare time flitting about getting into situations with which he can't cope and doesn't understand, and his butler Jeeves, a shrewd and immensely competent man who can cope with anything and understands everything. Representative volumes are *My Man Jeeves* (1919), *The Inimitable Jeeves* (1923) and *Carry on Jeeves* (1925). Wodehouse also wrote many lyrics for musicals in collaboration with composers such as Jerome Kern and Irving Berlin. Interned by the Nazis during World War II, he foolishly made some innocuous broadcasts from Germany, which led to his being branded (even more foolishly) a traitor. Both Evelyn WAUGH and George ORWELL wrote spirited defences of him, effectively disproving the treason charges.

Wolfe, Thomas [Clayton] (1900–1938) American novelist. His major achievement is a huge four-volume series of largely autobiographical novels, i.e. *Look Homeward, Angel* (1929), *Of Time and the River* (1935), *The Web and the Rock* (1939) and *You Can't Go Home Again* (1940). Wolfe's novels were very popular in their day, despite critical complaints that they lacked form or structure (the first draft of *Look Homeward, Angel* was said to have filled suitcases, and the role of his editor, Maxwell Perkins (1884–1947), was crucial in the development of his fiction).

Wolfe, Tom [pseud. of Thomas Kennerly Jr] (1931–) American journalist and style guru. Wolfe's studies of American culture, e.g. *The Electric Kool-Aid Acid Test* (1968) and *Radical Chic and Mau-Mauing the Flak Catchers* (1970) are important and entertaining analyses in the nonobjective mode of "New Journalism," a term immortalized in the title of Wolfe's anthology of his contemporaries' writing, *The New Journalism* (1973). His only novel, *The Bonfire of the Vanities* (1987), a nightmarish yet brilliantly witty study of the disintegrating social order of New York, achieved great popular and critical success in the late 1980s.

Wollstonecraft, Mary *see* **Shelley, Mary Wollstonecraft**.

Woolf, [Adeline] Virginia (1882–1941) English novelist, critic and short-story writer. She married the novelist and social reformer **Leonard Woolf** (1880–1969) in 1912, and their home in Bloomsbury in London became the centre of the so-called "Bloomsbury Group" of writers and artists, of whom the most important was Virginia Woolf herself. Her novels are written in a fluid, poetic style, and are recognized as being among the most innovative of the 20th century. They are particularly noted for their use of "stream of consciousness" narration (*see* William JAMES), and include *Jacob's Room* (1922), *Mrs Dalloway* (1925), *To the Lighthouse* (1927), *Orlando* (1928), *The Waves* (1931) and *Between the Acts* (1941). Her literary criticism was collected in several volumes, e.g. *The Common Reader* (1925, 1932), and is often enthralling and lively, if occasionally a bit intolerant (*see* BENNETT), as are her *Letters* (six volumes, 1975–80) and *Diary* (five volumes, 1977–83). She also wrote several important feminist works, e.g. *A Room of One's Own* (1929). She suffered greatly from mental illness, and drowned herself. *See also* Vita SACKVILLE-WEST.

Wordsworth, Dorothy (1771–1855) English writer, sister of William WORDSWORTH. She lived with William from 1795 until his death, and kept journals which were not published until after her death. The most famous of these is the *Grasmere Journal*, which contains many superb passages describing people and landscapes, which her brother used as the basis for some of his poems. She is now recognized as one of the finest prose writers of the early 19th century.

Wordsworth, William (1770–1850) English poet. Like many young men of his generation, he was a great admirer of the French Revolution, and became disillusioned with revolutionary principles when the Terror began in 1793. He met COLERIDGE in 1795, and they published their great joint volume *Lyrical Ballads* in 1798. Wordsworth's contributions to the volume reflect his view (in the preface to the 1802 edition) that poetry should be plain and accessible to all men, and be written in the everyday language of men (poetry is defined, famously, as "emotion recollected in tranquility." The book is regarded, with BLAKE's works of the 1790s, as the first great flowering of English literary Romanticism. Other great Wordsworth poems include "Resolution and Independence" and the "Intimations of Immortality" ode, and such sonnets as his stirring tribute to Toussaint L'Ouverture, the Haitian revolutionary leader, and "The world is too much with us." Wordsworth's masterpiece is the long narrative poem *The Prelude: or, Growth of a Poet's Mind*, the first version of which was finished (but not published) in 1805. Wordsworth toyed with the poem over the years, and a revised version was published in 1850. Few other poets have so successfully blended into a coherent whole the personal with the natural and social worlds, as Wordsworth does here, whether in questioning his motives while picking up stones from the ruined Bastille, or in remembering a dark vision from childhood of the "unknown modes of being" of nature. Wordsworth became poet laureate in 1843, succeeding his friend SOUTHEY. Like Southey, he had become a staid conservative, much vilified both by contemporaries such as BYRON and by the new wave of radical poets (e.g. Robert BROWNING, who attacked him in "The Lost Leader"). KEATS, SHELLEY and Blake, however, while disagreeing radically with Wordsworth in many ways, were definite about his significance as a great new voice in poetry. As Keats put it in one of his letters, his thought reached "into the human heart." After Wordsworth, English poetry was never the same again. *See also* Dorothy WORDSWORTH.

Wright, Joseph ["Wright of Derby"] (1734–97) English painter. He spent most of his career in his native Derby, apart from travels to London and Italy (1773–5). He did genre paintings, portraits and landscapes, the outstanding features of which are his extraordinary light effects, e.g. *An Experiment on a Bird in an Air Pump* (c.1767).

Wyatt, Sir Thomas (1503–42) English poet and diplomat. He spent most of his adult life in the dangerous diplomatic service of Henry VIII, when he was not being imprisoned by him. Wyatt was very probably the former lover of Anne Boleyn, Henry's second wife, and how he avoided execution is still a mystery. Wyatt's main claim to literary fame rests on several striking love poems, e.g. "They flee from me that sometime did me seek," and his role as popularizer of the sonnet form in English (he translated and imitated PETRARCH's sonnets). He was a powerful and original poet, with a vivid turn of phrase, e.g. "Drowned is reason that should me comfort."

Wycherley, William (1641–1715) English dramatist. His two best-known comedies are *The Country Wife* (1675) and *The Plain Dealer* (1676), both of which have had many modern productions. Wycherley's plays were regarded as being among the most licentious of RESTORATION drama, but have grown steadily in reputation in the 20th century. Wycherley's relentless, sardonic mockery of social conventions and hypocrisy works very well on the stage.

Wyeth, Andrew (1917–) American painter, who was trained by his father, the illustrator **Newell Covers Wyeth** (1882–1944). Andrew's works are austerely realistic, meticulously painted in watercolour or egg tempera from a generally earthy palette. He painted landscapes and interiors devoid of human presence, and his use of an off-centre compositional device creates a nostalgic, haunting atmosphere. This strange quality also informs his portraits, including the famous *Christina's World* (1948).

Wyndham, John [pseud. of John Wyndham Parkes Lucas Benton Harris] (1903–69) novelist and short-story writer. Wyndham's best-known works are the science fiction novels *The Day of the Triffids* (1951), *The Kraken Wakes* (1953), *The Midwich Cuckoos* (1957) and *Trouble with Lichen* (1960). He preferred to describe his works as "logical fantasies" in which a highly improbable event occurs, e.g. the world is suddenly invaded by giant, mobile carnivorous vegetables (as in *The Day of the Triffids*), and the consequences are explored in a naturalistic manner. The most notable of his other works is the short-story collection *Consider her Ways* (1961), a rare example by a male author of a common feminist fable, the future all-female world.

Y

Yeats, Jack Butler (1871–1957) Irish painter. The son
of the Irish artist **John Butler Yeats** (1839–1922) and
the brother of W. B. YEATS, his early work was as a
painter in watercolour and as an illustrator in pen and
ink. He also worked as a cartoonist and created the
first cartoon version of Sherlock Holmes for *Comic Cuts*
magazine (1894). By 1915, he was painting regularly
in oils and developing a vivid, spontaneous and colourful style, mainly in landscapes.

Yeats, W[illiam] B[utler] (1865–1939) Anglo-Irish
poet. He studied art for three years at Dublin (his
father and his brother, Jack Butler YEATS, were well-
known artists), but became a writer in the early 1890s.
His early works include several very important collections of poems, e.g. *The Wanderings of Oisin* (1889),
The Rose (1893) and *The Wind Among the Reeds*
(1899), which reflect the poet's concern with Irish myth
and legend. He also edited two noteworthy editions of
BLAKE in the 1890s. The influence of Blake upon Yeats
was profound; Yeats followed Blake in establishing a
private, arcane mythology in which to express his
ideas, and, like Blake, his lyrical gift, e.g. the magical
"faery" poem "The Stolen Child," was as evident in the
early work as in the later. It should be noted that
Yeats' later complicated, arcane system of "gyres" and
occult symbolism, as in *Michael Robartes and the
Dancer* (1921), can be safely ignored; like MILTON's

equally esoteric mechanisms in *Paradise Lost*, the structures are only of relevance to dissertation-hounds and are no real barrier to the uninitiated reader; it should also be noted that Yeats admired Blake so much he gave him an Irish father, a piece of whimsical myth-making that is still repeated as fact in reputable works of reference. Several of Yeats' plays, first performed at the ABBEY THEATRE, which he helped to found, are also of great importance, particularly *Cathleen ni Houlihan* (1902), a celebration of Irish patriotism which he later feared had sent men to their deaths against the British. Many of his poems, e.g. "Easter 1916," "Among School Children," "The Second Coming," "Coole Park at Bally-lee, 1931," the "Crazy Jane" poems, "Lapis Lazuli" and "The Circus Animals' Desertion" are among the great-est poems in the English language. His prose works are also of great importance, notably the remarkable collected *Autobiographies* (1955), which includes many valuable portraits of his contemporaries. Yeats' poli-tics are too complex to explain briefly; he certainly flirted with fascism (*see* ORWELL's essay "W. B. Yeats"), but became a highly respected member of the Irish senate (his speech in the senate in defence of divorce and of the Anglo-Irish heritage is a masterpiece of political rhetoric). His relationships with other writers, and with artistic movements, especially SYM-BOLISM, are equally complex. Yeats was very much his own creature, and too conscious of the great literary heritage of the English language to take modern move-ments too seriously; he paid tribute to innovators such as JARRY, but wondered what could follow: "After us, the Savage God." He was awarded the NOBEL PRIZE for literature in 1923.

Yonge, Charlotte M[ary] (1823–1901) English novel-ist. Of her many novels, the only one that is still regu-larly printed is *The Heir of Radclyffe* (1853), a study of the influence of a good-natured (but bad-tempered) man upon his apparently good (but actually devious) cousin. The dominant theme in Yonge's fiction is her strong belief in the transforming power of Christianity. She was a High Anglican, and part of the profits of *The Heir of Radclyffe* went to fit out a missionary ship.

Yorke, Henry Vincent *see* **Green, Henry**.

Z

Zamyatin, Yevgeny Ivanovich (1884–1937) Russian
novelist, short-story writer, dramatist and critic. His
best-known work is the grim anti-utopian (*see* MORE)
novel *We* (part publication 1920–1), the influence of
which was acknowledged by ORWELL (on *1984*), and
unconvincingly denied by HUXLEY (on *Brave New
World*). The novel, like *1984*, was read as a diabolical
fantasy by Western readers and as virtually pure naturalism by its Soviet readers. It was first published in
its full version in the mid-1920s, outside the USSR, by
which time Zamyatin's position had become a highly
dangerous one. Stalin let him emigrate, and he died in
Paris.

Zangwill, Israel (1864–1926) English novelist, dramatist and journalist, best known for his novel of Jewish
life in the London slums, *Children of the Ghetto* (1892).
The most notable of his plays is *The Melting Pot* (1909),
which describes America as "God's Crucible, the great
Melting-Pot where all the races of Europe are melting
and re-forming!"

Zola, Emile (1840–1902) French novelist, regarded as
the most prominent exponent of NATURALISM in the
novel (*see* MARX). His huge sequence of 20 novels,
entitled the *Rougon-Macquart* series, describes the history of the Rougon and Macquart families within the
setting of what he called the "natural and social
history" of Second Empire France, *c.*1850–1870,

"natural" in this context denoting a deterministic view of human nature and the pernicious effects of hereditary faults. The novels include his masterpiece *Germinal* (1885), a moving account of the brutalized lives of miners and their families, which ends with a superb evocation of future revolution. Zola's works had an enormous influence on other naturalistic writers (e.g. DREISER), but few of his imitators produced anything as good. Zola was a highly able propagandist for socialism and for social justice in France; he had to flee France and take refuge in England for almost a year following the publication of his letter "J'Accuse," a brilliant defence of the Jewish officer Alfred Dreyfus, who had been falsely accused of treason.

Zucchi, Antonio *see* **Kaufmann, Angelica.**

Zurbarán, Francisco (1598–1664) Spanish painter, who lived and worked almost entirely in his native Seville. He painted mainly religious works, apart from a few still lifes and *The Labours of Hercules* series, commissioned by Philip IV. His starkly lit figures of monks or saints were painted in an austerely realistic style, and conveyed an atmosphere of spiritual intensity, e.g. *St Francis*. From 1640 he was rivalled by MURILLO, whose popularity soon outshone his completely, and he retired to Madrid in 1658. Much of his work was exported to South America.